B Science Fiction and Horror Movie Makers

Interviews with
B Science Fiction and
Horror Movie Makers

*Writers, Producers, Directors,
Actors, Moguls and Makeup*

by Tom Weaver

Research Associates
John Brunas
Michael Brunas

McFarland & Company, Inc., Publishers
Jefferson, North Carolina, and London

Library of Congress Cataloguing-in-Publication Data

Weaver, Tom, 1958–
 Interviews with B science fiction and horror movie makers.

 Includes index.
 1. Science fiction films—United States—History.
 2. Horror films—United States—History. 3. Motion
 picture actors and actresses—Interviews. 4. Motion
 picture producers and directors—Interviews.
 5. Screenwriters—Interviews. I. Title.
 PN1995.9.S26W44 1988   791.43'09'09356   88-42641

 ISBN 0-89950-360-8 (50# acid-free natural paper)

Printed in the United States of America.

McFarland & Company, Inc., Publishers
 Box 611, Jefferson, North Carolina 28640

Dedicated to

Mark Martucci

He never believes me when I tell him this,
but I couldn't have done this book without him.

——— *Table of Contents* ———

vii

Introduction

The late 1940s were the dog days for the horror and science fiction film. The Universal monster rallies had come to an inevitable end, the Val Lewton B-picture unit at RKO had lamentably ceased production, and even bush-league Poverty Row studios like PRC and Monogram realized that audiences had finally succumbed to horror movie burnout. Occasionally one of the cheaper indies turned out a third-rate film like *Scared to Death* or *The Creeper*, but by and large the genre was in a state of limbo.

Then came the '50s.

With public consciousness now preoccupied with the A-bomb and UFOs, a fresh new wave of science fiction films began in 1950. Major releases like *The Day the Earth Stood Still, Destination Moon, When Worlds Collide* and *The Thing from Another World* rubbed elbows with creative little B's *(The Man from Planet X, Five)* and desultory Z's *(Untamed Women, Mesa of Lost Women)*. The floodgates burst. Important studios like MGM, Paramount and Warner Bros. acquiesced to audience demands and created well-mounted, respectable science fiction efforts. Universal, never quite able to shake off the tag of Hollywood's least prestigious "major," rejoiced in the comeback of the kind of film that helped build its fortunes twenty years before, and embarked on its own popular series of horror-accented sci-fi thrillers.

A good deal of the really interesting and innovative work, however, came from the low-budget independent studios like Allied Artists and the newly conceived American International Pictures. From 1955 to well into the 1960s, these distributors and others like them turned out an incredible number of pictures, surpassing even the horror heydays of the early 1930s and the early-to-mid–1940s. Despite their wildly varying quality (from gems like *Not of This Earth* and *I Was a Teenage Werewolf* to genuine dogs like *Teenage Monster* and *From Hell It Came)*, these films developed a following whose loyalty stands undiminished after three decades.

This book pays homage to the many people that have contributed toward producing a body of work whose entertainment (if not always artistic) values have only increased through the years. Assembled herein is a cross-section of talents: writers, producers, directors, actors, actresses, even a movie mogul and a makeup man. We've kept our questions and interjected comments as terse

ix

and to-the-point as possible, our goal being to present a book in which the filmmakers and performers do nearly all the talking.

Fans of Hollywood gloss, be warned: This may not be the sort of interview book you're used to. There are no tales of multimillion dollar productions or of pampered glitterati, no elegant Tinseltown soirées, big premieres or jet-set ostentation. Most of the films discussed in this book are medium- to low-budget productions, some of them made by people who are at best footnotes in the big book of Hollywood history. Perhaps it *does* require something of an open and tolerant mind to see the good in pictures about Styrofoam crab monsters, Martian Jell-O, hubcaps, sparklers and bathospheres from outer space, thirtyish teenagers and bald midgets armed with vacuum cleaners. But this is not meant as any sort of apology. It takes far more talent and imagination to make a good film on a low budget than to make one with all the materials and means of a major studio at one's disposal.

The twenty-eight question-and-answer sessions in this book were conducted over a period of nearly five years, many in person and the rest via long-distance telephone. Prior to every interview, we researched and reviewed every fantastic film of each individual, and prepared lists of relevant questions. Although our emphasis is squarely on the 1950s era, many of our interviewees worked in the science fiction or horror genres long before and / or long after the '50s, and all of these additional films are fully discussed as well. The majority of these interviews originally appeared in such magazines as *Fangoria, Starlog, Fantasic Films, Filmfax* and others over that same five-year period. In compiling these articles for this book we have gone back to nearly all of our interviewees to pose additional questions and to bring the interviews up to date. Some of the interviews are now more than double the length of what initially appeared in the abovementioned publications.

It's been a fun and rewarding five years hunting down cult actors and actresses, favorite writers and directors and all the rest. Many are still active on the Hollywood scene, making them relatively easy to find, but others, long retired, led us on merry chases which ended in places like avocado farms, video stores and the Pacific Northwest. Of course there were disappointments along the way, from the polite and pleasant (and perhaps understandable!) refusals of people like Peter Graves and Ed Nelson, to the angry slamming-down-of-the-phone on the part of a certain male star of *The Atomic Submarine*. But these little letdowns are all part of the game, and we remain pleased and proud of the group we have gathered.

Certainly a tremendous amount of work remains to be done, and we hope to continue our tracking-down and interrogating for other interviews. Part of our inclusion criteria this time around was that each of the interviewees should have something of an identification with the horror or science fiction genres, or at least a sufficient number of credits to guarantee a multi-page write-up. But we also recognize that there are some very colorful and interesting one-shot sci-fi filmmakers and performers lurking in those Hollywood hills, and we hope to begin documenting their B movie experiences for the sake of posterity. None of these people is getting any younger (nor, come to think of it, are we); and we've already come "this-close" to missing out on a few of the people we *have* talked to. The enthusiastic response to our past work has made us feel that it's important as well as entertaining to gather these reminiscences for future fantasy film historians and fans.

No book of this type could possibly be written without the help of a veritable army of fellow fans, Hollywood contacts, well-wishers, glad-handers, film and tape sources and so on. Our sincere thanks are extended to Acquanetta, Bill and Roberta Amazzini, Ron and Loraine Ashcroft, Mr. and Mrs. Ewing Brown, Roger Corman, Edward and Mildred Dein, Carl and Debbie Del Vecchio, Richard Devon, David Everitt, Tim Ferrante, Mike Fitzgerald, Robert Franklin, Karin Garrity, Alex Gordon, Coleen Gray, Jonathan Haze, Scot Holton, Tom Johnson, Little Joe the Honey Bear, Bill Littman, Arthur Lubin, Greg Luce, Alex Lugones, Dave McDonnell, Mark McGee, Scott MacQueen, Greg Mank, Jacques Marquette, **our moms,** Cody Morgan, Jeff Morrow, Lori Nelson, Paul Parla, Gil Perkins, Rex Reason, Mary Runser, Sam Sherman, John Skillin, Michael Stein, George Stover, Maurice Terenzio, Tony Timpone, Katherine Victor, Virgil Vogel, Bill Warren, Ed Watz, Jon Weaver and Wade Williams. Some individuals deserve *extra* special thanks, like Robert Skotak, who loaned us rare and valuable behind-the-scenes photos, and Mark Martucci, who gave us unlimited access to his incredible video collection. James LaBarre guided us through the ins and outs of using a word processor and printer, and never seemed to mind that we were less interested in learning the system than in having everything done *for* us, time after time. Many thanks, James.

And of course we are grateful to our twenty-nine interviewees, who made all of this possible. This book is our thank-you to these highly creative and resourceful people (both before and behind the cameras) who prevailed over low budgets and abbreviated shooting schedules and produced films whose fan followings endure to this day.

Tom Weaver
John Brunas
Michael Brunas

*I always kind of had the feeling that when people
looked at some of these science fiction things,
we were going to get a big laugh.*

John Agar

ONE OF THE BEST-KNOWN stars of 1950s fantasy films, John Agar's science fiction credits range in quality from the top-of-the-line productions of Jack Arnold *(Revenge of the Creature, Tarantula)* to the bottom-of-the-barrel efforts of schlocksters like Bert I. Gordon and Larry Buchanan. While Agar has never appeared in a sci-fi classic, few of his acting contemporaries are as closely identified with the genre, and none can equal his output—a long list of memorable titles that also includes *The Mole People, Daughter of Dr. Jekyll, The Brain from Planet Arous, Invisible Invaders, Hand of Death* and more. With Richard Carlson, Beverly Garland and Kenneth Tobey, John Agar is one of the icons of '50s horror.

Agar was born in Chicago, the eldest of four children of a local meat packer. His 1945 marriage to "America's Sweetheart," Shirley Temple, brought him into the public eye for the first time, and a movie contract with independent producer David O. Selznick quickly ensued. Agar debuted opposite John Wayne, Henry Fonda and Temple in John Ford's *Fort Apache* (1948), initial film in the famed director's Cavalry Trilogy. Other early Agar roles included *She Wore a Yellow Ribbon* and *Sands of Iwo Jima* (both starring "the Duke") and the film noir *I Married a Communist*. His marriage to Shirley Temple ended in 1949, while his movie career continued. Agar made his fantastic film debut in the eight-day Sam Katzman quickie *The Magic Carpet* (1951), an Arabian Nights adventure, and other minor fantasy films *(Bait, The Golden Mistress* and the sci-fi/comedy *The Rocket Man)* followed. His science fiction career was in full swing by June, 1954, when production began on Jack Arnold's *Revenge of the Creature*.

Jack Arnold is considered one of science fiction's top talents in certain circles. How did you enjoy working with him?

I've always had nothing but great respect for Jack Arnold. I did *Revenge of the Creature* for him and then the next year we did *Tarantula*, and we got along very well. So far as I was concerned, he was a very knowledgeable director and he gave his all trying to make 'em the best that he could. Jack is a great guy; I don't think Universal was too kind to Jack, I think he should have been given a lot more opportunities. I went over and saw him at Universal a few years ago; he was going to do a remake of *The Lost World,* then all of a sudden the powers that be cancelled the thing on him. Of course you know that Jack lost a limb [to cancer]. The people behind *The Lost World* were going to go over to England and shoot it and Jack really *wanted* to direct it, but they didn't feel that he could physically do it. Then they changed their minds about doing the picture at all.

Did you enjoy the location trip to Florida for Revenge of the Creature?

I had never been to Marineland, and that was a lot of fun. We all got kind of carried away on that picture—we started having water gun fights and, gosh, it got to the point where one guy got up on top of a cottage with a bucket of water and poured it all over a bunch of people!

Previous page: John Agar and Mara Corday react to the off-screen terror of *Tarantula*.

Lori Nelson told us that that was the most fun she'd ever had making a movie.

We just had a heck of a good time. My wife Loretta joined me down there, and as a matter of fact she had a little part in the picture. Remember the scene at the lobster house when the Creature abducts Lori, and I dive off the pier after them? After that there's a shot of a guy and a girl in a boat; the girl's my wife Loretta.

Did you have to learn to use an aqualung for the underwater scenes in Revenge?

I learned to use an aqualung before that. Shortly before I did *Revenge of the Creature,* I went down to the Caribbean and did a picture called *The Golden Mistress* [1954], and I had to learn to use an aqualung for the underwater scenes in that picture. Nobody down there seemed to know anything about them, so I just went into the swimming pool at the hotel we were staying at, and I learned to utilize it. It's not all that difficult, but the one thing I didn't know about using an aqualung is that you can get an air embolism mighty easy — if you surface too quickly and you're holding the air in, you can be in a lot of trouble. I got into a ticklish situation: The underwater cameraman and I were swimming around this sunken ship, about forty feet down. There were some breaks in the deck and shafts of sunlight were shining down into the hold, and the cameraman thought it would be interesting to get a shot in there. So I swam in there, clear to the bow of the ship; I went to take a breath, to get air — and I couldn't get it! So I had to swim about twenty feet to the hole, just to get out of the ship, and then I had to swim forty feet up before I could surface. And in coming up I could *feel* the pressure on my body easing, releasing. Luckily somebody was watching over me, and I guess He showed me what to do. I had the sense *not* to hold my breath, to let it out, as I came up. I could have gotten into some real problems there.

Wasn't it dangerous swimming in the Marineland tank with all those sharks?

I was told by the people who ran Marineland that those sharks were really not dangerous; I had a tiger shark, an eight-footer, swim right over my head and it didn't pay any attention to me. I know Ricou Browning, who did the underwater work as the Creature, was being pestered more by the big sea turtles than by anything else — they'd come up and nip at him! But I did have one experience that could have been a little disastrous — there's one part of the main tank that had a kind of rock formation just below the surface. During the scene where the Creature escapes — grabs Johnny Bromfield, throws him in the water and kills him — I was standing at the far end of the tank. *Why* I did this I will never know *[laughs],* but I dove back into the tank at that point, not realizing how close to the surface of the water those rocks were. If I hadn't flattened my dive at the last second, I would've hit it flush. This is just speculation, but if I had hit there hard and maybe gotten a bloody nose or something,

John Agar in a publicity pose for *Revenge of the Creature*. (Photo courtesy Steve Jochsberger.)

it might have been a different kind of story, according to what I've heard about sharks and the way they smell blood out in water.

What can you tell us about working with Ricou Browning?
    Ricou was one of the most fascinating people insofar as his swimming was concerned—he had lung capacity that was just incredible. They would drop an oxygen hose into that tank and he would breathe through it; the oxygen was coming out of there with pressure and it would fill up the Gill-Man suit. So after he'd gotten the amount of oxygen he wanted, he then had to press the suit and get all the bubbles out. Then he would go and do the scene. I could stay underwater for over two minutes if I wasn't doing anything, but this guy was swimming and using a lot of energy. How he did that was just really amazing and marvelous to watch.

Richard Carlson, who starred in the original Creature from the Black Lagoon, *once admitted that the Gill-Man suit seemed so real that he got spooked shooting scenes in the studio tank.*

Well, when you see something that unusual, even though you *know* it's all make-believe, it *is* kind of a strange experience. If this *were* a real creature, what it could do to you wouldn't be pretty. So I can understand Richard Carlson saying that, especially in an underwater situation.

Recent Hollywood rumor has it that Clint Eastwood, who has a bit in Revenge, *also played the Creature in the on-land scenes.*

I don't remember Clint ever putting the suit on, but he may very well have; I do know that Ricou Browning never played the monster on land. Clint didn't go to Florida with us, so when the Creature broke away from Marineland Clint wasn't in the suit then. Now, he may have put the suit on for the scenes we shot back here; I don't remember him doing that, but that's not to say he didn't.

Would you agree that Tarantula *is your best science fiction film?*

Yeah, I guess that would be the one; *[laughs]* I really don't know. I am the *worst* judge of what I've done; I look back on all my pictures and insofar as I'm concerned I can see where I could have been so much better, could've done such a better job than what I did. I can *always* see that.

I had never planned to be an actor, and it was thrust upon me at a very early age. It was something I really wasn't ready for. Now I know exactly what George Bernard Shaw meant when he said that youth is wasted on the young.

William Alland, who produced Revenge, Tarantula *and other Jack Arnold films, once said that he feels slighted because Arnold seems to get all the credit for them nowadays. Was Alland a creative force as well?*

I agree wholeheartedly that William Alland was a force. He was the one that came up with some of the ideas and he produced the films, and he shouldn't be slighted at all. Those pictures, whether Universal wants to admit it or not, were moneymakers. There were three Creature pictures made, and I was told by a producer at Universal, Aaron Rosenberg, that *Revenge of the Creature* was the biggest grosser of all of 'em. I also heard that *Tarantula* was one of the top grossers of 1955; what they probably meant was that it was a top moneymaker in terms of what it *cost* and what it brought *in,* but I had heard that it was Number 5 in 1955.

The Mole People *is by far the least of your three sci-fi Universals. Would you put the blame on first-time director Virgil Vogel?*

Oh, no—Virgil Vogel is a nice guy and I don't blame that on Virg, *heck,* no. But to me, *The Mole People* was like some of those Larry Buchanan things

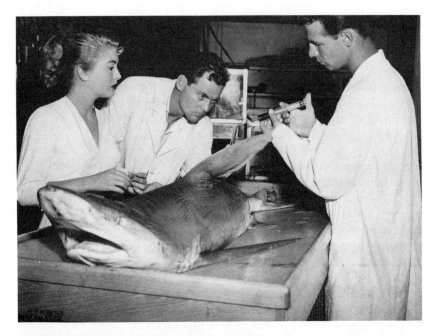

Top: Lori Nelson and John Agar in a serious moment from *Revenge of the Creature.* The lab technician (right) is Ricou Browning, who also played the Gill-Man. *Bottom:* Agar clowns with Mara Corday between takes on Universal's *Tarantula.* (Photo courtesy Steve Jochsberger.)

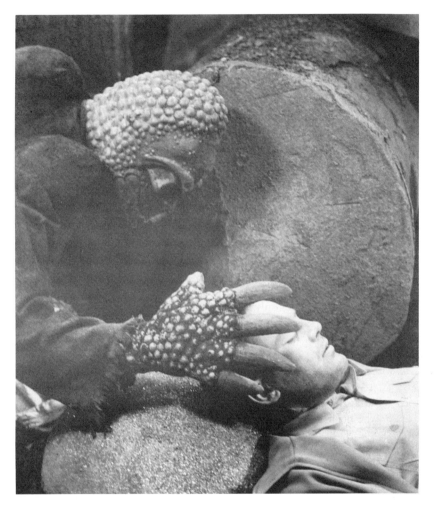

Agar is menaced by one of the humpbacked slave creatures in Universal-International's *The Mole People.*

I did down in Texas for money. In fact, it was right after *The Mole People* that I left Universal. I was there at the same time that they were grooming Tony Curtis, Rock Hudson, Jeff Chandler, George Nader — and *I* always kept gettin' the science fiction pictures. While I was under contract, the only Universal picture I did that wasn't sci-fi was a Western called *Star in the Dust* [1956]; that worked out well, and I felt that I didn't want to be just science fiction all the time. Bill Alland, for some reason, wanted me in all of his science fiction pictures, and when they came up with *this* one ... well *[laughs],* the story just didn't gel with me at all. People coming up out of the ground looking like moles, and an underground civilization. . . .

Too far out?

Yeah. I remember, too, that there was some silly dialogue in *The Mole People,* and I went to Bill Alland and told him, "Bill, people don't *say* things like this." He said something to the effect that he paid a guy a lot of money to write that dialogue, and I said, "Well, you got cheated!" And I think my nose got out of joint one time when I was on the set and Rock Hudson came over. He looked around at the production that was going on and he said, "How'd you get into *this* thing?" It was the kind of derogatory way that he said it—I don't know whether he meant it or not, but *[laughs]* that frosted me a little bit. I just never thought that *The Mole People* was as good a picture as *Revenge of the Creature* or *Tarantula.*

As a Universal contract player, were you in a position to turn down an assignment?

When you're under contract to a studio or to a producer and they assign you a project, if you don't do it they can put you on suspension and for the duration of that film you go without pay. I never turned anything down. They were paying me, and I figured that they were doing what was best for everybody concerned—not only for the studio but for me as well, because I was a member of their team, so to speak. Maybe I was naive, but I trusted them to guide my career.

Did you feel that the mole monsters in The Mole People *were effective?*

They were all right for the time; they didn't have the technology we have today. But at that time I thought that Universal had some of the best technicians in the business, as far as science fiction was concerned.

How was the special effect of men being dragged down under the earth achieved?

They put a rubber mat down over a hole in the floor; the mat had an X-shaped slit in it. Then they covered it with some kind of light material—it could have been Styrofoam—that was supposed to be earth or gravel. Even when someone was being pulled down through from below, the earth was held up—a lot of it could not fall through at once. The remaining earth would then cover up where they went through.

Why did you leave Universal after The Mole People?

I talked with Jim Pratt, who was the vice president over there, and I told him, "You know, I understand that you-all are grooming particular people, but I just don't want to *do* all these science fiction pictures." So when my option time came up, I said that I'd just as soon not stay on, and I didn't. I don't know, maybe I made a mistake, maybe they might've turned around and given me other things to do. I've made a lot of mistakes in my life *[laughs],* and maybe that was one of 'em.

Agar lent his talents to a number of B-grade sci-fi films of the late 1950s, including director Bert I. Gordon's *Attack of the Puppet People*.

One of your first pictures after leaving Universal was Daughter of Dr. Jekyll. *Were you disappointed to still be in that sci-fi/horror rut?*
Well—yeah. I really didn't want to do any more of those pictures, but *[laughs]* at least I made more money on *Daughter of Dr. Jekyll* than Universal was paying me!

What do you remember about your co-star, Gloria Talbott?
I really thought she was going to go on to do better things, but then what I guess happened was that she got married and got smart, and got out of the business. She was a very nice gal and we tried to do the best we could with *Daughter of Dr. Jekyll.* Some of those things work and some of 'em don't.

Did Daughter of Dr. Jekyll *work?*
Not really. I did that picture strictly for the bread. I didn't *fluff* it—I did the best I could with what I had to work with—but it wasn't my cup of tea. I just didn't believe it.

When you weren't appearing in a science fiction film, it was usually a Western or a war picture. Were you more comfortable in those genres?
To me, it's a lot easier to play in something that's real—a natural situation—than it is to deal with abstracts and things of the unknown. It's sort of difficult to make them come to life *[laughs]!* I always kind of had the feeling that when people looked at some of these science fiction things, we were going to get a big laugh. On a couple of occasions, some of the things that were supposed to frighten people really looked rather ludicrous—funny, rather than scary. I feel it's more natural to deal in something that people understand, rather than something that human beings don't come in contact with. It's a touchy situation to be in.

Did you enjoy playing a villainous Jekyll and Hyde–style role in The Brain from Planet Arous?
Yes, and I wish I had gotten more opportunities to play *against* type. I'll tell you one thing, that picture was a very painful experience for me. When that alien being took over my body, they inserted these full contact lenses in my eyes. They'd painted 'em silver and they forgot that that doggone paint would chip off. Every time I blinked, some of that silver would come off the lens and it was like having sand in my eyes. But it was the best they could do; that was 1957, and they didn't know that much about contact lenses. It was very, *very* painful.

What did you think of that film's floating brain prop?
Oh, I thought it was terrible—just *awful!* They really could have done a heck of a lot better than that—it looked like a balloon with a face painted on it. And that's probably about what it was, too *[laughs]!* I can't really remember exactly what it was, I just know it was ludicrous.

How did you get along with Bert I. Gordon on Attack of the Puppet People?

I don't know whether Bert Gordon liked me very much; we got into a little difficulty one night because he had promised me that I was only going to have to work until a certain hour. I was on a bowling team then and I was supposed to meet my wife and the team at such-and-such a time. Well, they carried me over past the time; Bert kept putting it off and putting it off, and I told him, "Look, you promised me I could be out of here by now, and you're foulin' me up!" I don't think Bert ever forgave me for that. I stayed and finished the work, but I don't think he thought I was giving one hundred percent. *Puppet People* was half of a two-picture deal I had with American International; the other one was called *Jet Attack* [1958], with Audrey Totter. That *Puppet People* was kind of a nonsense picture.

Was it difficult working with Puppet People*'s oversized props?*

No, but that question reminds me of another time that Bert Gordon passed some kind of a comment. I had to climb a rope and pull myself up onto this giant table, and they were betting I couldn't do it. Bert Gordon was saying, "He'll never pull himself up there," and I said, "The hell I won't!" Don't tell me I can't do something, 'cause that's just when I'm going to go break my neck to prove I *can* do it. And I did it!

How much real guidance would an actor get from a director like Invisible Invaders*' Edward L. Cahn?*

Edward Cahn was Mr. Speed-O; he'd jump up and almost get in the shot before he'd yell "cut"! But in all fairness I have to say that directors like Eddie Cahn didn't really have a chance. They had a schedule to contend with, and they wanted those films finished *ka-boom*. I think he did the best he could with the time he had, but in something like *Invisible Invaders* it's pretty much, "Learn the lines and get 'em out." They just didn't have the money to stay there and work on it.

Did you go to see all of your movies when they were first released?

A lot of the pictures I made were not released—they *escaped [laughs]!* I didn't *avoid* looking at them, but there were some where I knew full well what they were going to be like before they were ever released.

You've been directed by a lot of actors in your time—Abner Biberman, Edmond O'Brien, Hugo Haas and, on Hand of Death, *Gene Nelson. Did you ever think about directing a picture yourself?*

Well, I had a thought about doing it back then, and then I decided that I preferred to be in front of the camera rather than behind it. But the temptation was there for a time. Speaking of Gene Nelson, *Hand of Death* was his first shot at directing, and I thought he did a very good job for his first go at it.

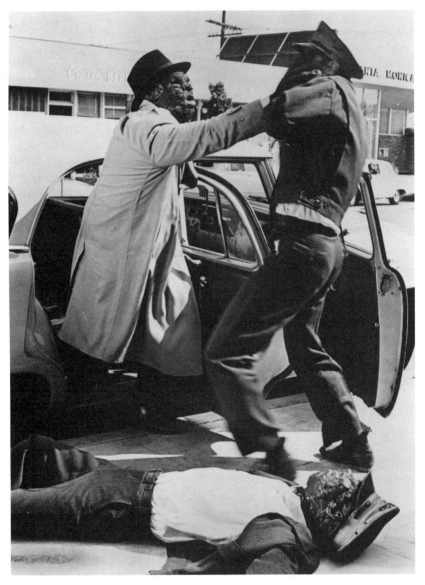

A monstrous Agar rebels against rising taxi fares in Fox's *Hand of Death*. (Photo courtesy Steve Jochsberger.)

Tell us a little about playing the monster in that film.

First they got some long johns and padded 'em to make me look like I weighed about four hundred pounds. Then they had this grotesque mask — a complete hood — and very large hands, to make me look burned. Our oldest boy, Martin, was maybe two or three years old at the time, and he came on the set with his mother and heard his dad's voice coming out of this monster get-up—and it scared him half to death! I had a tough time explaining it to him.

Was that an enjoyable change of pace, or was it too uncomfortable an experience?
Oh, no, it wasn't that bad—except at the very end, when I finally died. We went out to Malibu for a scene where I run into the ocean trying to get away from the police, and they shoot me. When I fell, the waves started knocking me around, and with that mask over my face I didn't know *where* I was! My eyes were set way back and the mask was sticking way out in front, and the only thing I could see was just directly straight out. I couldn't see the waves coming—that water was crashin' on me, and I was floppin' around, supposed to be dead *[laughs]*—! That was quite an experience.

How did you get involved on Journey to the Seventh Planet?
A guy named Sidney Pink had made some kind of a deal to make that picture over in Denmark, and he contacted me about going over there and starring in it. He had already done one over there, a thing called *Reptilicus*—they showed it to me over in Denmark, and *[laughs]* I didn't think too much of it. Anyway, my wife and our son Martin went with me and enjoyed the trip very much. Something that I'll never forget is that when we flew from L.A., we went the Polar route and I got to see the Northern Lights—the Aurora Borealis. I think that was the most incredible thing I've ever seen. When we came back here, we went over to American International and we looped a great deal of that picture—almost all of it. I don't know what the trouble was, but American International wanted it all redubbed, so that's what we did.

Compared to The Brain from Planet Arous, *what did you think of* Seventh Planet's *giant brain prop?*
Actually, I believe that giant brain was done here, not in Denmark. The one in Denmark was worse than the one they did here *[laughs]*! They thought they could improve on it here, but as I remember it wasn't too good, either. So we did shoot some new shots for *Journey to the Seventh Planet* over here and they slipped a couple of 'em in.

Can you give us some background on the Larry Buchanan pictures you did in Texas?
What happened on those was that American International gave Larry Buchanan a budget to work with and scripts of pictures that they had already done. Larry, God bless him, is a nice guy but he really was not a director. He did the best he could, but he didn't even know enough not to "cross the line," which is one of the simplest things there is in directing. In the beginning, he didn't understand *that [laughs]*! The first picture I did for Larry was *Zontar,*

the Thing from Venus; Curse of the Swamp Creature came next; then we did a war film called *Hell Raiders* [1968]. Of course I never thought those things would ever see the light of day—that was the only reason I did 'em!

You were working on actual locations most of the time, weren't you?
We did work mostly on location, although there were a couple of sets. We went out to Gordon McLendon's ranch on *Hell Raiders;* for *Zontar,* they used a park in Dallas, and we did work on a couple of stages in that. A lot of *Swamp Creature* was done in a little town called Uncertain, Texas—it was called that because the people that founded it weren't sure whether they were in Texas or Louisiana.

What about an obscure film called Night Fright, *made by many of the same people but not by Buchanan?*
I don't recall too much about that movie. It was produced by an attorney down there and directed by Jim Sullivan, who was an assistant director for Larry Buchanan.

How did you land your role in Dino De Laurentiis' King Kong?
I went out to Metro-Goldwyn-Mayer, read for it along with fifty other actors, and the director, John Guillermin, said he wanted me to do the part. But to this day I simply cannot understand why they wrote my scenes the way they did. Toward the end of the movie, Jeff Bridges and the others are running around New York wondering where Kong has gone, and then they realize that he'll think of the twin peaks and go to the World Trade Center. So Jeff Bridges calls me from out of the blue, but the audience doesn't know who in the heck I am. When King Kong was brought in and showed off, I was not in any of those scenes, and I never made contact with Jeff Bridges—but he calls *me* and puts all that trust in *me.* I never could understand that! My character was supposed to be a Jimmy Walker type of guy. Then at the very end, after Kong's been killed, they tried to show that I was really not concerned about the girl [Jessica Lange] or what she'd gone through, I was just trying to get publicity because I was a politician. But that scene didn't come off, either, and I knew it wouldn't. I just believe that, insofar as that character was concerned, they really weren't thinking. But, hey, I took the money and ran.

To most of us who enjoy the B-grade science fiction films of the '50s and '60s, your name seems synonymous with that type of film. Do you appreciate or resent the association?
No, I don't resent being identified with them at all—why should I? Even though they were not considered top-of-the-line, for those people that like sci-fi I guess they were fun. My whole feeling about working as an actor is, if I give anybody any enjoyment, I'm doing my job, and that's what counts.

Considering the fact that you started out in first-rate pictures with people like John Ford and John Wayne, are you at all happy with the direction your career took?

Well, I think a lot of success was thrown at me too quickly and I wasn't ready to receive it. It was my fault if it didn't work out better; I can't blame anybody but myself.

How do you keep busy today?

I've been working with Brunswick Recreation Centers, with their Club 55 program, for the last few years. I travel around, kind of like a public relations guy, and try to get prime-timers — senior citizens — involved with the sport of bowling.

When you were making these sci-fi pictures twenty and thirty years ago, did you have any idea that they'd still be seen and appreciated in the 1980s?

[Laughs.] Well, I don't know; you didn't think about those kinds of things at that time. They're making a lot of science fiction pictures nowadays that they don't call me about — maybe the fans appreciated me in these films, but the people in the business today certainly haven't said anything about me doing any work for 'em. I think I have much more to offer as an actor now than I ever did as a young man; now would be a time for me to be a character actor. It hasn't worked out that way, but you never know what's going to happen. As long as there's breath in the body, I am still hopeful.

*Satisfaction is a matter of what your needs are,
and what you're accustomed to.... When I was kicked out
of college and went bumming for a year, riding freights and so on,
it didn't take a hell of a lot to satisfy me—just a full meal!
Now, later on, when I was eating very well ...
it would take a hell-of-a-lot* better *meal...!
So since the background keeps shifting,
you cannot establish an absolute.*

Samuel Z. Arkoff

IF THERE WAS EVER a movie mogul who needed no introduction to fans of exploitation films, it is Samuel Z. Arkoff. A prime purveyor of exploitation pictures for nearly a third of a century, the Iowa-born Arkoff co-founded American International Pictures with his partner, the late James H. Nicholson, in 1954. Under the aegis of Arkoff and Nicholson, the company survived in a constricting industry by catering to the whims of the teenage trade. AIP's long (350-plus) roster of kitsch classics, running the gamut from horror to rock'n'roll, from juvenile delinquency to Italian musclemen, and from Edgar Allan Poe to Annette Funicello, have already forged their own unique niche in film history.

After Nicholson's 1971 resignation, Arkoff assumed full control of the company and remained in charge until the 1979 merger with Filmways prompted his own departure. He is now the head of Arkoff International Pictures, where upcoming projects (with titles like *Phobia, Buried Alive* and *They're Here*) offer solid evidence that Arkoff has no intention of straying from his time-tested formula for movie success.

As someone who's always made movies for the youth market, what were your favorite types of films when you were growing up in Fort Dodge?

I'm a picture buff—I didn't have any favorites. I liked pictures if they were well done at all. But you have to remember that that was a whole different era. I mean, I can remember the advent of sound! I went through all the experimentation with sound, when they had it on disks; in fact, I can recall going to a picture starring Richard Barthelmess—it might have been *Weary River* [1929]—and I remember a scene with Barthelmess and his leading lady in a boat. And because it got a little out of sync, the love speeches he was making were coming out of *her* mouth, and vice versa *[laughs]!* Now *those* were interesting days!

When you and Alex Gordon were planning to make a movie around Mother Riley Meets the Vampire *footage, did you get to meet Bela Lugosi?*

I had a number of conversations with Lugosi, who was a very interesting man; by this time, of course, he was "playing the role" of Lugosi—you know what I mean. In fact, I was the lawyer on *Bride of the Monster,* which was one of the last pictures that Lugosi did before he died. The director on that was Ed Wood, who has since come to prominence. Ed was quite a character, a very interesting fellow, and now, through pictures like *Glen or Glenda* and the like, he has sort of a reputation—although in his own era he never made very much dough.

When you started American Releasing Corporation in 1954, it was clearly a bad time in Hollywood for independents.

When we started in '54, there were virtually no independents at all! The

Previous page: Movie mogul Samuel Z. Arkoff (seen here minus his trademark cigar) proclaims that "everything in our whole American economy is exploitation!"

only independents had been Bob Lippert, who was an exhibitor, and Sam Goldwyn; David Selznick had lost his patron, John Hay Whitney, and was just going through the motions. Other than those, the only independents in those days were the one-lung producers who used to go to Griffith Park or one of the movie ranches, and for twenty-five or thirty thousand bucks each make two Westerns, back-to-back, with the same cast, the same horses and virtually the same story. Maybe they'd change a villain or something, and sometimes they didn't change a damned thing.

We started at a time when everybody said it was crazy to start a picture company. Thousands of theaters were going out of business. Young adults were getting married and moving out into new housing in the suburbs. They were sitting out in their millions of new homes, having babies and watching TV. The only real constant audience which Jim Nicholson and I recognized — one which the majors didn't — was the youth, who *didn't* want to stay home, who had to get *out*. Drive-ins were opening up all over but of course at the beginning they bought pictures at the end of their run for flat prices. They were known as "passion pits," and they didn't give a damn about the pictures they showed — a picture was a way to attract the kids who had wheels.

And it was this youth market that you and Mr. Nicholson zeroed in on.

That's right. In the old days, all the way up to the late '50s, there *were* no youth pictures as we understand them. Fundamentally, there were Disney types of pictures for the small kids and there were regular "family" pictures for everybody else. A typical youth picture would have been an Andy Hardy film. Look at it this way: Andy's father was played by Lewis Stone, an impressive fatherly figure who also happened to be a judge. *Think* about that. Andy says to his father, "I'm going to do such-and-such a thing." The father says, "You'd better not, you'll get into trouble." Andy and his friends go off, get into trouble and can't get out, and now Andy comes back to his father and says, "Dad, you told us not to do this, but we did it. Now we're in trouble, and I hope you can get us out." And so the judge says, in a severe but sympathetic tone, "Okay, I'll get you out of trouble," which he does. "Dad," says Andy, looking up at his father, "I'll never do that again." And the whole adult audience creams in its pants.

That is what the youth picture essentially was — a moral lesson, a lecture. But by the late '50s the kids were beyond lecturings. And this led up to the '60s, which of course was a decade like no other decade in American life. When we made the *Beach Party* pictures, those pictures were not basically about the beach. They were set at the beach, but basically they were about kids who didn't have parents. Why? Because these were youth pictures made for youth. Not the youth of Disney, not the youth that all these moralists, these *spinsters* wanted "family" pictures for. Fundamentally what we were doing, starting in the '50s when we did *Hot Rod Girl*, *Dragstrip Girl* and all of those, was making pictures for teenagers who didn't want to have a lecture crammed down their

Youth-slanted double-bills like *Teenage Werewolf* and *Teenage Frankenstein* helped AIP to flourish while other Hollywood studios floundered.

throats. This is not only true of our pictures, it was true in real life, because it was in the late '50s and the '60s that you began to have youth going out on their own.

Tell us a little about your early dealings with Roger Corman.

We had a four-picture deal with Roger, and he had a certain amount of money—something less than $100,000 a picture—as a budget for the total four. When he got to the fourth picture, *The Beast with a Million Eyes,* there was only about $29,000 or $30,000 left. So he did the whole picture, non-union, in Palm Springs, running away from the Screen Actors Guild and the IATSE. But when we got to the end there was no more money left and there was no monster. What we ended up using was a *teakettle,* with a lot of holes in it. Not a million holes, of course *[laughs],* but a lot, and the thing was obscured by the steam that was coming out of all the holes. That's ingenuity. Joe Levine, who was our franchise holder up in Boston and a great exploitation man in his own right, really got enthused about the piece of artwork we had made up for that picture. He and another big New England exhibitor had worked out this big campaign, and they were going to have a special promotion up there in that circuit. Joe brought the exhibitor out to see the picture. And when he saw it, he was somewhat crestfallen *[laughs]!* But the picture did very well, considering; it was a hell of an idea.

A lot of the basic concepts of your '50s films are still being used today.

You're right about that. Other than the sci-fi films, which of course have progressed because we've learned a great deal about other planets and so on . . . you name me one horror or science fiction concept that wasn't used in the '50s—that wasn't either started or used in the '50s. Pretty hard to do, huh?

Most of the ideas in many of these films today are really not ideas that were advanced by Spielberg or Lucas—although I won't take anything away from 'em. But the fact is that most of those ideas came out of the '50s. For example, in *It Conquered the World,* we had another odd monster—it looked like a pumpkin head—that enslaved people through little arrows that pierced the backs of their necks. That was one of the first times that was ever used—but it's been used in a lot of much bigger pictures since. So the *idea* was the thing in those days. Also, the state of the art in the '50s was not what it is today. Even if we had had more money, we could never have come up to what they're doing now.

The bigger sci-fi pictures in those days were the George Pal pictures.

Which, in their own way, were pretty good. Much better, in a sense, than ours, I'm not arguing the point, but they also had probably ten, fifteen times as much money going into them. But George was a good man and a friend of mine—in fact, just before he died we were talking about doing a picture together. But my whole point was that it was the *idea* that was important in those days. Now, along come these new state-of-the-art special effects—you might say that *Star Wars* was probably the pinnacle. I can remember everybody's awe at the special effects in that picture—and they *should* have been in awe, because that was an integral part of the story. It was one of the most judicious meldings of basic story and special effects that I think we've had.

Except that now it's gotten to the point where it's special effects for special effects' sake.
    And that's bullshit! And I'll tell you why: because the public gets tired of special effects. I thought we came to the zenith in the summer of '85, when they came out with those three special effects youth pictures all in one week— *Weird Science, Real Genius* and *My Science Project*. Three in one week! In the first place, it's too many—the same market, all aiming at the same youth sci-fi audience. Now, all youth doesn't go for sci-fi. And also you have to be careful when you meld genres. You can do it—we've done it, too—but you have to be cautious because if you go a little overboard, you're going to lose the "other" audience, you may even lose both of 'em, as far as getting the big numbers is concerned. So now what we have is that we're getting pictures where the special effects outweigh and out-proportion the rest of the piece. *Young Sherlock Holmes* [1985] is another example—if you're going to make a Sherlock Holmes picture, then *make* one! What that really was is another of those so-called adventure pictures masquerading under a Sherlock Holmes title. For the Holmes people it was completely unsatisfactory, and for the people who wanted a special effects, adventure type of piece, it was not satisfactory either, because it was harboring under Sherlock Holmes, who means nothing to the big bases of teenagers today. What does the average eighteen-year-old kid know about Sherlock Holmes? It's completely outside of their ken.
    Also, when they do all of these mechanical things, they're losing something that's very important: the interest of the audience in the movie's characters and their identification with people in trouble. It's very thin, very superficial. In the *Sherlock Holmes* piece, were you really *with* anybody? Nobody went to enough care to get you interested in the people, so you never really gave a shit. You've got to *care* about people, you have to be *concerned* when they have a problem. Oddly enough, it's almost like going back to the very origins of the business when you had superficial comics doing these chases and brawls. Today, you're supposed to be awed—or overawed—by the special effects. Well, I'm telling you that there's a limit beyond which the special effects just aren't going to take anybody. And I think that most young people today have seen just about all the special effects they care to.

Getting back to American Releasing and the mid–'50s, how exactly did you go about pretesting your movie concepts?
    We started with a title, and then we'd make up some kind of a slick

drawing. And then we'd send it around to half a dozen exhibitors that we thought were more than just real estate men and concession operators, and a few other people on the other side of the business, too, and we asked them whether they thought this had a *look*. It's always surprised me that so many of the pictures in our business are made without the sales department or the merchandising department being consulted. We didn't take a script and shoot it, and then, when the picture was done, send it to the advertising department and say, "Now, figure out how the hell you're gonna sell it." That's putting the cart before the horse, but a lot of companies still do that today.

I'm a great believer in "If you can't sell it, don't make it." American industry has used that kind of concept for years—they go out, test the market, talk to people and so on. But nobody in the picture business seems to want to test anything anymore. Now they want to go out with one thousand or two thousand prints and a big national campaign, *boom*. We tested. People think you can make a little picture and send it out, and then *[majestically]* the public *responds,* and word-of-mouth spreads. That's true, within reason. But if you go out with a little picture and go into a theater and spend a little money—as befits a little picture—how's the public going to come? What's going to bring 'em? A picture with no handle? That's why you have an exploitation picture—because if you don't have a big star or a pre-sold book and all of that, you *have* to have that handle.

What do you say to people who think that exploitation is a bad word?

Everything in our whole fucking American economy is exploitation! It simply means to exploit what you have; you have to have something to sell, you have to have a handle. We knew that stars weren't necessarily a handle, but the presence of a star or two helps make the picture look bigger, so the public will give it a chance. Then at least you have a chance, with enough advertising, to bring people into the theater, and then get word-of-mouth going. What happens with a little picture is, nobody comes the first week, the theater doesn't do much business, gets rid of that picture and gets another one in the second week. There's that old saw, "If there's no one to hear, there is no sound." If there's nobody to see it, where's the word-of-mouth going to come from? There's no blowhole somewhere that keeps telling what a wonderful picture it is. The whole point about it is, you need a gimmick. We didn't have stars—we created stars, but we didn't have 'em. So that was really how we sold those pictures.

Was ARC the first production company to try that approach?

Oh, no, I don't think so—but I think we brought it to a polish *[laughs]!* There was Barnum and Bailey, there was Mike Todd, there were all kinds of people throughout history who beat the drums—exploitation is not a new word. For me to say that we started the concept of exploring the worth of an idea based on a title and some rough artwork would not be fair; I can only say that maybe we added a little more gilt to the process.

For all of this business savvy, American Releasing got off to a pretty shaky start.

The exhibitors wanted to play all of our pictures as second features. Well, a second feature gets a flat price—$100, $200, maybe even $500, but it isn't going to get the percentage. We could never have made a go of it with second features; after a few early pictures like *The Fast & the Furious* [1954], *Apache Woman* [1955] and maybe a couple more, we realized that with second features we were going to go under. So we sat down and said that what we were going to do was to make exploitation pictures, put two of 'em together and then hold firm—we would play the two pictures for a percentage. Basically, we would be giving them two pictures for the same percentage they used to pay for one, which meant that they didn't have to pay for the second feature, we were *giving* it to them. And what's more, we told them, we were going to make it like a combination. What the majors used to do was to take one picture, which was (let's say) a Western, and then make the second feature completely different than a Western hoping to get a more diversified audience that way. That was really bullshit. The way to do it, particularly if you're appealing to youth, was to make two pictures on the same subject. So our first combination was *Day the World Ended* and *The Phantom from 10,000 Leagues.* Those two cost about a hundred thousand bucks apiece.

How did this new strategy work?

In the beginning, we couldn't even book 'em! The exhibitors said, "No, we don't want to play them together as a combination, we'll book them as second features." We just resisted and resisted, and I want to tell you, it got to be pretty tense. We were just sitting there and not getting any action from the exhibitors, who after all were very powerful. Finally we got a date in Detroit in the first week of December, which is *not* the best playing time in the world in Detroit. And there was a newspaper strike to boot! So we got up a promotion through the streets of Detroit—we had some kind of a horror caravan, with a monster and all that kind of stuff, and we had flyers that we dropped everywhere. And we did very well. With that one run we broke the barrier, the exhibitors booked them together, and we were off and running.

Wasn't The Phantom from 10,000 Leagues *a pick-up?*

There were a couple of guys, the Milner Brothers, editors who wanted to make a picture, and so we went to them. We made a deal for them to make this other picture and we put it together with ours, and we divided sixty-forty—we got the sixty because ours, *Day the World Ended,* was a little more expensive than theirs. So actually it was made to order—they made the picture but we had a hand in it. Lou Rusoff was the writer on *Phantom;* he was my

Three-eyed mutant Paul Blaisdell absconds with an unconscious Lori Nelson in the climax of *Day the World Ended.*

brother-in-law, and he wrote a lot of those pictures for us. He died just after he made *Beach Party,* around 1963.

Why did you change your company name from American Releasing to American International?

We tried to get the AIP label in the beginning, but there was an American Pictures so we couldn't get it. We took the title we could get, which was ARC, and then the other company apparently went out of business and we got the other title.

Was AIP a reasonable success from then on, or were those early years still lean ones for all of you?

They were lean years, for a lot of reasons. We didn't start with any money—we put bits and pieces of things together. For example, I'd go to the franchise holders in the U.S. and I'd get maybe $40,000 in advance for a picture to be delivered. And then I would go and get maybe $14,000 for the U.K., half of it in advance. And then I'd get a little money out of foreign—not much. Then I'd get about $25,000 from the laboratory in cash, plus a deferment, and then I'd get actors and others to defer their salaries for a time. And we'd put together fifty, sixty, seventy thousand dollars toward a $100,000 picture—

that's how we made our pictures. And we kept expanding, so even if we *had* been successful, we wouldn't have had any money. Probably the best thing that ever happened to us was the fact that we never had any room to breathe. We kept fighting and going ahead, we didn't spend much dough on anything — we certainly didn't spend it on ourselves! — and we just put every dollar back into the business.

Several of the people we've talked with about Roger Corman have resented his attitude and his methods.

Well, in the first place, let me tell you something. Roger's been a good friend of mine for a long time now — I met him when he was twenty-eight and I was thirty-five, so I've known Roger for thirty-three years. And Roger's a hell of a guy. Roger and I have had a lot of successes together; he made maybe forty pictures for us, give or take. I assure you of one thing — Roger's doing what he wants to do, for whatever reasons he has, because he's fully capable of doing anything he wants to do.

What sort of arrangement did you have after the initial four pictures?

Our relationship was just a working arrangement that was never really in writing. In fact, he formed a distribution company before New World called Filmgroup. During those days when he was making pictures for Filmgroup, he would make cheaper ones for himself and Filmgroup, but the minute he went above a certain amount he would come to us and we would do it. And then when he decided to get out of Filmgroup, he brought us over those pictures, and we released those for a time. We had a very informal arrangement and it was a wonderful relationship — still is a wonderful relationship, although we haven't done any pictures together recently. I think the last picture we did together was *Boxcar Bertha* [1972].

After what happened on Gas-s-s *[1970], he said he'd never do a movie for AIP again.*

I don't even think Roger was too fond of *Gas-s-s;* I thought that the title was about what the picture was. But, look — I'm very fond of Roger, I'm not going to pillory him for the press or for anybody else. We had our differences from time to time — very few differences, considering how easy it is to have them on something as highly charged as making a picture. We did a lot of pictures together, we had a great relationship, we have a great relationship now. He's a terrific guy and I'm proud to call him a longtime friend.

Were you impressed with his ability to grind out product quickly and inexpensively?

Of course — there was nobody better than Roger. He produced and directed four and five pictures a year, he was a hard worker, he always brought them in on budget — which is more than I can say for practically anybody else.

To tell the truth, there were times when he could've spent a little *more* money—and, boy, you don't hear anybody ever say that about pictures, especially me! But I thought there were a couple of pictures where he could have used a few more people in 'em—you know, to sort of fill up the scene *[laughs]!*

Would you agree that some of his early films have stood the test of time better than many of the other older AIPs?

That's not necessarily true. I like Roger's, but what about *I Was a Teenage Werewolf?* Herman Cohen did some very nice pictures—*Teenage Werewolf, Teenage Frankenstein, Horrors of the Black Museum* and so on. Those stand up very well. But Roger did more of the black-and-whites than any other single director did. I'm not taking anything away from Roger, but we did have other directors as well.

Tell us about your brief appearance in Corman's Hawaiian-made Naked Paradise *[1957].*

We went over to Hawaii—me, my two kids and my wife, Jim with his wife and three kids. Roger told me one day to come over to where he was shooting, and he gave me this one line to read to Richard Denning: "It's been a good harvest, and the money is in the safe." Now *that's* a key line *[laughs]!* That was my first and last role; I've never been asked back into any of 'em since!

Did you enjoy visiting the sets or meeting the stars of these early films?

What stars?—what kind of shit is that *[laughs]?* Look, I have nothing against actors—although I wouldn't say that some of my best friends are actors—but we'd meet 'em in the normal course of business. Actors are people—I'm not awed by them, certainly not overawed or anything like that. That's for fans—I'm not a fan.

Alex Gordon tells the story that AIP really didn't care to have veteran actors in their early films.

Well, for Christ's sake, Alex loved old actors—he used to drag these old actors around, and I sometimes thought he went out to the graveyards to find 'em *[laughs]!* He idolized old actors, he really did—that was Alex's bag. I wasn't against them, I just was against building a picture around 'em. Let me give you an example: When he brought around Anna Sten and used her in a movie called *Runaway Daughters* [1956], he thought that was a great coup. I thought it was a *coup de grâce!* She meant nothing *[laughs]*—nobody in the fornicating audience had the slightest idea of who Anna Sten was! She was never successful—Sam Goldwyn tried to build her up, brought her over from Europe, used her in three or four pictures, spent a lot of money on her. None of her pictures ever crashed through—and she'd played opposite some very good stars. She was a nice lady and I had nothing against her, but when Alex wanted to give her top billing and all. . . ! He also used to bring Raymond Hatton around a lot. Well, I remembered Raymond Hatton, he used to play in pictures with Wallace Beery. But at that point the young audience didn't even know who Wallace Beery was, and *he* was the *big* star!

I had nothing against oldtime actors; if Alex wanted to put an older actor into a role, fine, but don't try to base your pictures on them, particularly when you're trying to go for a young audience. I am not ashamed to say that I didn't want to play to empty theaters. And therefore you had to cast people who would bring audiences in; we didn't have stars but we created them, and they had a market. Like Annette Funicello: Annette did the Mouseketeer bit for Disney, and we turned her into a completely different kind of personality—Mouseketeer was little kiddie-time. But fundamentally I appreciate what Alex was doing; he just happened to love old actors.

What prompted his decision to leave AIP?

It was a completely voluntary act on Alex's part—he wanted to be bigger himself. We considered him a part of an organization, that he had certain functions and that he did them well. He really wanted, I think, to be kind of a sole star. So when he asked to get out, I told him, "Don't do it—you're making a mistake." But he wanted to do it, and so we bought him out. I still see Alex every now and then, I *like* Alex—but I don't think he should have left.

Because there was a sequel to The Amazing Colossal Man, *people assume that that was one of your biggest early moneymakers. Was it?*

Let me tell you our theory. The majors today make sequels, but they never *plan* for sequels, as a rule. A picture goes out and does very well—they make a sequel. Basically, they're looking for a follow-up to a successful picture. *We* were looking to establish a vein of ore that we could mine. A sequel didn't necessarily mean that the first picture was particularly successful; just as long as it was successful *enough,* then we'd make a second one. While *The Amazing Colossal Man* made money, it wasn't that it made so much money we *had* to do it—we were trying to open up a vein.

So then what were some of your better-grossing early double bills?

You have to remember that satisfaction is a matter of what your needs are, and what you're accustomed to. I can remember when I was kicked out of college and went bumming for a year, riding freights and so on, it didn't take a hell of a lot to satisfy me—just a full meal! Now, later on, when I was eating very well—and showing the evidences of it! *[laughs]*—it would take a hell-of-a-lot *better* meal to make me think it was a good meal! So since the background keeps shifting, you cannot establish an absolute. Take the gross on a picture: As pictures began to cost more, you had to gross more. So some of the earlier pictures which were kind of a breakthrough, like *Day the World Ended,* you

One of AIP's most memorable '50s productions was Bert I. Gordon's *The Amazing Colossal Man* with Glenn Langan.

always remembered as being very important to you. Now we surpassed the gross of *Day the World Ended* relatively soon after that—but even in that short amount of time our pictures had already started costing more.

We were told that the double bill I Was a Teenage Frankenstein *and* Blood of Dracula *had an interesting story behind it.*

There was a famous exhibitor in the Southwest by the name of Bob O'Donnell—he was the head of Interstate, which was *the* big company at the time. He was having an argument with some major companies about film rentals, and so he told us—on Labor Day—that if we could make a couple of pictures by Thanksgiving, he would play us in his Flagship Theater. We had never played that Flagship Theater, so we made those two pictures for him by Thanksgiving!

Made them from scratch?

Oh, no—the scripts for those two were already in the works before he asked. Look, we made *I Was a Teenage Werewolf,* which was successful—were we *not* going to do *Teenage Frankenstein?*

Why did Herman Cohen make a number of his pictures in England?

Well, because England was a good place to make 'em. That was a market that liked horror films, so you worked with them on these as co-productions, each party bearing half the cost. It made economic sense to make pictures in England.

AIP's formula for success seems so straightforward and so common-sensible; why weren't the other studios able to fully duplicate your success with exploitation films?

Because a lot of producers like to be dignified. They're basically narcissistic, a great many of them—they want to be considered cultured people, like so many other people in the United States. Fundamentally, a lot of them didn't want to do exploitation pictures. In fact, for years one of the great problems was that, even after the television era came in and it was known that it was primarily the youth who were going to the theaters, they were still doing remakes of pictures like *The Barretts of Wimpole Street* and all that kind of bullshit. That's what people want to make—it gives them a dignity.

But a lot of the smaller studios, Allied Artists in particular, were churning out their own horror/sci-fi films at that same time.

That's right, and by the spring of 1959 we knew we were in trouble. We had been making these combinations and being successful with them, but all of a sudden the market was inundated with copies of them. And a lot of these other pictures didn't have any originality—they were more or less copies of ours. What we did then was one of the most important things we ever did: We said, "Look, the combinations aren't working any more. This is the way to go broke." So at that time we made two steps. First we said goodbye to the combinations. Then we decided that we were going to put the money that we used to put into *two* pictures into just *one* picture, and then we'd go out with it plus an older picture as the second feature. In other words, in June we'd come out with a new picture, and March's top-of-the-bill would become June's second. And then June's top-of-the-bill would later become September's bottom-of-the-bill.

That was also about the time AIP started picking up a number of foreign-made films.

Oh, sure. For instance, Joe Levine had picked up a Hercules picture and did well with it. There were a lot of Hercules pictures being made, so we also got a Steve Reeves Hercules picture. But we didn't want to make ours Hercules, so in the dubbing we changed it to Goliath, and the picture became *Goliath & the Barbarians* [1960]. We also picked up a picture called *The Sign of Rome* [1959], which had no gladiator, but in the dubbing we had the guy in it talk about the days when he *was* a gladiator, and we called the picture *Sign of the Gladiator [laughs]!*

Was Black Sunday *a pick-up, or was AIP in on that one from the start?*

That was a pick-up. I remember seeing that picture on a deadly cold morning in Rome. At that time, the Italians couldn't have both air conditioning and heat; when they'd turn off the heat in the spring, they'd never put it on again until late fall. So what happened was, they turned off the heat, and there was a cold spell. I can remember sitting in this damned screening room at eight o'clock in the morning—shivering, our overcoats on and everything else—and then this picture, *Black Sunday,* came on. And I'll tell you, it was really one hell of a picture. Mario Bava was really a master; if he had been an American or British director, I think he would have made it big. He had a real feel for this stuff.

How did you enjoy working with Vincent Price on Roger Corman's Poe films?

He was really quite a bright man—very educated, very cultured. We had a long relationship with Vincent, and I really thought he was a spectacular man in every respect. The same goes for a lot of the other horror people, but Vincent is in sort of a class by himself.

You know, it's very interesting that some of our best horror stars have really been very good actors in another milieu. Vincent started out doing serious stuff—he played on Broadway opposite Helen Hayes, playing Prince Albert to her Victoria in *Victoria Regina.* Lugosi had been a serious dramatic actor in Europe, and Basil Rathbone had been a stage actor. Rathbone had no humor; he was in a couple of our pictures. Vincent had a lot of humor, and

Pit and the Pendulum with Vincent Price and Barbara Steele ranks as one of Arkoff's favorites among his three hundred–plus American International Pictures.

so did Peter Lorre—he was really my favorite. We brought back almost all the great horror stars: Vincent, Boris Karloff, Lon Chaney, Jr., Peter Lorre and so on. The only one alive today is Vincent, and the odd part is that all the others died after making our pictures *[laughs]!* I don't know whether there's any direct connection. . . .

Can you tell us a little more about Karloff?
    A very dignified, very warm man. Naturally, I didn't know him at the start of his career; I met him for the first time in the late 1950s, when he was already up in years. But he had a wife who took good care of him—a very sweet lady. And, again, like Vincent, he was a cultured man. You know, it's really amazing about the horror stars, that so many of them were miles above the average actor. Vincent certainly is, and I thought Boris was. They were dignified men, they really were, and you treated them like dignified men. Those were good relationships, and I have very fond memories of working with them.

So no trouble with any of them?
    Peter Lorre gave us a little bit of trouble; I think he would have liked to have gotten some more standard, "non-horror" roles toward the end—although as you know his first big hit was as the child murderer in *M* [1931].

And although I knew Basil Rathbone less than I knew the others, I felt that he was still playing other kinds of roles a little bit. My guess is that he was doing horror more for the money than because he really loved it; I always had the feeling about Basil that he would just as soon have been in a different type of picture. I think Vincent genuinely relishes it, and that Boris sort of did, too.

Critics complain that Vincent Price camped it up in the Poe films. Do you agree?

Well, I think that became a little truer as the years went by—and I think that's a natural kind of thing. I think if you do anything for a long time, that ultimately you have to satirize or spoof yourself. As the world gets more involved and intricate, I think that's a natural tendency. You see, if an actor is really a good actor, he doesn't really want to play everything the same way the second time.

I know that there's a funny story you tell about Conqueror Worm.

A very bright young director, Michael Reeves, wrote a script which he sent to us. It was based on a best-selling book in the U.K., *Witchfinder General,* a story about a witch-burner in Cromwell's era. Reeves sent it to us with the intent of getting some financing. The book had never been published in this country, and I just didn't think anybody in the U.S. gave a damn about Cromwell and such. By this time Jim Nicholson and I were fairly expert on Poe, so we looked at the poems and found one called *Conqueror Worm,* which fit pretty well in a way—although I guess a title like that could've fit a hell of a lot of things *[laughs]!* So we went in on it, and it was released in the U.K. and such as *Witchfinder General*—the book had a substantial audience over there—and in the United States as *Conqueror Worm.*

The funny part you're talking about was that Nat Cohen, with whom we'd made a number of pictures, had distribution rights in the U.K. and in various military installations. The picture played on bases and ships as *Witchfinder General.* So this whole group of sailors saw this piece under that title. And then a few weeks later they're in Hong Kong and they go into a theater to see a picture called *Conqueror Worm* — the same picture — and they damn near tore the theater up *[laughs]!*

Which were the bigger grossers, the Poe films or the beach films?

I think the beach pictures domestically and the Poe pictures internationally.

In what way did Sidney Pink's Reptilicus *initially fail to meet AIP's standards?*

Because it was shot in *Danish* English. Scandinavians have a particular kind of accent when they speak English—like a singsong. Sidney Pink made this picture in Copenhagen, and on one of my trips to Europe I made a stop there and Sidney, very proud of *Reptilicus,* ran the picture for me. And I said, *"Sidney*—we'll never get by with this!" He had been over there—where everybody talked like that—and he didn't realize that any American audience would have broken up immediately, particularly in that kind of picture. Sid didn't want to change it, and he sued us for not taking the picture. I told him, "Sidney, I'm not going to accept it—it says right in your contract that this English has to be English. This isn't English!" He was so clearly wrong, but he sued us—he was really bound and determined, so help me God! But on the courthouse steps—or almost—he decided in favor of the better part of valor *[laughs]!*

Did it bother you when people used to say you made irresponsible and inflammatory pictures?
    That was ridiculous. You want to know something? It used to irk the *shit* out of me that we actually had at one time spinster types who used to picket the theaters where they played our monster pictures. These damned pictures now play on Saturday morning TV and afternoon matinees, and are even thought of as camp by the *kids,* for Christ's sake *[laughs]!* What the spinsters would do is, they would read the SEE's—SEE! this and SEE! that. They used to be kind of lurid, and these spinsters would believe that shit. Do you know that there were hundreds of papers in this country during the *Beach Party* days, which were the early-to-middle '60s, that brushed the navels out of the ads? Is it believable today? There must have been a whole generation of kids who thought that navels were dispensable, not realizing that without them their birth would have been somewhat questionable!

Why did Jim Nicholson leave AIP, and how did the company change for you after he left?
    Basically I believe Jim left because it was getting bigger than he really wanted. He wanted to go off and do some pictures himself, and he did make a few successful pictures for Fox before he died. Of course the company did change for me after he left because he and I were practically interchangeable in some ways—although there were certain things that we did by ourselves. Jim certainly was without peer when it came to devising titles and that kind of stuff, and also for heading up the merchandising, artwork and so on. He didn't do the actual artwork—most of it was done by a fellow named Al Kaylis, who was very good—but Jim was really the key behind that. Do you remember the *Beach Blanket Bingo* campaign—"Ten thousand kids meet on five thousand beach blankets" *[laughs]?* Well, that was terrific, and that was Jim. At the beginning I did the legal work, but by this time we had our own legal department. I was really in charge of all of those areas, and of course I handled the problems, which were daily. That was not Jim's forte, he didn't like to be involved in problems.

So we had our respective divisions, but basically I would say we spent two, three, four hours a day every day together and made joint decisions. In fact, we were the only company I know that had joint chief executive officers. We continued on being very friendly after he left; in fact, I delivered the eulogy at Jim's funeral, which unfortunately came much too early.

Why did you resign from AIP after the merger with Filmways?
Because I couldn't get along with one of the asses who was heading Filmways. Being an independent to the end, I resigned.

What percentage of AIP pictures have you personally seen?
Oh, I've seen 'em all. Every one of them, sure. Now, I can't say that I necessarily always enjoyed them *[laughs]*...!

Which were your favorite AIP pictures?
I don't look at pictures from the standpoint of favorites. It was when we would hit upon a new genre, *that's* what gave me the big thrill — like when we did *Beach Party* and it worked. Our objective was to be able to open up a vein so we could mine the ore until the vein ran out. So when we hit a new genre — when we made our first motorcycle picture or beach picture or Poe picture, as examples, and those things clicked so you could make a whole string *more* — those were my favorite moments.

I don't mean to harp on this question, but there must have been some pictures that you especially liked.
Well, I had a few favorites — I thought *Pit & the Pendulum* was really very good, the best of the Poes. I thought *Dressed to Kill* was a hell of a picture, and so was *The Amityville Horror,* which was the biggest picture we ever had — in fact, the largest picture any independently produced, independently distributed company ever had in this country. One that really gave me a kick — because we didn't expect it to be that good or that successful — was *Love at First Bite* with George Hamilton as Dracula. A lot of people tried to ape that afterwards. It's tough to mix genres; lots of people have tried to meld horror with comedy, and it doesn't work very often. A horror picture really should have moments where you kind of rest up and laugh — even if it's a nervous laugh — and then go on to another horror. Some of these pictures which have been made in the last decade or so are simply one blood-drenched corpse after another. That's not really suspense, that's just plain bloody gore. They're unleavened — they need a little yeast. *Friday the 13th* started a whole inundation of that kind of piece, and there's still a market for it, although the market isn't as big as it was. But I think that basically those are over the hill.

Your own The Comedy of Terrors *did a good job of mixing genres.*
You've got to make them larger than life, but not preposterous. One of

the great problems with young writers is that they have a tendency to think that they can spoof everything to a fare-thee-well. Well, you can't do that. Spoofs are very difficult; they used to say, "Satire is what closes on Saturday night." Since *Love at First Bite* there've been half a dozen pictures out where they've tried to do the same thing, and not a single one really worked. One of the reasons that they haven't is because they get too wild. Your piece has to be anchored in realism — then it's funny. But if it gets too far off that foundation, it becomes unbelievable.

What can you tell us about Arkoff International Pictures' initial production Night Crawlers?

We're doing that film for Cannon, a company that Golan and Globus say was based on American International. I'm willing to take the credit as long as they're doing well; if they don't *[laughs]*, I'm going to deny any resemblance! By the way, before he ever made a picture in Israel, I put Menahem Golan on a picture called *The Young Racers* [1963]. That film was directed by Roger Corman; first assistant was Francis Coppola; and Menahem was in there, really, as kind of a water boy — gradually, I think, he got a little more dignified status. His wife was also script girl. And the lead was Mark Damon, who now heads up P.S.O. Can you top that cast?

Is it a tough game today for independent producers?

It always goes up and down for the independent. But there's room for him, in one sense, that there isn't in American industry. Now, you take big American industry — take the automobile business. There's no room for the little guy. The thing about the independent in the movie business is that there's no way that a major can cut him off. An independent may have trouble, but there's always an independent picture coming down the pike that can get into the theaters, or into home video, or what have you. So no matter how difficult it is, there's room in a game like this because there's no way that anybody can spread-eagle the whole field. There's always a place for an independent, because there's always somebody who's going to come out of the woods with a picture that's a little different. Sure, it's a tough game; the amount of money that you put into these things, plus the prints and ads, is really ridiculous. If we had any sense, we could make more money with parking lots! It's just that there's something about this picture game that we like.

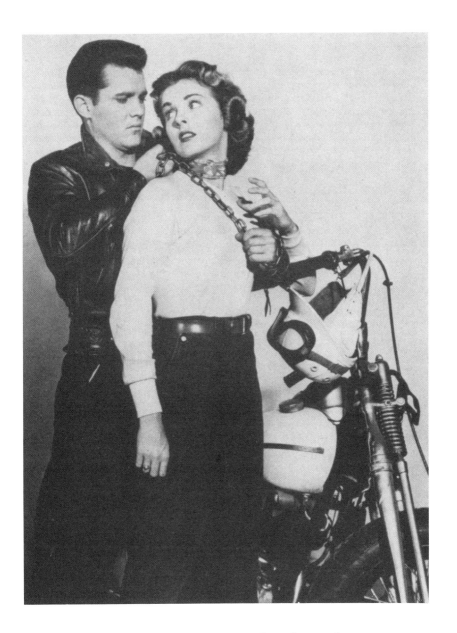

*This is a terrible thing to admit, but maybe
the key to my success with exploitation films
is that I always liked those movies, and I
never had any real reason to turn them down.
I just enjoyed doing them.*

John Ashley

AS AN AIP TEEN STAR, John Ashley appeared in such '50s kids-in-trouble pictures as *Motorcycle Gang, Hot Rod Gang* and, for Filmgroup, *High School Caesar*. In 1958 he was introduced to horror movies in *How to Make a Monster* and continued to thrive in the genre until the early '70s. In between the occasional A-picture assignment like *Hud* (1963) and his regular appearances in AIP's beach pictures, Ashley worked with such zero-budget luminaries as Richard Cunha *(Frankenstein's Daughter)* and Larry Buchanan *(The Eye Creatures),* and went on to carve a lucrative niche for himself in the Philippines as both a star and producer in a unique series of horror pictures that included *Mad Doctor of Blood Island* and *The Beast of the Yellow Night.*

Oklahoma-bred Ashley got his start in the movie business while on a vacation in California. A friend from Oklahoma State University got him onto the set of the John Wayne movie *The Conqueror* (1956), and Wayne in turn steered him toward a job on television in the William Castle series *Men of Annapolis.* One day, Ashley went over to the AIP offices to pick up his girlfriend, who was auditioning for a part in *Dragstrip Girl* (1957). AIP house writer Lou Rusoff saw Ashley waiting in the hall, decided the young man was the type the studio was looking for to play the *Dragstrip* male lead, and teen-pix history was made.

How did you enjoy working at American International?

It was a lot of fun, because it was a new company. Sam Arkoff, Jim Nicholson, Leon Blender and Milt Moritz were basically the cadre there. They made movies very quickly; they would come up with a great title, draw up an advertising concept, and then make the picture. Everything was *fast* — we shot them in ten days, black-and-white — but it was a great learning experience.

When I first went to work for American International, there were three little outfits working under the AIP banner: Alex Gordon and Lou Rusoff, who was Sam Arkoff's brother-in-law, had a little entity; Herman Cohen had another; and then there was Roger Corman, who had his little company. Roger and I became friends. I never worked for Roger as an actor, but then later on, when I got into producing, we did several projects together over in the Philippines. A couple of 'em were horror films, a couple of 'em were just exploitation.

How did you land your "special guest appearance" in How to Make a Monster?

How to Make a Monster was Herman Cohen's picture, and at the time I was under contract to AIP and had done two or three films for them. Herman came to me and asked if I would do this role — a musical number — and just play myself. That was casting more or less against type at that point, because I had been playing delinquents and heavies. I was beginning to do a little singing — I had a deal with Dot Records — and I think maybe that triggered it

Previous page: A publicity photo taken during Ashley's days as a movie juvenile-delinquent at AIP. The gal is Jean Moorhead.

a little bit. Also, I had been down to the wire and lost the title role to Michael Landon in *I Was a Teenage Werewolf,* and Herman had kept saying, "Don't worry, we're going to work together." So, *How to Make a Monster* was the result.

Did you take an interest in behind-the-scenes goings-on at AIP, with an eye toward getting into the production end of the business someday?
No, I really didn't; basically, I was just having fun doing it. The first time I really began looking behind the scenes was when I started making the films in the Philippines. Most of those pictures I *was* financially involved with; I normally came up with half of the money, and then Corman, or Larry Woolner at Dimension, or AIP came in with the other half. That was when I really began to get involved in the production end.

How did production values on Astor's Frankenstein's Daughter *compare to those at AIP?*
AIP was low-budget — one hundred grand made a movie — but at least they shot on sound stages, and the size of the crew was bigger. *Frankenstein's Daughter* was *really* rock bottom. But the people involved were very nice, especially Dick Cunha, the director. You know, it's strange — I don't have a lot of memories about that picture, except that Harold Lloyd, Jr., was in it, and Richard Dix's son Robert, and Sandra Knight, who was quite nice. But it *was* quick, a little more down-and-dirty than AIP.

Did you get to know any of the classic horror stars who made cameo appearances in your beach pictures?
No, nothing other than meeting them on the set. Boris Karloff *[Bikini Beach]* I had met several times because he had done pictures for Corman. Vincent Price *[Beach Party],* the same. I was a big fan of Peter Lorre *[Muscle Beach Party],* but I only met him when we did the show. They were all very nice and friendly, talked to the young people and offered them advice on how to do a scene.

What was it like to be in your early thirties, yet still playing a teenager on-screen?
Strange. At the time I was never really consciously thinking, "Okay, I'm gonna try to play twenty." Maybe in my mind I felt I *was* ten years younger than my actual age! It never really hit me until we were doing the beach pictures. We were doing, I think, the third one, and I was thirty years old.

We shot the beach pictures in the wintertime, so they'd be available for release in the summer. So it was always colder than hell. They'd slap body makeup on Frankie Avalon and me, 'cause it was winter and nobody had a tan. I remember we were doing a scene one day when it was *really* cold, and the director, Bill Asher, told me and Frankie to do the dialogue and then just walk right on down the beach and into the water. So we did the dialogue and headed for the water, waiting for Asher to yell "cut." Our backs were to the camera so we were walking and talking, and Frankie said, "Man, can you believe us? Two thirty-year-old guys out here in body makeup and red trunks, and Asher's waiting for us to walk in that water!" Asher didn't yell "cut," we kept getting closer and closer, right down to where that fifty-degree water was starting to lap at our toes. Frankie and I just shoved our surfboards into the sand, turned around to look at Asher, shook our heads and walked out of the shot.

How did The Eye Creatures *come about?*

There was a guy named Larry Buchanan that came up with a formula of taking some of the early movies that AIP had done, *Invasion of the Saucer-Men* in this instance, and remaking them, shooting them in 16mm, with essentially just one supposedly recognizable name. I went down and did *The Eye Creatures,* which probably ranks right up with some of the all-time worst horror films ever made. Steven Terrell had originally played the lead in *Saucer-Men,* and here I was doing it again. We shot at the ranch of Gordon McLendon, a very wealthy fellow who had a beautiful ranch called Cielo, just outside of Dallas. We shot the entire film right there on his ranch, and it was a great treat for me because I was his guest there and I had this incredible bungalow suite — it was like staying at a very opulent hotel and having room service whenever you wanted it. Everybody else in the film was local, all from Dallas little theater and Dallas stage. The picture was made for an extremely low price — I mean, we shot it in sixteen, and I think the cost was *less* than $50,000, including the answer print. The monster looked like something out of the Michelin Tire ad!

What kind of shooting schedule was involved?

It was two weeks. Buchanan was a nice guy, and it was a real "at ease" pace; I mean, we just kind of worked until we felt like, "Okay, that's enough," then we'd break. It was very small crew, and quite well organized — Buchanan had it together.

How did you begin your involvement in the Filipino horror films?

The first picture I did there, *Brides of Blood,* was for a company called Hemisphere. I was going through my first divorce when a casting director called me and said, "Listen, would you like to go to the Philippines and do this horror film?" I said, "Yeah, why not?" I wanted to get out of town anyway.

The original deal was for four weeks, I think. So I went over there and started doing the film. They ran into some financial problems in the course of

Now a highly successful TV producer, former actor John Ashley has supervised such small-screen series as *The Quest, The A-Team* and *Werewolf*.

making the movie. We got about halfway into the picture when all of a sudden my agent called me and said, "We didn't get your check for last week, so don't go to the set." I had gotten to know Eddie Romero, who was the producer/co-director on it, very well, and I liked the Filipino people a *lot*—it was like a second home to me. I explained it to Eddie and he said he didn't blame me. So basically I would sit around—we wouldn't shoot until my agent would call me and say, "Okay, I just got another week's pay, go ahead and work another week." Four weeks wound up to be like ten, eleven weeks.

I finished the picture, came back and was living in Oklahoma, running some motion picture theaters. I had really forgotten about *Brides of Blood;* I thought it would probably never get released. Some time later, a distributor friend of mine called me from Kansas City and said, "I've got a picture opening here in town that you did in the Philippines. Would you come up and make some appearances at the drive-in?" This guy was a friend of mine, so I said sure. We went out and did all that, then he said, "Have you ever seen the movie?" I hadn't. So we sat in his car after one of the autograph sessions and watched it. He said, "Jeez, what'd this movie cost?" I had no idea, but I told him it couldn't have been that much. *Brides of Blood* wound up doing some business; they had some kind of gimmick with plastic wedding rings and stuff like that. My distributor friend called me again and said, "Listen, if I can come up with a group of investors and make a deal with you, would you go back to the Philippines and do another one?" I said yeah; if the money was there and he could get it together, I'd be interested. So that's really how it started. We then did *Mad Doctor of Blood Island* and *Beast of Blood,* both for Hemisphere.

How many pictures did you eventually make there?
   In the Philippines? I think I did about twelve or thirteen over there. They're a little confusing, because the original titles have since been changed for television.

What were the budgets on the last two Blood Island *pictures?*
   Certainly not in excess of $120,000–$125,000. I remember the most expensive Filipino production I was involved in was *Savage Sisters* [1974], which cost $230,000–$250,000.

Did you have cooperation from the government on these pictures?
   Yes, we always did. They were very good, particularly in the early days, because the scripts were so generic. Later on, when we started doing *Savage Sisters* and others which involved a military posture within the film, we had some minor problems there, but normally we had great cooperation. Several times when we were down there shooting, martial law was in effect and they had curfews. We were able to make arrangements with the government to allow us to work after hours.

But at this point, you still had no financial involvement?
   Not until *The Beast of the Yellow Night.* The fellow who owned Hemisphere in New York was rather ill, and Eddie Romero just said to me, "Look, why don't *we* do these together? I'll furnish the below-the-line costs, you guys come up with the above-the-line." So I did. Corman had just started New World, and *Beast of the Yellow Night* was one of the first releases that they had out.

Did you enjoy playing the monster in Yellow Night?
   It was a lot of fun to do. I used a double in a lot of the long shots, but

John Ashley takes on all comers in the Filipino-made *Mad Doctor of Blood Island*.

in the scenes where the beast was talking, obviously that was me. But I didn't make the transformation until near the end of the film, which was about a guy who made a deal with the devil for his soul. As he gets worse and worse, finally there's this transformation.

Beast of the Yellow Night *is remembered as being one of your better-written vehicles.*

I agree with you. It was a screenplay that Eddie Romero had written, and it certainly was the most cerebral, if you can call any of these pictures that.

Didn't Roger Corman visit you down in the Philippines while you were shooting Yellow Night?

Yeah, he called me and told me about this picture [*The Big Doll House*, 1971] that they were going to do in Puerto Rico. I told him, "You ought to come down and take a look at the Philippines. I mean, it's all right here" — 'cause the picture was set in a jungle, and in a women's prison. So he flew to the Philippines, took one look and asked me, "Would you stay around and exec-produce the show?" So two of my partners and I put up the above-the-line, Roger put up all the rest of it, and I stayed and supervised that one. Then I went ahead and did *Black Mama, White Mama* [1972] for AIP; then, back to Roger for *The Womanhunt* [1972]. That was originally a screenplay called *Women for Sale,* and it was very much in the *Big Doll House/Big Bird Cage* syndrome: white women being kidnapped and sold into the white slave trade.

Then *The Twilight People*. When Larry Woolner, who had been working for Corman, split, part of their split was, he got *The Twilight People*. He distributed it, and it did well.

Isn't The Twilight People *one of your personal favorites among the Filipino horrors?*

I think so. I just remember it was a lot of fun to do, and there weren't a lot of problems on it. And we did it so quickly! We were sitting around one day at lunch, Larry Woolner and Corman and I, in an Italian restaurant up near Corman's old offices on Sunset. We had walked down from his office, and were having salad. One of us said, "Well, what can we do now?" And somebody said, "What about *The Island of Dr. Moreau?*" And, "We can't do that, but what about half-beast, half-human?" And we just sat over lunch and made the deal. We wrote the script and, like a month later, we went over and shot it. It went very smoothly. It came back and did real well, real quick.

Tell us a little about your dealings with Corman.

The thing that's fun about Corman is, Roger's a tough deal-maker — a very fair deal-maker, but he's tough — but once you make your deal, he leaves you alone and doesn't bother you. He lets you go off and make your movie. And I think that's why so many people have started with him, because he does let you go off and do it your way.

Eddie Romero had directed Terror Is a Man, *a picture very similar to* Twilight People, *back in 1959.*

Conceptually, it was Roger, Larry and I who said, "Let's do *Dr. Moreau*," but I do remember Eddie saying that he had directed a picture called *Terror Is a Man*, and that there were some similarities.

Probably only because he ripped off Dr. Moreau, *too.*

Exactly. Everybody rips off somebody.

Was makeup a major expense on The Twilight People?

No, as a matter of fact, it wasn't. There was a local makeup man in the Philippines named Tony Arteida, a very, very creative fellow. All that stuff he did right there for us, with molds and appliances. The guy that we hired to play the Ape Man, he had that Neanderthal look to begin with *[laughs]*! And, strangely, it was not time-consuming — I mean, we never seemed to be waiting for the makeup to be put on. And I remember when I first saw the film, I thought, jeez, it worked better than I thought it would when we were doing it.

What were your budgets on some of these later pictures?

The Twilight People was like $150,000. We got up to around $200,000 on *Beyond Atlantis,* because we had a lot of underwater stuff. And then *Savage Sisters* was the biggest of the bunch.

Censorship problems in the Philippines made that one of the places where your films could not be shown without major cuts.

True, we did have some censorship problems in the latter stages. In the beginning, we didn't; it was pretty open. Later on, after the Philippine government began to crack down on the local films, they determined that our films were *imports* to their market and they could not set double standards.

Weren't you originally scheduled to direct Beyond Atlantis?

There was some talk about that, yeah, 'cause I really liked the script and I thought maybe I would direct it. Then the production end of it got so spread out that I felt that for me to attempt to produce, direct *and* appear in it would really be difficult. So I changed my mind.

Did a better-than-average cast help that picture at the box office?

Interestingly enough, *Beyond Atlantis* was *not* a success, because we attempted to break the mold. Our original concept was to find these people underwater, and for the most part they were going to be at least topless. We got into the script—which was really a rip-off of *The Treasure of the Sierra Madre* [1948]—and Larry Woolner all of a sudden said, "I think maybe we've got something here that's a little bigger than what we've been doing." And then we got Pat Wayne involved; one of the provisos of Pat doing it was that it had to be PG-rated. We had to make a decision: If we wanted Pat, who was very right for the role, then we couldn't go with an R rating. So we went ahead and got Pat, and George Nader, and did it as a PG. I still believe that, had we done it a little *harder,* it probably would have done better. At least we'd have had a picture that was a little more exploitable.

One of the things that trapped us, I think, was that underwater footage is very tough to get, but when you do get it, it's *gorgeous.* But watching it is like watching slow motion. You spend all this money and time, so you feel like, "I don't want to take it out of the picture." I think that slowed the film down a lot. We also had a lot of problems with getting apparatus that these people could wear that wouldn't fall apart underneath the water, and the eyes on the fish people were very hard to do on the budget that we had. It wound up slipping a little bit from the original concept, but we just decided, "Let's try it." It was a bad call. I think that's the only picture that I had money in that didn't make it.

A few years later, you wrapped up your Filipino production sideline.

The last thing I did in the Philippines was my involvement in *Apocalypse Now* [1979]; Coppola and his people used my Philippine company as a kind of base of operations, so that they could deal through me. While I was killing some time waiting for that to start, I did a local Filipino film that has never been released over here. It is a *wild* film — we did some things in there that you can't *do* anymore. For example, I played a doctor — I always seem to wind up playing doctors! — and we had a scene in which we got a human body, did an examination and then literally took the body apart. We did it with an actual human corpse — we made a deal, arranged to get a dead body from one of the prisons, and exhumed it. It was very graphic, very gory. A local guy released the film in the Philippines, then went to Hong Kong to redub it and do some work on it. He ran short of money, I think, and never could put it together.

So what brought you back to the States permanently?

I had maintained a residence in the Philippines and I would be there three, four months a year, then back to Oklahoma where I had my theaters. The theater business changed radically, I needed more time to devote to the theater end of it, and so I just couldn't afford the luxury of being able to take three or four months off.

What is the key to your success in the exploitation field?

That's an interesting question — I really don't know. This is a terrible thing to admit, but maybe it's that I always *liked* those movies, and I never had any real reason to turn them down. I just enjoyed doing them.

[Zsa Zsa Gabor] was very difficult all through the picture
[Queen of Outer Space]. The producer, Ben Schwalb,
went to the hospital with ulcers halfway through the picture,
I was left to cope with her alone, and she damn near gave me ulcers!
It always bothered me that here on this planet Venus,
she was the only one who spoke with a foreign accent.

Edward Bernds

ONE OF THE MORE PROLIFIC WRITER/DIRECTORS of the 1940s and 1950s, Edward Bernds is best remembered for his work in comedy: two-reelers starring the Three Stooges, *Blondie* and *Bowery Boys* features and many other shorts and features starring prominent funnymen (and women) of the period. It is curious that such a filmmaker should also be fondly remembered by fans of horror and science fiction films. Bernds' first fantastic production, *World Without End,* was a well-done "end-of-the-world" melodrama that stands with some of the better sci-fi efforts of the mid–'50s. Bernds later reinforced his reputation in the genre by directing the effective — although seldom revived — *Space Master X-7,* and by writing and directing *Return of the Fly,* a straightforward *Fly* sequel preferred by some to the original.

Bernds was born in 1905 in Chicago, Illinois. While in his junior year in Lake View High School, he and several friends formed a small radio clique and obtained amateur licenses. In the early '20s there was a considerable prestige for amateur operators ("hams") to have commercial radio licenses, and Bernds was in a good position to get into broadcasting when he graduated in 1923, a year when radio stations began popping up all over Chicago. He found employment — at age twenty — as chief operator at Chicago's WENR. When talking pictures burst onto the scene in the late '20s, Bernds and broadcast operators like him relocated to Hollywood to work as sound technicians for the movies. After a brief stint at United Artists, Bernds quit and went to work for Columbia, where he worked as sound man on prestige pictures like *It Happened One Night* (1934), *Mr. Deeds Goes to Town* (1936), *Lost Horizon* (1937), *Mr. Smith Goes to Washington* (1939) — and on less-celebrated pictures like Boris Karloff's *The Black Room* (1935) and other B horror films. Bernds later graduated to directing two-reel shorts and then to features, and helmed his first science fiction film, *World Without End,* in 1955.

How did World Without End *come about?*

A producer at Allied Artists, Richard Heermance, invited me to write and direct a science fiction picture. Heermance's starting point on the project had been some stock film from a Monogram science fiction picture of a few years before, *Flight to Mars.* It's strange how some producers, at least at that time, got hooked on the idea of saving money by using stock film. This stock wasn't that great, just a few miniatures of a rocketship in flight, and a crash landing. You could duplicate those stock shots for a few thousand dollars; are you going to make a $400,000 picture on the basis of saving a few bucks? I'm grateful that it was the starting point and gave me an assignment that I made a little money on, but the logic of it escapes me.

I had no directive on story, that was *my* starting point: astronauts encountering a strange planet. It was awfully tough to do anything new; the name of drama is conflict, and when the only conflict is with monsters, it isn't entirely satisfying. I was reading a nonfiction paperback book about science for the layman by Arthur C. Clarke, and there I came across the Einstein theory

Previous page: Director Edward Bernds (right) mingles with players Eric Fleming, Zsa Zsa Gabor and Paul Birch on the set of *Queen of Outer Space.*

that if you move fast enough, time slows down, and if you approach the speed of light, time stands still. And it hit me instantly that the place for our astronauts to land was back on Earth, only far in the future. So help me, it may have been done many times since — certainly that was used in *Planet of the Apes,* and Rod Serling used it many times in his series *The Twilight Zone* — but it was utterly new to me at that time, and it opened the door to the whole thing. The entire picture took on sharpness and meaning. I was glad to get the assignment, the money was satisfactory, and although the budget and schedule were more "B" than "A," it was to be made in Technicolor CinemaScope — A-picture mounting for a B-budgeted picture.

Your script was reminiscent of H.G. Wells' The Time Machine — *later made into a movie starring, coincidentally,* World Without End's *Rod Taylor. Did you derive any inspiration from the Wells story?*

I had read Wells' *Time Machine,* but it never occurred to me that there were any similarities. Wells' *Time Machine* was purely a fantasy about a magical bicycle-like device that could transport one backward and forward in time. I wanted my picture to have an arguably scientific basis.

The estate of the late H.G. Wells took Allied Artists to court over similarities between his Time Machine *and* World Without End.

I didn't know anything about that. There's no resemblance at all between Wells' book and *World Without End.* The idea of time travel is certainly not copyrighted. If anybody could sue anybody, I could sue Rod Serling for *Planet of the Apes,* because they definitely used my ideas about space travel and time travel in making that picture.

What about the production end of World Without End?

Not enough time, not enough money — the eternal complaint of the director. Heermance wasn't the ideal producer — to my mind, Ben Schwalb, the man who produced most of my Allied Artists pictures, was. Ben and I worked as a team, and he wanted quality just as badly as I did. Heermance wasn't interfering or destructive, it's simply that he seemed to be more interested in cost than quality — which is kind of strange, because *World Without End* may have been one of his first producer credits, and you'd think that he'd want it to be very good. If it was, he could take the bows, and if it went over budget, he could always blame the director. That was standard Hollywood procedure. But I did need more time on the film.

What would you have done differently with more time or money?

There are two things I remember especially: first, the closing sequence, which we shot out at the historic Iverson's Ranch. The closing scenes of a picture are the ones that people walk out of the theater with, the ones they remember. Ben Schwalb agreed with me. But on *World Without End,* with

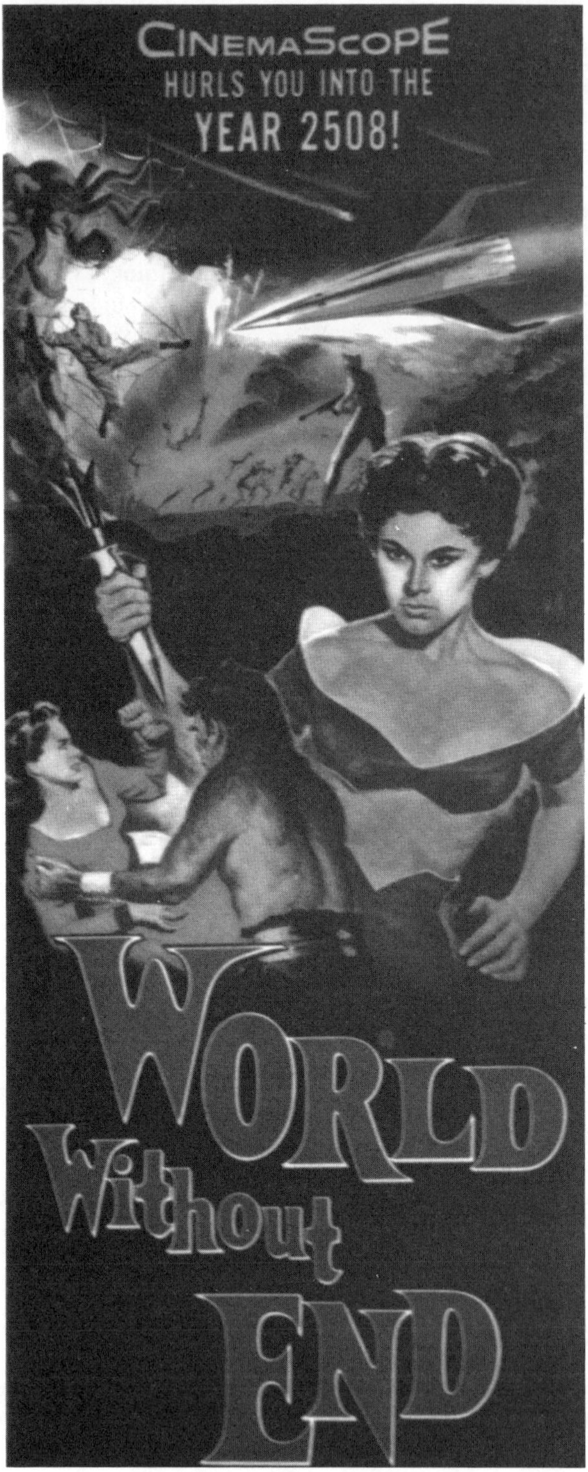
CinemaScope
HURLS YOU INTO THE
YEAR 2508!
WORLD
Without
END

a much greater potential for the picture to be a big moneymaker, Heermance cut down on the set for the final scene and the time I had to shoot it. I had wanted to *show* the world being rebuilt: trenches dug, buildings started, workmen swarming over them. I wanted to take a lot of care with those closing scenes. But there was no consultation, no give and take, no weighing of cost versus quality—just cut the sets and extras down, shoot it in half a day.

The second thing was the special effects. I wanted the operation of the spaceship to be as authentic and exciting as it could possibly be. My script detailed an elaborate and impressive series of special effects. What I got was a man who contracted with Heermance to supply all the special effects in the spaceship at a rather low price. They were disappointing. I did persuade Heermance to give this special effects man a couple of days to prepare, and then they gave me a day to shoot inserts—close shots—of radar scopes, speed indicators, oscilloscopes and so on, without actors. A day like that costs just a few thousand dollars instead of the cost of a full production, which might be ten times as much. The contractor wasn't even ready *then*. I did the best I could with what he did provide.

The scenes of the spacemen battling the mutates were well mounted and exciting.

We did get a pretty good crowd there; those were all stuntmen and they all took falls, and that cost money even in those days. We did have pretty good production there. It was strange—on some things Heermance splurged, and other things he clamped down on. He was not consistent.

Was it time-consuming having to make up all those mutates?

It required three or four makeup people to take care of those guys, but of course these stuntmen were cooperative. They'd help themselves—put the masks on, smeared the dark makeup on their bodies and so on.

You know, I invented the name "mutates" for *World Without End.* Now, of course, the accepted term is *mutants,* and it's kind of embarrassing to find myself out of step with accepted usage. I made up the word, and perhaps I made it up wrong. But *is* it wrong? True, there are supplicants, mendicants and applicants; but there are also advocates, associates and delegates. But I guess I'm outnumbered.

What about the giant spiders, which you later used in Queen of Outer Space *and* Valley of the Dragons?

Their legs were supposed to be operated by selsyn motors. The mandibles—the jaws of the big spiders—were spring-loaded, and snapped shut by magnets. The jaws worked all right, but the motor-driven legs . . . sometimes

Opposite: Bernds' first and best science fiction film was Allied Artists' *World Without End* with Hugh Marlowe and Nancy Gates.

Edward Bernds (right) confers with executive producer Walter Mirisch during the production of *World Without End* (1956). Mirisch rose from humble beginnings at Monogram and Allied Artists, and later produced such films as *The Magnificent Seven*, *West Side Story* and *In the Heat of the Night*.

worked, sometimes didn't. The actors had to provide most of the struggle; they put most of the energy into the fights with the spiders. But they were good for a tremendous scream. What a gratifying thing that is, when you're watching one of your own "scare" pictures in a theater and you get a spontaneous scream from the audience. That is *great*.

My dialogue director was Sam Peckinpah, who later became a big-shot director noted as a kind of a stormy petrel. I found that he was a very mild, self-effacing kind of a guy when he worked with me. Sam worked on several of my pictures as dialogue director, and I helped him get what I think was his first job as a director. Years later, when I was at Columbia, I think in connection with *The Three Stooges Meet Hercules,* I got in an elevator with him; he had grown a beard, but I recognized him, and I said, "Hello, Sam." And he looked at me, didn't say a word, and walked out. I don't know what the hell was eating him. He had developed a reputation as an intransigent "angry young man" director. He could not possibly have *not* recognized me, so it kind of amused me — if he wanted to be a Hollywood character, well, that was all right with me.

Were you happy with your World Without End *cast?*

I wanted Sterling Hayden for the lead. The producer thought Hugh Marlowe was a bargain, and Hayden would have cost about four times as much. Hayden at that time was a splendid figure of a man and to my mind he gave an aura of strength, intelligence, integrity. I think he would have been great in it. I also preferred Frank Lovejoy for the part of Borden. He wasn't a star or a name actor, but I considered him a fine performer who'd provide the strength and believability the part demanded. But Lovejoy's agent demanded four times as much as we paid Hugh Marlowe — a bargain that I feel hurt the picture.

Why were you so disappointed in Marlowe's work?

Heermance and his boss Walter Mirisch thought Marlowe was a bargain because he had been in a very, very fine picture for Joe Mankiewicz, *All About Eve* [1950]. I had seen *All About Eve,* too, and I thought Marlowe's performance in it was very good, but there's a hell of a lot of difference between playing a Broadway writer in a picture where you can take infinite pains and time to get a performance, and what we had to do, where he had to play a virile, gutsy spaceship commander. I was disappointed in him, for a great many things. He was not prepared, he didn't know his lines, and that's unforgivable. He was lazy. We spent a lot of time out on location — hot, dusty, disagreeable old Iverson's Ranch — and, as you remember the picture, when they came down from the spaceship, they were loaded down with packs and weapons and things like that. Between takes Marlowe would shuck the pack, put his weapon down, find shade somewhere. Eventually we'd have to go send for him, find him. Then it took time to get the pack on again. This was unpardonable — the minutes that you lose are precious. Then when he'd get on the set he frequently didn't know his lines, he'd blow scenes. And most of all he didn't generate the strength that I wanted. The first time he opened his mouth, my heart sank. Believe it or not, some of that rankles to this day because, after all, the film exists to this day.

When an actor behaves like that, he tends to infect others. Chris Dark was like a spoiled kid: If Hugh Marlowe could goof off and sit in the shade and forget where he put his pack so the prop man had to find it, why, he tended to do the same thing. Rod Taylor was all right, he was very new to the business and anxious to please. Nelson Leigh was an old pro who, despite the discomfort, did his work, knew his lines, was ready when we needed him even on that hot, uncomfortable set.

How did World Without End *do at the box office?*

World Without End made a lot of money for Allied Artists, it got good reviews, and I'm grateful that discerning critics like it — but I still have the feeling it could have been better. I just needed more time — I *know* more time would have resulted in a better picture. Would it have grossed more? I don't know. Heermance's attitude was that a picture of this kind would gross a certain

amount and that any extra production cost would cut into profits. He may have been right, I don't know, but to this day I wish I had made *World Without End* with a producer like Ben Schwalb, who always wanted a picture to be as good as he and I could possibly make it.

How did you become involved on Queen of Outer Space?

As you probably know, [Hollywood producer] Walter Wanger thought that his wife, Joan Bennett, might be having an affair with her agent, so he shot the agent in the crotch—aiming at the seat of the difficulties, so to speak. Hollywood agents being what they are, a lot of people probably thought that he should get a medal, but instead he was sent to jail. I guess the man wasn't wounded too badly, and Wanger was out in a year or so. He needed a job, but the studios where he had been such a big man didn't want to give him a break. The president of Allied Artists finally did hire him, though, and Walter Wanger came to AA as a producer. He brought with him a ten-page outline by Ben Hecht called *Queen of the Universe*. I don't know how Ben Schwalb came to produce the picture instead of Wanger, but that's what happened. Charles Beaumont wrote the screenplay. I guess I had been working somewhere else and I came to the picture after the script was written. Ben and I agreed that it needed work—that, as a straight science fiction melodrama, it wasn't very good. By the way, I read the screenplay *before* I read Ben Hecht's original.

What kind of story was it that Ben Hecht wrote?

Hecht's original wasn't a motion picture story at all. It was just a satirical look at a planet ruled ineptly by women. There wasn't anything there for Charlie Beaumont to use except the idea of a planet ruled by women, so the screenplay was pretty much an original. But Ben Schwalb decided that it would have a better chance if we lightened it up—spoofed it—and we did. My friend Elwood Ullman and I did some rewriting—I wish we had done more. I think the light parts of it worked, but the melodramatic parts were . . . a little heavy for my taste.

There may be a reason that Charlie Beaumont's version was, in my opinion, and in Elwood's, and in Ben Schwalb's, dead serious and dead dull. I met Charlie a couple of times just after he finished the script, and he looked terribly unwell. He was about twenty-eight years old when he wrote *Queen of Outer Space,* and at the age of twenty-eight he should have been in the absolute prime of life. Charlie died, much too young, in 1967.

How did you enjoy working with your stars Laurie Mitchell, Eric Fleming and Zsa Zsa Gabor?

Opposite: A Ben Hecht outline entitled *Queen of the Universe* furnished the basis for Bernds' *Queen of Outer Space* with Zsa Zsa Gabor. Allied Artists dispensed with Hecht's title because they felt it denoted a beauty pageant.

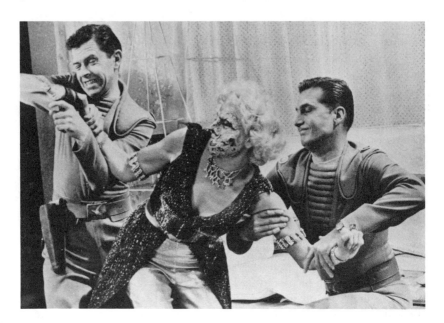

Dave Willock and Eric Fleming struggle to wrest a ray-gun away from burn-faced *Queen of Outer Space* Laurie Mitchell. (Photo courtesy Steve Jochsberger.)

Ben Schwalb had cast Laurie Mitchell in some of his previous films and liked her work. I interviewed her, I liked the way she read the part, I agreed to cast her and I wasn't disappointed. She did pretty well in what was pretty much of a thankless role as Queen Yllana. Eric Fleming was the male lead opposite Zsa Zsa Gabor—I believe it was one of his first movie roles—and he was a model of professionalism: always prepared, dialogue solidly memorized, all business despite Zsa Zsa's flightiness. Later, when he was the lead in the TV series *Rawhide,* I learned that he had become arrogant, hard-to-handle—undirectable, to quote Gene Fowler, Jr., who had directed a couple of *Rawhide* episodes. That's typical of actors who work in successful TV series.

You mentioned Zsa Zsa's flightiness...?
She's a beautiful woman, no doubt about that, but she was not very young even in 1958. We had some of the most beautiful women we could find, any number of beauty queens, and I think the competition was a little steep for her. She was not thoroughly professional, she didn't have her lines well prepared, she had a kind of a giddy attitude toward things.
We cast members of Queen Yllana's "posse" for size and good looks. We wanted beautiful Amazons. One that I remember very well was Tania Velia—Miss Belgium—who didn't have a particularly pretty face, but who had one of the most spectacular figures known to man. As they say in New York City, "What a built!" And, as I said, Zsa Zsa didn't exactly like the competition. I

can tell you that when Tania Velia came into view, no male, cast or crew, had eyes for anything but Tania and her gorgeous superstructure.

Prior to production, I was seeing Zsa Zsa through wardrobe at Western Costume Company, and she began to make demands: Her clothes had to be made for her, she would not wear stuff from stock and so on. While she was trying something on or discussing something, I got to a phone and told Ben Schwalb that she was threatening to quit the picture if we didn't do everything she wanted. I told Ben, "This is our chance to dump her. If she wants to walk, let her walk." Ben said, "No, we need a star—without a star we haven't got a picture. Look, stars are that way—humor her." Well, she was very difficult all through the picture. Ben went to the hospital with ulcers halfway through the picture, I was left to cope with her alone, and she damn near gave *me* ulcers! It always bothered me that here on this planet Venus, she was the only one who spoke with a foreign accent.

I don't claim by any means that *Queen of Outer Space* is a good picture. Trying to paste satirical material onto a creaky melodramatic structure just didn't work very well. If the picture's shown on TV I won't watch it, because Zsa Zsa Gabor still gives me a swift pain. And, secondly, the film was shot in CinemaScope, and TV murders the composition. The better I staged and composed the shots, the worse the TV proportions butcher them. I was also disappointed with that big set at the end. Although the art director, Dave Milton, did the best he could with a whole stage, what we needed was a set like one that they would have in a James Bond picture. But we didn't have James Bond money!

What's the story on Space Master X-7?

Space Master X-7 was made for Robert L. Lippert's Regal Films, I think on a budget of about $90,000 which was low even then. Twentieth Century–Fox financed and released Regal Films but had nothing to do with the films until Lippert turned them over as a finished product. To my knowledge, Fox didn't even have veto power over cast, and I don't think they even looked at the final cut of the pictures!

Really!

The Twentieth Century–Fox executives, even the lower-echelon ones, never looked at the final cuts. There may have been several reasons for that; maybe even the lower-echelon producers were too snobbish to get involved with Lippert's low-budget process, or perhaps they felt they were not equal to making decisions at that level of filmmaking. But most likely Bob Lippert—a rough, tough customer—just didn't want any kibbitzing on his films, and his autonomy may have been part of his deal. If there were any such thing as reincarnation, that man would have been a pirate in an early incarnation.

My producer, Bernard Glasser, bought the script for *Space Master*. It was written by my old friend Dan Mainwaring, in collaboration with a man named

George Worthing Yates. Their title for it was *Doomsday* something-or-other. They had written it on "spec"—that is, they had not done it on assignment, but to be sold on the open market. It hadn't been sold, and my guess is that Glasser didn't pay much for it. He *couldn't* have, with only $90,000 to make the whole picture! I guess I was working cheaply, too. I did an extensive rewrite job—no extra money for that, just my fee as a director. Mainwaring and Yates had written it without regard for expense, they wrote it as a big-budget production. I had to make it fit our budget and a shorter running time.

Again, as with Queen of Outer Space, *you didn't take any screen credit for working on the script.*

There were and still are credit-grabbers in the business who seize every opportunity to take credit that they may or may not deserve. I always prided myself on *not* grabbing credits—I considered it part of my job to make the script work the way I wanted it to. Strangely enough, Dan Mainwaring, who had been a good friend of mine, was kind of touchy about the whole thing—I think he thought that *he* should have rewritten it. But he was probably at least a $750-a-week writer, which we definitely couldn't afford. Dan was kind of a neurotic person, and he was furious. I guess he was realistic enough to know there wasn't enough money for him, but just the idea that anybody would touch his *gem*...!

What kind of revisions did you make?

I don't remember many details—it was a long time ago. I think I eliminated a train sequence; perhaps I substituted a plane for it. I recall using a four-engine propellor plane, probably a DC6, at Long Beach Airport. I was working under terrific pressure, making production decisions about casting, wardrobe, sets, special effects—our assistant director was trying to make up a schedule and a budget without a script to work from! I had to give him much of the information he needed verbally.

Was Space Master's *documentary style your idea, or was it spelled out that way in the screenplay?*

I think the script was mostly my creation—that is, the style, if any, and the viewpoint were mine. We couldn't afford to be anything *but* documentary—we were all over L.A.! *Space Master* was a prime example of what could be done with very little money.

Despite the low budget and the pressure you spoke of, Space Master *turned out quite well.*

Space Master was an example of independent moviemaking at its best. At Lippert, you had freedom to do it as you saw it. True, you only had $90,000 to spend *[laughs]*, but Glasser and I could do anything we pleased with it! All we had to do was bring back a good product for the ninety G's. *Space Master* was made with near hundred-percent efficiency and near hundred-percent freedom. Bob Lippert and his story editor, Harry Spalding, looked at the rushes, made occasional suggestions, but in the main Glasser and I made the picture our way, Glasser attending mostly to money matters and I mainly to the creative aspects. Of course, these functions overlapped at $90,000 — sometimes creativity had to make concessions to the hard economic facts of life, and sometimes creativity won out over dollars and cents. But Glasser and I were a pretty good team: He knew that if we were to get more assignments, our pictures had to be as good as they could possibly be on a quickie budget, and he contrived to squeeze every bit of production value possible out of every dollar. This squeeze was assisted to quite an extent by our hiring of Norman Maurer as a production assistant. His presence on the picture requires some explanation: Maurer was the son-in-law of Moe Howard of the Three Stooges.

And Moe Howard has a small part in Space Master.

Right. Moe did that part not because he needed the money, but because he loved acting — he really did. The thing he missed most about the Three Stooges two-reelers being terminated at Columbia was that he couldn't work any more. We'd been friends ever since I began directing the Stooges, so I was glad to cast him in the part of the cab driver. I had met his son-in-law, Norman Maurer, and knew him as a professional artist of considerable talent. Moe told us that Norman wanted to get a foothold in the production end of motion pictures and asked us to take him on as a production assistant. An artist can be a great asset to a motion picture, so we were glad to do it. Norman was a hard worker and made a big contribution to *Space Master X-7;* he gave the special effects men sketches of the Blood Rust, sketches that we could agree on before any money was spent on experimental presentations. Later, thanks to the start that *Space Master* gave him, he was associate producer on *The Angry Red Planet,* and was the producer of *The Three Stooges Meet Hercules, The Three Stooges in Orbit* and *The Mad Room.*

I guess that's about all for *Space Master* except that, for a picture made so many years ago, the script seems to be reasonably accurate, scientifically. In writing science fiction scripts I always tried to be true to the scientific facts and procedures as I knew them at the time. Another reaction that I had when I reread it was, how in the world did we ever do this in eight days?

Was Kurt Neumann, director of the original The Fly, *assigned to direct* Return of the Fly *before his untimely death?*

I don't think so. He died in 1958 and we made *Return of the Fly* in 1959. Kurt was only about fifty years old when he died, an untimely death, as you said. I made two other pictures for Robert Lippert in 1958, and I spent a good part of the year with Lippert's organization. I was working there when Kurt died, and attended his funeral. I think I would have known if I was, in effect, replacing him — I just don't think so.

Did you screen the original Fly *in preparing* Return of the Fly?

Although I know I've seen *The Fly,* I honestly don't recall whether I screened it for that purpose. The way I wrote *Return of the Fly* originally, we were going to use some of the film from *The Fly* as a lead-in, but for some reason we weren't permitted to do that.

Vincent Price liked my script for *Return of the Fly* — he wouldn't sign to do the film until he read a script, so as soon as I had a first draft I sent it to him. Then, after he'd read it, I visited him in his *palatial* home — that's a fancy word, but believe me, his place *was* palatial — and he said he liked the script. We discussed it at considerable length, he said he'd sign and he did. Some time later a problem came up: What Vincent read was a first draft, and like many first drafts it was a little overlong, and some cuts were made to trim it down and some changes made to bring about budget economies. Vincent liked some of the scenes we had cut, and he objected. If I recall correctly, they were mostly scenes with Danielle De Metz — scenes of warmth and charm, but, when you're pressed for footage, not truly essential to the progression of the story. But I conferred with Vincent from time to time, and I made changes that satisfied him.

What was Price like to work with?

A delight, no less. Thoroughly professional, always prepared, giving his best to every scene. His wasn't even the biggest part in *Return of the Fly,* but his star status and the strength he brought to his performance lifted it out of the B category it might have fallen into. The whole cast was good to work with — Brett Halsey was excellent, as always. I guess the number of times Brett and I worked together attests to the fact that I liked his work. David Frankham, who played the villainous Alan, was new to me, but he was everything I wanted as the charming, plausible, good-looking young Englishman who turns out to be a despicable double-crosser and killer. I wanted the contrast between the charming, pleasant Alan and the killer Alan to be a startling one, and David was everything I hoped for when I wrote his scenes. Danielle De Metz was very young, very pretty; practically no experience, but her youth and beauty were a plus. Maybe the fact that she wasn't an experienced actress made her performance seem more innocent and more real. I liked her looks and her acting, and I liked *her.* That's why I later cast her in *Valley of the Dragons.* I saw her just recently on TV in a British-made Richard Burton movie, *Raid on Rommel* [1971] — I hardly recognized her.

I've still got a copy of the script I used to shoot *Return of the Fly,* and glancing at it reminds me that we tried to cast Herbert Marshall to repeat his role as Inspector Charas from the original. I *must* have written with Marshall in mind because the role in my script is referred to as Charas throughout — but in the dialogue the character played by John Sutton was named Inspector Beacham. I'm not sure why we didn't get Marshall — John Sutton was very good but Marshall would have added stature to the part, and another link to the first

Fly would have been a definite plus. I was given to understand that Marshall was not well enough to take the part, but he made a half a dozen more pictures before his death in 1966, so I suspect that maybe his price was a factor in not hiring him. I wasn't told that; I'd have fought to have him, even if we had to strain the budget, if I'd known it was a matter of money.

What do you remember about the stuntman that played the Fly, Ed Wolff?

He was a circus giant, and he had very low endurance. With that head on and that heavy costume, we had to be very careful with him — we were afraid he'd have a heart attack and die! When we required him to run or anything, we'd have to give him several minutes to rest up. Like many giants, he was very weak.

Did Robert Lippert have any creative input at all on these Regal Films?

No. Our dealings were with the story editor, Harry Spalding, who was an excellent man to work with. A lot of story editors try to prove they're smarter than the people they're dealing with, but Harry was anxious to cooperate, and his suggestions were generally helpful. I was told that Lippert never read a script, that he depended on Harry to read the scripts and then tell him what they were about.

Wasn't Return of the Fly *shot on the Twentieth Century-Fox lot?*

Yes. We who worked for Robert Lippert were kind of "second-class citizens" as far as Fox was concerned — pariahs, so to speak. Fox didn't want us on the deluxe Westwood lot, but when the time came to do *Return of the Fly* they wanted us there. I believe this was a tough period for Twentieth and they wanted us to absorb some of their overhead. I'm sure Lippert made some kind of a deal where we weren't stuck with the full Twentieth Century-Fox overhead — he probably got some kind of concession. *Return of the Fly* was made at the Fox Westwood lot, with Fox personnel all the way through, even a cameraman. Fox just simply couldn't do things in any way except top-notch, and so our sets for *Return of the Fly* were as good as an A picture's would be.

It seems to me the Twentieth Century lot was a rather dismal place when we shot *Return of the Fly* there. Not much production, and many of the crew worried about their jobs. Buddy Adler was the ostensible boss — I knew him from Columbia, and as a matter of fact I directed a couple of second units for him there — and I considered him an all-American no-talent. In shooting second units I simply could not get a decision from him. He was so afraid of Harry Cohn that he was afraid if he made a decision and something went wrong, that Harry Cohn would rip his hide off — which Cohn was quite capable of doing.

The Fly *being the big moneymaker that it was, why did Twentieth Century-Fox entrust the sequel to Lippert's organization?*

Why we got *Return of the Fly* I don't know; maybe Fox thought that it was going to be a slough-off, just something to cash in on the popularity of the first one. But I also think it was kind of a bad time for Fox and they thought that they could capitalize on us, at a reasonable cost, and get a reasonable product. I think they *did*—the sequel, in spite of being in black-and-white, made them a lot of money.

Did you ever see the second Fly *sequel,* The Curse of the Fly?

I thought it was very bad. Everything about it was bad—it was so dull that I found it hard to stay with. It went nowhere—there was no storyline established—and I can't for the life of me see how Harry Spalding could have written it. Harry was so perceptive as a story editor, I can't see how he couldn't be perceptive about his own work.

Did you enjoy working in the science fiction genre?

Oh, sure. I think I was pretty well qualified—in radio from the days of crystal detectors; I was the chief engineer of a radio station in Chicago at the age of twenty; sound technician from the end of the silent era in 1928 until 1944. I believe that what the science fiction writer needs most is a sense of story and enough science to make the story work. Of course a critic might well ask, "How scientific is the basis for *Valley of the Dragons?*" The answer is, of course, that the basis of *Valley of the Dragons* is utterly unscientific and—*ridiculous* is probably not too strong a word for that. Science really takes a beating in that picture *[laughs]!* But it entertains people, and still makes money for Columbia.

Valley of the Dragons *uses so much stock footage from* One Million B.C. *that I assume it was the available stock which shaped your screenplay.*

Yes, *Valley of the Dragons* was built around the *One Million B.C.* stock footage. The story is this: Producers Al Zimbalist and Byron Roberts had formed a partnership to make an independent picture, preferably for a major studio. I knew Al Zimbalist, I was on the Allied Artists lot when he produced and Don Siegel directed *Baby Face Nelson* [1957], a highly successful low-budget picture. Byron Roberts had served as a production manager on some of my Lippert pictures, so I knew them both. Al Zimbalist's son Donald was a college student at that time, on vacation in England. He found an obscure book stall in London and picked up an old copy, possibly a first edition, of a Jules Verne book called *Hector Servadac, Or, Career of a Comet.* It was never published in the United States, probably because it was violently, *viciously* anti–Semitic. I'd never heard that about Jules Verne, so this was shocking; I suppose that's the kind of thing that prevailed in the France of his day. Well, Donald Zimbalist bought the book and Al, who was a born promoter, had two things to work with: First, the Jules Verne name meant box-office at that time, the title was unused, unknown, and the work was in the public domain.

Second, Al had an option to use any or all of the *One Million B.C.* film. Al and Byron needed somebody to put the two elements together to make a package, to present to a studio. So you're absolutely right, the stock did shape the story.

If all Donald Zimbalist did was bring home a book, why does he get story credit on Valley of the Dragons?

His dad asked for it. Al wanted Donald to have a screen credit, he pleaded with me to let Donald have story credit, and he finally talked me into it. Donald had nothing to do with it except finding the book. I was always a chump for a request like that, I guess. The thing I didn't anticipate was that the residuals went to him. I think of Donald Zimbalist every time I get a residual check on *Valley of the Dragons*. That film has tremendous vitality on TV—I get checks that *surprise* me. I also get residuals on the Elvis Presley picture *Tickle Me* [1965] that Elwood Ullman and I wrote, and it seems to me that *Valley of the Dragons* makes me more money in residuals than *Tickle Me* does! But every time I get a residual check, say for a hundred dollars, it kind of gripes me to know that Donald Zimbalist, wherever he is, is getting twenty-five. I may have got, through the years, a couple thousand dollars in residuals, and I guess Donald's got around five hundred. Well, maybe he needs it...!

Anyway, I used the Jules Verne premise of the comet scooping up the men and taking them into outer space—a pretty wild premise, but it worked all right for us. The story was then shaped around the stock stuff. I wrote a ten-page outline, and Al Zimbalist took it to Columbia in New York—to *New York,* not to Columbia in Hollywood—sold the deal and signed a contract to make the picture as an independent production. The Columbia executives here in Hollywood were not pleased at all: Al had gone over their heads to make the deal, and their noses were somewhat out of joint. I think they'd have been glad to see us fall on our faces, figuratively speaking. To get the deal, Al had agreed to a ridiculously low budget—I believe it was $125,000—and agreed that any over-budget sum would come out of his fee and Byron Roberts' fee as producer and associate producer, respectively. They couldn't touch my money for writing and directing because the Writers Guild and Directors Guild contracts with the studios wouldn't permit that. I couldn't work as "spec," as it were; I *had* to be paid.

You made Space Master X-7 *for $35,000 less than that.*

$125,000 under major studio conditions was, as I said, ridiculously low. That much money at Columbia wouldn't buy as much production as $90,000 did under the Lippert-type independent operation. We had all those expensive, inefficient departments to pay for. The bigger the studio, the bigger the overhead. Columbia was by no means the biggest studio, but it was big enough to really make the overhead rough. Al had made one smart move: He had bargained with New York to limit the charge for studio overhead. I never knew just what that limit was, but it was a life-saver. The Columbia executives expected us to go over budget, but we fooled 'em. The big lucky break we had was that we were able to use a half-million dollar mountainside set standing at Columbia that had been built for *The Devil at Four O'Clock* [1961]. That meant we didn't have to go a single day out on location; we shot all of our exteriors on this magnificent half-million dollar set. It was a tremendous money-saver. The cast was good, we had a reasonably fast cameraman, and we did the impossible: We brought the picture in on budget, Al and Byron didn't get pried away from any of their fees, and I had the satisfaction of thwarting the Columbia brass who were waiting for us to go over budget.

Among your five sci-fi films, which is your favorite?

World Without End. I had high hopes for it, and I took great pains in writing it. Of course there are disappointments in *World Without End;* I've already told you of most of them. It occurs to me that some of it may sound like the plaintive wail of a chronic complainer. It's true as I said that the everlasting complaint of the director, at almost every level, is, "not enough time, not enough money." But I directed forty-odd films and I was up against that kind of pressure on most of them; I coped as best I could and I don't think I complained unduly. Only on *World Without End* did I feel so strongly that with a little more time, a little more money and most of all with a little more support and belief in the project on the part of Dick Heermance, we could have had a better picture.

If I were active as a director today, I would revel and delight in the chance to use the great special effects available to the director of today. What a lift really great special effects might have given to *World Without End* — as a matter of fact, they would have helped most of the science fiction pictures I did. Oh, but why dream? *All* of my sci-fi films, even *World Without End* and *Return of the Fly,* were comparatively low-budget productions. The $90,000 it cost to make all of *Space Master X-7* — *all* of it — wouldn't buy a four-minute sequence of *Star Wars* or *Raiders of the Lost Ark.* And here's a sobering thought — sobering to me, anyway: unless I could crack that A-picture barrier now — *today* — I wouldn't have access to those great special effects, would I? And I didn't crack that barrier when I was active, so what the hell, there's no use crying over spilled milk, bygone years, bygone opportunities and films that might have been better.

*[Roger Corman] gave me a lot of freedom,
and also a chance to play parts that Universal
would never have given me. Oddball, wacko parts,
like the very disturbed girl in* Sorority Girl
*and things like that. I had a chance to do
moments and scenes that I didn't get before.*

Susan Cabot

THE LATE SUSAN CABOT was born in Boston and raised in a series of eight foster homes. She attended high school in Manhattan, where she took an interest in dramatics and joined the school dramatic club. Later, while trying to decide between a career in music or art, she illustrated children's books during the day and sang at Manhattan's Village Barn at night. It was at this same time that she made her film debut as an extra in Fox's New York–made *Kiss of Death* (1947) and worked in New York–based television. Max Arnow, a casting director for Columbia Pictures, spotted Cabot at the Village Barn, and a co-starring role in Columbia's B-level South Seas drama *On the Isle of Samoa* (1950) resulted. While in Hollywood, Cabot was also signed for the role of an Indian maiden in Universal's *Tomahawk* (1951) with Van Heflin. Studio executives viewing *Tomahawk* dailies were impressed with her screen possibilities and signed her to an exclusive contract.

At Universal Cabot co-starred in a series of films opposite leading men like John Lund *(The Battle at Apache Pass)*, Tony Curtis *(Son of Ali Baba)* and Audie Murphy *(The Duel at Silver Creek, Gunsmoke, Ride Clear of Diablo)*. Inevitably she became fed up with the succession of Western and Arabian Nights roles, asked for a release from her Universal pact, and accepted an offer from Harold Robbins to star in his play *A Stone for Danny Fisher* in New York. Taking advantage of being in New York again, she resumed her musical studies and entered acting classes with Sanford Meisner at the Neighborhood Playhouse. Roger Corman lured her back to Hollywood for the lead in the melodramatic rock-and-roller *Carnival Rock* (1957), and she stayed on to star in five more films for the enterprising young producer-director. Cabot's three fantasy films—*War of the Satellites, The Wasp Woman* and the cumbersomely titled *The Saga of the Viking Women and Their Voyage to the Waters of the Great Sea Serpent*—were made by Corman at this time.

After a highly publicized 1959 fling with Jordan's King Hussein, Cabot divided her time between TV work and roles in stage plays and musicals. During the last three years of her life she raised $500,000 for the American Film Institute's educational, training and preservation programs. Susan Cabot died on December 10, 1986, at age fifty-nine.

How did working in these Roger Corman films compare to working at Universal?

Totally *mad.* It was like a European movie—I mean, we'd have some sort of a script, but there was a lot of, "Who's going to say what?" and "How 'bout I do this?"—plenty of ad-libbing and improvising. But Roger was really great in a way; he was very loose. If something didn't work out, he changed it *[snap of the fingers],* right away. He gave me a lot of freedom, and also a chance to play parts that Universal would never have given me. Oddball, wacko parts, like the very disturbed girl in *Sorority Girl* [1957] and things like that. I had a chance to do moments and scenes that I didn't get before.

Although Roger was—I suppose, still *is*—some kind of maverick, he's very

Previous page: **During her Universal-International heyday, Susan Cabot played co-starring roles in Westerns like *The Duel at Silver Creek, Ride Clear of Diablo* and *Gunsmoke* (pictured).**

bright and fast-thinking. He treated a lot of us shabbily in ways, and I'm sure we were asked to do things above and beyond what a major studio might have asked. But we all wanted the pictures to work, so we just pressed on.

How did you approach the role of the evil high priestess in Saga of the Viking Women?

I felt she was a misfit in that society; she had powers and a higher intuition, and a psychic sense of direction that the others couldn't pick up but she did. I especially liked the scene where I pleaded for the rain, and the rain came — I really tried to make that like a prayer. That kind of worked.

Did you enjoy playing villainous roles in Saga, Sorority Girl *and* Machine-Gun Kelly [1958]?

I loved it from the standpoint of their being a challenge, but it was very hard for me to play an unfeeling character — to do or say something cruel to another person, not feeling it in my bones or in my heart, and know that that other person is suffering. I've been victimized by people like that, and it hurts.

Any special recollections about Saga?

I remember the scene where the Viking women set out to sea in search of their men. There were, I believe, eleven girls in a Viking-type ship, and we were pulled out to sea, tugged by a rope attached to another boat. And the man who was towing us fell asleep! We started screaming at him, but the sound of the ocean drowned us out. Before we knew it, the bottom of our boat started to fill up with water, and we had nothing to bail it out with! I had boots on — I pulled them off and used them to get some of the water out — but all the other girls had sandals. We looked back to the shore, but the crew had already become minutely small in the distance.

We spotted two surfers not too far off, and Abby Dalton and I started screaming and waving our arms wildly. No response. Meanwhile, we had lost sight of the crew — we had sailed completely out of the cove and around, in front of a mountain.

How many of the girls knew how to swim?

Two — Abby Dalton and me! The surfers finally heard us and came over. They took a couple of girls and headed toward shore, and Abby and I took Betsy Jones-Moreland. By the time we finally got to land — the base of a mountain jutting out into the ocean — the tide was beginning to rise, fast, and the tiny strip of sand that was left began disappearing under the water. We couldn't just sit there, waiting for a miracle; we had to start climbing up the face of the cliff. And this was a high, hard climb — I mean, once you were halfway, and you were tired, you couldn't go back down again, you had to keep going up. It was very scary.

When we finally got to the top, we heard the sound of buses approaching, people running, trying to find us. I think I just yelled my head off at Roger—I just *blasted* away—because Roger had a habit of doing things like that. Tiny little things—like the time Abby and I almost went over a cliff on horses! They didn't show this in the film: The bunch of us girls had to ride through a mountain cave on horses, heading for an opening in the back. Roger was on an adjoining mountain filming the cave opening. *Nobody* told us there was a drop. Abby and I rode to the edge and stopped—but all the other girls were coming up on us, pushing in together! Abby and I had to try and hold everybody back, otherwise we'd have all gone over.

How about the scene where you're killed by the hunting dogs?

In order to make the two Great Danes run after me, the trainer wanted me to carry chopped liver in both hands—which is really yucky—to the spot where they were going to kill me. We rehearsed it a few times, but when the cameras were rolling the dogs wouldn't jump on me—they kept licking my face! I'm an animal lover, and I guess they knew it *[laughs]*! I made believe I was struggling, but it didn't work because the dogs didn't look the least bit ravenous, they looked like they were smiling. Finally I had to suggest to the crew, "Look, why don't you have two guys *throw* the dogs up at me?" So that's what we did—two guys came forward from the crew, each one took a dog and they threw them at me. I caught the paws of one dog, and started wrestling and screaming—but the dogs were still *[pausing to pant and lick at the air]* acting like puppies, having a ball! That was the only way we could get the scene on film.

When you finally got to see the finished film, what did you think of the special effects?

What special effects? The *sea serpent?* Oh, really *[laughs]*! Although, when we were in the boat, in front of the process screen, and that monster came up behind us, there *was* a start—we *were* scared for a moment. We were in the boat, on a sound stage, and people were shaking it, throwing water at us, blowing the wind fans. And when the monster came up, all of us shrieked—it was startling, even though it was on a flat piece of paper. Even though it might be a lousy film, or not well directed, or whatever the faults are—when you're involved in a situation and in a character, and in the period of the piece, that *can* happen.

How did you enjoy working with the Corman stock company?

I enjoyed our group—I think we had a super bunch, good talents. Barboura Morris was a lovely actress, a very sweet lady and a nice friend—but she always seemed very sad to me. I'm so sorry she's gone. Dick Miller was a nice guy, very cooperative; Richard Devon, an excellent actor; I loved Ed Nelson. Everybody worked hard, we worked spontaneously, we interplayed with each other—we had a real good group.

Hustled into production to capitalize on interest in the new space program, *War of the Satellites* pitted Cabot and hero Dick Miller (center) against alien *Doppelgänger* Richard Devon.

Any memories at all about War of the Satellites?

I was fascinated with the spacesuits that we wore; that was kind of nice. And I liked the way the special effects people did the splitting, when Richard Devon divided himself into two characters.

I'm sorry Roger didn't enlarge upon that plot; I think he had a little seed of something that could've been really good in that film. I remember the scene where I made a speech at the United Nations, and it posed an interesting question: If you have the ability to do something incredibly fantastic — and nobody else has it — how do you handle the responsibility, and not abuse the power? I liked some of the things Roger was trying to say with that.

Gene Corman had bit parts in Machine-Gun Kelly *and* The Wasp Woman. *Did you get to know him as well?*

Gene was a lovely person and a fine man, and I respect his work. I liked Gene very much; he seemed the antithesis of Roger. Gene was a very low-key, gentle man; Roger seemed a driven man. Roger wanted to accomplish a lot, he had to have a lot of drive to do it, and he pushed through. He not only pushed through, he *punched* through! With a lot of energy — and a lot of disregard, at times.

Did you and Roger date?

We had a few dinners, yes. And argued about the treatment of our fellow

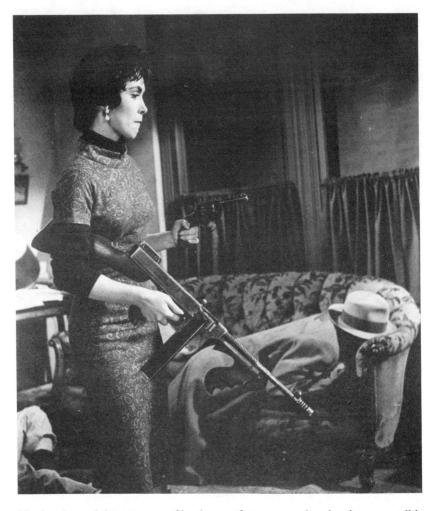

The late Susan Cabot gave one of her best performances as the scheming gun moll in Roger Corman's *Machine-Gun Kelly*.

actors. Having a social conscience—me, that is, I don't know about Roger—and being, I think, the only one he had signed under personal contract, I felt like a mother hen, and thought perhaps I could influence him to take it easy on the actors. Everybody wanted to please him, to make the pictures a success—but when he'd disregard somebody's safety I'd get real mad. And so we would argue a lot about that.

What would his comeback be?

    "Oh, don't be so sensitive"; "we're just making a movie, don't take it so seriously." Things like that. But I have to say one thing about Roger: When

Hideously transformed by wasp enzymes, Cabot moves in for the kill on helpless Lani Mars in *The Wasp Woman.*

Sandy Meisner, who is a very respected acting teacher, came out here, many years ago, Roger began to go to his classes to learn how actors act and think and how they work things out. So I had to hand it to him — he was really trying to improve himself and develop, and see things from the actor's point of view. When a director does that, he becomes a better director.

Tell us about working with Charles Bronson on Machine-Gun Kelly.

He was very nice and very interesting — we shared a lot of feelings about certain things going on in the world. He spoke somewhat of his past; I came from a rough past also, so there was a kind of bond or camaraderie there. I was raised in eight foster homes — I don't talk about this very much — and we shared a lot of pain about some of that.

What can you tell us about The Wasp Woman?

That was a lot of fun and a real challenge. In that film I played Janice Starlin, a character who, through injections of wasp enzymes, goes from a woman of forty to a woman of twenty-two. I had to play the two roles differently. Older people usually move and speak more slowly, and I just used a slower pace, a more considered way of thinking for the "old" Janice. Acting spontaneously, full of life, doing things off-the-top — that was how I played the "young" Janice. Since I'm small — I'm 5'2" — another challenge was figuring out a way to attack 6'4" men and make it look credible. The only way I felt I could

Susan Cabot in 1985.

convincingly down a bigger person was through swiftness — by coming at them so fast, like a bolt of lightning, and staying right on target. It worked.

So you did do all your own stunts in the film?

Every bit of running, jumping, tackling, fighting and falling you see in that film, I did myself. One thing I remember in particular was that, as I attacked each character, I was supposed to bite their necks and draw blood. As I pierced the neck, to get the drama of the moment Roger wanted to *see* the blood. And so as I attacked everybody, I had Hershey's chocolate in my mouth — which I proceeded to *blurp,* right on people's necks *[laughs]!* What we did for Roger Corman — I mean, things that you could never do in a real studio but you did for this guy! Everything seemed unreal with him.

Your best scene as the Wasp Woman came at the very end of the film.

Well, after I'd done all those ghastly things I had to get my lumps at the end, right? That's a story in itself: The whole finale was going to be done in one shot — one shot! — and if anybody goofed, it *stayed* goofed. The hero would burst into the lab where I was lurking, and the fight would begin. We'd battle with a stool, back and forth, then somebody would throw a bottle of "acid" at me. After the bottle hit, I was supposed to duck out of camera range for just a few seconds while a prop man put liquid smoke on my antennae — the smoke showed the effects of the "acid." Then I had to go out through a window, backwards.

We started shooting the scene — Anthony Eisley discovers me in the lab, the fight begins, the stool, everything. Then they threw the bottle — which was supposed to be a breakaway bottle. Well, things started happening at that moment. Somebody had filled the bloody thing with water, and it hit like a rock! I thought my lower teeth came up through my nose, and I was sure I was bleeding under the mask. When you saw me holding my face in that shot, it was because I was hurt very badly. But I continued to go through the scene! Out of camera range, the prop man put the liquid smoke on my antennae—too much liquid smoke! I went crashing backwards out the window, and two men caught me on the other side. I started choking on the liquid smoke, but I couldn't tell them! The mask did not have a mouth—it only had two little nostrils and two globular eyes, and it was glued very tightly all around my neck. The smoke was going in the nostrils, and there was no place for it to go out! I was clawing and scratching, but I couldn't talk! At last somebody got the message and they poured water on me. I had to tear part of the mask off in order to breathe, and when I did I tore away some of my own skin. That left a big purple bruise on my neck for a very long time.

Did *Roger* do anything? Did *Roger* send me flowers? What year is it now *[laughs]*?

What made you decide to quit Hollywood after 1959?
I felt that I had more within me to explore, as a music and art major and as a person. And the way my film career was headed, I didn't feel that that was going to offer me a way to develop any more, except on a very superficial level. I mean, how many *Wasp Woman*s can you do *[laughs]*? I wanted to get back to New York—the Museum of Modern Art—my art studies. I began to study music again. I just went back to the things I really loved. I also traveled, and toured with a lot of musicals.

Do you ever consider getting back into the picture business?
I'd like to reenter the film industry, and work again. But any kind of work I do has to have dignity in the environment of that work. That's very important to me, because there's been such an abuse of actors in the history of Hollywood. But if the right part came along—colorful, fun, good people—then, yes. Sure.

Among the six films you did for Roger Corman, which ones are your personal favorites?
Machine-Gun Kelly, Carnival Rock, Sorority Girl and *The Wasp Woman*. *Machine-Gun Kelly*, as a whole, was the most satisfactory. There was kind of a fun thing going on between the characters of Kelly and Flo—Bronson and myself—and there was a fondness there. I think that came out of the fondness that Bronson and I had for each other—we had an affection at that time. It was fun singing in *Carnival Rock*, and I had some really good scenes with David Stewart. *The Wasp Woman* was totally isolated from a normal kind of feeling, and that was a wonderful growth experience for me; I think that was the most

fun part I've ever had. To be able to go from a forty-year-old character to a twenty-two-year-old one was a challenge. Then, to be a monster—one of the very few female beasties in movies—was great fun. *The Wasp Woman* is very special.

. . . The Astounding She-Monster?
I remember that the director, Ron Ashcroft,
planned to make that feature in a week's time
and I think we ended up making it in five days.
That *was the astounding part of that picture!*

Robert Clarke

WAGING WAR with *Planet X-men*, *Captive Women* and *She-Monsters* in settings that ranged from *The Incredible Petrified World* to *Beyond the Time Barrier* has earned actor Robert Clarke an honored place in the pantheon of '50s monster fighters.

The Oklahoma-born Clarke abandoned his plans for a career in engineering when he caught the proverbial acting bug in college. Beginning in Hollywood as a $100-a-week stock player at RKO, he racked up early acting credits in such mid–'40s genre fare as *A Game of Death*, *Zombies on Broadway* and *Genius at Work*, as well as in Val Lewton's *The Body Snatcher* and *Bedlam*. Clarke graduated to lead player via strong co-starring roles in *Outrage* (1950) and *Hard, Fast and Beautiful* (1951), well-made dramas for Ida Lupino's Filmmakers production unit, and then starring roles in shoestring swashbucklers such as *Tales of Robin Hood* (1951) and *Sword of Venus* (1952).

In 1951, Clarke began his starring science fiction career with *The Man from Planet X*, and immediately followed up on this impressive start with the top role in the same producers' *Captive Women*. In the low-budget arena, he later toplined *The Astounding She-Monster*, *The Incredible Petrified World* and his own productions of *The Hideous Sun Demon* and *Beyond the Time Barrier*. Those were years of memorable experiences with the greats (and not-so-greats) of the genre.

How did you enjoy working with the Val Lewton unit at RKO?

Very, very much. Val Lewton was such a thoughtful type of individual, and he had a great capacity for kindness. He had very high ideals, and of course his artistic endeavors were far above those of most horror film producers.

Can you tell us a little about working with Boris Karloff on The Body Snatcher *and* Bedlam?

He was just delightful. At the end of one of the pictures, I think it was *The Body Snatcher*, they had a wrap party and Karloff was autographing pictures. I asked for one, and on it he wrote, "To Bob Clarke—Be as lucky as I am. Boris Karloff." Karloff was such the antithesis of what he portrayed on the screen: He had a very gentlemanly attitude, and in working in a scene with him he never tried to upstage you or to get the best of the scene. He was awfully kind, and his dressing room door was always open to anyone who wanted to say hello or chat with him. I never worked with any man that I had more admiration for.

Do you have a favorite Karloff anecdote?

Yes, I do. Karloff told me about the time that he went back East to do *Arsenic and Old Lace*. He hadn't been on the stage in so many, many years that he was literally suffering from stage fright. In fact, they let him sit in the audience the first few days of rehearsal. He told me, "I walked the streets of

Previous page: Robert Clarke and Marilyn Harvey flank the fallen body of alien Shirley Kilpatrick in a pensive scene from the micro-budgeted *The Astounding She-Monster.*

Among Clarke's first horror credits were supporting roles in Val Lewton productions like *Bedlam*. In this classic shot, Clarke (right), Jason Robards, Sr. (far left), and an unidentified player gang up on sadistic Boris Karloff.

New York all night long—I couldn't get up my nerve. Opening night, someone *pushed* me on the stage and I don't remember a thing—except that I had diarrhea for three weeks!"

How about Bela Lugosi on The Body Snatcher?

Karloff used to call him "Poor Bela." And "Poor Bela" had *such* terrible problems with his back, and he was on drugs because of it. During the time that I was involved on *The Body Snatcher,* he hardly came out of his dressing room unless the assistant director called him. They had a daybed in there, and he was flat on his back on that couch nearly all the time. He talked very little to anyone, and obviously he wasn't well at all. It was very difficult for him to perform.

Most of your Body Snatcher *scenes were with Henry Daniell.*

He was a smooth, accomplished and very professional actor. I was a bit overwhelmed, as were the other young stock players, Bill Williams and Carl Kent, by his extreme professionalism because he was a bit condescending in his attitude. The scene that we were involved with was mostly his scene—he was showing us how to perform the operation on the little girl. I had one line—"Bravo!"—and when I missed my cue, he went right by my line in his dialogue. But Bob Wise, the director, spoke up and stopped him, and said,

"Wait a minute—Bobby Clarke has a line there. Now, let's go back and start again, and let Bob get his line in." Unlike Karloff, Daniell was not the type to have empathy for young actors; "aloof," I guess, would be the best word to describe him. It was *his* scene, we were just window-dressing, and he couldn't care less whether we were there or not.

You had a more substantial role in Bedlam.

We were out at the RKO-Pathé Studios in Culver City, where *Gone with the Wind* [1939] was shot, and we were on one sound stage for over a month. Mark Robson, the director, was a marvelous man, he worked so carefully with us as actors. Today, directors don't have the time to do that. I remember a scene where we were playing a card game called paroli and, being demented, instead of betting money I was betting dogs—whippets and bassets and such. Robson made practically every little move for me—"When you place a card here, you do *this,* and then *that,*" and so forth. It's been over forty years, but I'll never forget how careful and meticulous he was. Robson, and Val Lewton, too, were both caring people, and they treated actors with respect, which is wonderful. I've had a couple of occasions in my career where the director would sit back near the camera and holler at you. I must give credit to Mark Robson for making my role in *Bedlam* more than it could have been; Robson gave me the kind of direction that brought out the best in me.

Was Val Lewton a hands-on, on-the-set producer?

I don't recall that he was so much that, no. He appeared on the set occasionally, but he wasn't looking over Mark Robson's shoulder; he had confidence in Mark and gave him full rein as director. And of course every day at the rushes, Lewton had a good opportunity to get a first-hand look at Robson's work, which was marvelous.

How did you get involved in The Man from Planet X?

Malvin Wald, a screenwriter and a partner in Filmmakers, told me that the writer-producer team of Jack Pollexfen and Aubrey Wisberg were looking for both male and female leads for that picture. Not too long ago, Jack Pollexfen said that Margaret Field—Sally's mother—and I were two of over a hundred actors and actresses that they interviewed. Margaret and I had recently done a picture together called *A Modern Marriage* [1950], she and I were both interviewed—I think together, as a matter of fact—and we were hired for the job.

Can you tell us a little about Pollexfen and Wisberg?

Jack was kind of a shy and diffident individual—erudite in his background, someone who you could imagine would plow through volumes and volumes of research material to get correct detail into his scripts. Wisberg was the more outgoing of the two; he was a bit more of the spokesman, it seemed to me. Nice men both, but very different from each other.

How did you enjoy working with director Edgar Ulmer?

Edgar and I worked very, very well together. He was never given the kind of opportunities he really deserved because he could make pictures so inexpensively that that's about all he ever got to do! He was so talented, in so many different areas. For example, on *Planet X* he painted the glass shots of the brock [a castle on the moors] — he did that as well as direct. The script originally was very, very talky — *long* speeches — and I'm sure he had a hand in the rewrite, too.

The one major flaw in Planet X *is that the dialogue is so overwritten. Do you remember that?*

I do, because it was hard to learn. The style was too literary, too wordy. Edgar Ulmer did his best to trim it, but I'm sure he was fighting with writers who thought every word was a pearl.

Where was Planet X *shot?*

Again, on a sound stage at RKO-Pathé. Except for maybe two or three shots outside, that's where we were for the six days it took to make the picture — they had it smoke-filled all day long, making it look like the moors. The inside of the brock were sets from the Ingrid Bergman *Joan of Arc* [1948]. Remember the village seen in the film? That was a painted backdrop! Talk about inexpensive — they really cut corners! And I got paid only $175 for the *whole picture*. The S.A.G. minimum then was $175 a week; today it's $375 a day. We got scale — and we worked from 6:30 in the morning till eight or nine at night every day, six days straight. *With* overtime, I think my check was for $210, and no residuals, ever.

Do you recall anything about the actor who played X?

Only that he complained — constantly — about how little money he was making. He had to be earning less than we were, and he didn't get billing, which I thought was unfair. People have asked me what his name was, and I've since forgotten — he was about the size of a jockey. He didn't like wearing that suit, and the mask was hot and very uncomfortable. He had a right to complain, and he did — a lot! A nice fellow, very cooperative, and he did his job well, but as far as I can tell he went on to great oblivion *[laughs]!*

Was it an enjoyable experience working on Planet X?

Oh, yeah. It was very, very hard work, but it was exciting because to us — to Margaret and me, especially — it was an opportunity that we thought might be the first step on the road to stardom. *The Man from Planet X* has certainly found a place in the annals of the science fiction genre, and I think it's one of the best films that I was in, especially when you take into consideration the budget and so on.

Clarke battles the vanguard of an interplanetary invasion in the cult classic *The Man from Planet X*.

Captive Women *cost twice as much as* Planet X, *but wasn't half as good.*

I'd agree with that. Part of the fault was the fact that the director, Stuart Gilmore, was being given one of his first directing opportunities. Howard Hughes was the owner of RKO then, Gilmore had been a film editor for Hughes on *The Outlaw* [1943], this was one of Gilmore's first pictures and he was *lost.* Completely. The poor man had tremendous problems; there were too many people in the cast, too many actors with no dialogue in the scenes, and then the fact that they had over-extended themselves for special effects.

The trouble with that picture is that is blends science fiction with religion — a curious combination.

Yeah, the whole film was ineffectual. Pollexfen and Wisberg were trying to make a better picture — sometimes Hollywood thinks that if you spend more money, you make a better picture. Well, this was one instance where that didn't happen. Gilmore was in over his head — he didn't know directing, and

I don't think he did too many pictures after that because he got a bad taste in his mouth from this one.

Wasn't there some rewriting while the picture was in progress?

Seemed to be, yeah. They would see the rushes and then we'd get new dialogue, new scenes. Part of it was that Bill Schallert's role was expanded—in some of the dailies that they saw he was coming across so well that they made the part bigger. He certainly deserved that kind of treatment; he'd also been in *The Man from Planet X,* and did an excellent job in both.

Tell us about working with Lon Chaney, Jr., on The Black Pirates *[1954].*

It was fun. He referred to himself as "the son of the *good* actor"—and then proceeded to have a big belt of booze *[laughs]!* But Lon was a fun-type man. One very unusual thing I learned about him was that he had a strange fear of going hungry. I had a friend who used to go fishing and hunting with Chaney, and this fellow told me that between L.A. and his ranch in San Diego Lon had several freezer-lockers *full* of frozen food—fish and meat and game— that he had either caught or he'd had butchered and stored, because of this inherent fear of going hungry.

What do you remember about The Astounding She-Monster?

I remember that the director, Ron Ashcroft, planned to make that feature in a week's time and I think we ended up making it in five days. *That* was the astounding part of that picture!

What kind of crew were you working with on films like She-Monster?

On *She-Monster,* we had a very minimal crew—one gaffer, a helper for him, one cameraman and one sound man. Just like with Jerry Warren, there was practically no crew at all. But Ronnie was resourceful—my gosh, was he ever! One of the things that he had envisioned was that the She-Monster would crash through a large window into the mountain cabin. They made the glass out of sugar and water and all, and as they were putting it in place they dropped the thing! If it had been me, I would have said, "Oh, hell, forget it," but Ronnie managed to put the few little fragments that were left back into the frame of the window and had her jump through. And then he edited it so that it looked pretty good.

Wasn't there a problem with the She-Monster costume?

The gal playing the She-Monster, Shirley Kilpatrick—a very well-endowed, buxom, beautiful girl, as I recall—had to wear a silvery, metallic-looking suit so that she would appear to be a monstrous yet appealing type of alien. It fit very tightly, and the first time she moved the doggone thing split, right up the back. She was so generously endowed that they couldn't do anything but put safety pins to hold it together in the back. So you'll notice that the She-Monster always backs away from the camera—you never see her retreat from the scene other than she *backs* away—and the reason she was backing away was because, otherwise, she'd be showing her backside!

Those few little anecdotes are what I remember best about *Astounding She-Monster*—those, and the fact that the damn picture made so much money! I guess it was partially because of the title; it certainly was not a good horror film, but it sure made the bucks. Ashcroft paid me $500 a week, which I thought was a good salary for this type of picture, and he promised me 4 percent of his producer's share. Thanks to his honesty and integrity, over the period of the next eighteen months or so I made a couple thousand bucks!

Wasn't that what prompted you to produce The Hideous Sun Demon?

That percentage prompted me to do a couple of pictures on my own, *Sun Demon* and *Beyond the Time Barrier*, because I felt that Ronnie did pretty well with a picture made on a low budget and that I could do something as well or better. Ronnie liked to make films fast, and he did make them acceptable enough so that they would play, but I wanted to make something with a little more quality, which I believe I did with *Sun Demon*. I think Ronnie would agree that mine had more substance to it, story-wise and so on.

Who originally came up with the idea for Sun Demon?

I did. Actually, it isn't all that original in a sense because the basis is really *Dr. Jekyll and Mr. Hyde.* I had the idea for the plot, and then I had a writer, Phil Hiner, help me. I had known him in Chicago, when I was in the Signal Corps there in 1941–42. We just did a flipflop of the Robert Louis Stevenson plot—instead of the Jekyll and Hyde thing, where a man drinks the potion, we made it a scientist working with fissionable materials who has an accident with radioactive isotopes. That upsets his chromosome balance so that he reverts, in the sun's rays, to a reptilian type of monster. Phil and I wrote a treatment and he did a first draft screenplay called *Saurus,* which in Latin means reptile.

What were your first steps toward getting into production?

As a result of the friendship that I made with Malvin Wald, I went down to the University of Southern California and took a class under him in screenplay writing. As a result of *that,* I met several of the young fellows who were going to school there in the cinema department—Tom Boutross became my film editor and co-director, Robin Kirkman was associate producer and Vilis Lapenieks the photographer. They were all students there; in fact, they all lived in an apartment complex called Cinemanor.

I told them about the idea that I had of wanting to do a feature picture. Robin Kirkman, very, very fortuitously, said that he would like to invest. The two of us formed a partnership and the company was called Clarke-King Enterprises. Though he took credit as associate producer, Robin Kirkman really

Actors Robert Clarke and Robert Bice with unidentified woman in wardrobe for *Captive Women*. (Photo courtesy Robert Skotak.)

functioned more as a co-producer, and was a great help toward finishing the picture. As many pictures do, we ran out of money, and he was able to fund the finishing of the picture.

The fellow who got screenplay credit, a U.S.C. student named E.S. Seeley, was a friend of Robin Kirkman's. Very erratic and quite a difficult fellow — a real character. He did the final draft, and then we had it rewritten *again* by Doane Hoag, a man who worked in industrial films quite a bit. He did a good job polishing up the dialogue.

The tarnished character you play in Sun Demon *seems more true-to-life than the usual sci-fi protagonist. Who brought that to the script?*

Well, if I may take personal credit, I think that was my own input. I wanted to make it a more realistic, multi-dimensional character, with some bad qualities as well as some good.

How long did shooting take?
We shot on weekends. We'd have a spot picked for our shooting that weekend, we rented our camera, lighting and sound equipment on a Friday afternoon and we actually got two days of shooting for one day's rental. We thought that was pretty clever. We shot twelve consecutive weekends—we didn't shoot during the week because runaway production, or nonunion production, was not as prevalent then as it is now. We were nonunion—these kids from U.S.C. were all students, and they were paid something like twenty-five dollars a day and were delighted to be doing it. We were one of the first to use practical locations—when we needed a scene in a bar, we went to Santa Monica and asked a guy how much he would charge to let us come in and shoot the scenes in his bar.

Why did you feel you needed a co-director?
Mainly because, when I was in the monster outfit, it was extremely difficult to be doing that and also laying out the shots and so on. And it was also kind of an accommodation for Tom Boutross—he was the editor, and he thought a co-director credit would be a nice gesture. But Tom did a *lot* in the editor's room to make that picture work.

Where were some of your other locations—the Sun Demon's house, the beaches, the oil fields where he hides out and the gas storage tanks where he's killed?
The Sun Demon's house was located in the old part of Los Angeles, on a street called Lafayette Boulevard; the house is no longer standing. It was one of those big old mansion-type houses with four stories; then it was a rooming house. I remember telling a lady that I had been there shooting a TV series, *I Led Three Lives,* and I said I was interested in renting the house for a movie. She said, "Will you pay me as much as they did?" and I said, "Well, perhaps—how much is that?" And she said, "Twenty-five dollars a day." So *[laughs],* we wrote some extra scenes to have played right there in the house, because the price was so right! We worked there five or six different weekends! The exteriors, however, were an old mansion, once owned by Antonio Moreno, up in the Los Angeles–Glendale Hill area; it was a Catholic school then. We went out to Bass Rock, which is where we shot a lot of the exteriors where I'm walking along, looking over the cliffs. The beach scene with the girl was not far up the beach, near Trancas—a very fashionable area now. The oil fields were in the Long Beach area of what had been Signal Hill in the early 1900s. Many of those old wooden derricks still stand and still pump oil. The gas storage tank, which was located near the Union Station train depot, was made

THE BLAZE OF THE SUN MADE HIM A MONSTER!

After years as an actor, Clarke tried his hand at producing and directing on 1959's *The Hideous Sun Demon*.

available to us through the Southern California Gas Company. The height of that gas tank was something over three hundred feet, and when I took the dummy of the Sun Demon up to throw it off, my voice, as big and loud as it is, could not be heard by the camera crew down below. We had a very difficult time communicating.

And your budget?
   Believe it or not, we started with $10,000 cash. Robin Kirkman and I each put in $5,000. That must seem ridiculous, but Roger Corman made *Attack of the Crab Monsters* for, I think, around $15,000, cash. Eventually our overall cost came to a little under $50,000. I even borrowed several thousand dollars from my brother and sister. Our lab bill came to around $8,500, and they were very lenient and allowed us to pay that off over a period of a couple of years.

Where did you get your largely unknown supporting cast?
   We got them through members of the crew that knew of aspiring actors and actresses around U.S.C. We told them that this was a nonunion picture and we had them come out and read. We selected Nan Peterson because of her voluptuous figure; Patricia Manning was quite good. I don't know if

they've done anything much since. Peter Similuk, who played the gangster, hadn't done much and he didn't come off all that well. Another fellow that didn't come off awfully well was Robert Garry, who played the scientist explaining my problem at the very beginning. The little girl, Xandra Conkling, is my niece; she's a grown young lady now and has four children. Her mother, in the film and in real life, is Donna King, my wife's sister. She was one of the original King Sisters during the big band days with Alvino Rey. My wife's mother, Pearl Driggs, was the elderly lady sitting out on the hospital roof when I get the first attack from the sun. The King Sisters' real name was Driggs, which they changed for obvious reasons—who'd go to see the Driggs Sisters?

Another King Sister, Marilyn, is credited with writing the song Strange Pursuit, *heard three times in the film.*
    Marilyn is the youngest King Sister. She wrote it, and did her accompaniment. When they came out with *It Came from Hollywood* [1982] she was able to get a few hundred bucks out of them for the use of the song.

Did you play the Sun Demon throughout the film, or did a stuntman take your place?
    All the stunts—all of the running, jumping and fighting—I did myself. No other actor played the Sun Demon. The suit was made on the base of a skin-diving wetsuit, and it was hotter than blue blazes! It was so hot that my perspiration ran down my body and *[laughs]* into my trunk area, shall we say, and during the fight we got so much energy going that one of the still shots shows me standing up there with this wet appearance—it looks like I couldn't make it to the men's room, but actually it was perspiration.

Was the construction of the Sun Demon suit a major expense?
    For us it was a major expense—five hundred bucks was what it cost. I went to see Jack Kevan, the fellow who did *Creature from the Black Lagoon,* and he said, "To make what you want, I would charge you at least $2,000." He was not overpricing it, but luckily I found this fellow Richard Cassarino, who was a film buff and a sometimes-actor.

Do you mean Gianbattista *Cassarino, who is listed in the film's credits as art director and assistant to the producers?*
    Gianbattista Cassarino was his *nom de screen.* A very happy Italian guy. He made a plaster mold of my head and then fashioned the mask on that. He was an artistic guy who contributed a lot to the picture—he was a set designer to some degree, and he also played the policeman that I fought on top of the gas tank. "Ben Sarino" [makeup man listed in the film's opening credits] was probably another *nom de screen* for him because we didn't want it to appear that one person was doing so many different jobs!

Makeup man Richard Cassarino puts last-minute touches on Clarke in *The Hideous Sun Demon*. (Photo courtesy Robert Skotak.)

Why did the film require three cinematographers?

Because some of them were not available weekend after weekend. When we'd say, "We're going to shoot next weekend," some of these fellows would say they weren't available, so we'd get somebody else. We didn't actually start with Vilis Lapenieks, but we found that his was the best work. John Morrill did at least half of it. Stan Follis worked with us throughout the picture as assistant cameraman and did some first unit work.

Did working with a largely inexperienced crew create problems?

We shot on the beach, live and with a sound recording, but the sound of the ocean drowned us out and we had to loop every line. One sequence in the oil derrick housing was shot silent and we had to loop it. That was a mistake; it was so late in the evening we let the sound crew go home, then realized we had this yet to do.

Missing from most prints of Hideous Sun Demon *is the scene where you pick up a rat and squeeze it so that its blood oozes through your fingers.*

It happened on the spur of the moment. We were trying to make a macabre type of sequence out of it. Similarly, when as the monster I killed the dog, that was somebody's idea of showing the violence of the monster, that the man had changed into a real malevolent type of creature. We didn't hurt the rat—we put some ketchup or something on it and squeezed it so that the ketchup would come out between the fingers. Actually, we probably shouldn't have used it; it was not in good taste and I'm glad that it has been cut. I don't even recall how we got the rat in the first place! But it *was* allowed to go free.

And how did Beyond the Time Barrier *come about?*

After we finished *The Hideous Sun Demon,* I was looking for a distributor. I went to Sam Arkoff and Jim Nicholson, and I made an arrangement for Nicholson to take the print and show it at his home. His daughters liked the picture very much, so Nicholson said, "Take it in and let Sam Arkoff see it." Afterwards, Sam asked, "Well, what do you want to do with it?" and I told him I wanted to use it as a door-opener, to produce other pictures. He wasn't interested at all; he said they had about all the producers they could use. But he still said he would like to distribute the picture.

I told him I'd think about it, but in the meantime I was put in touch with a company called Pacific International. John Miller and Mike Miller were trying to be another Arkoff and Nicholson, but as it later turned out they just didn't have the moxie or the know-how to do it. They were preparing a picture called *A Date with Death* [1959] starring Gerald Mohr and Liz Renay, who was Mickey Cohen's girlfriend, and they told me they were going to need a companion feature. I indicated that I might be interested if they'd make me the right kind of deal; I told them I'd like a three-picture contract, and they said, "Well, fine — if you don't require any money up front for your *Sun Demon,* we'll release that with our picture as a double bill." So we went on location to Roswell, New Mexico, to shoot *A Date with Death,* in which I had a supporting role, and then the picture I got to make for that company was *Beyond the Time Barrier.*

No temptation for you to direct, as you did on Sun Demon?

No, no — directing *and* acting is a tremendous chore. We got Edgar Ulmer, who had directed *Planet X,* as director and a friend of mine, Les Guthrie, as production manager. Working with Ulmer again was a lift because he was an extremely imaginative, creative director who got the most out of whatever was available and gave his all to the pictures. His wife, Shirley, was our script supervisor and his daughter, Arianne Arden, played in the film, as the femme fatale Markova.

Where did your Time Barrier *script come from?*

That was an Arthur C. Pierce script which I had read and liked; I optioned it and submitted it to the Millers. They had five other scripts under consideration, but this was better than any they had and they selected it. In addition to providing the script, Arthur Pierce came down to Dallas, was involved in some of the production and worked as an assistant editor later, in postproduction. He also did a brief cameo appearance as one of the mutants.

What prompted the decision to make the film in Dallas?
The money was coming from Texas and they wanted to make the picture there. I think the budget was $125,000 and the schedule was about nine or ten days. We shot at the old 1936 Centennial Fairgrounds. The big, convention-type structures there were big enough to simulate sound stages, but the problem was that the sound in those large, empty buildings was like something out of a deep well—"echoey" and booming. The production crew had to hang a lot of old Air Force surplus parachutes all around to absorb some of the sound.

Where did you shoot your air base scenes?
Those were done at Fort Worth's Carswell Field, an actual Air Force base for B52's; it was secured for us by Les Guthrie's father, "Pop" Guthrie, who'd been the location manager at Warners. The wrecked air base of the "future" scenes was nearby; Les Guthrie had gone on a location scouting trip and found this old World War II airstrip, with the remnants of the buildings and all, just as if it had been made for us! It fitted in beautifully with our story.

Who designed your futuristic Time Barrier *sets?*
As I remember, it was our production designer, Ernst Fegté, who conceived the whole thing. He had been under contract to Paramount as a set designer, and he brought in these sketches, with the motif of the inverted triangles and all. Edgar Ulmer, being an artist and a former set designer as well, immediately loved his ideas.

Shortly after Time Barrier, *you announced another film,* The Frozen Continent, *which was never made.*
That was a story treatment that Arthur Pierce had; I got an option on it and provided the financing for him to do a fifty- or sixty-page treatment. It was about an advanced civilization in a city beneath the sea in the Arctic. I was interested in raising money to do it or doing it through Pacific International as another feature, but that company's success was short-lived. Pacific International got into a bankruptcy situation because of lack of business ability in the area of distribution, and in a matter of eighteen months or so they went bankrupt. Once they went under, I didn't receive anything except my actor's salary, $1000 a week for two weeks, for *Time Barrier,* and I lost quite an amount of money, about $50,000, on *Sun Demon.* American International released *Beyond the Time Barrier* along with another Pacific International picture, *The Amazing Transparent Man,* because they bought them, at auction almost, for whatever lab costs were involved. They made out like bandits.

The way things turned out, do you ever regret having broken into production with The Hideous Sun Demon?
Oh, no. I would never say I was sorry because if I had not done it, I think

I would have been sorry and would be saying that I wish that I had tried it. It was an interesting experience. I wish, of course, that it had turned out more profitably and that it had led to other things that would have been more mainstream. With Roger Corman, pictures like these were stepping stones to bigger productions. But I took such a terrible bath with the bankruptcy on both *Sun Demon* and *Time Barrier* that I just felt there was no way to make another one and come out with anything.

How did you get involved on The Incredible Petrified World?

That was a picture I made for Jerry Warren. Jerry was a guy who made a dozen or so pictures which earned money for him in the days when little pictures would play at drive-ins. He put so little money into them, and they were made with such terrible limitations. But he did put a lot of effort into them — I'll credit Jerry for having a great deal of drive, and for working as hard or harder than anybody else. Jerry came out to see me, brought a script of *Incredible Petrified World* and told me that if I'd defer, he'd pay me after we got through the picture, which he did.

Petrified World was shot in Colossal Cave in New Mexico. We drove over there in cars and stayed in some sleazy little motel, and it was hard — *very* hard — work. Jerry would feed us hamburgers for dinner and hamburgers for lunch — and maybe for breakfast, too! And I remember when we got over there I was astonished that the crew consisted of *a* cameraman, who did his own lighting, and *a* sound man. When one of us wasn't in the scene, *we* would hold the boom *[laughs]!* So that was it — a cameraman, a sound man and Jerry, who was a screaming director.

Katherine Victor describes him the same way.

I've always kidded him about that; I've told him, "You turn into a real Mr. Hyde when you get that camera switched on — suddenly you go crazy!" — which he does, he gets so emotional. When he'd holler at me, I'd holler back at him; there's no need for that, except that Jerry gets excited. But it would get me upset, internally, for him to be so obstreperous.

What about working with John Carradine?

What I remember best about Carradine is how strong his concentration was. Carradine was in the scenes we shot here in L.A., and I remember one night, in front of a garage, he had to do a long speech, almost a soliloquy, explaining some plot point. And he was so into that — right out there, practically in the street, without any setting of any kind or any actor to work with. He was just a marvelous actor.

How about on a personal level?

I enjoyed working with him very much. He was a true professional, and he gave every bit as much working for Jerry Warren as he would working for

Cecil DeMille or John Ford. He did not stint in the slightest in his performance. He was cooperative, easy to work with and he was not condescending —
he was something of a star and we weren't, but he treated us as equals and
fellow actors. I have great respect for him.

Would Jerry Warren holler at Carradine, too?
    I can't recall him hollering at John; in fact, I question that he would.

Do you have fond memories of making films like The Astounding She-
Monster, Secret File: Hollywood *[1962] and the Jerry Warrens, or were they all
so rushed and so poverty-stricken that all the fun goes out of them?*
    I did these quickies because I was raising two boys and trying to help sup-
port my wife; the money was there, and it seemed to be the thing to do at the
time. I wouldn't say they were fun; you don't get to feel that you're doing
something that might lead to better things, as I did on the Ida Lupino pictures.
I got more enjoyment and gratification out of *The Man from Planet X* and
Beyond the Time Barrier than I got out of these quickies that we did.

In the mid–'70s you planned a return to producing with The Sorceress. *Can
you tell us about that?*
    There's not a lot to tell. I again got Arthur Pierce to write a treatment of
a story idea that I had come up with: it was about a young woman who had
these powers of sorcery. We tried to modernize it for the day; this was about
the time of Sissy Spacek's *Carrie* and pictures like that. We thought a film
about sorcery and magic powers, things that could be achieved through special
effects work, would have a good commercial reception. But I wasn't very successful at getting the necessary backing for it.

Your last sci-fi role was in Jerry Warren's comeback film Frankenstein Island.
What memories do you have of that film?
    Well, again, of Jerry's obstreperous ways as a director. He would get so
involved that he would forget to use a certain amount of control in his direction
to *anyone* — actors, camera, etc. He would get quite carried away. But there
were good people on that particular film — Andrew Duggan, Cameron Mitchell, Steve Brodie and John Carradine. We went down to Escondido every
weekend; [actor] Robert Christopher and I would drive down together. Bob
Christopher also put in a lot of money and helped Jerry bail the thing out and
get it finished. I'm sure that Bob wishes now that he hadn't; I talked to Jerry
not too long ago, and he said that as far as any theatrical release is concerned
he may as well forget it in today's market. They did make a sale to video
cassette, but he said all that did was get him out of hock with the lab, and on
the deal that they made with television, they got it in a good package but now
they can't collect the money from the packager.

Frankenstein Island *was your first starring feature since* Terror of the
Bloodhunters, *almost twenty years. Was it good to be back in the lead, or did
the low-budget trappings detract from the experience?*
    I think you just answered your own question *[laughs]!* The quality of a
film has a lot to do with whether you can feel good about it. I had hopes for
Frankenstein Island because one great thing about Jerry is that he has a lot of
enthusiasm and he can get a lot on the screen for the kind of money he spends.
But it soon became pretty apparent that this wasn't going to get much beyond
what any of his others had achieved, and it wouldn't reach *Planet X* or *Time
Barrier* or even *Sun Demon* as far as quality. It's slow, it's stodgy, it just plods
along; Jerry cut and cut it, but it's still very ponderous.

Can we look forward to seeing you in any new horror/sci-fi films?
    About two years ago I went to Kansas City to star with Ann Robinson in
a film for Wade Williams called *Space Patrol.* For various reasons the producers
were not very happy with the results, so now it's going to be seen as a movie-
within-a-movie — they wrote a new script and shot forty-five minutes of
footage, and the film is now called *Midnight Movie Massacre.* It now takes
place in 1956, and it's about twelve people who go to a midnight show where
the film Ann Robinson and I did, *Space Patrol,* is playing. Essentially *Midnight Movie Massacre* is a black comedy about a monster that lands behind the
movie house and eats the people, one at a time, as they leave the theater. Wade
says he still used quite a bit of the footage that we're in, and we still have the
major lead billings. It should be out some time in 1988.

*A lot of the talent that Roger and I sponsored
was really germinated and brought about because
we didn't have the financing that other companies had.
Instead of the ability to write that check, we had to
go out with the ability to recognize that talent.
And it worked out well for all of us.*

Gene Corman

WHILE ALL SORTS of media attention has been lavished on Roger Corman, relatively little has been written about his producer-brother Gene. Not only has Gene been an active moviemaker in his own right, he actually preceded his older brother Roger in the film business and played a key role in getting his famous brother's first horror/sci-fi picture released. Both in the area of exploitation and mainstream films, Gene has been producing movies for over thirty years.

Gene Corman first brought the family name into the film industry as a motion picture agent. Beginning in 1956, he and his brother joined forces as producers to make such films as *Hot Car Girl*, *Night of the Blood Beast*, *Attack of the Giant Leeches*, *Beast from Haunted Cave* and *The Premature Burial* for distributors like Allied Artists, AIP and Filmgroup. Gene returned to the exploitation field in the early '70s at MGM when he produced several blaxploitation features such as *Hit Man* (1972) and *The Slams* (1973), as well as Paul Bartel's kinky thriller *Private Parts* (1973).

In the meantime, Gene Corman's more mainstream career was getting underway and has since come to dominate his filmmaking activities. *Tobruk* (1967) was an early success, followed later by such pictures as *F.I.S.T.* (1978) and *The Big Red One* (1980). Presently he is vice-president of Twentieth Century–Fox Television, but he doesn't let that mainstream success make him shy away from talking about his early days shooting monsters on a shoestring in Bronson Canyon.

As youngsters, did you and Roger share any interest in movies and filmmaking?

No, neither of us really was involved or even thought about filmmaking. We were born in and, for the first ten or twelve years of our lives, grew up in Detroit, Michigan. Our dad was a civil engineer, so you can see that there was no way, in Detroit, and with his background, that we would even have considered motion pictures.

If Roger hadn't gotten into the movie industry, do you think you would have?

I was in the motion picture industry *before* Roger was. I had become a motion picture agent and Roger, I think, was working for a steel company or an electrical company. He had graduated an engineer, but then had really no interest in pursuing it. So I preceded him into the business.

I remember when Roger made his first film, *Monster from the Ocean Floor*. He had done it independently, for very little money, without distribution. Obviously, the next order of business was to sell or to make a distribution deal. Being an agent, I negotiated the very first distribution sale for Roger and that film. Herbert Yates, the president of Republic, had an interest in it, but I sold it to Bob Lippert, who in the '40s and '50s had a company that was, in a larger way, an AIP-type outfit. Bob was one of very first who had franchised offices and/or states' righters working with him. As a matter of fact, it was funny — when I made the deal with Bob for *Monster from the Ocean Floor*, we

Previous page: Gene Corman.

made it for something like $110,000 as a pick-up. He was very pleased with that price. Then, when he got back to me with the contracts, he had changed the deal on the basis that we had not *spent* $100,000 on the film. I said, "Well, that was not the question! After looking at the film you were delighted to put up $110,000 as a pick-up." He said, "But now I've found out that you spent less than that—you spent probably seventy or eighty thousand dollars. I'm going to readjust it." To tell the truth *[laughs]*, I think Roger had spent like $35,000 on it, so everybody did well anyway.

What kind of response did Roger get from family and friends when he broke into filmmaking?
  Everybody was somewhat in awe—they didn't quite understand. But since I had preceded him into it by a year or two, and seemed to be doing nicely, they were supportive. To all loving parents, the most important thing is that their children find a lifestyle that is compatible and that is meaningful for them. Even though our father had been an engineer and Roger had studied to be one, once Roger was out in the real world he decided that that wasn't for him.

How did you first become involved in the production of Roger's films?
  I was vice-president of MCA for about seven years. Early on, it seemed to be an area that excited me, and I had a very responsible position. I represented Joan Crawford, Fred MacMurray, Ray Milland, Harry Belafonte, Richard Conte—I had a very strong list of stars at that point. But it wasn't really anything that I saw as terribly creative. And I found, as an agent, that I was functioning as a producer. For instance, with Joan Crawford, who had more careers than probably any other major star that I know of. Joan went through a quiet period after she left Warner Bros., and there was a question of how to place her, what to do with her. There was a Western book I had read, *Johnny Guitar* by Roy Chanslor, that was really suitable as a film vehicle for, say, Clark Gable and two women. I gave it to Joan to read, with the idea that maybe we would move it in a different direction: Maybe *she* would be the lead—*she* would be Clark Gable—and we'd put two other *men* in! I was representing Nicholas Ray at that point, too, so I put the whole project together. And I found I was doing the same with Fred MacMurray, and with Ray Milland when he left Paramount. I was, then, a producer! So I then moved, with Roger, into making the teenage protest films. It was a natural adjunct; having represented Nick Ray through *Rebel Without a Cause* (1955) and several of his other pictures, I knew through first-hand experience what the sum and substance was about. True, the first picture that we made together, *Hot Car Girl* (1958), had a very modest budget, so we were not able to do anything on the same scale as what Nick had done, but it served us well.

Actor Leo Gordon, who wrote Hot Car Girl, The Giant Leeches, Tower of London *and many of your other films, had to be one of the burliest, most brutal-*

looking movie tough guys in the business. It's almost impossible to picture him sitting down writing a screenplay.

Leo was a very burly, tough fellow, but—his background belied his looks. He was an avid reader, and he would read on many levels. And he was a very witty, interesting conversationalist. In many ways, his appearance in those tough-guy roles probably worked to his disadvantage, because to have Leo walk into a story conference was somewhat intimidating! I remember on *Tobruk,* having Arthur Hiller, who is really a very fey, gentle soul, taken aback when he met Leo—it took maybe two or three story conferences before he could come to grips with the size and bulk of Leo! The way he presented himself was intimidating.

When writing the original story for Night of the Blood Beast, *were you at all influenced by* The Thing?

How could you not be? We had to be, if only indirectly or subconsciously. That was a classic film then, a classic film today. The only disappointment is, when they remade it, they failed to understand what Howard Hawks was trying to convey. We shot *Blood Beast* in Bronson Canyon, and we also went up into the Hollywood Hills and used a radio station, right above the HOLLYWOOD sign, for the film's tracking station. Since we had a great deal of day-for-night to shoot, we were always chasing the shadows up there, trying to block out the sun *[laughs]!* That was one of the more mobile units I've ever been involved with. Normally, everybody chases the sun; *we* were chasing the shadows!

Why did you settle for a leftover monster costume in Blood Beast, *rather than an entirely new creation that might have served the picture better?*

Money. We found through experience that if you exceeded a certain figure, you were not going to get that additional money back. You must remember that most or all of these films were handled by states' righters or franchise holders, so you knew pretty well going in what your cost had to be. I think all our early films were in the area of thirty or thirty-five thousand dollars, plus the lab deferment. So for each picture we had a cost of approximately $50,000. The cost of trailers and advertising would then bring it up some more.

Were you present on the sets of your various pictures?

Always. I was a hands-on producer, and to this day I am still a hands-on producer. In my opinion, you cannot be an absentee producer.

One of your most accomplished films of this era was I, Mobster *[1958].*

I made the deal for Roger and myself to do that picture for Twentieth Century–Fox and Eddie Alperson, who had a budget unit independently financed by Fox.

For *Night of the Blood Beast*, Gene and Roger Corman got some extra mileage out of a monster costume made for the earlier *Teenage Caveman*. The uncomfortable-looking victim is Michael Emmet.

Would you have liked to continue making films for mainstream studios like Fox?

Yes. With a major studio comes major financing. And with major financing you have security—you can hire a better writer, possibly go for a book. All along the line you can strive for a greater degree of excellence and professionalism. For the most part, a lot of the talent that Roger and I sponsored was really germinated and brought about because we *didn't* have the financing that other companies had. Instead of the ability to write that check, we had to go out with the ability to recognize that *talent*. And it worked out well for all of us.

So I, Mobster *did whet your appetite to do more ambitious films?*

Yes. As a matter of fact I did do two or three other films for Fox, including one that [production chief] Buddy Adler particularly liked, *Valley of the Redwoods* (1960). That was a film I shot in Eureka, California, in CinemaScope, for something like seventy or eighty thousand dollars. It was so well received that Buddy wanted to make an overall deal with me, with the idea of doing more important films. Unfortunately he was stricken shortly after that and died within a year. I'd also made *Secret of the Purple Reef* (1960), a 'Scope, Technicolor film for Fox, shot in Puerto Rico.

You went back to science fiction again for Attack of the Giant Leeches *and* Beast from Haunted Cave.

At that particular period, the science fiction pictures were a very salable commodity. We had enjoyed a series of successes with them, we found them easy—*fun*—to make, and more readily marketable than most other types of films. If you got away from that kind of horror or science fiction, you found yourself truly competing with the major studios, and in that arena it was impossible. One, you didn't have the production values, and two, you could not afford the stories or the actors. For some reason the other studios had laid back and let science fiction alone for a great deal of the time.

Didn't you originally plan to star Ed Nelson in Giant Leeches?

It seems to me that Ed was going to star in it, but something came along that paid money *[laughs]!* And I think all of us might have gone with him had we been able to get paid as well!

Much of Giant Leeches' *running time is squandered on a white trash love triangle, but there are a number of grisly highpoints.*

It just seemed that in that kind of film you had to have two or three memorable moments—scenes that the audience would go away thinking about, talking about. Somehow, when you place people in jeopardy with leeches—with things that are distasteful—and then combine that with water, you somehow touch a very Freudian-ly responsive chord in people.

Can you tell us a little about how and why you and Roger formed Film-group?

Roger and I had made so many films, and the distributors were legion. If they stayed in business, there was always a question of "creative bookkeeping." If they didn't stay in business, there was the problem of trying to find out where the bank accounts were. Necessity was the mother of invention. We decided, if we were that unhappy with distributors, that it was a logical thing—if we had the product, why not have the distribution? Then we would know where the money was, because we would be the bookkeepers. So we did this. At that time, I knew a lot of the heads of the theater chains, so I could pick up a telephone and book. I became less enchanted than Roger did because I found myself suddenly involved more in that end of the business, and it wasn't something that appealed to me. If that had appealed to me — that kind of . . . less-than-creative part of the business — I would have stayed an agent! That brought Roger and me to see that our goals were not necessarily always going to be the same. So then I went off and made films for Fox.

Did you or Roger work on any of the Filmgroup releases that did not bear a Corman name — pictures like The Wild Ride, The Girl in Lovers Lane, T-Bird Gang *and others?*
We kind of supervised 'em, helped put the crews together and offered a little bit of input, that sort of thing. But not much other than that.

What was the rationale behind taking Beast from Haunted Cave *on location to South Dakota?*
We were looking to find a different background. I mean *[laughs]*, we had used Bronson Canyon and all of the caves to such a point that even *I* was getting tired of that backdrop. I don't think I've returned to Griffith Park since! Bronson Canyon, the Arboretum — we'd outgrown those, because we'd done pictures there so many times. It just seemed that we had to do something different.

We had gotten some information from the Chamber of Commerce in South Dakota, and I think it had to do with the Black Hills, around Rapid City. Once we got there, we found that the Black Hills were such that, visually, you couldn't *hold* them. They're wonderful if you're standing five miles away, but once you're down there, close, you're always in shade, and it just didn't seem to work as well as I had hoped.

Then we found out there was a gold mine in Lead, South Dakota, so obviously that intrigued me and I wanted to use that mine. But there was no way I could get the permission. One of the officers of the mine told me of an old mine in Deadwood, twenty miles away. So we used the interior of *that* mine, and the mountain and snow around it. This was the first time I had tried to shoot in snow, and it was very difficult. But the picture had a whole new look.

Were you happy with Chris Robinson's spider-monster costume?
Yes, we were very, very satisfied. Chris at that time hadn't come to us as an actor, he'd come to us as a model maker. He approached me because he had seen or heard of the other sci-fi / horror films that I had made with monster costumes, and told me they could have been done better — which was true. I said I would have welcomed that, but with the constraints of a budget we had always come up with less than what was designed or sketched. With that in mind, he came forward with the monster costume for *Beast from Haunted Cave* — he did the costume, *and* played the monster in the film.

The exasperating thing about Beast *is that its climax is so frantic and the film ends so abruptly that it's not even clear who lives or dies.*

I think we tried to do that purposely, on the basis that we might have come back for a sequel. That would have been the only reason we might have done it that way.

With very few exceptions you seemed to shy away from availing yourself of Roger's stock company of actors. Why was this?

I think we were trying to expand the look of our pictures. So each one of us looked to see whether we could add to that covey of so-called stock players. I was not intentionally avoiding using them; we were trying to expand our coterie of players because we were distributing through insular companies. You can't always offer the same players to the public.

Why do you and Roger play small parts in many of your own pictures?

Generally it would happen when an actor didn't show up, but also it did save a few dollars. I mean, we were there all the time on these films, so why not? I played small roles in *Machine-Gun Kelly* (1958), *The Wasp Woman, The Secret Invasion* (1964) and so on. And I must tell you, it also was fun!

Why did you and Roger feel you had to get away from AIP to do The Premature Burial?

I don't think we felt we *had* to do that, it just seemed that we were able to structure a better deal with Pathé American. Pathé had wanted to go into distribution, and had in fact distributed a few films.

One of the first "legitimate" old-time Hollywood stars to lend his name to exploitation films was Ray Milland.

I had represented him as his agent for many years, so it was a good experience. I thought he was very good in that film; his very presence gave it a different look, and it had a truer feeling of the period with Ray in the role. I think this was one of the first pictures of that type he had done.

Why did AIP wrest The Premature Burial *away from Pathé American in mid-production?*

I think they didn't want to lose their identification with what at that time was the upscale, more sophisticated type of horror film. As I remember, Pathé did the lab work for AIP — AIP was one of their biggest suppliers of raw stock to be developed and printed. And I think at that point they leaned on Pathé and said, "Look, you're in competition with us, especially with this kind of a film. There are a lot of other labs out there who are really courting us, and would like our business."

How did you feel when Jim Nicholson and Sam Arkoff showed up on the Premature Burial *set and told you that they had managed to take over?*

Left to right: Brendan Dillon, Alan Napier, Hazel Court and unidentified players look on as Roger Corman positions the casket in the Corman brothers' production of *The Premature Burial.*

[Laughs.] I guess we kind of chuckled, and went along with it. We knew that they weren't joking—but also, Roger and I had had a long relationship with them. Like lovers—you have a spat, but you always find a need for each other.

How did Tower of London *come about?*

Leo Gordon and I were trying to come up with a variation on that genre—*not* to do Edgar Allan Poe, because it seemed to me that Vincent Price had done enough of those. We were looking to find another venue; we talked about Nathaniel Hawthorne, and three or four other ideas. Then I said to Leo, "Why don't we go to Shakespeare, and see where that takes us?" *Macbeth* didn't serve us, but the story of *Richard III* did. So that was how that came about—we were exploring the same genre, but a different author.

What was your budget on Tower of London?

Under $200,000, that I know. Building those sets was our major cost. It seems to me we shot that at the old Producer's Studio. Roger directed, with probably a shooting schedule of fifteen days.

Presuming that audiences might be tiring of Vincent Price/Poe films, Corman turned
to Shakespeare and *Richard III* as the basis for *Tower of London* (also featuring Price,
above).

Why, so late in the game, was Tower *made in black-and-white?*

That was not our decision, that was Eddie Small's — Eddie was an independent financier for United Artists. The cost of a color print was considerable in
those days, and he took the hard line. That came as a surprise to us — none of
us had anticipated shooting in black-and-white. This all happened probably
two or three days before we rolled the cameras, when we were ordering the raw

stock. Roger and I had some very strong discussions with Eddie, but it was a case of, "This is the way it's going to be," and he wasn't going to change his mind. What Eddie obviously decided was that Vincent Price had a built-in audience, and that they would not realize up front that they were buying a black-and-white Price film. They'd be taking for granted that this was in color.

How would you rate Price's performance in the film?
I thought Vincent was very good in *Tower of London*. It seemed that he had a real feeling for that period, and for that character. I kind of liked that film, and I know Vincent was always pleased with that performance.

How did the picture do at the box office?
We opened big—for that kind of film—but the down-the-line play was not what it should have been, because at that point the distributor knew he didn't have a color film. That was one of the things that aggravated us to a further degree—the fact that we were *right*, and it turned out to be "a Hollywood rip-off." The picture opened the way all Price pictures did, but did not have that solid, down-the-line play. *Tower of London* didn't do it—and, following that, it didn't do it in television—because it didn't have color.

One of your most intriguing films from that period seems to be The Intruder *[1961].*
The Intruder was a film that Roger and I always wanted to make, and it violated some of our basic precepts. We got ourselves so caught up in *The Intruder* that it was the only film that he and I personally financed that lost money.

Was Roger exaggerating when he told an interviewer, "We all risked our lives on this one"?
[Laughs.] We were run out of Sikeston, Missouri, the Klan came after us, they threatened us—Christ, I'd never gone through such an experience before in my life! And wearing glasses was no protection!

You had a curious supporting cast that included writers Charles Beaumont, George Clayton Johnson and William Nolan.
They were all as dedicated to this project as we were, and we were all friends. Also, Roger and I truly had no money to make this picture. So we called upon as many friends as possible. Each one felt strongly about the film, and they could play specific roles because those roles mirrored, in fact, their own personalities. And if their performances might not be up to what Mervyn LeRoy might have called for, they gave that picture a gritty reality. I think that in many ways the lack of professionalism helped that film.

What inspired you to make a career of the business end of motion pictures, rather than the more creative facets of writing, directing and so on?

That was where I first started—I would be producing and Roger directing—and so it seemed the logical road to continue down. Now that I look at it in retrospect, I probably should have directed, and I have had two or three different opportunities. Specifically when? When I had my own unit at MGM, in the early '70s. I was very autonomous there, and I could have done anything that I wanted as long as the budgets didn't exceed $500,000. So I guess it was just a case of where I found myself, plus the fact that I've been fortunate enough not to have any real problems getting films that I wanted made, made.

Which of your many films is your favorite?
My personal favorite is *Private Parts.* Among the older, "monster"-type things, I think *Attack of the Giant Leeches* is my favorite—although, maybe if I *saw* it again, I wouldn't *[laughs]!* We just had fun—we had such little money, and I remember the director, Bernie Kowalski, shaming me into getting into my bathing trunks and pushing a camera barge with a cameraman and crew on it through the water so they could film.

Roger's remained a sort of maverick while you've moved on to more mainstream projects. Are you happier where you are now?
Probably. I've had some nice experiences, and some of the films have been well-received—I think of *A Woman Called Golda,* in which I was fortunate enough to work with Ingrid Bergman, and we both won Emmys that year [1982]; and I did *The Big Red One,* which was America's entry at the Cannes Film Festival. It's been very comfortable and enjoyable, and I've met a lot of interesting people.

Do you think the day will come when you'll work with Roger again?
You know, we have not made a film together since *I Escaped from Devil's Island* [1973]. And, whether I've been at the Cannes Film Festival or just talking to the students at U.S.C., everybody keeps asking, "Isn't it time?" And Roger and I keep thinking, "It's *time!"*

So you do think it'll happen again soon?
I would think so, but I'm not at all sure when. We do talk, now and then, about trying something, doing something, and I think it would be kind of fun to do it all again.

The creeping terror that rose from the depths of the unknown!

GIANT FROM THE UNKNOWN

*There was X number of dollars, and you don't
run over on these low-budget films — you shoot the
opening scenes and the end scenes, and then
fill in the picture in between. And so if you
run out of days, somehow they'll dissolve between
what you missed and the next scene in there.
Fortunately we didn't miss anything, or if we did,
it wouldn't have* been *missed.* Believe *me.* —Richard E. Cunha

Richard E. Cunha
and Arthur A. Jacobs

GIANT FROM THE UNKNOWN, She Demons, Frankenstein's Daughter and *Missile to the Moon* — four horror pictures that any fan of '50s exploitation is sure to remember fondly. Unfortunately, little has been written in horror retrospectives about the director of these movies, Richard E. Cunha. A notable exception to this lack of Cunha exposure was a passage in a recent book on exploitation films which reported that "the late" Richard Cunha was "amazed, shocked and hurt over the bad reviews his horror films garnered. Despondent over the turn of events, he traveled to the Peruvian jungle and has never been seen since." Well, it seems fair to assume that Cunha *has* been seen by a number of people, such as those connected with the television commercials he made for twenty years after completing his last feature in 1961, as well as those people who now patronize his Video Depot shop in Oceanside, California. All in all, we are happy to report that Richard E. Cunha has managed to escape the exile and death designated for him by an imaginative "nonfiction" author, and has lived to tell the tale of his film exploits.

The Hawaiian-born Cunha received his film training in the newsreel and motion picture units of the United States Air Corps during World War II. He made his first step into the civilian film business by making industrial films and commercials, and then moved on to shoot, write and direct such early TV shows as *The Adventures of Marshal O'Dell* and *Captain Bob Steele and the Border Patrol* for Toby Anguish Productions. Cunha and his friend Arthur Jacobs then plunged into the adventurous arena of shoestring '50s exploitation by forming Screencraft Enterprises. Jacobs, who produced Cunha's first two pictures, joins the director for our discussion of *Giant from the Unknown* and *She Demons,* while Cunha, by himself and apparently still living, tackles *Frankenstein's Daughter* and *Missile to the Moon.*

How did you come to form Screencraft Enterprises?

Arthur A. Jacobs: Toby Anguish was getting ready to retire from the business, and Dick and I decided that we would like to take over his studio. I had had a small editorial service, and we decided to join forces, Richard and I, and take over the complete operation that Toby had, which included the stage, the dubbing facilities, the editing rooms and everything else.

Richard E. Cunha: We had a nice stage, it was two thousand square feet — forty by fifty — and it was great for all the kinds of things that we did back in there. We took over the studio and we used it as a production service — we rented out the stage, and we also did editing and dubbing for people.

Jacobs: Right. And we did the editorial on the last thirty-nine *Lone Rangers,* remember? Just prior to making *Giant from the Unknown.*

Cunha: So that's how Screencraft got formed — it was left over from Toby Anguish Productions, and so we inherited a great deal of studio facilities, and —

Jacobs: *Inherited,* Richard?! We hocked our souls for them *[laughs]!*

Cunha: It was all sitting, and so we got into film production. We made

Previous page: The first Cunha-Jacobs collaboration, made in the hope that "maybe we could make a dollar-and-a-quarter out of it."

some television commercials; I remember we did some Texaco commercials with Harry Von Zell. . . .

Jacobs: Cheerios . . . Wheaties . . . we did quite a few now that I think of it.

What prompted you to make a full-length feature film, Giant from the Unknown?

Cunha: We had a friend, Ralph Brooke, who was interested in movies and things, and he kept egging us on and saying, "Why are you guys messin' around here, wouldn't it be better just to make a movie, or do *something?*" He finally convinced us that it would be kind of fun to do, and that maybe we could make a dollar and a quarter out of it. And that's when we decided to make *Giant from the Unknown* — what did we first call it?

Jacobs: *The Giant from Devil's Crag.* We were all sitting in the office one day — let's see, there was you and I, and Ralph, and [screenwriter] Frank Taussig — and we wondered, "What kind of a picture do we want to make?" And then we said, "Well, we should make a monster movie." Then, "What *kind* of a monster?" At first we tried to get a script already written; we had about a hundred scripts come in, and not one of them could we use.

Cunha: One had a giant lizard, and we couldn't afford the lizard *[laughs],* or *any* of those giant whatevers! About that time Bert I. Gordon was making films with giant spiders and animals and things. We figured we didn't have the talent for special effects, so we needed some kind of an inexpensive monster. And we thought, just a *giant* — we had seen a fellow, I think he was 7'7", that rolled around Hollywood for a while — and we decided that a monster that'd be inexpensive would be a big, tall guy. We interviewed quite a few people and ended up with Buddy Baer.

What was your budget on Giant from the Unknown?

Jacobs: I think it was budgeted around $55,000. And we had $30,000 cash. If I remember correctly, the final cost was $54,000 on that picture, and so we had about $24,000 that we owed when we finished — but we had deferments at the lab and so forth.

And your shooting schedule?

Cunha: We had six days of shooting — however, we had prepared the picture for at least a month ahead of time, and we tried to figure the schedule so that it would work out regardless of what happened. We shot at Big Bear, about one hundred miles or so from Los Angeles proper, up in the mountains, and we also shot a great deal in Fawnskin. The snows were a little late that year, and I know the resort areas were all anxiously awaiting the snow so that the skiers would come up. They were glad to have us at that time because it was just dried up, between seasons, so we were able to get a good deal on the motel that we stayed at. That helped a great deal.

We sent the word out on our first day of location that we were going to shoot at Paradise Cove, on the beach there. That was strictly to confuse the union representatives and the agents and so forth. And everyone was so surprised when we got on the bus and headed in the opposite direction from Paradise Cove! That gave us a two-day start on all of the unions before they really did find out where we were hidden, off in the mountains — and, by God, they found us!

Jacobs: They did find us!

Cunha: They finally located us, and we had to hide most of our equipment...

Jacobs: We had the trucks hidden in the woods, and, fortunately, we had used the five-dollar extras the first day.

Cunha: Yeah, we got them out of the way, because that was all very illegal...

Jacobs: All of our pictures looked like union representative conventions [laughs]!

Cunha: Okay, so we shot the film in six days; we averaged about twenty-one pages a day.

Jacobs: Except for that Wednesday when you shot twenty minutes of film — which I'll never forget as long as I live!

Cunha: Well, that was a very big day and we had to do that to get out in time.

Jacobs: From the time we decided to do the picture until the time we finished the answer print was sixty days — two months altogether.

Mr. Cunha, why did you photograph as well as direct Giant?

Cunha: I *was* the cinematographer on *Giant* and I *became* the director on *Giant!*

Jacobs: It was cheaper!

Why does Bob Steele, who played the sheriff, wear such a horrible white makeup in the film?

Cunha [laughs]: I remember the makeup man coming over to me after working on Bob and saying, "It's not my fault — he told me to do it!" When they get to be a certain age, a lot of people think white makeup makes them look younger. Bob just had this compulsion to put that on, and we kind of had to live with it!

What can you remember about your other stars — Ed Kemmer, Sally Fraser and Morris Ankrum?

Cunha: Ed Kemmer was fantastic — he was eager and Johnny-on-the-spot. And Sally Fraser was neat, too — she hadn't done a great deal prior to that but you wouldn't know it from the way she worked and her very professional attitude. Morrie Ankrum was actually recuperating from an operation when he did *Giant,* and he was just a real trouper. We were in kind of a rugged area there, but outside of the fact that he mentioned it to us once and his agent said to try and take it easy on him, he wouldn't let anybody know that he was in any pain or anything. He was just great.

Jacobs: And Buddy Baer was actually too sweet to be a monster. He was such a nice guy.

Cunha: He was a gem. He really pitched in and did everything.

Jacobs: What was the name of the fellow who made all the fiberglass stuff that we used? He did all the shields and the helmets and everything else.

Cunha: Harold Banks. He did all the armor, the hat, the swords, the extra pieces, the skull. It was our first experience with fiberglass—that was brand new at the time, they weren't making props out of fiberglass.

Jacobs: We couldn't afford the real ones, and he said he could make them out of the fiberglass. And I remember it stunk up the whole studio *[laughs]!* But he sure did a good job on it.

Cunha: He did a fantastic job. We saved a lot of money there.

Had you ever used makeup artist Jack P. Pierce prior to Giant?

Cunha: No, we never used Jack before. He was available, so we got in touch with him and he was very excited about it and was glad to get involved in it.

Jacobs: A *marvelous* man.

Was the Giant's *makeup a Jack Pierce original, or was his appearance spelled out in the screenplay?*

Cunha: No, we had no idea what the monster should look like, it was all determined by who we cast. And so when Buddy worked out so great, we said to Jack, "Okay, we'll go out and get the locations and set up and do some filming, and you bring out a monster." And he did, and it worked out great. I'm not even sure if we did any tests on that—did we ever do an experiment with him to see what he would look like?

Jacobs: No, Jack Pierce took Buddy aside, put him in the chair, and started working on him. I think it took about two, three hours.

Much of Giant *is photographed outdoors, to great effect, but several brief scenes are ruined by the use of obvious, painted backdrops. Why were these necessary?*

Cunha: We had to buy an inexpensive set and we had a few pickup shots that we had to do in there—when the Giant was shot, and some of the chases. To be able to pull it in on this kind of money it was necessary to use a painted backdrop and, again, a very fast schedule to get on there. Art and I ran the film just last night to remind ourselves what it was all about, and we were reminded of the big fight scene inside of the mill, which was a mill built for...

Top: When Astor Pictures insisted on a *Giant from the Unknown* co-feature, Cunha and Jacobs responded with *She Demons. Bottom:* Nazi diehard Gene Roth gets his just deserts at the fangs and claws of the *She Demons.*

Jacobs: *The Trail of the Lonesome Pine* [1936].

Cunha: It was originally built for that and it was left over there, and we worked till midnight shooting the fight sequence and discovered at the end of the night that the shutter in the camera was closed, and we had absolutely nothing that night. We had to come back and we had an abbreviated session the next night and the fight was cut down considerably from what it was before.

That was one of the picture's most atmospheric scenes, filmed in what certainly looks like an actual snowstorm.

Cunha: When we finally did get the snowstorm, it worked in great with the film; we were fortunate enough that it lasted for the sequence. I think we just barely got it all in before the snow left us. I don't recall having to make any phony snow.

Jacobs: We had a couple scenes that we had shot that didn't have snow in 'em, so we had to add snow optically, otherwise it wouldn't match. Richard, you sound like we were *anticipating* a snowstorm. If you remember, when we woke up that morning and there was snow on the ground, you lost ten pounds and turned gray *[laughs]!* We were halfway through the filming and there was no snow at the beginning! That worked out fine, though.

How did your second feature, She Demons, *come about?*

Cunha: We made *Giant from the Unknown* strictly on speculation. We said, "Okay, we're gonna make a picture"—which we were told was *not* the thing to do—and then we were going to put it under our arm, and Art took it back to New York.

Jacobs: It took longer to sell it than to make it *[laughs]!*

Cunha: Yeah, right! But we had a lot of confidence in it, and with the $54,000 budget we thought sure that we'd be able to come out of it okay. When Art got to New York—I think you ran it for various distributors, but Astor Pictures....

Jacobs: I had worked for Astor once, a long time ago—that's how I was aware of them.

Cunha: And so Astor came up and said, "Yeah, fine and dandy, we'll accept *this* picture only if you'll make some more for us," because they wanted to put 'em out in twosomes. And that's how the second picture, *She Demons,* came about.

What was your budget on this one?

Jacobs: They gave us $80,000 for *She Demons,* I think we spent $65,000.

Cunha: But that included our salaries for producer, director, and all that. By that time we figured that I was busy enough directing, and Meredith Nicholson, a very good friend of mine, did the cinematography on *She Demons.*

But this time you co-wrote the screenplay.
   Cunha: I think at that time I did it because it was necessary.
   Jacobs: Who else was gonna do it *[laughs]?* Somebody had to!
   Cunha: I did it because we needed a script, and . . . I was there.

She Demons *contains much more humor than any of your other films. Was this part of your contribution?*
   Cunha: I think those are my private little jokes. I was trying to get even with the world at the time and just having a good time. These were really tongue-in-cheek films, and we enjoyed doing them a great deal and had as much fun as possible.

What was Irish McCalla like to work with?
   Jacobs: *Sheena, Queen of the Jungle [laughs]!*
   Cunha: I guess of all the people that we used in the first few films, she was . . . well, she wasn't *difficult. . . .*
   Jacobs: No, she really wasn't, Dick, when I think back on it—not compared to some of the kids today. She had already had some notoriety, so, really, it wasn't too bad. You have to remember that actors and actresses are strange people anyhow, aren't they, Richard? They're all difficult, at best.
   Cunha: She had always been a great pinup girl, and she had great boobs and stuff, but then she had this child and she lost everything up top. And we had the worst time trying to get this silly sequence of her nude back. We just had a *terrible* time! It was like she was doing a porno or something! Everybody had to hide, we had to get the guys off the set—we had pasties on her and everything else. It was just the fact that she had lost her bustline and she wanted everybody to remember her like she looked when she was a pinup girl.

What were some of your locations on She Demons?
   Cunha: Paradise Cove was our primary beach location. The jungle sequences we did in Griffith Park, in Ferndale—the regular public trails there. One thing we had to do that they reprimanded us for was putting the dry ice into the stream there. They had already told us not to monkey with the water but of course as soon as we were alone we threw that stuff in—but they caught us.

Probably the best-remembered scene in She Demons *comes when Leni Tana tears off the bandages across her eyes.*
   Jacobs *[to Cunha]: Who* was Leni Tana?
   Cunha *[laughs]:* She was the lady that wore the bandages through the whole picture.
   Jacobs: Oh? I always thought that was your *wife!*
   Cunha: Leni Tana didn't want to wear all that terrible makeup under-

neath the bandages, and so my wife *was* the face for the "reveal" scene! However, Leni Tana walked around with the bandages the rest of the film.

Did the Diana Nellis Dancers, who did the dance routine in the picture, also play the disfigured She Demons?
Cunha: Yes, they did. That was all part of the same group; we had our little company, if you please, and—
Jacobs: And one bongo player! That was our whole rhythm section, one bongo player!

Why did you two separate after this first pair of pictures?
Cunha: As we had mentioned, we had been doing a good deal of post-production for Jack Wrather and the *Lone Ranger* company. And so, after we had finished these two pictures, Art had the opportunity to go with Mr. Wrather.
Jacobs: I spent nine and a half years with the Wrather Corporation, ending up as vice-president in charge of production and distribution. I set up domestic and foreign distribution of their television company, and I was involved in the production of *Lassie* for many years. After I left them, I went to work for Danny Thomas, Sheldon Leonard, and Aaron Spelling, at Paramount. I was there for several years. And at that time I decided that I'd really like to see what happens to a picture when it's finished. I got into independent theatrical distribution in the U.S. In 1975 my wife and I moved to London, where I was an independent producer's representative. Right now I'm back in the States, I'm selling independent productions, and for fifteen years I've been trying to get Dick Cunha to make another picture with me *[laughs]!*
Cunha: That brings us into the metamorphosis into Layton Film Productions. At that time, when Art had the opportunity to go with Jack Wrather, we dissolved Screencraft, and Marc Frederic, who was an investor, then formed Layton Film Productions.
Jacobs: Which was the name of the street he lived on, if I remember correctly.
Cunha: Yes, that's right—Layton Drive. He and I formed Layton Productions, and I made another three pictures *[Frankenstein's Daughter, Missile to the Moon* and the detective picture *The Girl in Room 13]* with him.

What were your budgets and shooting schedules on Frankenstein's Daughter *and* Missile to the Moon?
Cunha: All of our budgets were under $80,000, and we tried very hard to bring them in for approximately $65,000 or less. I think we were successful in most cases. When we turned the negative over to Astor after the picture was accepted, we were paid $80,000. Our shooting schedules were always six days. I believe on *Missile to the Moon* they gave us an extra day of preproduction

where we did some of the monster scenes out at Red Rock Canyon, about eighty miles from Los Angeles.

What were some of your locations for Frankenstein's Daughter?
Cunha: The exterior scenes were done at Marc Frederic's home. The interiors were a set. Our art director, Don Ament, was a super guy; I worked with him subsequently at E.U.E. Columbia for many, many years. Don was just a fabulous guy — he would go around and see what sets were available cheap, and then redesign 'em so they'd work out for us. He was great at that.

Can you tell us a little about your cast?
Cunha: They were all keen. John Ashley ... Sandra Knight ... Sally Todd ... Donald Murphy was absolutely great. I don't recall what happened to any of these people; it always seems whenever I make a picture, that's the person's last picture *[laughs]!* It must be something I do...

Where did you get the props for your laboratory scene?
Cunha: We got a character that was furnishing those to the studios, and we took what the studios wouldn't take — for a price, you know. We'd say, "We can't afford your real prices, so give us the junk from your backyard," and he'd say, "Okay, if you guys clean 'em up, make 'em look pretty good, you can have 'em." So we did it, and returned them to him in twice-better shape than he gave them to us.

Probably the best-remembered scene from this picture is when Donald Murphy gets the acid thrown in his face. Was that really Murphy under the makeup?
Cunha: Yes, it was. And as I recall — *vividly* — the makeup man on that, who by the way was Paul Stanhope, created that remarkable effect with torn Kleenex tissue. I was quite pleased with that, that worked out very well. We did want Jack Pierce to do the makeup on that, but he was not available for the picture.

Paul Stanhope was your makeup man? The credits list Harry Thomas.
Cunha: Stanhope was just not ready for us; he was used to *old* motion picture time. So when somebody fired a gun and I'd get twenty-one pages a day, he just fainted on us. That's when Harry Thomas came in.

Was it Stanhope who did the makeup for Sandra Knight's she-monster?
Cunha: No, that was Harry Thomas.

Harry Wilson, who played Frankenstein's Daughter, had been Wallace Beery's stand-in for twenty-five years and had dubbed himself "The Ugliest Man in Pictures." Can you tell us about him?

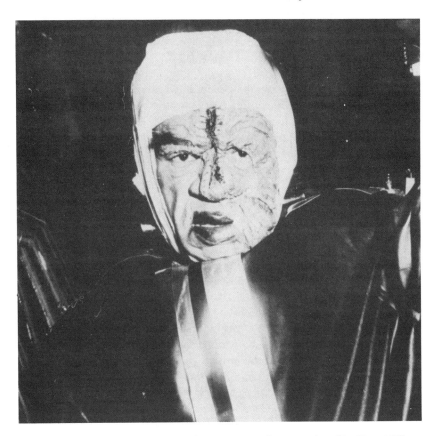

The female monster in Cunha's *Frankenstein's Daughter* was played by Harry Wilson, a one-time stand-in for Wallace Beery.

Cunha: He was a very patient man, and he suffered a great deal with that makeup and the suit that was required for him. And with the speed that we had to shoot at, it wasn't like he could rest between takes. He was always right on call and, as I recall, he was right there all the time. George Barrows played the monster in the scene where he was on fire. Barrows also did a lot of the fight scenes in *She Demons*.

Was it Paul Stanhope or Harry Thomas who did the — very unusual Frankenstein's Daughter makeup?
Cunha: Stanhope. That wasn't an unusual situation at all, it was a situation where we just got trapped, again, without any money. We had no preparation time, and Frankenstein's Daughter was designed on the set on the first day of shooting. And suddenly someone came up to me and said, "Look—here's your monster!" And I nearly *died*. We said, "No, that's not quite what we need, but by God we can't do anything about it!" And we

pushed the guy on the set and started shooting — the show must go on. So the monster wasn't designed like that, it just . . . ended up like that, and once we achieved that [laughs], we had to keep it!

One of the best elements from Frankenstein's Daughter *and* Missile to the Moon *is the Nicholas Carras music.*
   Cunha: He was introduced to us, and we liked his style. He was a swinger, and as eager as we were to try and accomplish something on a minimum budget. It seems to me that we paid him about nine or ten thousand dollars for the total music score on each of those two pictures — that included the writing, the musicians and everything. He did a fantastic job.

Whose idea was it to have you remake the earlier Astor release Cat Women of the Moon *as* Missile to the Moon?
   Cunha: It was Astor's idea. They thought, well, shucks, it'd be a good idea to redo the movie, they could get a little bit of sex in and have some pretty girls wandering through the scenes. And it *was* patterned after their movie.

Where did you get the giant spider used in Missile to the Moon?
   Cunha: We rented it from Universal Pictures. In those days we used to go around to all the prop shops, nose in the back rooms and see what we could get cheap. That spider was in Universal's prop shop, and it was in terrible disrepair; we just managed to put it together the best we could. As I recall, we paid practically nothing for it, and they were kind enough to let us use it. It wasn't even written into the picture until we found it in pieces at Universal.

Who designed the Rock Creatures, and what were they made of?
   Cunha: They were made of sponge rubber that was cast. Harold Banks made those for us. He was the very creative man who made the fiberglass outfits for *Giant from the Unknown.*

Wasn't it tough on the people who played those monsters — working in Red Rock Canyon in midsummer?
   Cunha: The worst — absolutely the worst. And if you'll remember we had one scene where we had to plaster them to the sides of giant rocks, for them to break out. And, you know [laughs], it took a while for the plaster to dry with them in there! They'd be yelling, "Get us out of here, get us out of here!" So, yes, that was very, very difficult for them, but they were all good guys. We laughed over a beer about it later.

What was it like working with so many beauty queens in one picture?
   Cunha: A real pain. None of them were actresses as such, they were all beauty queens who couldn't hit marks and couldn't say lines — it was quite frustrating.

Was any inspiration derived from a then-current Allied Artists release, Queen of Outer Space, *which had the same premise as well as some of the same players?*

Cunha: No. I don't remember the picture, and I certainly didn't go see it.

Of your four horror films, which one is your favorite?

Cunha: My favorite was and always will be *Giant from the Unknown* because that was the most fun to make. We did it in a spirit of fun, we had the most cooperation—that was a ball.

Were you disappointed with any of these films?

Cunha: I think the biggest disappointment to me was *Frankenstein's Daughter,* only because of our monster creator; I can't blame anyone for that, we just didn't have enough money to create a monster that would represent Sally Todd. So that was my biggest disappointment. And, as far as *Missile to the Moon* is concerned, again, the money was so meager that it was just impossible to create the proper atmosphere for a spaceship—although I think, on the money we *did* have, the interior of the spaceship worked well. It included many pieces of grip equipment, as I recall, and we used a big dimmer bank for some of the controls on the missile. And we just scraped together whatever we could to make do, and that's all there was. There was X number of dollars, and you don't run over on these low-budget films—you shoot the opening scenes and the end scenes, and then fill in the picture in between. And so if you run out of days, somehow they'll dissolve between what you missed and the next scene in there. Fortunately we didn't miss anything, or if we did, it wouldn't have *been* missed. *Believe* me.

H.G. Wells' The Time Machine *is a classic of science fiction.*
I first read it when I was about fifteen years old
and it has always been one of my favorite stories.
So it was a challenge to turn it into a film
without degrading the quality.
I hope I did so.

David Duncan

AS IS THE CASE in all other types of moviemaking, the screenwriter of a science fiction film is often overlooked in favor of the director. To help correct this common oversight, we present an interview with David Duncan, a novelist turned screenwriter who has contributed to many well-remembered science fiction/horror films of the late 1950s and early 1960s. His credits include *The Monster That Challenged the World, The Black Scorpion,* the Americanized version of *Rodan, The Thing That Couldn't Die* and *Monster on the Campus.* His best work is the script for George Pal's science fiction classic *The Time Machine.*

Duncan didn't start to write full-time until the age of thirty-three, in 1946, after around ten years of work in government administration and public services. He began screenwriting in 1953 but "did not start writing science fiction for the movies until one of my SF novels, *Dark Dominion,* was serialized in *Collier's,*" Duncan recalls. "You know how they categorize people in Hollywood: suddenly I was a science fiction writer, which I had never been before."

Did you write most of these sci-fi pictures on speculation, or were you brought aboard by producers who told you basically what they wanted?

I wrote either on a salary or a contract basis. For my original screenplays I wrote what I pleased. Others were based on books or other material where the producer owned the motion picture rights.

What exactly did you contribute to The Monster That Challenged the World?

When I went to work on the story and screenplay the plan was to make the picture in Japan, and so everything I wrote was done with this in mind. As well as I recall, everyone including myself was pleased with the finished screenplay. I was paid off and had lined up another assignment when the blow fell. For reasons I don't know, the Japanese filming had to be called off, which meant that the screenplay had to be completely rewritten for a local setting. I labored at it for a few days free of charge but everything I wrote was dead, dead, dead. Pat Fielder, a very attractive young woman, was doing secretarial work for the producer at the time and asked if she could have a shot at it. Her request was granted, with very happy results for Pat.

Pat Fielder claimed that you wrote an article about ancient shrimp eggs for Life, *and that was what inspired the movie.*

No, I didn't write for *Life* about shrimp eggs. It may have been the writer-photographer David Douglas Duncan, with whom I was sometimes confused in those days. I recall that he did a book on Picasso and *Publishers Weekly* ran a review of it headed by a picture of me.

Them! *had a large influence on sci-fi films of the '50s, especially* The Monster That Challenged the World *and* The Black Scorpion. *Do you recall whether you saw the film and used it as inspiration?*

Previous page: **David Duncan today.**

Ten feet, fifteen hundred pounds and $15,000 worth of fiberglass fury, this giant mollusk prop provided more-than-ample menace in the David Duncan–scripted *The Monster That Challenged the World.*

Yes, I saw *Them!*, one of the best. And I certainly used it to the extent that it demonstrated that the longer one could keep the nature of the menace a mystery, the better.

Some film experts insist that parts of The Black Scorpion *were "written around" certain special effects shots which were filmed before a script existed. Do you recall whether you were told to incorporate any specific scenes into your screenplay before you even began writing?*

After almost thirty years, my memories of the actual writing of these screenplays is pretty dim. I seem to recall that there was an unusable script on hand in the case of *The Black Scorpion,* and I remember a huge floppy spider that producer Jack Dietz insisted on introducing far sooner than I thought it should be. I've never seen the film.

Did the men who would eventually direct your screenplays — Edward Ludwig, Will Cowan, Jack Arnold, etc. — meet and consult with you prior to filming?

The only one of the three directors you mentioned that I knew personally was Eddy Ludwig *[The Black Scorpion].* Directors don't like to have writers around when they start filming. At least no director ever wanted me around or bothered to consult with me. Except George Pal.

I had written a historical drama called *Sangaree* [1953] for Bill Pine and Bill Thomas — "The Two Dollar Bill" — and I went back to work for them again about two months later, when they were shooting the film. I took a break and walked down to where they were filming to see what was happening, and on the set I noticed a sign in a window, "George Washington for President." I tore back to the office and told Bill Thomas, "My God, they've got a sign out there, 'George Washington for President.' He wasn't president until three or four years after this picture is set, and he didn't have to run for president anyway — he was elected unanimously and had no opposition. This'll make the whole picture look silly."

So Bill Thomas grabbed the phone, called the set and stopped them from shooting. Then he went out there to see what was going on. I don't know what this delay cost him, but they stopped production for an hour — it must've been quite a lot. He came back, gave me a glowering look and said, "That sign isn't even in camera range — some extras put it up for fun!" That's one reason they don't like writers on the set.

What are some of the ins and outs of writing dialogue for dubbing into a foreign film like Rodan?

Working on *Rodan* was the most boring job I ever had in my life. The film goes into a Moviola that can run it forward or backward and repeat scenes as many times as needed while the operator stares at the mouths of the Japanese actors and attempts to find English words that fit the mouth movements. There are only three letters in the English alphabet that close the mouth completely — B, M and P — but there must be *dozens* of Japanese characters that do the same thing because when the sound was turned off the actors appeared to be saying something like, "Mama, mama, mama," over and over again. Actually, most of the dubbing was done by a co-worker whose name, I think, was O'Neal. *He* should have received the credit.

Most of your other sci-fi credits around that time were for Universal-International.

Howard Pine, son of Bill Pine, was working as a producer at Universal studios, and he had them put me on salary to come up with some original science fiction screenplays. I wrote *The Water Witch*, which became *The Thing That Couldn't Die*, and *Monster on the Campus*.

Where did the idea for The Thing That Couldn't Die *come from?*

Not long before I wrote *The Thing That Couldn't Die* I'd read a book on dowsing [finding water through the use of a divining rod] by Kenneth Roberts and tried to do a little dowsing myself, in the backyard of our Los Angeles home. Nothing happened. So I turned on the garden hose and carried my wand over it a few times. Nothing. About that time my youngest daughter, six or seven years old at the time, came out of the house. Without telling her

A real-life scientific discovery helped sow the seeds for Duncan's *Monster on the Campus* screenplay.

what I had in mind, I placed the forked wand in her hands and asked her to walk over the hose with it. She did so several times and started giggling. "How funny," she said. "Every time I cross the hose the stick tries to jump out of my hands." I was quite impressed. I think that was the genesis of the screenplay. No, my daughter didn't become a dowser. She's now an attorney living in St. Louis.

Can you tell us how Monster on the Campus *was conceived?*

Not long before writing *Monster on the Campus* there'd been quite a lot in scientific publications about a live coelacanth having been caught off the coast of Madagascar. The coelacanth was a species of fish thought to have been extinct for several million years. It was that which suggested the story.

One of the weaker elements in Monster on the Campus *is the utterly careless way Arthur Franz infects himself—getting the dead fish to "bite" him, dripping its blood into his pipe and so on.*
I didn't know the fish bit Arthur Franz, I thought it was only the blood in his pipe that turned him into Pithecanthropus. But you're quite right, that could have been done much better.

Did you also write The Leech Woman *around this same time?*
No, I wrote that long after I had done *Thing That Couldn't Die* and *Monster on the Campus.* Apparently someone at Universal liked what I had done on those two, and a producer by the name of Joseph Gershenson re-hired me.

Unlike Thing *and* Monster, The Leech Woman *was not an original.*
Oh, no. They gave me some material—in fact, I think they gave me a screenplay that had been written by somebody named Ben Pivar. It wasn't a very good screenplay—really, it was unshootable. In redoing it, I suppose I changed the story somewhat. I rewrote it on a two-week assignment and never saw it until a couple of months ago, when I happened to catch it on TV. Isn't it *awful?*

Several of your sci-fi films are surprisingly violent for their time.
I never cared for violence in movies, although I love suspense. In science fiction monster films, it's the special effects guys who have all the fun and are usually responsible for the gruesome stuff.

Did George Pal give you enough creative freedom when you worked with him on The Time Machine?
It was great working with George Pal, and there were no restraints on my writing. The only restraint was that I had to write the screenplay in the upstairs bedroom of my house, whither George came occasionally for discussion. He didn't want anyone to know what we were doing; on some previous occasions, his ideas had been preempted by quickie producers before he could get them on film. However, I liked the bedroom. I could work in my pajamas.

Tell us how you went about adapting the original H.G. Wells novel into a screenplay.
Like most of Wells' science fiction novels, *The Time Machine* was as much a social document as a tale of science adventure. It was written around the turn of the century—about 1895, as I recall. Anyhow, the Industrial Revolution was in full swing at the time, with laborers working long hours at low pay in

underground mines and dingy factories while the elite basked in the sunshine at the workers' expense. Wells was something of a socialist; he conceived a future where this industrialization brought about, through the forces of evolution, a split in the human race. The proletariat became a race of underground Morlocks while the elite, being utterly dependent upon them, lost all incentive for anything except pleasure. While remaining human in appearance, they degenerated mentally and morally into thoughtless childishness.

However, by 1959 when the screenplay was written, this forecast of the future no longer carried any plausibility — if it *ever* did. Labor unions were strong, wages were high, while shorter hours, vacations with pay, pension plans and a host of other fringe benefits had moved most blue-collar workers into the middle class.

Fortunately, however, the ill wind that was blowing then and has been blowing ever since, blew *The Time Machine* some good. The '50s and '60s were the years when schoolchildren were being taught to hide under their desks (unbelievable!) and the populace at large encouraged to dig backyard bomb shelters and prepare to dive into them when the air raid siren warned of an impending attack by atomic bombs.

So you substituted that situation for the economic one in the original story?

Right. Over a period of time the people above ground became conditioned to seeking the lower regions when the air raid siren sounded; over the same centuries those who had originally constructed the vast underground shelters became the carnivorous Morlocks. That was a principal change from the Wells novel.

Then you added a great deal to the story.

Of course. In the novel the only truly human character is the Time Traveller, to whom Wells didn't even bother to give a name. George Pal decided to call him George. A number of other characters then had to be created for the opening and closing scenes of the play. One of them Pal kindly gave the name of David.

For the rest, the action generally followed the Wells novel, or at least what was suggested by the novel. In the novel, for example, the Time Traveller descends into the realm of the Morlocks only long enough to realize that if he remains there he's likely to be eaten, and so he beats a hasty retreat. This would never do for a motion picture. There had to be a major underground sequence.

It's impossible for me to write dialogue and stage directions without knowing what the stage looks like, and no scene designers had been put to work yet. So I spent a couple of hours with pencil and paper sketching out a picture of the Morlocks' underground world. When George saw it he took it home with him. The following Sunday morning, when I went to his home for a

Rod Taylor lashes out at attacking Morlocks in 1960's *The Time Machine*. Duncan considers his screenplay (adapted from the H.G. Wells novel) for this George Pal classic his best work in the genre.

conference, I was flattered to find him out on the lawn before his easel translating my sketch into a full-color finished version upon which the actual set was later based.

Didn't you and Pal discuss the possibility of giving the film's framing sequences a contemporary setting?

Yes, but only briefly. We both agreed that the Victorian beginning made the film more believable by allowing the Time Traveller to pass through that part of the twentieth century with which the audience was already familiar. That made it possible to bring it *real* history, such as the world wars. It also gave viewers the pleasure of witnessing the Time Traveller's astonishment at technological advances which, to them, were already commonplace.

Did you have a hand in designing the Morlock makeup?

No, I had nothing to do with that. But I do remember being on the set one day during shooting when the Morlocks had everyone roaring with laughter at their offstage antics. I recall George saying something to me to the effect, "My God, do you think the motion picture audience will react that way?"

Did The Time Machine *reach the screen exactly as you had written it?*

No, there was some tampering with the script after I was finished with it.

I recall going to the premiere with my wife Elaine, and at some point in the far-future part of the story the Time Traveller came out with a line to the effect that the Eloi were at a cultural level on a par with the people on the isle of Bali. Elaine gave me a ferocious jab with her elbow and I whispered frantically, "I didn't do it! I didn't do it!" The Balinese were building temples while the Time Traveller's ancestors were still chasing deer with stone-pointed sticks.

You received the Georges Méliès Award for your Time Machine *screenplay.*
   I didn't receive that award until the mid–'70s, long after we'd moved to Oregon and after I'd stopped writing for films or TV. My reaction was, "Why the hell didn't they give it to me while I was still active and it might have done me some good?"

Many fans see The Time Machine *as George Pal's best feature. Did Pal ever try to seek out your services for any other collaboration?*
   We talked of other projects several times but nothing more developed.

Did writing Fantastic Voyage *entail much anatomical research on your part?*
   I do remember having a number of anatomical books on hand while working on it. I also remember taking my microscope to the studio one day to show the art director what living red blood cells look like. I insisted that he examine his own cells rather than mine.

Would you care to elaborate on the way that film was, according to many, mishandled?
   I think the big mistake in making *Fantastic Voyage* was in trying to integrate a spy story with what should have been purely a pictorially beautiful science fiction picture. The spy-sabotage element was added by the second writer, who received the screenplay credit. I believe another mistake was the abrupt manner in which the human body was entered. This was like introducing the monster of a monster movie in the opening scene.

Did you go to see your own movies when they were released theatrically?
   The only one of my movies I ever saw at a premiere was *The Time Machine.* I've never seen *The Monster That Challenged the World* and didn't even know that was its final title until you mentioned it. Nor have I ever seen *The Black Scorpion. Rodan* I had to see at least twenty times while dubbing it and never want to see it again. The others I've seen on television.

What occupies your time nowadays?
   You've been keeping me busy quite a while now. For the rest, I garden a lot, especially in the spring, spend quite a bit of time with my microscope

studying the Protozoa I culture in a tiny artificial pool on the hillside, take an auto trip with my wife every now and then, read a lot and once a year watch the World Series on television.

Which of your science fiction films is your personal favorite?

  The Time Machine, by a huge margin. The Wells novel is a classic of science fiction. I first read it when I was about fifteen years old and it has always been one of my favorite stories. So it was a challenge to turn it into a film without degrading the quality. I hope I did so.

I finally got to the point where it was like,
"Oh, well—some people work at the shoe store,
some people work in the butcher shop.
I'll work in the studios, and a job's a job."
There are naturally aspirations and so forth that you have,
but it's better than working in a restaurant!

Anthony Eisley

ALL TOO UNDERSTANDABLY, Anthony Eisley prefers to be remembered as the suave, stalwart star of television's *Hawaiian Eye,* rather than as leading man to insectivorous ingenues *(The Wasp Woman)*, walking trees *(The Navy vs. the Night Monsters)*, giant apes *(The Mighty Gorga)* and mustachioed sea serpents *(Monstroid)*. But as the 1950s horror boom extended into the 1960s, the mantle of monster exterminator formerly worn by the likes of John Agar, Richard Carlson and Kenneth Tobey was inherited by Eisley when he starred in a long succession of low-budget sci-fi/horror adventures.

The future stage, screen and TV star (real name: Fred Eisley) was born in Philadelphia. His father was general sales manager and "trouble-shooter" for a large company, and his work kept the family on the move, up and down the East Coast, throughout Eisley's young life. As early as the days of school plays, Eisley knew that he wanted to be an actor, but because he lacked show biz contacts he felt nothing would come of his aspiration. He later took drama courses at the University of Miami, "not because I thought I could really be an actor, but because I was taking the easy way out to get a degree."

Finally following up on his longtime ambition, Eisley landed a job with a stock company in Pennsylvania, where he worked opposite James Dunn in a stage production of *A Slight Case of Murder.* Later roles in long-running plays like *Mr. Roberts, Picnic* and *The Desperate Hours* ensued, along with some early movie *(Operation Pacific, Fearless Fagan)* and TV *(Racket Squad)* work. His first genre assignment was in Roger Corman's mini-budgeted *The Wasp Woman,* and the rest is exploitation history.

How did you enjoy working with the legendary—notorious—Roger Corman on The Wasp Woman?

This reveals some lack of depth in me, I suppose, but I thought it was fun—a hell of a lot of fun—because he worked like a house afire and I like to work fast. On the stage I had spent eight years playing four parts; I'd had a great deal of luck in being in hit plays that consumed a lot of time, but after that period was over I found it much more enjoyable to learn something, do it, forget it and go on. So whipping through that picture with Corman was a lot of fun; in fact, he did some pretty strange things. He would set up one camera angle on a particular setting that may appear in the picture five times. And then you would do all five scenes, changing your clothes between each scene. Then he'd set up the *other* camera angle, over your shoulder, and you'd do the five different scenes *again,* changing your clothes five times again! There was no sense of continuity or anything, but to me it was fun to do it in little bits and pieces.

What do you remember about your leading ladies Susan Cabot and Barboura Morris?

Susan Cabot was one of Roger's stock company at the time, and I don't think she was happy with the picture. And not being happy, she was more

Previous page: Anthony Eisley strikes a ready-for-action pose in the zero-budgeted *Journey to the Center of Time.*

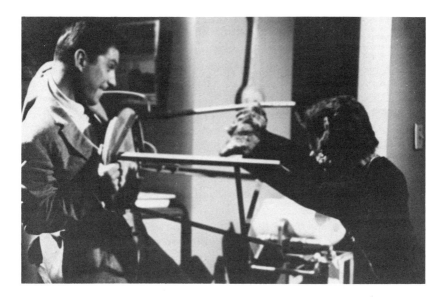

Eisley and she-monster Susan Cabot battle it out at the climax of director Roger Corman's *The Wasp Woman.*

inclined to go sulk in a corner rather than converse with anybody. I think she was unhappy, probably just fulfilling some contractual obligation, and she was not that sociable because I think she was pretty p.o.'ed at Roger most of the time—for what reasons, I don't know. Barboura Morris was just a sweet young girl; she had done quite a few pictures for Roger, and I've often wondered what happened to her career after that.

Any other Wasp Woman *memories?*
There is one funny thing I remember. At that time I was very gung-ho, and any time something came up that involved any element of danger I thought, "Hey, man, this is great, I'm gonna show 'em"—which is something you grow out of eventually. There were no stunts, per se, on *The Wasp Woman,* but they had a scene where I had to break through a glass office door and rescue the heroine. They shot that very early on and I insisted that I would kick through the glass door for real, which I did. And it was real glass—budgetwise, they didn't even have the money for candy glass. But thereafter they put opaque paper over the door—glued it on, instead of replacing the glass—and shot many scenes which preceded that breakthrough in the picture. So if you look, you'll notice that whenever the door opens or closes, the "glass" balloons back and forth like the jib on a sailboat! Talk about low-budget, I had never seen such cost-cutting as Roger Corman did. But there was no question that that guy really knew what he was doing—he was miraculous at turning out acceptable product in no time at all.

Early on, what sort of niche did you hope to fill as a movie/TV actor?

I was hoping to be a light comedian, which of course didn't happen. What actually brought me to the attention of Warner Bros. is that I did the play *Who Was That Lady?* at the Players Ring Theater in Los Angeles; Jerry Paris and I were the co-leads in it, and we were very, very funny. Then when I got a Warner Bros. contract which more or less came from that show, I had visions of being the next Jack Lemmon. Instead they put me in *Hawaiian Eye,* and I have no complaints about that, but it wasn't what I thought they would have in mind for me. So I never really got to do what I felt that I did best.

Why did you leave Hawaiian Eye *after the third season?*

It was a political thing. A guy at an ad agency who handled one of our sponsors never liked me, for what reason I don't know. When *Hawaiian Eye* was about to be picked up for the fourth year, the ad agency guy said that the sponsor would pick up the show only provided they bring in Troy Donahue. At that time Troy and Connie Stevens were hot on the big screen. Well, now you had Bob Conrad, Grant Williams, me and, in order to be picked up, they had to have Troy Donahue come in. At that point it simply became a question of seeing whose option came up first. My option came up like three weeks after this edict was handed down, so they just dumped me. Of course it wasn't that simple, but that's the basic story.

Shouldn't a popular series like Hawaiian Eye *have led to a career in a better grade of film than those you ended up in?*

Yeah! *[Laughs.]* You're right, my career never took off again like I felt that it should have. I think the big thing was the image that I came out of *Hawaiian Eye* with. It was a very limiting image.

Were there some lean years after Hawaiian Eye?

Oh, yeah, it was always up and down. Then I had some years where I made a hell of a lot on commercials, which I never thought were great fun, but it kept things going for me. It was always a seesaw ride, it was never what it should've been. But I have no complaints.

What recollections do you have of The Navy vs. the Night Monsters?

The producer recut that picture after it was made, and totally destroyed any validity it might have had. That picture, as Michael Hoey wrote and directed it, would have been a very good little thriller. First of all, you never saw these trees in explicit detail—you had a sense of mystery about what was killing the people on this island. As originally shot, the island radio tower was destroyed by a plane crash, and there was no contact between the island and the outside world. I, as executive officer of the island military base, was not prepared to assume command, and I had nobody I could turn to. So we played it at a level of fear and panic that wouldn't exist if we could have contacted

The Navy vs. the Night Monsters pitted Eisley against walking trees, a hostile sex kitten and a blundering executive producer.

some base on the outside. Then, months after the picture was shut down, the producer put in this stupid stock footage of bombers blowing up the island at the end and shot these monotonous talking scenes of generals on the telephone that were not at all germane to the original story. As a consequence, in the final cut we actors were playing at a level that the situation didn't call for at all! That was very, very upsetting.

When you talk about the producer, you mean Jack Broder?
Right. He wanted more running time, I guess, but mainly he wanted to use that stock footage of the airplanes. The picture should have ended on a note of mystery: Will they be able to overcome this menace or not? But he had to continue the picture with all that airplane stuff. I'm not saying that the picture ever could have been any kind of a gem, but it had a validity that it subsequently lost because of the stuff he added.

Jack Broder had produced quite a few low-budget pictures, and I was always mystified as to why he never made any sense — you'd normally figure that a guy who produces pictures must know something *about* them! Because he felt we had been taking too long and because he was so concerned about his schedule, he would walk in, in the middle of a scene, and insist that the set be torn down — which would happen! And then a few days later he'd realize the scene had to be finished, and they'd have to put the set up again! He did things like this constantly! Another time he was sitting in the projection room looking at dailies—Michael Hoey and I were there, too, watching this fight scene that I had with Ed Faulkner in the picture. After it was over Jack said, "That was terrible!" Mike said, "I thought it looked all right—what's the matter with it?" and Jack said, "I can't hear the punches!" *[Laughs.]* I don't know what the hell he was ever doing making pictures.

Who directed all those extra scenes you talked about?
    I think they were directed by Arthur C. Pierce, who also directed *Women of the Prehistoric Planet.* The opening scenes in the airplane, scenes of the guys with the weather balloons, all this was thrown in after the fact. I don't know what the hell any of that stuff was, it was totally boring.

What do you remember about star Mamie Van Doren?
    Her nose was out of joint about everything in the world at the time. I have no idea why, but she wouldn't even say hello! You'd play a scene with her and it was like she was in another world, and she was offended at people talking to her even when you were just doing dialogue! It was just incredible; I don't know what her problem was, but she couldn't wait to leave. That was very uncomfortable.

One of our favorites among your films was your Italian-made James Bond imitation Lightning Bolt.
    To me, that was sort of a disaster. Again, we're not talking great art here, but we made that picture two or three years before it was released over here, and by the time it came out it was too late to capitalize on the early success of the Bond pictures. By the time they brought it over here they had lost the interpositive or something, and they had to go back to Italy and piece something together—they had to reassemble it like it had been a decayed old silent picture they were restoring! They got it here a year or two too late to release it successfully—at least that's my opinion. Also, in having to piece it together like a puzzle, the editing became pretty jumbled and ragged. I understand that *Lighting Bolt* was a moneymaker in Europe, but it did miserably here. As a matter of fact, in the L.A. area they released it on the bottom of a double bill *with* a James Bond picture, which was sure death!

I always thought that picture was a lot of campy fun.
    Oh, that's exactly what I thought. It made no sense, but campy fun, yes! And that was one of the most fun experiences that I ever had. First of all, at the time we made it I felt that it could possibly be a success in the U.S.—I thought it would make more sense than it ultimately did, and I thought that I could do my own looping well enough to make it come off. But in terms of the action in it, I thought it was a gas. I was still young enough to enjoy all the running and jumping, and except for one diving tackle and a few cuts that were reshot with a double after I'd returned to the U.S., I did it all myself.

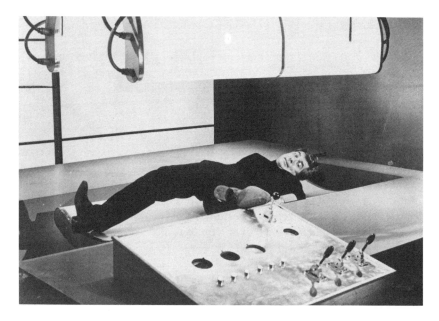

Eisley struggles to escape a frozen-alive fate in the Italian-made James Bond imitation *Lightning Bolt.*

The scene at the bottom of the water-filled silo was actually shot sixteen feet underwater, at the bottom of what had once been an official Olympics pool in Rome. I worked in short cuts, occasionally getting a gulp of air from a garden hose dangling from the surface and just out of frame.

A day or two before that sequence, we had been shooting some scenes at an actual brewery in Rome. Between shots the Italian stunt guys and I were playing a makeshift "tag" game on moving conveyor belts. I got a foot stuck in a roller on one of the turns and screamed bloody murder till they threw the "stop" switch. Nothing was broken, but my foot swelled up terribly. So, in the underwater sequences, a sharp eye can detect that I'm wearing a shoe on one foot, and a painted sock on the other! Another thing that was fun was that gantry sequence — they tore the roof off the studio and built an actual gantry, about eighty-five feet high. I think more than anything else I enjoyed the riding up and climbing on that thing, and the fight at the top. As I said, I don't think I've had more fun on a picture than on *Lightning Bolt.*

Why did you have red hair in that picture?
[Laughs.] It was a co-production with the Woolners in the United States; the Woolners brought me over there to do it and the director, "Anthony Dawson," who is really Antonio Margheriti, thought I looked too Italian! He insisted upon the hair. It was supposed to be blond, but it came out wrong.

Would you agree that Journey to the Center of Time *is probably your dullest film?*

[Laughs.] Yeah! There's only one explanation for that whole thing, and that is that they spent $1.95 on the entire picture, and shot it in a studio the size of your den! But under the circumstances I think everybody did the best they could.

What kind of director was Center of Time's *David L. Hewitt?*

David Hewitt at one time was a special effects man, and he's the sweetest guy in the world. I really like Dave, and we always had a lot of fun. He made these pictures for nothing, and when you look at them you say, "My God!" But if anybody would ever give this guy enough money to put what he wants on the screen, I think he could make quite a good picture. He's always operated totally on a shoestring; he's a hell of a lot of fun to work with, but you don't do it with any kind of expectations.

You later did another picture for Hewitt, The Mighty Gorga, *which is very rarely seen.*

I know of a guy who at one time got ahold of it and was apparently peddling it in Europe, but to my knowledge the picture was never finished. It was basically a *King Kong* rip-off, but I don't think they ever finished the special effects. The guy who was selling it probably sold it in packages, and then ran like hell!

Where was that shot?

I think we shot that out in the Simi Valley somewhere. As I said, Dave Hewitt used to be a special effects man, and he would fake all sorts of things. I think we were just out in some field that he rigged up to look like a jungle somehow, and I remember he got some animal shots by having me walk around a zoo! Dave's a hell of a good guy, and a talented guy, but I don't think anything he's ever tried to do ever translated on film 'cause he's never had the wherewithal to do it.

Were you interested in horror and science fiction films, or were these just jobs?

Jobs. I enjoyed them — had a hell of a lot of fun with them — but I didn't seek 'em out!

What do you remember about The Mummy and the Curse of the Jackals?

I don't mean this disrespectfully, but the director was quite senile at the time. Putting together the cast for that film, he contacted me and Scott Brady. Scott was to play the guy who becomes the Jackal Man, which of course was just a rip-off of the Wolf Man, and I was going to play his friend. But what happened was that Scott got something better, I wound up playing the Jackal

Man and they got Robert Allen Browne to play the friend. I was very glad to have a job—and making these low-budget things was always fun because it's like playing cowboys and Indians rather than working. But when I found out I was going to be the Jackal Man, the one thing I instantly thought was, "Oh, God, I can't sit through all that makeup stuff!"

Early in production they shot a transformation scene where I was lying on a table; they were putting one layer of makeup on at a time, shooting a few frames of film at a time, and that took all day. Well, as I said, the director was sort of losing his faculties, and I realized after a few days that he really didn't know what the hell was going on at all times. They had a second mask—just a quick pull-over thing, for my stunt double to use—so, to be very honest, the stunt double and I got to be friends, somewhere along the line I realized the director would never know, and I never put that makeup on again! Every time I became the Jackal Man, it was the stunt double. And the director never knew it! That took the curse off of that picture.

That film was never released, and has only recently come out on video.
To my knowledge the picture was never finished, and I have no idea what's out on tape. What I always understood was that it was uncuttable— there was so much stuff that did not match at all. For example, the director shot one sequence at midnight, an exterior, that was supposed to be *high noon*—and that was a plot point! We knew as we were doing it that this was never going to make it.

Were you involved in the monster scenes shot on the Las Vegas Strip?
No—but that's another story! I was shooting out at a shack someplace one afternoon when the director became frantic about being behind schedule, turned to the assistant director and said, "Let's set up a second unit downtown and get that stuff with the monsters running around." So the assistant called downtown, got all the permits and everything, they split up the crew and sent 'em downtown. I still had a whole day's shooting left to do where I was. An hour later a call comes from downtown to tell the director that they needed me. He had set up a second unit to save time, and I was supposed to be working both places! So I never went down there, and I have no idea what they shot. That was the absolute epitome of total confusion.

Why was the film never finished?
It just became hopeless *[laughs]*, and I'm sure they ran out of money and everything else.

What can you tell us about your frequent co-star John Carradine?
John is the sweetest guy in the world, just a delightful man. He's a true product of the old theater—Shakespeare and so forth—and he has anecdotes that are simply priceless. You know he is so crippled and pained with arthritis

it's amazing to see him rise above it and triumph over it. He's the oldtime trouper through and through, and as such you have to respect and admire him. He definitely will die with his boots on—that's the only way he would have it. It's that kind of thorough professionalism that just makes him a joy to be around.

How did you become involved on The Witchmaker?

That was made by friends of mine, and it was sort of a mutual project. I was not one of the instigators—Alvy Moore and L.Q. Jones, both of whom are actors, scared up money and actually did a film, which very few people can do. That was made on location in Marksville, Louisiana, and that again was a hell of a lot of fun. Not because we had a great script to work with or any particular budget or anything like that, but because practically all the people involved there *were* actors, and we could all share the experience of trying to make something out of what little we had.

Was that all shot in Louisiana?

Yep. From the motel where we stayed, it was about a half mile by motor-boat, through the bayous, to the cabin location. So we had the advantage there of being in an authentic locale, which sort of gives you a little edge to start with.

Dracula vs. Frankenstein *was no better than a lot of these other cheapies, but at least it had some strong cast values.*

That, to me, has to be the absolute worst. I made a picture called *The Blood Seekers* which did not involve Dracula, Frankenstein or several of the other elements that are now in there. J. Carrol Naish and Lon Chaney were in it, and it was about the pair of them killing girls to use their blood for some kind of experiments—we've heard *that* plot before! It was a pretty raunchy little picture, but it made sense. Director Al Adamson and Independent International started cutting, reshooting, adding more and more plot elements, pieced it all together and tried to make a story out of it. I had no idea what the hell they had in mind. When I finally saw the picture I can't say I was terribly shocked, 'cause I didn't expect it to be a work of art in the first place, but between that half-assed looking Frankenstein and the strange young man who played Dracula and some of the other elements they brought in, I thought, "Well, there's one picture that I would rather nobody *ever* see!"

Can you tell us about working with Chaney?

Lon Chaney died a few months after we finished that; he was probably the most fascinating man I had ever worked with. He was very, very ill then—he would have to lie down after every take—but to talk with him and to hear his stories was just incredible. He was a wonderful, lovely, unbelievably interesting man. I think in the few days that we were on the set he was very ill,

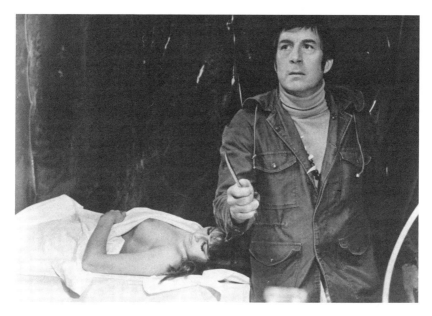

Eisley feels he reached his professional nadir with the execrable *Dracula vs. Frankenstein.*

but for that short period of time we became friends, and I was terribly saddened when he died.

Wasn't his voice pretty much gone by this point?

Yes, he spoke in a whisper, which is why they made his character a mute. You may recall that he and I had a little bit of a physical encounter in the picture. Lon was going to be doubled in that sequence, because he really was ill. Some time before they were supposed to do that sequence, he whispered to me that, once more before he — he didn't say *died,* but that's what he meant — he would really like to do a fight scene, and that they wouldn't let him do it. I thought, jeez, this guy has been around so long, he's a legend of a sort — why not give him his last wish? Back in my *Hawaiian Eye* days Bob Conrad and I had done a good portion of our own fights and so forth, so we knew the basic techniques. I went to Al Adamson and told him we could shoot this thing in really short cuts, and there was no reason that Chaney couldn't do it. So we did do the fight that way, and he was exhausted. The next day he came to the set and told me he'd gone home the night before and almost drowned in the bathtub, he was so tired — his wife had to wake him up! But he told me, "I'm so glad we did it, because that was the most fun I've had in ten years."

What do you remember about Al Adamson?

I had never gotten that close personally to Al; I never disliked him, but I kept an emotional distance from him because I felt that he had excruciatingly

Ad for *Dracula vs. Frankenstein.*

bad taste. I wanted to reserve the right to say, "No, thanks, Al, I won't do that." So I never warmed up to him too much.

What do you recall about the unreleased 1,000,000 A.D. *[1973]?*
    [In stitches.] That was a scam—although not on my part! This was the same film salesman who was selling *The Mighty Gorga* overseas; he came up

with a scheme to shoot a trailer for a nonexistent picture, show it in Europe, take advance orders on the picture, get the money and then come back and make it—which never happened. John Carradine, Jo Morrow and I went up to Victorville, California—we were there two or three days—and what we were shooting was this *trailer*. I don't know whether he even had a story! I remember us crawling out of a plane; being chased by a bunch of prehistoric women; and Carradine, as some sort of an old sage, making a speech on a rock. But that's it—there *is* no picture!

Monstroid *was really rock-bottom, and even you looked unhappy.*
   I was—that was a disaster. The producer, Ken Hartford, raised enough money to get us on location and buy ten feet of film, I guess, to start out—it was one of those situations where there was just no way of ever really doing it right. Most people going in felt that they could get a few bucks out of it and forget it, and that nobody would ever see it. Of course the only flaw in that theory was that apparently he did get it finished to some extent and some people have seen it—but you can only hope there aren't that many! That was a terrible experience.

What made it so bad—poor working conditions?
   That, and total idiocy on the production end. Expecting people to do things that are impossible, and having no understanding of what the quote-artistic-unquote people are trying to do. All Hartford cared about was his cockamamie monster—if he could have had ninety minutes of the monster swimming in the pond there, everybody could have gone home and he'd have been very happy.

Hartford gets director's credit, but Herbert Strock told us that he *directed it.*
   Strock directed everything. Then later Hartford shot a couple scenes in Griffith Park with his own kids and claims to have directed it. It's totally falacious.

Your newest sci-fi film is Fred Olen Ray's Deep Space. *How did you become involved with him?*
   You won't believe this. Through my agent, I got a call to go see Fred Olen Ray, whom I had never met before. Fred said that he had always liked my work, so on and so forth, and that he had just run a tape of one of my pictures. I asked him which one, and he told me it was *The Mummy and the Curse of the Jackals!* Can you imagine? Some guy sees that and says to himself, "I want to use that actor!" *[Laughs.]* But at any rate, he went on to say that he makes two or three pictures a year, and that he just wanted to meet me. A few weeks later, he called my agent again and offered me a part, with star-type billing, in *Deep Space.*

I really enjoy seeing you in pictures, but I get so depressed at the pictures themselves.

[Laughs.] Me, too! I finally got to the point where it was like, "Oh, well — some people work at the shoe store, some people work in the butcher shop. I'll work in the studios, and a job's a job." There are naturally aspirations and so forth that you have, but it's better than working in a restaurant!

What are you doing to keep busy nowadays?

Up until this past year or so I've kept comparatively busy doing guest star shots on TV. Then in the last year I just got tired of the rat race in general and I moved down here to Palm Desert. Also I became a stunt driver a couple of years ago; I don't publicize it because you don't have to work a lot to make a good living, and because I want people to continue to think of me as an actor. I guess I've become philosophical about it: I enjoy the sunshine, it's a healthy place to live down here, and I've gotten out of the rat race completely. I don't feel like going around any more to casting offices where they have a twelve-year-old kid in charge and he wants to know who you are. So I decided I'll work quietly as a stunt driver, two or three days a month, and that's all I need. The rest of the time I'm gonna sit down here and relax, where people aren't so crazy.

I really probably shouldn't say that — it may sound a little bitter. And while I don't mean to say that there aren't areas of bitterness in my memories of my career, all in all I've had a lot of fun, and I've met and worked with some great people. And if a great part came along and somebody would let me do it, I'd love to. But I've gotten beyond the point of really feeling any great concern about it. I've had a good time and I've got a lot of years left just to sit back and enjoy myself.

*It disturbed me for a while [that Ray Bradbury got
all the credit for writing* It Came from Outer Space];
*all my friends and all the people "in the know" knew
what the facts were, but I doubted that the public knew.
When Bernard Shaw and Joe Blow write something,
they're going to give all the credit to Shaw!*

Harry J. Essex

AT THE HEIGHT of the 1950s science fiction boom, writer Harry J. Essex was involved with two of the best-remembered and most influential films of that period: director Jack Arnold's 3-D productions of *It Came from Outer Space* and *Creature from the Black Lagoon*. Although these two credits alone would assure Essex's place in sci-fi history, he also contributed to *Man Made Monster* and *What Ever Happened to Baby Jane?* as well as handling writer-producer-director chores on the more recent *Octaman* and *The Cremators*.

New York–born, Harry Essex planned on a writing career throughout his young life. Among his first jobs were stints on the New York newspapers *The Daily Mirror* and *The Brooklyn Eagle*, short stories for *Collier's* and *The Saturday Evening Post* and even a Broadway play entitled *Something for Nothing*. "It was a resounding *failure*, both out of town and in New York, but it was an achievement for a kid who was not even twenty-one to have played on Broadway." Writing for the movies was uppermost in Essex's mind throughout the period, but the big break never came, and World War II intervened. Then, five or six days after his discharge, he ran into an old acquaintance whose new job was finding playwrights to turn into screenwriters for Columbia Pictures. His friend greeted him with the question, "How would you like to go to Hollywood?" and Essex was off and running.

Several years before your Hollywood career officially began, your name turned up in the credits of Universal's Man Made Monster. *How did that come about?*

That was written while I was still working at *The Daily Mirror*. There were three of us sitting around an office—myself, Sidney Schwartz, who also worked for the paper, and Len Golos, a press agent. We were bouncing story ideas around, and I came up with the notion to do a thing called *The Electric Man*. It was based on a true story I'd read about: A government organization was performing tests on the electricity in the human body, how much we use up throughout the day and how we "recharge the batteries" by sleep at night. Out of that was born the idea of *The Electric Man*—if there was some way to recharge the body's electricity, we wouldn't have to eat or sleep.

Were you writing with the intention of selling it to the movies?

Yeah, it was a movie treatment. The three of us sat there and developed the story. Well, actually, Golos wasn't much of a writer, he was a press agent, and just in for a free ride. It was really Sidney and I—we'd been collaborating on stories prior to that, and we kept thinking about the movies, of course. The story was submitted to an agency, under the title *The Electric Man*, and sold to Universal. We didn't get much money for it at the time—I think we got something like $3,300—but it was my first big sale. *Man Made Monster* got some excellent reviews—I remember that *Time* and *Life* liked it very much—and it was pretty much exactly what we had written. That was my very first screen credit.

Previous page: **Harry J. Essex.**

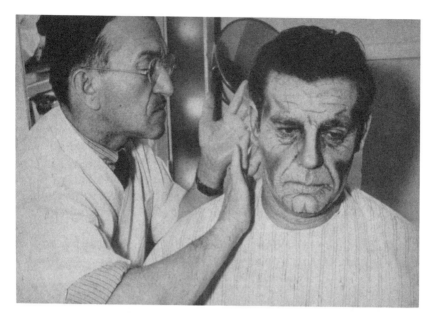

Top: Universal's resident makeup genius Jack P. Pierce puts some finishing touches on *Man Made Monster* Lon Chaney, Jr. This 1941 thriller was Harry Essex's first screen credit. *Bottom:* Leading lady Anne Nagel helps an encumbered Chaney take a drag on a cigarette behind the scenes on *Man Made Monster*.

Was it producer William Alland who took you on as a writer on It Came from Outer Space?

Really, it was the studio that assigned both Alland and me to the job. But of course I'd have to meet with Alland first, to see if we got along. A couple of years ago I ran into him at a marina out here; we stopped and talked, and I asked him why he was no longer in the business. He said he couldn't tolerate it anymore, it was an impossible business. Well, the truth is that I always found *him* a little impossible! He was an ambitious man, very sensitive—he'd weep at the drop of a hat—but underneath it all he was ruthless. But he never achieved enough importance or power that he could practice at *being* a ruthless man! But when I ran into him at the marina he was very gentle and very sweet; we talked about the old days and that was about it. He was a very strange little guy—he's no longer around, and I have no idea where the hell he is.

Since Ray Bradbury wrote some treatments for It Came from Outer Space, *why wasn't he allowed to do the screenplay?*

Ray never did a treatment, he did a three-page short story.

I've seen copies of full-length It Came from Outer Space *treatments, with Bradbury's name on them as author.*

No, it's *my* treatment. Ray's story was a very short piece, and I did the treatment, which was accepted. Some time later, when we were invited to attend the preview, some very formal invitations were sent out, and there was Ray Bradbury's name above mine, which would generally not be the case. But of course I could understand what the situation was—I mean, we're talking about an internationally popular writer, a famous man! There was enough credit for everybody; the people inside the business knew that I had written the screenplay, and that was all that mattered.

Did Bradbury even attempt to write a screenplay?

Yeah, he tried to write a screenplay, and it was just no good. He's not a screenplay writer. But as a matter of fact it was through *It Came from Outer Space* that Ray got a very important job, writing *Moby Dick* [1956] for John Huston, who probably thought that he *had* written the *Outer Space* screenplay. And *Moby Dick* was a fiasco and a disaster. Ray is primarily a novelist and short story writer, and there's a difference between dramatization and just pure narrative writing.

It didn't bother you at all, that so much of the credit for the success of It Came from Outer Space *was heaped on Bradbury?*

Well, it disturbed me for a while, yeah; all my friends and all the people "in the know" knew what the facts were, but I doubted that the public knew. When Bernard Shaw and Joe Blow write something, they're going to give all the credit to Shaw! There was nothing I could do about it, but it did bother

Telephone linemen Joe Sawyer (left) and Russell Johnson are attacked by the xenomorph in *It Came from Outer Space*. Writer Harry Essex insists that, contrary to reports, it was he and not novelist Ray Bradbury who was responsible for the screenplay.

me. But Ray and I remain friends to this day; in fact, we tried recently to do something together called *Chrysalis*, based on a short story of his. But we never could sell it. We came close several times, and on one occasion we almost had a deal, but I think we outpriced ourselves. We asked for something like $300,000 for it, and that soured the entire deal.

Did Universal treat It Came from Outer Space *as a picture with strong potential?*
Yes, they knew immediately that they had something important. And it *was* — it turned out to be an extremely successful picture, especially considering the fact that it cost very little to make and didn't have any important stars.

Your Outer Space *script calls for "an instant's sight" of the alien creature, but in the picture itself the aliens are clearly seen on several occasions.*
That's something the director decides on. I don't know why Jack Arnold decided to show it several times; I will say that he was a very bright, very careful man, and I'm sure that if he thought it had to be seen several times, then it was probably to the picture's benefit. How can you fault anybody who makes a successful picture for what he does? We called that monster "The Fried Egg,"

by the way. The big trick in *It Came from Outer Space* was that the aliens could assume the features and physical shape of humans. That idea, as you know, has since been used a hundred times by other people.

Were you a visitor to the set of It Came from Outer Space?
    I was there constantly. Jack Arnold was a very dear friend and a very gentle man. And the star, Richard Carlson, and I also became good friends. Later on in the '50s, as a matter of fact, Carlson was supposed to do a picture based on a piece of mine called *The Dune Roller*—a science fiction story—and when that came to naught he bought the script. And then when he didn't do it I bought it back from him and eventually did it myself [as *The Cremators*]. Carlson had great problems, he drank a lot—really, he was a terrible drunk, but a very sweet, kind man. I liked him very much.

Was he already a drinker when you did It Came from Outer Space?
    When I first met him he was already involved in drinking, how deeply I don't know. I didn't socialize with him, we were just good friends on the set. They all liked me at Universal, since I had had two of the most successful pictures there [*It Came from Outer Space* and *Creature from the Black Lagoon*]. And we're talking about days when these pictures cost less than a million dollars—we're talking about three, four, maybe five hundred thousand dollars for a movie that would make millions, and are still making money to this day.

What can you recall about Creature from the Black Lagoon?
    I remember that when I was assigned to do *Creature*, it was a very, very poorly written short story—just the basic idea of a fish that had been discovered in the jungle. Universal had bought the story for very little money and assigned me to it, and I was bitter and angry. I didn't want to do anything with a title like *Creature from the Black Lagoon*, it was an embarrassment to me! But they pleaded with me to do the picture, and so I began to redevelop the whole damn thing. It's pretty much formula, for the kind of horror stories we used to do in those days, except in this particular case I added the "Beauty and the Beast" theme. The whole idea was to give the Creature a kind of humanity—all he wants is to love this girl, but everybody's chasing him! It's an old formula of mine that I've used with great success.

Did Universal have the same high hopes, going into Creature, *that they had for* It Came from Outer Space?
    No, *Creature from the Black Lagoon* was a picture they just wanted knocked out, and that was that. But it grew and grew. Jack Arnold again was the director, and we had Dick Carlson in this one, too—they gave us the same company! Universal wanted the same success, and it turned out to be even more successful than *It Came from Outer Space!* They didn't anticipate it—

The one classic movie monster to emerge from the 1950s, the *Creature from the Black Lagoon* was the brainchild of scripters Harry Essex and Arthur Ross.

Ray Bradbury wasn't involved this time—but it broke through, it just played forever and it's playing now. I don't know why it should have been that successful, but to this day it's kind of a cult picture.

Were you a fan of the 3-D technique that was in vogue at that time?
    For some strange reason, so many of my pictures—more than anybody

Essex revamped the popular "Beauty and the Beast" theme in fashioning his screenplay for the 1954 thriller *Creature from the Black Lagoon.*

else's, I guess—*were* 3-D. I was involved with three of the most successful 3-D pictures: *I, the Jury* [as writer-director; 1953], *It Came from Outer Space* and *Creature from the Black Lagoon.* I found 3-D kind of a novel thing—although it gave me a headache, looking through those damn glasses!—but I felt at the time it couldn't be successful. While it was interesting, and gave the pictures another dimension, there were too many problems, and I knew that eventually the idea of the double cameras and the double projectors and the need to revamp the movie houses would be too much. And I was proved right.

Weren't you involved, without credit, on What Ever Happened to Baby Jane?

That's one of the bitter memories of my life. I came across a story by a man named Henry Farrell, *What Ever Happened to Baby Jane?,* and I thought it would make a hell of a play. I went to an agent, Sid Beckerman, and told him my idea. I had a good reputation and people were willing to take me at my word, so he optioned the book and gave me a minimal amount of money to sit down and prepare a play. I finished the first act when Beckerman called me up and said that somebody was offering me $10,000—*not* to bother finishing it, but just for the material, because they wanted to do it as a movie. Who the man was, he wouldn't tell me. I said, "No, I want to do it as a play." Later he called me back and offered me $15,000, and I still said no. Finally it got up to $28,500, and Beckerman told me, "Look, I want you to know now that I'm not going to produce it. I think you ought to take the money." So I took the 28.5 and turned in my play. Well, I was later to find out that the man was Robert Aldrich. He was getting the material as I was turning it in to the agent and loving it, and was talking to the two stars, Bette Davis and Joan Crawford. They literally gave me the business. But I was greedy, and a lot of it was my fault. So I took the 28.5 and I turned in my play.

Why no screen credit at all on the film?
    Because what I wrote was a play and was not done in screenplay form, the [Writers] Guild had no jurisdiction. If I had written "Dissolve in" and "Dissolve out" a few times I could have demanded credit.

In 1971 you wrote and directed a semi-remake of Creature from the Black Lagoon *called* Octaman.
    Octaman was a chance for me to direct and to become co-producer — with this same man Beckerman, as a matter of fact *[laughs]!* He called and asked me what I was doing, and why don't we get together, etc., etc. I said, "Let's do some kind of a takeoff on the science fiction junk that's around." So we went and did *Octaman*. But that, too, came a-cropper; it didn't turn out the way I wanted it to, there just wasn't enough money for the thing. You can't do these things for ten dollars, you just can't. Our shooting schedule was probably sixteen to eighteen days, and the budget was about $250,000. We shot it on the Universal lot and in Griffith Park.

Were you pleased with the Octaman outfit used in the film?
    No, I wasn't. But the people who did the Octaman outfit were the same people who were later to become famous because they did *E.T.* and all the other important science fiction stuff. But their Octaman suit was too cumbersome, too difficult, and just wasn't good enough.

And how did The Cremators *come about?*
    I really did *The Cremators* because I wanted to give my son David another shot at acting: He had played the Indian in *Octaman,* and he was in this one as well. I wrote, produced and directed *The Cremators,* which was shot in Westlake, in Griffith Park — the caves again — and in Agoura. Shooting took thirteen days, maybe less.

The Cremators *was based on the short story* The Dune Roller, *which we talked about before.*
    The original short story was written by a woman named Judy Ditky. I bought the story from her — for $500, I remember *[laughs]* — but I couldn't get a major studio to do it. Richard Carlson bought it from me and had plans of doing it, as I told you, but nothing came of that and I ended up with it again. Eventually my agent made a deal for me with Roger Corman, who was running

New World Pictures at the time. Corman and I didn't get along from the beginning—I mean, we just couldn't stand one another! He knew we were going to do the film for very little money, and I felt he just didn't give the picture a fair shake. I produced and financed *The Cremators,* figuring that I would control it that way. Well, what I had forgotten was that Corman would control it by distributing the thing—he'd put some of his own pictures as the main feature in a double bill, and put *The Cremators* in as a second. That meant that I'd get a flat fee, $100 or $150 a night, while he played his own pictures on top for the percentage!

What kind of money were you working with this time?
      We did *The Cremators* for $50,000—the fact that *anything* came out of it was a miracle! We shot the thing in a hurry, and for very little money. But if we had had the right money and the right sets and the right everything, we could have had a very interesting picture.

Looking back over your career, which would you say is the picture you're best known for?
      I would have to say *Creature from the Black Lagoon.* As I mentioned, it was based on the "Beauty and the Beast" legend, a fairy tale that's been in existence for hundreds of years and has always been a successful story. Basically, I suppose, most of the public thinks of itself as the Beast, and when Beauty comes along we all hope to achieve what these symbolic characters did. And so *Creature* has become the sort of cult picture that young people just love and accept.

The memories of working with Roger Corman are pleasant
because I got along with him very well. He was fun
to be around and work with. We always did these films
on a cheap budget, and people were always
mad at Roger because he'd hardly feed us!
And no matter what happened to you,
you worked regardless.... You could be dead
and Roger would prop you up in a chair!

Beverly Garland

FOR MOST FANS of '50s horror there are just no two ways about it: Beverly Garland is *the* exploitation film heroine of the period. A principal member of Roger Corman's early stock company, she was the attractive, feisty leading lady in such Corman quickies as *It Conquered the World, Gunslinger, Naked Paradise* and *Not of This Earth*. In between Corman assignments she braved the perils of the Amazon River on writer-director Curt Siodmak's *Curucu, Beast of the Amazon*, and a less-harrowing Hollywood backlot swamp in Fox's *The Alligator People*. Her 1960s film work included *Pretty Poison*, *The Mad Room* and the multi-storied *Twice Told Tales* with Vincent Price. Overall, this list of titles is unmatched by any other '50s genre actress.

Born Beverly Fessenden in Santa Cruz, California, Garland made her feature film debut in a supporting role in the film noir *D.O.A.* (1949) with Edmond O'Brien and Pamela Britton. During the next few years she appeared in many small parts and acquired the screen name she is now known by when she married actor Richard Garland. Her first experiences in science fiction were small parts in *The Neanderthal Man* (1953) and *The Rocket Man* (1954). Her exploitation film career went into full gear in 1955 when she signed to star in Roger Corman's Louisiana-made *Swamp Women*.

What do you remember best about the five films you made for Roger Corman?

Roger made us work hard and long, I remember that! He was always fascinating to me, a fascinating man—and a good businessman! He had such incredible energy, it was tremendous—he was a dynamo to be around. I always knew he was going to be a huge success because there was no stopping him. He just made up his mind that he was going to be a success and that was it! I think his real talent is getting the money together and producing. But he also knows his craft. He knows how to direct, he knows just about everything there is to know about films. If the picture broke down and everybody went on strike, I'm sure Roger Corman could put it together one way or another. He could probably write the script, cut the film, write the music—maybe the only thing I think Roger couldn't do was *act!*

Did you enjoy working with him on these films?

The memories of working with Roger are pleasant because I got along with him very well. He was fun to be around and work with. We always did these films on a cheap budget, and people were always mad at Roger because he'd hardly feed us! And no matter what happened to you, you worked regardless. But that was all right with me because that was the type of person I was anyway—I don't like to fool around, I like to get the work done. I found Roger to be very professional—except when it came to putting us up in a good hotel or feeding us a decent meal or paying us any money! But that's how he got

Previous page: Scream queen Beverly Garland was the spunky and attractive leading lady in such '50s favorites as *It Conquered the World, The Alligator People* and *Curucu, Beast of the Amazon* (pictured).

With her second husband, Richard Garland (left), Beverly Garland appeared in the 1951 stageplay *Dark of the Moon*. The spooky guy is Lloyd Meyer.

started in the business so you can't fault him for that. After all, you didn't have to work for him. People shouldn't have complained — it was their own decision to work for Roger, no one forced them. I didn't ever bitch because I could see what he was trying to do. And he had a lot of people around him that were not particularly professional, so he really *had* to have the whip out to get the work done.

Roger and I had a good relationship, and we worked very well with each other. I think he made some of the best B movies around, and they weren't all monster films. Roger had, and still has, a sense of what the public wants, and he was right there to supply those types of films. He's become a very wealthy man and I think he is married to a great gal. I've never met her but she's a director, too, I believe. She has babies and continues to work, and that's the kind of high-powered, bright woman that Roger would need.

In your Corman movies you yourself generally played plucky, strong-willed, sometimes two-fisted types.

I think that was really what the scripts called for. In most all the movies I did for Roger my character was kind of a tough person. Allison Hayes always played the beautiful, sophisticated "heavy," and I played the gutsy girl who wanted to manage it all, take things into her own hands. I never considered myself very much of a passive kind of actress—I never was very comfortable in love scenes, never comfortable playing a sweet, lovable lady. Maybe if the script wasn't written that way, then probably a lot of it I brought to the role myself. I felt I did that better than playing a passive part.

What do you recall about your first Corman film, Swamp Women?

Swamp Women! Oooh, that was a terrible thing! Roger put us up in this old abandoned hotel while we were on location in Louisiana—I mean, it was really abandoned! Roger certainly had a way of doing things back in those days—I'm surprised the hotel had running water! I remember that we each had a room with an iron bed. Our first night there, I went to bed, and I heard this tremendous crash! I went screaming into Marie Windsor's room, and there she was with the bed on top of her—the whole bed had collapsed! Well, we started laughing because everything was so awful in this hotel, just incredibly terrible, and we became good friends.

You did all your own stunts in these films, didn't you?

At the end of *Swamp Women* I was killed with a spear and fell out of a tree. They got me up in this tree and Roger said, "When you're killed, you have to drop"—and this was a big tree! I'm not exaggerating when I say it was at least a twenty foot drop. I said, "Well, will somebody be there?" and Roger said, "Yes, they'll catch you." And by God, they had three guys underneath. And when they "killed" me, I just fell—dead weight on these three poor guys! Roger said to me, "You're really one of the best stuntwomen I have ever worked with."

But you actually did get hurt doing your own stunts in Gunslinger *[1956], didn't you?*

I will never forget that. I was supposed to come running out of a saloon, get on a horse and ride out of town as fast as I could. I looked at this horse, and it was quite large! And I said to myself, the only thing I can do is to make a flying leap and get on him and go. So I come out of the saloon, down the stairs and I leap—and *over* the horse I go! I went right over the other side of the horse! Roger said, "Okay, let's do it again." *Oh, God,* I thought! So I came running down the stairs again in those boots, and as I did my ankle just twisted underneath me and I sprained it badly—but I managed to get on the horse!

When I went home that night I thought it would feel so good to put my ankle in a warm bath, so I did—and I left it there for about an hour. And the next day, my ankle was about twice its normal size! And I had to work! This was toward the end of the picture, so I couldn't be replaced, and practically all the remaining scenes were fight scenes—you know, with all the prostitutes, getting them out of town and such. Somebody had to drive me to work. When I got there, Roger looked at it and said, "Well, we have to start shooting."

Top: Garland is about to encounter the claw of the carrot creature in a tense scene from *It Conquered the World. Bottom:* Garland struggles in the grip of space vampire Paul Birch in the cult favorite *Not of This Earth.*

Naturally, Roger! You could be dead and Roger would prop you up in a chair! So I said, "All right, what do we do? There's no way I can walk." I couldn't even get my boot on! So Roger agreed then to call a doctor, and the doctor brought this giant novocaine needle. They shot the novocaine into the bone, which was the most painful thing. Breaking an ankle is nothing, but shooting novocaine into the bone is absolutely out of this world! If you ever want to feel pain, just have someone do that to you. But then I felt marvelous! So they took the boot and split it in the back and taped it on my foot, and I worked all day. I did all the fight scenes, and I ran and jumped and did whatever — and I couldn't walk for a week after that! I had screwed up my ankle so bad!

The first scene we shot of *Gunslinger* was another unforgettable one. It was a love scene where John Ireland and I were leaning on this tree. It was 6:30 in the morning, we were colder than good God's head and our teeth were chattering. When it was time to say our lines we somehow had to manage to stop the chattering. And as we started to do our love scene, these huge red ants began crawling all over us — so not only was it freezing cold, but these ants were biting the living hell out of us! You can actually see the ants on us when you watch the film!

Do you recall seeing the smaller version of the Venusian monster which Corman initially planned to use in It Conquered the World?

I remember the first time I saw the *It Conquered the World* monster. I went out to the caves where we'd be shooting and got my first look at the thing. I said to Roger, *"That* isn't the monster...! That little thing there is not the monster, is it?" He smiled back at me, "Yeah. Looks pretty good, doesn't it?" I said, "Roger! I could bop that monster over the head with my handbag!" This thing was no monster, it was a table ornament! He said, "Well, don't worry about it because we're gonna show you, and then we'll show the monster, back and forth." "Well, don't ever show us together, because if you do everybody'll know that I could step on this little creature!" Eventually I think they did do some extra work on the monster: I think they resprayed it so it would look a little scarier, and made it a good bit taller. When we actually filmed, they shot it in shadow and never showed the two of us together.

Did you enjoy working with Corman regulars Dick Miller and Jonathan Haze?

They were the funnymen in *It Conquered the World, Not of This Earth* and some of the other films I did for Roger. They were really nice guys. They were proteges of Roger's and he always put them in his pictures. I remember them as being sweet guys, really nice young kids.

Were you and Roger dating by this time?

Well, we really weren't dating, but — *kind* of. I mean, he wanted me to find him an apartment, decorate it, things like that. At one time, Roger wanted to put me under contract. I was with Bill Hays, who was handling all my money at the time, and he said, "Beverly, I don't think that's what you want to do. If you do that, I'm afraid you'll stay in B movies and that's really not where you want to go. Let's see if you can move from there." So I didn't go under contract with Roger. But I dated him a little—nothing very serious. We were very good friends—I loved his mind, and I think he liked my mind. I loved to talk to him about his deals, and what he was doing. We seemed to get along very well. But he always had a girlfriend, and I was always dating somebody else.

Where was Not of This Earth *shot?*
We filmed that at a beautiful old Tudor-style house in Hollywood. The interiors were all done in that home, too. Oh, I remember the pool sequence! I had a scene where I had to jump into the swimming pool and everybody, the cast and crew, thought that that was very sexy, that I had that bathing suit! That was a very sexy scene back them. Really! And even I was embarrassed—it *was* very sexy then. Also the scene in the bedroom—that was a bit much for its time. I'm wearing a robe and I'm putting on stockings while Jonathan Haze is talking to me from the other side of the dressing screen. Those funny scenes that were supposed to be so sexy—oh, God!

Corman and star Paul Birch had some sort of argument during the making of Not of This Earth, *and Birch walked off the picture. Do you recall any of this?*
I don't remember a lot of it except that Paul Birch, I think, felt that he was doing a B movie and that it was a little bit below him. I think he felt, "I am an actor, and I don't need this stuff." You know, when you work with Roger Corman, there isn't time to think—I mean *[talking faster and faster]* you do it and do it fast and you better know your crap and you better get in there and get it done. That's the way Roger is. I understood that; that's how I work, and that didn't bother me. I believe Paul felt that he didn't like the pace. Also, he was very unhappy about his eyes—he had to wear those contact lenses, and you have got to realize that in those days contact lenses were not like what we wear today. Back then it was really like putting *plastic* in your eyes! I mean, it was tough! Paul could only wear them for about two minutes before he would have to take them out. Then we'd have to wait around for a while before he could continue again. We did long scenes, and he was very uncomfortable, and it was hot—it's always hot when you work with Roger Corman, for some reason *[laughs]*! So I think there were lots of things Paul didn't like, he got more and more frustrated, and finally said, "To hell with it all. Goodbye!" Luckily, there was enough film taken already with Paul so that we could go ahead without him. They dressed a stand-in to look like Paul, and used him in three or four scenes, I believe. Roger can get around just about anything.

Had you gotten to know Paul Birch during the shooting?
I didn't do a lot of talking to Paul because he was not very happy *[laughs]*.
I just felt that the best thing was to stay out of his way—so I did.

Did you enjoy going on location for Naked Paradise?
Absolutely. That was the last movie I ever did for Roger, and he took us
all the way to Hawaii to film it. We filmed on the island of Kauai, stayed at
the Cocoa Palms Hotel and had great accommodations. Roger really did this
one up the right way. I don't know if it was because we were at this beautiful
location and Roger simply felt like spending more, but it was one of the best
locations ever—especially for a Roger Corman film. It was just a good movie
to work on.

Which of these five Corman films was your favorite?
I liked *Gunslinger* the best. I liked playing the sheriff and I loved that love
scene with John Ireland. *Naked Paradise* was also good, but any actress naturally likes the movie that she has the most to do in, and *Gunslinger* was *my*
movie.

*In the '60s, when Corman moved on to a better class of pictures, he left most
all his '50s stock players behind.*
Absolutely. And I have no idea why. I guess he thought we weren't good
enough for him. Too bad. We were. We were *very* good for him, and we'd
worked very hard for him. And later on he never even asked me if I would be
interested in doing anything. He never even *asked*.
You know, we were with him at the beginning when we would work with
scripts that weren't finished. We never had dressing rooms, we never had a
john, we never had anything. And we never stopped! We worked our butts
off for this guy. And then when he began to move into better pictures, I don't
think he had *any* of us work for him. Maybe he felt we were all B players, and
he didn't want B players. He dropped us all—and I've always kind of resented
that. There were times when I really needed a picture, really needed to work.
A lot of us have had good years and bad years. I had some bad years, and Roger
was never around. I might not have done a later picture for him, but I sure
would like to have been asked.

Did you enjoy working with Curt Siodmak while making Curucu, Beast of the
Amazon *in Brazil?*
You know, it was hard working with Curt. First of all, he was very difficult
to understand because he had a very thick accent. He was in a hurry to do this
picture—the heat was oppressive, we all got the turistas, we were all sick. He
had probably the hardest job because he had to be up every morning earlier
than anybody else, and he was the last one to go to bed. And he was not a

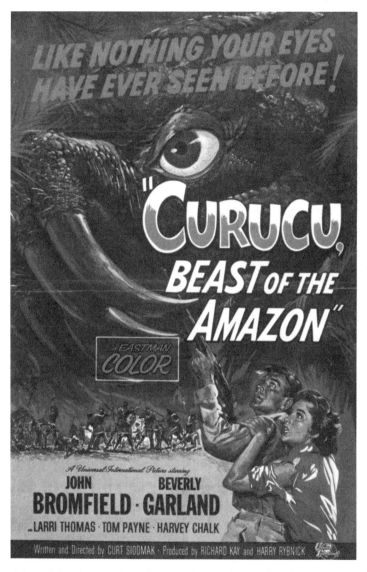

Garland braved the dangers of the Amazon River while shooting *Curucu, Beast of the Amazon* in Brazil.

young man when he did *Curucu*. As he told you when you interviewed him, he got very sick, and he came away from that picture never really feeling good again. And I can understand that.

He had a crew that was Portuguese, with just a few Germans. Between his German and Portuguese, he was able to communicate and do the best he could, but it was very hard for him. So I don't think that Curt was really thinking about trying to make an Academy Award picture — he was just trying to do the picture, get it finished and get out of there!

Where did you stay while making Curucu?

At a hotel in Belem, which is a port on the Amazon. And there were bugs everywhere! I mean, there was nowhere you could walk without bugs! And the temperature was like a hundred and twenty degrees — hotter than hell! At night you should have seen me: First I'd take the sheets and blankets off the bed so I could get all the bugs out. Then, to *keep* the bugs away, I'd light candles all around the bed — I looked like some kind of mummy that had been laid out! It was really something else!

The bathroom had a toilet and a sink and the rest of it was all shower. The shower nozzle was right in the middle of the room so when you turned it on everything was sopping. So really the shower happened to have a toilet and a sink in it! The whole room was a shower with a drain in the middle of the floor! So once you used the shower you might as well forget about going in there again — everything was sopping wet! At 4:30 in the morning I would go out on this teeny tiny patio with a coat rack, and I would hang my mirror on the coat rack and then put on my makeup by the light of whatever sun was coming up that day. Naturally *we* were on the shady side. It wasn't easy to get made up, but I did it!

John Bromfield had brought his girlfriend, Larri Thomas, down and got married — and they certainly weren't interested in having *me* around! I'd knock on their door and say, "Are you going to be doing anything tonight?" and they would go, "Oh, *Beverly!*" So I was really by myself — I had no one to talk to except Curt Siodmak. And he was really getting kind of friendly, so I thought the best thing to do was not to talk to him at all! So I spent three months in South America really all by myself. There was a darling German boy, but I never knew what he was saying to me — so I figured I'd better not get involved with *that*, either! It really was a strange picture!

Again, you did all your own stuntwork.

The thing I remember best about *Curucu* is that I had to have this huge snake wrapped around me in one scene. This snake was twenty-eight or thirty feet long! Off-camera, two native boys held its head and two more held its tail. After spending at least an hour preparing, they wrapped the snake around me, got me on the ground and started filming. So I started screaming — and Curt yelled, "Cut!" I said, "What the hell's the matter?" and he said, "Are you all right?" I said, "Yes, I'm fine — am I not *supposed* to be screaming in this thing?"

I was talking to Curt one day twenty-five years later, and he said, "You know, it's amazing you're still here." I said, "Thanks a lot, Curt! What do you mean by *that* remark?" He said, "Well, you know, that snake in *Curucu* was very dangerous." What he was saying was that the snake was a boa constrictor, and that if anybody had let go and it had constricted, that there was no way they could have freed me. Because once the snake constricts, it squeezes you to a point where it takes all the breath out of you—it's like being choked to death. Even if you kill it, it still can't un-constrict; it's stuck there until those muscles relax, which can take anywhere from twelve to twenty-four hours. And of course they had the snake wrapped around me about five times, so there would be no way to save my life. Curt said, "Gee, it was just wonderful that the snake never did that," and *[laughs]* I thanked him very much. He'd never told me that, and I never knew it! That was a wonderful little episode...!

What about the scene where the Indian village catches fire?
John Bromfield and I almost didn't make it out of there. These straw huts were built early on, when we first got there on location, and they just stayed out in that sun. And all this straw became so dry that when it caught fire it just went up immediately. John and I were way in the back and we had to run out—I thought we were never going to make it. I singed my hair and my clothes. Scary—it was a scary thing.

Much of Curucu *was actually filmed on the Amazon River.*
We were on the Amazon River in Belem. We took this horrible little fishing boat out—John Bromfield and myself, Curt Siodmak, the cameraman and one other assistant—and we shot all day on the boat. About 4:30 in the afternoon, because we were shooting and everybody was distracted, we hit a sandbar. So there we were, in the middle of the Amazon River, up on a sandbar and we couldn't get off. Someone said, "The thing to do is to stay here until the tide comes up. That'll probably be about 11:00 tonight." Well *[laughs]*, I didn't think I wanted to wait! Another boat came along and stopped a good distance away, in deeper water. They offered to take us back with them, but we'd have to get *in* the water and swim over *to* them. John and I looked at each other; we didn't know if we really wanted to go into the Amazon River, but on the other hand, if we didn't, we'd be there until eleven, twelve, maybe one, two a.m. A *l-o-n-g* time. So we got in the river and swam to the other boat. When we climbed out of the water, I had all these red spots all over me that itched like mad! I was just covered with little red marks left by the millions of bugs in the Amazon River.

After all this grief, Curucu *didn't even turn out all that well.*
We had a South American actor named Tom Payne who thought he was magnificent, and he chewed the scenery up like nobody's business. And John Bromfield, God love him, was certainly not an actor—a good-looking, wonderful person, but I really don't think he was much of an actor. Larri was good, but she only got to dance and that was the end of her. And the rest were just *peasants* who were *starving* to death, that we dressed up as Indians! They didn't know what the hell they were doing!

But it was probably one of the most exciting things that I ever did. I mean, I look back on it now and think about all the junk we went through, but it was thrilling and great fun. It was awful but it was wonderful, and I would never trade the experience for a million dollars. I loved every bit of it.

Outside of The Joker Is Wild *[1957] with Frank Sinatra, you've never had a strong part in a major film. Is that a sore point for you?*

Yes, it is. I did *The Joker Is Wild* for Paramount, and I had a very strong part, as you say. I think that if I'd stayed in this town and gone from Paramount to somewhere else and built that career, I might have climbed a few more steps up the ladder in the motion picture area. Instead I went to New York and did a TV series called *Decoy,* the story of a New York policewoman. It was syndicated instead of being sold to a network. But it was not sold in California and it was not sold in New York. For all intents and purposes, I had disappeared from this town, and everybody here must have thought I had died! Nobody knew where I was or what I was doing — they never saw *Decoy,* because it wasn't playing here. When I came back after a year in New York, people didn't even know I *was* back. It was almost like starting all over again.

What were some of your experiences on The Alligator People?

The hardest thing in that movie was simply to keep a straight face. I was all right from the beginning of the film up until I found my husband in the sanitarium, and then I just fell apart. That was the end of me! There was that one scene where I had to be a bit romantic and console my poor husband, and this was probably the most difficult scene I had to do in the film. This was when he was pretty much an alligator, and I had to say to him, "I'll love you no matter what," which I think took me a good half day to say. Laugh? I thought I'd *die!* They almost had to film that on the back of my head, but I managed to get through it. That was very hard.

Like E.A. Dupont, who directed you in The Neanderthal Man, *Roy del Ruth was a director who had seen better days.*

I liked him — he was a sweetheart of a guy and a good director. *The Alligator People* was a fast picture, but he really tried to do something good with it. And I think that shows in the film. It's not something that was just slapped together; I think he really did his best. It was such a ridiculous story, and some of that dialogue was enough to drive you crazy! But we all worked hard and we all knew that if we didn't do our job it would be the comedy of the season! So we had to really get in there and make it as honest as we could. I feel that Roy del Ruth really tried to do that, also. I had a lot of respect for him, and I liked him.

What else did you find funny in Alligator People?

I remember that when all these people started turning into alligators, they

Beverly Garland resists the romantic advances of one of *The Alligator People*. "The hardest thing in that movie was simply to keep a straight face," the veteran actress recalls.

had a place to go—a clinic or doctor's laboratory or something. So, that day of filming I walked onto the set and we were about to do the scene where I go to the hospital to see my husband who is slowly turning into an alligator. I walk in and here they have these guys in long white robes with some kind of hat thing over their heads—and, I tell you, they all looked like they had *urinals* on their heads! I started to laugh—I laughed so hard that tears came to my eyes! I said, "You've got to be kidding, fellows! All of these tall urinals walking around!" Well, we did not film for three hours, I was in such hysterics! Every time these things would walk down the hall, I would just crack up! I couldn't recite a line of dialogue! Then Roy del Ruth began to look at them, and it started to get to him, too! I guess we must have lost close to half a day of shooting time. Great control—that's what you needed in order to do some of these monster pictures without a smirk on your face! It was really too much!

Many viewers are disappointed with the way that film ends.

I felt when I read the script and when I saw the film, which was a long time ago, that it ended very abruptly. It all happened too fast; it was kind of a cop-out. But there really was no way to end it. What were they going to do— were they going to have us live happily ever after and raise baby alligators? There was just no way! So this was what they had to do.

Did Lon Chaney's drinking problem cause any difficulties?

I thought Lon Chaney was fabulous, fun and easy, and he certainly never drank on the set as far as I remember. It was fascinating to hear him talk about his dad and all the things he remembered about his father's career. He was a favorite person of mine. Maybe he worked with other people that made negative comments about him, but I just adored him and thought he was great.

Stark Fear *was advertised as a* Psycho-*style shocker, but it didn't live up to any of its publicity.*

Oh, my God—*that* awful movie! That was made in Norman, Oklahoma, by Ned Hockman, the head of a drama department there. We kept saying to him, "This script doesn't make any sense," and he said, "No scripts at the Cannes Film Festival make sense, and they all win. This'll be fine." We didn't think that his logic was too sharp *[laughs]*, but *he* seemed to believe so. It was a disaster. Although he was a teacher, for some reason he just didn't seem to know what he was doing. Skip Homeier finally ended up taking over the direction, and Skip didn't know anything about making a movie, either! It just got to be more and more of a mess, but we finished it. I remember seeing it in a theater here, and there were three people in the audience. The next day I came back to bring some more people, and the theater owner said he'd pulled it and was not going to show it any more. That was the worst movie that ever came out.

Did you enjoy working on Twice Told Tales?

Oh, I loved it because I loved Vincent Price. He is the most wonderful, sweet, adorable man! I don't remember much about that movie, I just remember working with Vinnie and how wonderful he was.

How well do you feel your Twice Told Tales *segment,* The House of the Seven Gables, *turned out?*

I didn't like it that well. There were a lot of scenes where I was just staring, in a trance, thinking back into my other life or some damn thing. A lot of that could've been cut, or directed differently. I didn't think it was the best movie I'd ever seen in my life, no.

How did you land your part as Mrs. Stepanek in Noel Black's Pretty Poison?

Someone had seen my work in something else and felt that I would be very good as Tuesday Weld's mother. Mrs. Stepanek was a marvelous character—I loved the part. I felt it was one of the best things I'd done.

Pretty Poison *has attained cult status in certain circles, but it flopped when it came out theatrically.*

I thought it was a great movie, well-directed. Noel Black did a great job.

But the studio got very upset with him because it took a long while to shoot. Studio people kept arriving and saying, "You're taking too long," and they had him under a lot of pressure. *Pretty Poison* was done on location in Great Barrington, Massachusetts, and any time you go shooting on location it's hard. Noel had some wonderful ideas, and some camera stuff that took time. He went to great pains with that movie and the studio got very upset with him. But I think the movie shows that he took the time.

So why wasn't the film more successful than it was?
    Pretty Poison came out a few years ahead of its time — people were really not ready for that sort of movie. It was one of the first of its kind, and it's been copied many times since.

Were you really pregnant when you did The Mad Room?
    Yes, I was — I was very pregnant! When they asked me to do this movie, I was three months pregnant and I didn't show. By the time they got around to me I was *six* months pregnant and I *did* show! And I certainly wasn't supposed to be pregnant in the film! So they had me in A-line dresses with lots of ruffles and things like that. I don't think it showed as much as I thought it was going to.

Your suicide scene in that film is one of the best parts of the picture.
    They really wanted the blood to flow when I slashed my wrists in that scene. So I was rigged with tubes that went up my dress and down my arm. It was late at night — this was the last shot we did — and something would go wrong every time. I had to do the scene over and over, each time having the tubes removed and adjusted, the "blood" cleaned off my dress, off of me — *ai-yi-yi!* We did this fifteen times, I guess, before the blood came out, and, you know *[laughs]*, it's always the time the blood comes out that you don't think your scream was as good as it would have been if the blood had come out the first time!

Wasn't there a great deal of behind-the-scenes feuding on The Mad Room?
    Well, the director, Bernard Girard, wanted to shoot it one way, the studio wanted him to film it another way — and Bernard did shoot it his way. Then when they edited it, they wanted to cut certain things out and Bernard wanted them in, and he got very upset with the cutting. So I think that he decided that if they were going to cut it their way, that he would like to have his name taken off of the film. And there are some things in the film that don't make any sense to me; I think that some scenes were cut very badly. When I saw the picture there were lots of things at the very end that I felt did not fit together right.

Do you ever look back on your B movies and feel that maybe you were too closely associated with them? That they might have kept you from bigger and better things?

No, I really don't think so. I think that it was my getting into television; *Decoy* represented a big turn in my life. Everybody did B movies, but at least they were movies, so that was okay. In the early days, we who did TV weren't considered actors; we were just horrible people that were doing this "television," which was so sickening, so awful, and which was certainly going to disappear off the face of the earth. *Now,* without TV, nobody would be working. *No-bod-y.* But I think that was where my black eye came from; I don't think it came from the B movies at all.

Which of your many horror and science fiction film roles did you consider your most challenging?

Pretty Poison. It was a small part, but it had so much to say that you understood why Tuesday Weld killed her mother. I worked hard to make that understanding not a surface one, but tried to give you the lady above and beyond what you would see in such a short time.

In the early days when I was representing Bela Lugosi, I used to have autographed photographs of all the people with whom I was associated hanging in my office. And I discovered early on that when Bela came to my office and saw his picture hanging next to Boris Karloff's, that he got very upset about the idea! So after that, whenever there was an appointment for Bela to come to my office, I would take down the picture of Karloff and substitute somebody else—and then hang it up again after Lugosi left!

Richard Gordon

OVER THE WATER and far away from the bustle of the Hollywood B-hive, Richard Gordon was busy carrying on the grand tradition of 1950s exploitation on his native English soil. Producer of such '50s favorites as *The Haunted Strangler, Fiend Without a Face* and *First Man into Space*, the London-born Gordon became interested in the movies at an early age and, together with his like-minded older brother Alex Gordon, became involved in film societies at school. Detecting greener grass on the other side of the ocean, the brothers Gordon relocated to the United States in the late 1940s. While Alex ended up in California (where he later helped to found American International Pictures), Richard remained in New York and started his own company, Gordon Films, importing and distributing British and other foreign pictures in the United States. This gradually led to his involvement in the setting up of co-production deals, at which point he decided that, "if I was going to do it for somebody else, I could do it myself!"

How did you get to know Bela Lugosi in the late '40s?

My brother Alex and I were both in New York, and one of the things we were doing was writing articles for British fan magazines. We were interviewing actors we could get hold of — people like Chester Morris, Kay Francis, Richard Arlen and William Boyd, who were appearing in summer stock or visiting the city. In fact, we interviewed Boris Karloff, who was appearing in New York in the plays *The Linden Tree* and *The Shop at Sly Corner*. And we went out to a summer theater on Long Island where Bela Lugosi was doing *Arsenic and Old Lace*, playing Jonathan Brewster. We managed to contact Lugosi and he agreed to an interview, and he and his wife took us out to dinner after the show! We hit it off very well, we developed a great friendship, and the result, shortly thereafter, was that Bela asked us if we would like to represent him in New York — sort of on a management basis — and try to arrange some deals for him. That was how I developed my relationship with him.

What sort of work did Lugosi end up doing in New York?

He did several television shows — he appeared on the Milton Berle show as a guest and he did a live Edgar Allan Poe adaptation of *The Cask of Amontillado* with Romney Brent. Meanwhile, we were trying very hard to set up a revival tour of *Dracula* for him in England, which I eventually succeeded in doing in 1951. Bela went over to England with great expectations. Unfortunately, the management that we set it up with turned out to be a very unreliable company which was very badly underfinanced. They figured that if they had Bela Lugosi, they didn't have to spend any money on anything else, and that Lugosi would sell himself! The result was that the production was very poor, the supporting cast amateurish, and the whole thing turned into a disaster. The tour closed before it hit London and Bela was left stranded

Previous page: **Horror great Bela Lugosi indulges in some behind-the-scenes clowning with an "unsuspecting" Richard Gordon on the set of *Mother Riley Meets the Vampire.***

without any money. To get him sufficient money just to get back home, I was able to arrange for him to do the film which became known over here in the U.S. as *My Son, the Vampire*. The original title was *Mother Riley Meets the Vampire*. *That* at least got him the money for him and his wife to get back to the States. Then, of course, he moved back to Hollywood and I sort of lost contact with him, but Alex remained in touch with him right through the years of Eddie Wood, Jr., right up to the time that Bela died.

What more can you tell us about Lugosi himself?
He was a very charming, very generous person. Although he was in severe financial straits at the time, if he suddenly got a job and a good check, like he did for the Milton Berle show, he'd go out and spend it all the next day having a big party and entertaining everybody. We had a very good time with him. The principal problem was that he was bitter about the way his film career had deteriorated. He had a slight resentment toward Boris Karloff, because he felt that Karloff had succeeded so much better than he had — not realizing, of course, that he himself was limited by his accent, which was something he could never overcome. He also never stopped reminding us of the fact that he had originally been selected to play the Frankenstein Monster [in *Frankenstein*] and was replaced by Karloff, and if that hadn't happened Karloff would probably still be a bit player on the Universal backlot. But what he never did mention was that in fact he *refused* to play the Monster — after *Dracula* he thought it was a demeaning role in that it had no dialogue and his face would be covered by makeup. So in some respects it really was his own fault.

How did your first science fiction film, The Electronic Monster, *come about?*
The Electronic Monster came about at a time when I was doing co-productions with Anglo Amalgamated Pictures, with Nat Cohen. The first picture we did was called *The Counterfeit Plan* [1957]. I got Zachary Scott and Peggie Castle to go over to England for it, and it worked out nicely: The picture turned out well and it was quite successful, so we decided that we wanted to do a couple of other pictures together. Nat Cohen had a lot of properties under option and in development, and one of them was *Escapement,* a novel by the English science fiction writer Charles Eric Maine. When Cohen sent me that to read and suggested it as one of the films, I liked the idea very much, and that was how *The Electronic Monster* came about.
When Nat sent me the first proposed story outline, I thought that it was an ideal opportunity to try and get Basil Rathbone to return to England to make a film by offering him the role of Paul Zakon. Nat enthusiastically endorsed the idea, and as Rathbone was living in New York at the time, Alex and I arranged to meet him for lunch. Unfortunately, Rathbone had very different ideas about the possibilities of a screen or stage comeback in England. Having not made a British film since the Frank Vosper adaptation of Agatha Christie's *Love from a Stranger* in the 1930s, he wanted to go back only if he

could star in a prestigious vehicle that would have a chance of critical acclaim and surround him with the proper publicity of a Hollywood star returning to England in triumph. He was too much of a gentleman to say that he wouldn't consider doing a B movie for us, but he very definitely said that he wouldn't do a horror picture or anything as melodramatic as *The Electronic Monster*. When pressed as to what he would consider a worthwhile vehicle, he admitted that his ambition was to do a role originally played by George Arliss, and the subject he had in mind was *Old English*. There was of course no possibility for us to set up a remake of such a production, so we parted on good terms but with no chance of a deal. The role of Zakon was eventually played by Peter Illing.

If Rathbone had accepted the part, would you still have cast American stars Rod Cameron and Mary Murphy in the hero/heroine roles?
Had we obtained Basil's services, the film would have been structured quite differently. The role of Zakon would have been developed into the central character, and we probably would not have used any American players in other parts since Rathbone's name had sufficient box-office value for the American market. I did not see Rathbone again until many years later, during a visit in Hollywood. I ran into him at the Hollywood Roosevelt Hotel where he was then living and appearing in films for American International — films not so different from what we had wanted to do! We did not refer to the subject of our luncheon conversation in New York.

What were your budgets on pictures like The Electronic Monster?
The production budgets on those early films were in the range of £50,000, which at that time was about $125,000. The shooting schedules were generally four weeks.

The Electronic Monster *is set on the French Riviera, but where was it actually shot?*
The whole thing was shot in England. Anglo Amalgamated had a long-term production arrangement with a studio in London called Merton Park Studios, and the entire picture was shot there, with some location work outside London.

Why did you have a different director and a different photographer in shooting the film's dream sequences?
To the best of my recollection it was because those sequences were being shot simultaneously with the rest of the film, and it was a sort of second unit operation. For economy's sake it was necessary to do it that way.

Except for the dream sequence, there was nothing science-fictiony about that film. Did you approve of Columbia's misleading title The Electronic Monster?

To be quite honest with you, *I* came up with that title *[laughs]!* Certainly I didn't want to call it *Escapement,* and I thought it needed something to sell it — particularly as there wasn't that much science fiction or horror element in the picture. I screened the picture for Columbia and they expressed some interest in it, *if* it could be combined with something else in a double horror show. So I acquired the picture *Womaneater* with George Coulouris and Vera Day and made a combination out of those two, to release it through Columbia. But, getting back to your question, we then felt that we needed a much stronger title for our top picture, so I came up with *The Electronic Monster.* In England it was known as *Escapement,* and then eventually reissued there as *The Dream Machine.*

Probably the best film from this early era was The Haunted Strangler *with Boris Karloff.*
    The Haunted Strangler was actually my first solo production. I had gotten to know Boris Karloff when we interviewed him in New York and had remained in contact with him. A writer in England by the name of Jan Read had written a story called *Stranglehold* specifically for Karloff, and had submitted it to him and suggested it as a starring vehicle. One time when I was speaking with Karloff and talking about the fact that I was getting ready to go into production on my own, he suggested that he would send me the story to read, and if I liked it he would be willing to commit to doing it. He sent me the story and I liked it very much. I got in touch with Jan Read, Boris and I agreed on a deal, and that's how the whole thing got started.

How did you raise the money to produce Haunted Strangler?
    Part of the money came from Eros Films in England, who had an agreement with me to distribute the film in the United Kingdom. The rest of the money I arranged through my own resources. We did two pictures that way, *Haunted Strangler* and *Fiend Without a Face,* which were shot back-to-back in England, had much the same crew, and used the same studios [Walton Studios]. They were designed as a double bill for distribution by Eros in England. *Haunted Strangler* was called *Grip of the Strangler* over there.

How did you like working with Karloff?
    Very much. He was a charming, delightful man, a complete professional, couldn't have been more cooperative. He was anxious to do everything himself if it was at all possible. There was a sequence in *The Haunted Strangler* where Karloff appears at a dance hall, kills a girl and jumps from a box onto the stage. Of course we had a double for him. Karloff took me aside and said, "You know, I'd really like to try to do this myself." I told him, "It's out of the question. First of all, with all due respect, I don't think you could do it, and secondly, even if you can, the risk of injury to the star of a picture is far too great." Well, he persisted and finally persuaded me that he should at least be allowed

to try to do it, and he did in fact do it! But it didn't play well—he lost his balance when he landed on the stage—and so in the film it is done by a double. But this was Karloff's attitude of complete professionalism, that he wanted to try everything, and was willing to extend himself to do whatever he could to make it a good film.

I'd been told that Karloff was spending a great deal of time in a wheelchair, even as early as the 1950s.

No, that's totally untrue. Karloff did not end up in a wheelchair until much, much later—not until the time when he made *The Sorcerers* in England and started having this terrible emphysema problem. Also, his leg had given him trouble all his life, ever since he broke it during the making of *Bride of Frankenstein*. That's why he had that peculiar walk which became his trademark—he never really recovered completely. That was giving him trouble in those later years, and then, as I said, around the period of *The Sorcerers* he started using a wheelchair. But when I was working with him in 1957 and 1958 he was in perfectly good health.

Karloff's performance in Haunted Strangler *is a very good one amidst many very hammy ones. What prompted this extra effort?*

I think first of all that he liked the story very much. I think he felt that it was a picture which could be something more than just a horror film, and that we were treating it as a serious picture and not just a schlock horror movie. And he entered into the spirit of the thing. Also, think of the professional people he was surrounded by—Anthony Dawson, Jean Kent and Elizabeth Allan. It was really a very fine cast for a picture of that kind, and in that budget category. Karloff just felt it was worth the effort to try and really make something out of it.

Much as I admire Karloff, it's almost embarrassing to watch his work in pictures like Voodoo Island, Frankenstein 1970 *and others he made around that time.*

Karloff's attitude, once he agreed to do a picture, was that he should always act to the best of his ability and give it everything he had—even if he knew it was going to turn out to be a rotten movie! On the other hand, I suppose it also depended on the directors that he had and the shooting schedules—maybe they didn't have enough time for rehearsals, maybe they rushed them through too fast. We were fortunate in having a very good director, Robert Day, who wasn't well-known at that time but has since made a big career for himself in Hollywood. He and Karloff worked very well together on *The Haunted Strangler.*

Producer John Croydon, writing in Fangoria, *mentions Karloff's "aversion to the film" and that he later denigrated his own performance in it.*

Boris Karloff volunteered to remove his own false teeth to create the ghoulish visage of *The Haunted Strangler.*

I read that, of course. But I must say that in all the years I talked with Karloff after *The Haunted Strangler,* he never said anything to me about it, and I never had the feeling that he was dissatisfied with the film.

Croydon also describes problems with Robert Day.

Actually, what happened was that John Croydon had a falling out with Karloff, and that was the real basis of the problem. It wasn't so much in *The Haunted Strangler* as it happened later in *Corridors of Blood,* but there *was* a personality clash between Croydon and Karloff, and it was that which really created some of the problems rather than Robert Day, who was just trying to do a good job as director.

What was your budget on The Haunted Strangler?

The sterling budget was approximately £70,000. We paid Boris Karloff $25,000 for *Strangler* and then $30,000 for *Corridors of Blood.*

What can you remember about Karloff's makeup in the horror scenes of Haunted Strangler?

The facial expression on the mad killer was very largely devised by Karloff himself. We didn't want to have to spend a lot of money on the type of trick photography that was used in films like *Dr. Jekyll and Mr. Hyde;* we were trying to find a simple way of doing it. And Karloff came up with the answer: With a few simple tricks like putting cotton wadding in his mouth and distorting his features, he came up with what you see on the screen in the finished picture. It worked very successfully and is done almost entirely without makeup.

Is it true that he removed his false teeth?

Yes, that was one of his ideas—even as a producer I would never have *dared* to ask him to do that *[laughs],* had he not volunteered! We were standing there talking with him and he suddenly said, "Let me try something." He turned his back to us, and when he turned 'round again he'd removed his teeth and distorted his face—and that was the beginning of it!

While Haunted Strangler *was in production, you announced that your next picture would be* Dracula's Revenge *with Karloff.*

We obviously wanted to publicize the fact that we would do another picture with Boris Karloff. I had been mistakenly informed by lawyers in New York that by that time the property *Dracula* was in the public domain, and that if we wanted to produce a version with Karloff we would be free to do it. So we announced *Dracula's Revenge,* and in fact we had a screenplay written by Jan Read. But then in the eventual research and in talking with MGM, we found that our information wasn't correct—the property was still controlled by Universal, who in fact had struck a deal with Hammer Films to do the Christopher Lee *Horror of Dracula.* So we abandoned the idea.

Would Karloff have played Dracula?

Karloff would have been Dracula, and he was quite keen on the idea. It would of course have been very different from the Dracula that Bela Lugosi played; perhaps if anything it would have been more like the *Nosferatu* character. Karloff thought it was a very good and challenging idea, but for legal reasons it wasn't possible to do it.

Your next film was Fiend Without a Face.

In those days everything, particularly genre pictures, went out in double bills. So we figured that in order to do well with *The Haunted Strangler* we

Gordon ran into troubles with both British and American censors over the grisly special effects of *Fiend Without a Face,* as in this scene where the title character attacks Launce Maraschal.

really should have a picture of our own to go with it; otherwise we would get double-billed with somebody else's picture and forever have to worry about allocations and so on. So that was the *raison d'etre* for *Fiend Without a Face:* it was simply designed for the double program with *Haunted Strangler.*

How did Fiend *come about?*
    In my constant search for properties I received from my brother Alex a copy of a magazine called *Weird Tales,* published in the early '30s, that contained a story called *The Thought Monster* by Amelia Reynolds Long. This was given to Alex by Forrest Ackerman, who at that time was representing some of the *Weird Tales* writers and trying to sell film rights for them. I read the story and liked it very much, and I thought it'd be a great idea for a low-budget science fiction movie. So, through Ackerman, I acquired the rights from Amelia Reynolds Long. Herbert Leder, who later went on to write and direct a few low-budget horror films on his own *[The Frozen Dead* and *It!],* did a screenplay for us which became *Fiend Without a Face.*

Your star this time was Marshall Thompson.
    Through my co-production activities I'd had dealings with people like Richard Denning, Wayne Morris, Zachary Scott, Rod Cameron and so on. Marshall Thompson was one of the available people, and I made a deal with him. He was a very quiet, reserved guy, and it was difficult to get to know him

because he kept mostly to himself, but I liked him and had no problems with him at all. In fact, I ended up making three pictures with him — *Fiend Without a Face, First Man into Space* and *The Secret Man* [1958].

What about your budget on Fiend?
Our original budget was only about £50,000; *Fiend* was supposed to cost less than *Haunted Strangler* and be the supporting part of the program. But because of the complexity of the special effects and the amount of time it took to do them, it eventually ended up costing about the same as *Strangler*. As I mentioned earlier, we shot it back-to-back with *Strangler*—we had, for instance, the same production manager, Ronnie Kinnoch, and largely the same crew. We had to have a different director, because Robert Day couldn't have shot both pictures at the same time. So we got Arthur Crabtree, who was quite a well-known director in England and had done some very good pictures.

Did special effects men Ruppel and Nordhoff help shape the story, or did their effects simply meet the requirements of a finished script?
When Ruppel and Nordhoff came into it, we had a finished screenplay and they pretty much had to stick to it. They were working on their effects continuously while we were shooting, and then most of the special effects scenes were finished after the principal shoot was over. It did take rather longer than we expected, and the picture went way over schedule in the postproduction because of the special effects. But it all worked out in the end. And certainly we were very satisfied with Ruppel and Nordhoff because in fact we used them again on *First Man into Space,* although the effects there weren't nearly as extensive as on *Fiend Without a Face.*

Did the gruesome special effects in Fiend *cause any censor problems down the line?*
They did cause some problems with the censors, yes; in fact, we had to make a cut version for England because the British censor didn't want to pass it the way it was. The censors in the United States also trimmed it slightly, for the MGM distribution, before we could get the Code seal.
After the two pictures were finished I screened them for MGM, they liked them very much and I made a deal with MGM to distribute them throughout the rest of the world outside the United Kingdom. And as a result of that, when it came to doing my next pictures with Marshall Thompson and Boris Karloff, which were *First Man into Space* and *Corridors of Blood* respectively, then MGM put up the money for those pictures.

How did the Haunted Strangler/Fiend Without a Face *double bill do at the box office?*
It did very well for us, particularly in England. Both pictures performed very well all over the world, and we were satisfied. If they hadn't been

successful, MGM wouldn't have agreed to do *First Man into Space* and *Corridors of Blood* with us, so they obviously felt that it was worthwhile and that the profit potential was there.

Who came up with the idea for First Man into Space?
First Man into Space was an idea that actually was conceived by my then-partner Charles Vetter. He came up with the original story idea, which he wrote himself, and we sold the idea to MGM.

How much did First Man into Space *cost compared to the others?*
Our budget on *First Man into Space* was a little higher. This was partly because of the involvement of MGM, which meant that there were certain overhead and interest charges, etc., to be added to the budget. The budget came up to around £100,000. Of those four films it was the one that cost the most. Most of *First Man* was shot in a mansion near Hampstead Heath, which is an area similar to New York's Central Park. Some of the exteriors, like the scene where the police car is chasing the monster, were shot on Hampstead Heath itself. And then finishing touches were done at the MGM Studios.

Bill Edwards, the actor playing the astronaut who becomes a monster, sounds as though he's been dubbed throughout the picture.
It's postsynched, not dubbed. It was too difficult for him to maintain the American accent while he was actually doing the acting.

Did Edwards also play the monster, or was that a stand-in?
He did play the monster—the budget wasn't *that* big that we could afford to have an extra monster actor! It was basically a suit that Edwards was put into, with small holes in the mask for him to see out through. One problem we did have was that he couldn't wear the outfit for very long because not enough air was getting through. It was extremely hot and uncomfortable, and would have given him breathing problems after a while, so he could only wear it for limited periods of time.

Was First Man into Space *shot entirely in England?*
No, there was some shooting done in the United States—not footage involving the actors, but some of the car run-throughs and things like that. Alex did this for me—he got a cameraman to go out to a location in New Mexico and shoot some long-shot car scenes. We also got a couple of establishing shots at an Air Force base in Brooklyn. And then we reconstructed the rest of it in England.
The funny thing was that when we eventually delivered the picture to MGM, they turned it over to their distribution department, which of course had no idea what the background of the picture was—they were just presented with the finished film and told to release it. Someone in the publicity

department looked at it and said, "It would be a great idea if we had the world premiere in Albuquerque, New Mexico, because that's where the film was shot." So they staged an opening in New Mexico and it got a somewhat sarcastic reception *[laughs]*, because the people recognized immediately that it *wasn't* shot there!

Mightn't you have been better off releasing the film under the shooting title, Satellite of Blood?

Satellite of Blood was not our shooting title, it was the title of a Wyott Ordung screenplay that Alex had sent me to look at. Ordung's ideas seemed to mesh very well with Chuck Vetter's, so we acquired Ordung's screenplay and incorporated elements of it into Chuck's. Ordung seems to have been very pleased with it, because I read an interview with him in *Fangoria* where he said that *First Man into Space* was his favorite among his own films. Getting back to your question, I *don't* think *Satellite of Blood* would have been a good title for our picture. I think *First Man into Space* was an excellent title.

Why were the horror and monster elements played down in the First Man into Space *ads?*

MGM thought it would have more appeal to a general audience and that it could play much more widely than a horror picture might. So they decided to play up the science fiction rather than the horror or monster angles.

Why doesn't your name appear in the on-screen credits of these early pictures?

There were two reasons. First of all, I had a line producer, John Croydon. The second reason has to do with the British Quota, which is a very complicated thing I'm not sure we want to get into now! Since I was no longer a resident in England and since we had to conform to certain British Quota requirements, it wasn't really feasible to put my name on these pictures. So just my production company's name is on them, and I didn't take the individual credit.

And whose idea was Corridors of Blood?

We were looking for another subject for Karloff, and John Croydon came up with the original story idea for *Corridors of Blood*. A woman named Jean Scott Rogers wrote the screenplay. Her idea was to make a very serious picture about surgery in the days before anesthetics, which of course wouldn't have made a very commercial picture. So we tried to inject horror and melodramatic elements into it.

Why was Karloff *paid more for* Corridors of Blood?

The start of production was delayed after Karloff had committed himself to the picture. We had a lot of problems getting *Corridors of Blood* off the ground, and he received $5,000 more because of the extra time.

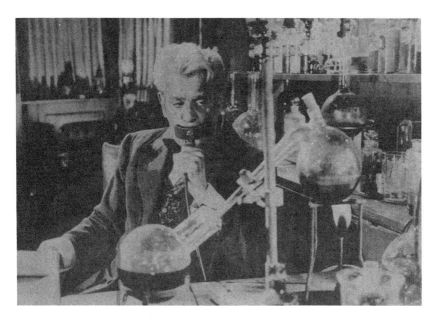

Early experiments with anesthesia lead to tragic consequences in Gordon's *Corridors of Blood* with Boris Karloff.

What were the problems in getting Corridors *started?*
We were in the middle of our negotiations with MGM for the financing of the picture when there was a complete change of management there. We were caught right in the middle — the picture was scheduled to start shooting at the MGM Studios in England, and then at the last minute it had to be postponed because MGM wasn't going to put up the money until all the documents were completed.

Corridors' *lurid title and ad campaign added up to audience disappointment in the film when people got a movie about anesthesia.*
I think the problem with *Corridors of Blood* is that it's really a hybrid film which isn't one thing or the other. It's not enough of a horror film like, let's say, *The Haunted Strangler,* and yet it's too *much* of a horror film to be regarded as a picture dealing seriously with surgery and with the medical profession in that era. To my mind the finished film falls in the middle, and I wasn't too happy with the way it turned out. But I thought that Karloff gave an extraordinarily good and convincing performance in it.

One impressive aspect of the film is its attention to period detail; it almost has the look of a Dickens film.
Because we were making it for MGM, it was shot at the MGM Studios in London, where we had the facilities of the MGM wardrobe department,

carpenters, backlot and everything else. I doubt that we would have been able to reproduce that as effectively if we'd still been shooting at a smaller, independent studio like Walton, where we'd made *The Haunted Strangler* and *Fiend Without a Face*.

What were Karloff's true feelings about horror films? Toward the end it began to seem that he really didn't have that much affection for them.

No, that's not true. First of all, he was very grateful for the opportunities they gave him to become a star. He wasn't at all resentful; he was very proud of his work in *Frankenstein* and some of the other films. And he had a great, affectionate regard for them. Naturally, he regretted some of the lower-budget horror films he was forced to make because of economic reasons. And later, when horror films started to turn into ultra-violent, slasher/gore movies, *then* he turned against them completely, and felt that it was a betrayal of the whole idea of making horror films. He thought that they were disgusting, and possibly something that he no longer wanted to be associated with. But certainly in the early days he was very appreciative of the horror films, and he felt that they provided him with just as good an opportunity to perform his craft as any other kind of film.

Also, he wasn't completely typecast in horror films, not like Lugosi.

Right. In fact, Karloff felt sorry for Bela Lugosi because Bela *had* been typed in that area. As horror films dropped in popularity in the late '30s Bela was forced to do cheaper pictures, and he really never got the opportunity to do anything else. Karloff was never resentful of Bela, he just felt sorry for him.

In the early days when I was representing Bela, I used to have autographed photographs of all the people with whom I was associated hanging in my office. And I discovered early on that when Bela came to my office and saw his picture hanging next to Boris Karloff's, that he got very upset about the idea *[laughs]*! So after that, whenever there was an appointment for Bela to come to my office, I would take down the picture of Karloff and substitute somebody else—and then hang it up again after Lugosi left!

Which film did Karloff prefer, Haunted Strangler *or* Corridors of Blood?

He much preferred *Strangler*. He was also unhappy about the mix in *Corridors of Blood*, and in fact that was where a lot of the real problems between him and John Croydon arose. Karloff blamed Croydon, but it wasn't Croydon's fault; if it was anybody's fault it was MGM's, because they said, "You've got to put more lurid stuff into it and you've got to build up the scenes in Black Ben's Den in the Seven Dials"—kind of create a little sex element, with the girls dancing and all of that. Of course that had nothing to do with the story, and it took away from the seriousness of the picture. Karloff was very disappointed with that—we all were! But when you're making a picture for a major

Devil Doll principals meet with members of the press on the first day of shooting. *Left to right:* Bryant Haliday, Sidney J. Furie, newsman, Kenneth Rive, Richard Gordon, newsman, and Lindsay Shonteff.

company and they're financing it, they call the shots. The picture didn't turn out the way any of us would have liked, and it also wasn't as successful as any of us would have liked. We had a very hard time getting it properly distributed.

Why such a long delay before U.S. release?
    Because MGM didn't know quite what to do with it. They didn't have a picture to go with it; naturally I suggested that *we* would make another picture for them, but by that time, with the changes of management and everything else, they were trying to get away from that type of filmmaking in their own schedule.

And since they had financed it, you were in no position to force the issue.
    Right. So *Corridors* sort of languished until MGM set up a separate unit, headed by Fred Schwartz, to distribute pictures that they didn't feel the mainstream of MGM distribution could properly handle — or perhaps didn't want to be associated with! Fred, who was formerly an exhibitor, came up with an Italian import called *Werewolf in a Girls' Dormitory* as the second feature, and the whole thing was a disaster. But that's how *Corridors* got released.

After a lapse of several years, you jumped back into production with Devil Doll *and* Curse of the Voodoo.

Devil Doll was a favorite project of mine. After we had finished the association with MGM and a suitable interval had elapsed, I was looking to get on with something else. I came across this short story called *Devil Doll* in *London Mystery Magazine,* liked it very much and acquired the rights for it. Then after we had the screenplay written, I made a deal with Ken Rive of England's Gala Films, to do the film in association with him.

Gala at that time had a contract with Sidney J. Furie, who had directed for them pictures like *During One Night* [1961] and *The Boys* [1961]. The original intention was that Sidney would direct *Devil Doll,* but while we were still in the early stages of preparation, he suddenly got an offer to do a big film with Cliff Richard. That film, in turn, led to his going to Hollywood and making *The Appaloosa* [1966] with Marlon Brando for Universal. So his career suddenly took a great jump. By mutual agreement we let him out of the commitment to direct *Devil Doll,* because he would have lost his other deal if we had held onto him. He suggested that a protege of his, Lindsay Shonteff, should take over the direction of *Devil Doll.* Lindsay *did* direct it, but Sidney, to his credit, was still very much around, kept an eye on things and guided Lindsay, because it was Lindsay's first actual directing job. So I would say—particularly if you look at the difference between *Devil Doll* and Lindsay's next picture *Curse of the Voodoo [laughs]*—that part of the credit for *Devil Doll* goes to the fact that Sidney Furie was on hand during production and guided it behind the scenes.

What can you tell us about your frequent star Bryant Haliday [Devil Doll, Curse of the Voodoo, The Projected Man, Tower of Evil]?

Bryant and I have had a lifelong friendship, and we still are very close friends—he lives in Paris now, and whenever I'm over there I always see him. Bryant was a stage actor and was the founder of the Brattle Theatre in Cambridge, Massachusetts—he was both an actor and a producer there, and was responsible for bringing some of the leading European theater companies to America, to appear at the Brattle. Together with a man named Cy Harvey, he was also the founder of Janus Films, the foreign film distributing company. They operated a movie house in conjunction with the Brattle in Cambridge—that was where a lot of these films had their first showings—and I actually got to know him through the distribution business of Janus Films.

And you used him in your pictures.

Bryant had made a couple of action pictures and thrillers in France, and he was always interested in trying to keep his acting career going. So it seemed a logical idea to me, when we were preparing *Devil Doll* and we were not really looking for a big American star to play in it, that he would be ideal for that part, and I think it turned out very well.

What became of your policy of putting American stars in your pictures?
    It didn't seem necessary any more. By then the whole trend of the business was changing — pictures that were made overseas with less-than-big-name American stars came to be regarded as television fare rather than theatrical fare. The idea of doing low-budget movies overseas and using American actors went out of style. Also, the actors became less available because of the amount of television work they were doing.

Were you inspired by older pictures like Svengali, The Great Gabbo *or* Dead of Night *in shaping your* Devil Doll *screenplay?*
    Naturally I was very familiar with those pictures, particularly *The Great Gabbo,* which has always been a big favorite of mine. Of course the ventriloquist sequence in *Dead of Night* has a strong bearing on *Devil Doll.* But what we used was what was in the original published story in *London Mystery Magazine* — we didn't try to plagiarize *Dead of Night* or any of those others. There's a limit to what you can do with the situation of a ventriloquist who eventually is dominated by his dummy, as you can see in the film *Magic* with Anthony Hopkins. Where our film is different was that in a way it was fantasy or science fiction — Bryant Haliday actually kills somebody and imprisons his soul in the body of the dummy, and this activates the dummy through some mysterious Eastern process. When the dummy talks back to Erich von Stroheim in *The Great Gabbo* or to Michael Redgrave in *Dead of Night,* it's because the ventriloquist has developed a split personality, and it's really *himself* projecting the voice *onto* the dummy.

Why have you never made a movie in America?
    I suppose it comes about through the fact that I started out making movies in England, became reasonably successful at it, had a British production company and had financing sources available to me in England. When you're onto something that seems to work, I always think it's logical to stay with it, rather than to try and make any drastic changes. Of course, there were certain advantages to working in England. First of all, production costs in those days were substantially lower in England than in the U.S. Also, there was something called the Eady Fund, which was a government subsidy that was available for British productions. It derived from a levy on cinema admissions: A certain percentage of the tickets sold at the box office was returned to the Eady Fund, and this money was paid out as a kind of bonus to British production based upon the box-office gross of the film in England. This helped to assure investors that they would get a return on their money.

What was your budget on Devil Doll?
    The actual British production cost, without my own services or those of Bryant Haliday, was about £25,000 — it was a *very* low-budget film. I flatter myself that it doesn't show it....

And it remains a favorite of yours?

Yes, it does—in fact, one of my future projects is to remake the picture, in color, as a much bigger film and in a modernized version. That's something I've been working on for some time.

And how did Curse of the Voodoo *come about?*

That started out as a finished screenplay called *The Lion Man* that came across my desk. Both the people at Gala Films and I liked it; it seemed to fit into the pattern of what we were doing, and also seemed like a very good follow-up vehicle for Bryant Haliday. So we went ahead and did it.

Curse of the Voodoo *always seemed like a picture with too much footage for so little plot.*

I'd go along with that. But that is, of course, one of the ways to make low-budget pictures—to have plenty of extra footage that takes up a certain amount of running time, without your having to do a lot of complicated shooting. The budget on *Curse of the Voodoo* was approximately the same as *Devil Doll,* and the whole picture was shot in England. A lot of the exteriors were shot in Regent's Park, in the center of London. The African footage, naturally, was stock footage that we incorporated into the picture.

What recollections do you have of the film Naked Evil?

Naked Evil came about through my friendship with Steven Pallos, who is a very successful English producer. It was originally a radio play by Jon Manchip White called *The Obi;* Steven sent it to me and said he thought it would make a good film.

This time around, I had very little control over the production and very little to do with the actual making of the film. I was really more of a co-financier/partner than actual producer. Steven was a very experienced producer, and I really was not of a mind to interfere with him. The big mistake that we made with *Naked Evil* was that we made it in black-and-white at a time when everything was switching to color. It was like those last silent films that were made when the industry had converted to sound! The year that we made *Naked Evil* was the year that black-and-white really went out of style.

So why wasn't it made in color?

Steven made a deal with Columbia Pictures to part-finance the film and to distribute it in the United Kingdom and the Eastern Hemisphere. When he went to Columbia and suggested that we should make it in color instead of black-and-white, and that we would need a certain amount of additional money to do it, they rejected the idea—they were only interested in using it as a second feature with one of their own films, and for that, color was not justified. Steve and I decided we were not going to do it on our own without their participation, so we went ahead and did it in black-and-white. But that was a mistake, and the picture did very little business as a result.

What inspired Independent International to later pick up Naked Evil?
Well, I suppose it was my salesmanship *[laughs]!* Sam Sherman, the head of Independent International, saw something in *Naked Evil* and felt he could turn it into a viable picture with some additional shooting. And I think he's been quite satisfied with the results.

Was it Independent International that added the color tint to the film?
The tinting was actually something that Alex had already devised in Hollywood for me — we tried it, but it still wasn't enough to get the picture off the ground. It was the addition of extra scenes that Sam Sherman came up with.

Your next two films were Island of Terror *and* The Projected Man.
Island of Terror came to me when Gerry Fernback sent me a screenplay called *The Night the Silicates Came.* I read it and really thought it was one of the best finished science fiction / horror screenplays that I'd read for a very long time. Gerry suggested that we should make the picture, and that Tom Blakeley of Planet Films would be a good partner to do it with. We went ahead and did it, and it's one of my favorite pictures.

How did you enjoy working with Hammer Films alumni Peter Cushing and director Terence Fisher?
I enjoyed working with them very much, but there's not too much I can tell you about them. We were shooting *The Projected Man* at the same time, and I ended up spending more time on *Projected Man* than on *Island of Terror* because *Island* ran very smoothly while on *Projected Man* certain problems arose: It started to go over budget and there were problems with the director. So I found myself trouble-shooting on *Projected Man* rather than worrying too much about *Island of Terror.*

How were the giant slugs in Island of Terror *motivated?*
Mostly with wires, being pulled along the ground — there was no stop-motion photography or anything like that. I thought *Island of Terror* turned out well — in fact, even when I look at it *now,* I must say that in my opinion, for a picture of its era it worked extremely well. It had a few really good shock scenes, and I was very pleased with the finished film. The first company I showed it to in the United States was Universal, and they bought it immediately for a very large sum of money.

You showed it to them singly, or on a double bill with The Projected Man?

Bryant Haliday makes a dramatic entrance in producer Gordon's *The Projected Man.*

I showed it to them singly, but I told them that I had *The Projected Man* coming along shortly. I also let them know that if they were interested in buying *Island of Terror,* I would really like to think in terms of providing my own co-feature. By the time we had negotiated the deal, *The Projected Man* was ready, and Universal accepted that as the other film.

What was the genesis of The Projected Man?
The Projected Man was a screenplay that Alex found in California. It was written by a man named Frank Quattrocchi, a Hollywood writer, and was of course written to take place in the United States. Alex sent it to me and I liked it; I sent it over to Gerry Fernback and *he* liked it, so we decided to have it rewritten for London locations.

One complaint fans have with The Projected Man *is that it's too similar to the earlier films* The Fly *and* 4D Man.
Well, I would certainly go along with that as far as *The Fly* is concerned; I haven't seen *4D Man. Projected Man* does have a very strong similarity to *The Fly,* but it came to us as a finished screenplay and seemed to be a perfectly logical film to make.

Earlier, you mentioned problems with your director on Projected Man.
The director, Ian Curteis, who had come out of television and had not had

any real experience shooting feature films, got into trouble toward the end of the picture. In fact, on the last few days the direction was taken over by John Croydon, who actually finished the film.

Why is the American running time on Projected Man *thirteen minutes short of the original British running time?*

The whole of our opening sequence was cut by Universal because they felt it took too long for the picture to get going. The sequence was a rehearsal for the experiment that comes later, so it *is* kind of a repetition, and Universal felt that it was unnecessary. Also, Universal didn't want a double-bill that ran three hours, and they didn't want to cut anything out of *Island of Terror,* so they decided to make the cut in *The Projected Man* to bring it down to a manageable double-bill running time.

Why after the 1950s have all your films been sci-fi/horror?

I've always tended to like that genre — I was successful with it, I told myself I'd become a sort of specialist in it, and it seemed to be better to stay with something you know you're good at, rather than experiment in other areas. Also, because I'd been successful at making horror and sci-fi pictures, I found it was easier for me to arrange financing and distribution making that kind of picture, rather than going off on a completely different tangent. And then, of course, operating within low budgets, horror and science fiction really were two of the best categories to be involved with because you don't necessarily need big stars, elaborate sets or complicated special effects. You could achieve something that would hold audience interest even if it was done on a low budget, without recognizable names and so on.

What were the beginnings for Secrets of Sex?

I had a very close friend in London, Antony Balch, who was a film distributor in England and was in fact the man who put out *Freaks* in England, when it was finally passed by the British Board of Film Censors 35 or 40 years after it was made. Antony had produced and directed some short films and done some experimental work, and he wanted to get into feature production. I had a lot of confidence in him as a director, and I thought it would be worthwhile to do something with him. He had an idea to do a low-budget film that would be an anthology of horror and sexy stories — he called it *Secrets of Sex.* We decided to do it together, with me producing and Antony directing. We made the film for approximately £40,000, which by then — 1970, '71 — was a *very* low budget.

Was the film successful at all?

It was very successful in England: It opened in a theater off Piccadilly Circus in London, where it ran for approximately 28 weeks! Between the money that it earned at the box office, plus the Eady Fund money, the entire

Richard Gordon, behind the scenes on 1971's *Tower of Evil*.

production cost of the film was recouped out of the one run in the West End of London! However, when I brought the film over here, I found that I couldn't get a Code seal on it—there was a certain amount of nudity and some erotic scenes, and the MPAA wouldn't pass it. Also, it was "too British"—it didn't appeal to the American distributors I showed it to. I made a deal with New Line Cinema, who tried to put it out nontheatrically, in 16mm, as a sort of midnight or cult movie, but it really didn't work. So I had it "on the shelf" for a year or two. Then, after I produced *Tower of Evil* and arranged for its American distribution, I suggested *Secrets of Sex* as a second feature for *Tower of Evil*. Of course that meant we had to reedit it, eliminating the sexy and erotic scenes and concentrating on the horror stuff, get it down to a shorter length, get it passed by the MPAA and change the title, and that in fact was what we did. We changed the title to *Tales of the Bizarre* and put it on the double-bill with *Tower of Evil*.

How did that particular film get started?
At that time I was friendly with George Baxt, the writer of such films as *Horror Hotel, Circus of Horrors,* Hammer's *Shadow of the Cat* and *Burn, Witch, Burn*. George and I were friends in New York and he knew I was always looking for subjects, so he came up with a story called *Tower of Evil*. I bought the story from him and then had him write the screenplay. Eventually that screenplay was rewritten by [director] Jim O'Connolly to fit the locations, the budget and the circumstances of the shooting. But it was George's story.
I showed the screenplay to Joe Solomon, who also liked it very much. Joe was the man who produced *Hell's Angels on Wheels* [1967], *The Losers* [1970], *Run Angel Run* [1969] and pictures like that, and I had been his foreign sales distributor ever since he started in business as a producer. He said he'd like to go in with me on it, and we went about setting it up.

Where exactly was Tower of Evil *photographed?*
Except for a few location shots that were done on the South Coast, it was shot entirely at Shepperton Studios. The island lighthouse was a set that was built at Shepperton. The establishing long shots of the lighthouse and the island in the water are actually all glass shots.

In 1973 you collaborated with Antony Balch again, on Horror Hospital.
After the success of *Secrets of Sex* in England and elsewhere in Europe, Antony and I decided that we certainly wanted to do another picture together. He was a great fan of horror movies — in fact, he used to say that his favorite movie was *The Devil Bat* with Bela Lugosi! We were both at the Cannes Film Festival in 1973, sitting around on the beach, between activities, throwing ideas around, when Antony suddenly said, "Why don't we make a picture called *Horror Hospital?*" I said, *"Fine,* I think it's a great title — but where's the script?" He said, "Well, first let's decide on the title, and if we agree that it's a good idea to make a picture called *Horror Hospital* then we'll get somebody to write us a script that'll fit that concept." So we kicked it around for a few days and came up with a storyline. There was a writer friend of Antony's who was also at the Cannes Festival, a fellow by the name of Alan Watson; we got him in on the meetings, and he seemed to be thinking along the same lines as we were, so we made a deal with him. While the script was written by Alan

Watson, I would say that there was a lot of input from both Antony and myself—perhaps more script input than I've ever had on any other picture.

It was a lot of fun making *Horror Hospital*—there was a picture where we had a wonderful time all the way through production. All the people involved—Michael Gough, Robin Askwith, Skip Martin, Ellen Pollock and so on—were all delightful to work with.

Can you tell us a little more about horror star Michael Gough?
Michael Gough was an actor with great classic background and stage training. Like Boris Karloff years earlier, he was the type of person who, once he agreed to do the thing, entered into the spirit of it and treated it just the same way as if he were appearing in a production of *Macbeth!* He didn't regard it as beneath him or as a joke or anything else. He was really very cooperative: He knew that Antony had had limited experience and that this was really his first proper feature film, and he went out of his way to be helpful to everybody. I can only say the nicest things about Michael Gough.

How did The Cat and the Canary *come about?*
The Cat and the Canary came about through my friendship with Radley Metzger, whom I've known for many years from the distribution side of the business. Radley and I had also talked about the possibility of doing a picture together and had been kicking around ideas. One of the things we talked about was the possibility of remaking some well-known horror picture, and it seemed a very good idea to try to do *The Cat and the Canary.*

What qualities led you to that choice?
Well, it hadn't been done since the Bob Hope version, it had never been done in color, it was a well-known title, had a certain reputation, and it was something that logically could or in fact *should* be made in England. It also invited the idea of getting together a sort of all-star cast—of course, the cast that *we* could afford was not on the level of *Murder on the Orient Express* or *Death on the Nile [laughs],* but let's say on the next level! We made a deal with Raymond Rohauer, who owned the literary rights, the screenplay was written by Radley Metzger, and that's how the production got set up.

Did your "all-star" cast take a big bite out of your budget?
The Cat and the Canary was certainly the most expensive picture I'd done up to that time, not only because of the cast but because of the circumstances of the production—it had a somewhat longer shooting schedule and required a more elaborate set-up. We *were* able to put together what I think was an exceptionally good cast: Carol Lynley, Michael Callan, Edward Fox, Olivia Hussey, Honor Blackman, Wendy Hiller, Wilfrid Hyde-White, Peter McEnery, Daniel Massey and Beatrix Lehmann. The casting itself wasn't all that expensive because, by the nature of the story and the way we scheduled

the production, most of the cast we only needed for certain limited periods of time, and we were able to shoot all their scenes together. In fact, Wilfrid Hyde-White only worked one day!

How did Inseminoid *come about?*
    Inseminoid was a project that Norman Warren brought to my attention. Norman, who had made a number of low-budget horror and exploitation films in England, sent me a script which had been brought to him by Nick and Gloria Maley, the special effects people. They had in fact written it with the idea that if they could get the production set up, it would be a showcase for their special effects abilities. Norman and I both liked the script, so I went to England and made a deal with Nick and Gloria. The Shaw Brothers in Hong Kong agreed to put up half the money and become partners in the picture, and that's how *Inseminoid* began.

Where was that film shot?
    Most of it was shot in the underground caves at Chislehurst, which are just outside London. It's a network of tunnels and underground caves that go back hundreds of years, and has become a sort of tourist attraction. Rather than try to build the underground settings in a studio, we decided that we would make a deal for the use of the Chislehurst Caves and build our sets there. The rest of the picture was shot at Lee Studios in Wembley Park—some of the interiors, closeups and whatever else we needed.

Did shooting in actual caves cause any problems?
    It caused a *lot* of problems. We had to go fairly deep into the tunnels to get to cave areas that were sufficiently large and open for us to be able to build the sets and to get the camera equipment and everything in there. As you can imagine, the air down there was not very good—there was a constant dampness and it was very cold—and by the time we had the lights and camera crews and everything else down there, it really was difficult for people to work without getting claustrophobic, and becoming somewhat neurotic about being buried under the ground! I don't know if this added to the performances or detracted from them *[laughs]*, but it was very hard, and at intervals people had to go back outside for a breather—it really was tough to work there all day long. In addition to that, the caves were constantly wet, and the sets had to be repaired again and again because everything was dripping with water.
    I think all this paid off in terms of what we got on the screen for the budget, but the circumstances were very difficult. It was much easier, of course, when we eventually went into Lee Studios, which is a regular motion picture studio, for the finishing work.

You also assembled what would, in time, become a much stronger cast.
    We got our stars Jennifer Ashley and Robin Clarke through a Hollywood

agency, and then of course we had Judy Geeson; Stephanie Beacham, although this was long before *The Colbys;* and Victoria Tennant, and this was long before *The Winds of War.* So as it's turned out, when you look at it now it really *is* an all-star picture!

But what a demanding, demeaning role for Judy Geeson!
She didn't regard it that way; she thought it was a very interesting part. She's a very professional young lady and a good actress, she thought it was a challenging role and she was happy to accept it.

And Inseminoid *remains your biggest budgeted picture to date?*
That was my most expensive picture, yes. *Inseminoid* was the original title and the title under which it was released in the whole world outside the U.S. and Canada. When we made a deal with Almi Pictures for the distribution in the U.S. and Canada and they didn't like the title *Inseminoid,* they came up with the title *Horror Planet.*

While doing a gratuitous horror film like Inseminoid, *do you miss the days of black-and-white, Lugosi, Karloff and implied horrors?*
Let me say that if I had my choice I would much rather make the more subtle kind of horror picture, a *Haunted Strangler* or *Devil Doll* or something like that. I don't really enjoy the slash-and-gore or slice-and-dice kind of picturemaking, I don't think it's any fun, but *if* I make another picture I think I will have to conform to the requirements of the box office.

What are your plans for the future?
There are two projects that I'm particularly interested in at the moment. One, as I mentioned before, is a modernized and updated version of *Devil Doll,* in color, on a bigger scale and with a bigger artist. That would *have* to be the more subtle kind of film, because it doesn't lend itself to an out-and-out gore approach. It wouldn't even be a "horror film" today, it would be a psychological thriller in the vein of *Magic* or what people call the Hitchcock type of movie. The other thing I've been thinking about is a remake or sequel to *Fiend Without a Face.* I've had several companies approach me about the possibility of doing a remake or sequel—because it's such a well-known title, it's become a sort of cult movie. I've been considering it very seriously, but I haven't got down to either devising a new script or making any active plans yet. I *have* had a new script written for the remake of *Devil Doll:* It was written for me by Stanley Price, who wrote *Arabesque* [1966] for Stanley Donen and who is quite a well-known writer in England. I think it's a very clever script that gives the story a different twist, and this is one of the things I hope to get off the ground within the next twelve months.

When I'm introduced to someone who knows my name
but doesn't know what I've done, they hear The Blob
and a sparkle comes into their eyes. The Blob *just goes
on and on and on; it's a respected movie and I've got to
think of it as the best thing I've ever done.
I will *top it, but I haven't done it yet.*

———— *Jack H. Harris* ————

ONLY THE SMALLEST HANDFUL of '50s science fiction films can rival the unique appeal of *The Blob*, 1958's phenomenally popular saga of drag-racing youth versus flesh-eating outer space slime. The pet project of first-time filmmaker Jack H. Harris, *The Blob* has achieved classic status, while the man behind it has parlayed his initial success into a long and lucrative career as a producer-distributor, seldom straying too far or too long from his sci-fi roots.

The Philadelphia-born Harris first entered show business by way of vaudeville, singing and dancing with "Ukulele Ike" Edwards' Kiddie Revue at age six. Working his way up from an early job as a theater usher, Harris went into publicity and learned distribution, eventually opening his own offices.

Dissatisfied with the minor black-and-white films foisted upon him, Harris quickly developed an itch to produce his own pictures. Linking up with the moviemaking ministers of Pennsylvania's Valley Forge Film Studios, producer Harris and director Irvin S. Yeaworth collaborated on *The Blob*, a film which eventually grossed more than a hundred times its $240,000 cost.

Harris followed up on this early success with *4D Man* and *Dinosaurus!* before circumstances temporarily curtailed his producing career in the 1960s. Returning to distribution, he has provided U.S. release for the British Bela Lugosi vehicle *Mother Riley Meets the Vampire* and the Argentinian Poe anthology *Master of Horror*, as well as for such home-grown fodder as *The Astro-Zombies*, the John Newland–directed *The Legend of Hillbilly John* and student films like *Equinox* and *Dark Star*.

Years later, Harris's own *Beware! The Blob* (a.k.a. *Son of Blob*) encored the '58 original, and in 1978 he exec-produced the stylish but sterile Faye Dunaway thriller *The Eyes of Laura Mars*. In this exclusive interview, Jack H. Harris talks candidly about his quarter-century's worth of fantasy fare and a business *The Blob* helped build.

Although made in Pennsylvania, The Blob *has the polished look of a Hollywood production.*

Absolutely. I had distributed five hundred pictures by the time I got to *The Blob,* I knew what I wanted and I insisted upon it. We were lucky enough to have a group of people I don't think you could ever assemble again. These people had done about a hundred and fifty short films, ranging from three to twenty minutes in length; they'd never done a feature film. But at least they did have the technical facility to understand what a camera was, and to know enough not to split somebody's skull with a microphone boom. Whenever we had a problem, we solved it with good, clear thinking.

You're talking about the people at Valley Forge Film Studios.

Right. The guiding light there was a guy named Irvin S. Yeaworth, Jr. He was a Methodist minister, and he had a group of strong believers in Jesus working with him. Their basic mission was to promulgate the Word. They were doing that pretty well, but starving to death at the same time. I convinced

Previous page: **Jack H. Harris schmoozes with starlets Sandy Brooke (left) and Susan Stokey during a break in the shooting of Harris' *Star Slammer* (1986).**

Veteran Hollywood character actor Olin Howlin played his last (and best-remembered) movie role as the first victim of *The Blob*.

them that we could take what facilities they had, add certain equipment I could bring in from New York and L.A., upgrade the actors and come up with films that a lot of people would come and see. And if they did it right, we'd do it again; and the more notice they got, the more Word they'd be able to transmit. It was not a sales pitch, it was a *fact*. And as things worked out it did them a lot of good, because they were able to do their primary thing, which was spreading the Word, because of the association that they had with Hollywood.

I knew a lot of pros and so did they, through religious connections, and everybody helped. But nobody could do anything about the twenty-two hour days we put in, seven days a week. But that's what made the difference. I believe that success is a combination of clear thinking, creative ability and hard work, and *[laughs]* I guess hard work is 90 percent. *The Blob* took thirty-one days to shoot and nine months to do the effects. And we invented a lot of things; some of them are still being used, and a lot of others we never bothered to tell people about.

Who originally came up with the idea for The Blob?
  The original notion was put together by a guy named Irvine Millgate. He was a consultant to the Boy Scouts of America, for their Visual Aids Department. With the help of the Cecil B. DeMille office, he had put together a film on the jamboree that took place in Hollywood in 1953. Every star in Hollywood was in it, but the Boy Scouts had a problem getting the picture out. They wanted it to play in theaters, so they came to me and used my distribution expertise to get it out in the marketplace. Millgate and I covered the country and got it played; we traveled together, on and off, for a year or more. He knew I wanted to make pictures, and he used to ask me what I wanted to make. I finally said, "Listen, what I want to think up is a movie monster that is *not* a guy dressed up in a suit — *not* a puppet — but some kind of a form that's never been done before. I want it to do things that will undo mankind as we know it if it's not arrested or destroyed. But I want the destruction to be something that Grandma could cook up on her stove on an experimental Sunday afternoon." We kept throwing things back and forth, back and forth, and I must admit we didn't come up with anything. One night, the phone rang at three a.m. — I was in New York, sleeping at one of the hotels there at the end of a long day — and it was Irvine. I said, "What is it?" and he said, "A *mineral* monster." I said, "I'm hanging up."
  He said, "No, no — don't hang up! This mineral, if you get involved with it, can absorb your flesh." I liked it. But I wondered, if you were wearing a nice suit, does it spit it out or eat that, too *[laughs]*? And how do you do it in? We had to work those things out. But I'd never seen anything like a mineral monster, so I knew we had better get serious. The next day he flew into New York and we worked on it all day. We figured out we couldn't burn it, shoot it or destroy it with acid, but we could immobilize it if we froze it. And that was our basic synopsis for a film we initially called *The Molten Meteor.*
  I introduced Irvine to the guys out at Valley Forge and they worked with us on the story. We built the story on a storyboard basis before a script was written; that was great because it gave us our major sequences and blocked everything out for the director [Yeaworth]. Theodore Simonson and Kate Phillips did the screenplay. Ted Simonson was a guy who's always written — he's another minister — and his writings were all religious in content until *The Blob* moved him in another direction. He's done a series of teleplays and other things since that time. Simonson could probably have turned it out, but we were all running scared. Kate Phillips and her husband, whose name I forget,

had done a lot of good things on television and were good friends and wanted to help, so we brought them in to do a polish.

Tell us a little about your casting of Steve McQueen.

The summer before, Neile Adams was doing a little favor for Yeaworth — she came down and appeared in a twenty-minute religious film that took 'em two days to shoot. There was this dirty jerk, an opinionated pain in the ass — her husband — who decided to be there at the same time. They couldn't *wait* to get him out of there, so they finally kissed *her* goodbye and kicked *him* out. I don't know anything about this; all I know is, I go to see *A Hatful of Rain* on Broadway because I had my eye on Tony Franciosa for the lead in *The Blob*. Ben Gazzara got sick and his understudy Steve McQueen — Neile Adams' husband — played the part. He was superb. I was all excited, and I told Irvin Yeaworth, "We found our leading man — Steve McQueen." Yeaworth cried out, *"What?!"* and told me the whole story — "He's a dirty guy, he's an opinionated ass, he's this, he's that." They all hated him — the idea of him going back there and living with them for week after week was unthinkable. They told me, "We know he's gonna rot in hell 'cause he's no good, but besides that we may kill him!"

I told them I wanted to think it over. That night, I went home and *Studio One* had a two-parter on about a father-and-son law firm. Steve McQueen had a role in that, too, and by the time it was over I was convinced, McQueen was the guy for our picture. So the next day Steve McQueen was signed to play the lead in *The Blob*.

Were you pleased with his work in the film?

He had done a little part in a Paul Newman film, *Somebody Up There Likes Me* [1956], and he had starred in a small picture for Allied Artists called *Never Love a Stranger* [1957]. So he did have some experience in front of a camera, and his stage presence was excellent. Really, the long and short of it was that he played Steve McQueen in everything — the same gestures, the same little smile, the same excitement level. That indicated star quality to me. But it didn't indicate it enough, because I had agreed to star him in two more pictures which were coming up — yes, *4D Man* and *Dinosaurus!* would have been the pictures — but he was such a royal pain and I hated him so much I didn't use him. I'm sure sad that I didn't — I've regretted that decision — but he was so impossible I wouldn't hear of it at the time. And not only that, I couldn't foist him upon the same people — I'd have had to find a whole new crew and director in order to use him. It was more important to get the pictures done, because I had commitments. I believe it was his insecurity that made him difficult to deal with. I must admit, the later productions went a lot smoother, but boy — as Walter Mirisch said, he's a pain in the ass but worth it.

What was the Blob made of?

The Blob was made of silicone, which was kind of a new thing at that time. We discovered that we could achieve varying degrees of consistency, from that of running water to hard glue, and we varied our consistencies to meet the requirements of each scene. There were a couple of scenes in which we used a barrage balloon, covered with goop and pulled along on a fishing line. And there were times when the Blob was air-brushed and animated—it all depended on the situation. Vegetable coloring gave it the red color; it got redder and redder as it grew and consumed more people. One thing we never resolved was, how do you keep the color in there? We just had to keep mixing it, like cake batter, otherwise it would all settle to the bottom.

How much Blob were you working with?
     The most we worked with was about a washtub full. Naturally we couldn't afford to cover a diner with the Blob, so what we did there was photograph the diner through a bent bellows to give it dimension. To correct any minute flaws we enhanced the photograph with touch-up and air-brushing. We then mounted it on plywood, set it up on an eight-foot-square gyroscope-operated table and tied cameras to the table, rock-steady. Then we were able to move the table in any direction we wanted; the Blob, of course, would always follow gravity. When we wanted the Blob to jump *on* the "diner," we put it on there and got it to jump *off* with a quick movement of the table. That footage, shown in reverse, gave us our effect.

From the original Paramount release through all your various reissues, how many box-office dollars has The Blob *pulled in?*
     My guess is that it's somewhere in the forty mill category. That took a lot of years, but it goes back to the days when admissions were a buck. So that's pretty good.

How did you come up with the idea for 4D Man?
     I was in a restaurant looking through a little pamphlet on the fourth dimension. It went into the molecular structure of matter, and said that if we could figure out how to arrest the molecular structure of two foreign pieces of matter, that these molecules could be allowed to intertwine. In other words, you could put a pencil through a table, why couldn't a person walk through a wall?
     So you walk through a wall, who gives a damn? We had to make it interesting, we had to provide menace. That's why we came up with the idea that, as a result of walking through walls and the like, our 4D Man was rapidly aging and could die very quickly of premature old age. *That* notion I gleaned from a book of *Ripley's Believe It or Not;* I remembered reading about kids who died at the age of seven of old age because of something peculiar in their physiological makeup. Through his touch, the 4D Man could kill a person and replenish his own life energy. We applied that to the storyline to provide conflict.

A prostitute (Chic James) withers from the life-robbing touch of Robert Lansing in Harris' *4D Man*.

Who cast Robert Lansing?

I picked up Bob Lansing from Broadway; I found myself choosing between him and Jason Robards. I thought Lansing had more of a romantic leading man–look about him. Robards went further in his career, although he's never been a command ticket seller, but Lansing's always been solid, and has never given a bad performance.

What were your budget and shooting schedule?

4D Man had about the same budget and shooting schedule as *The Blob*. The special effects took a hell of a long time.

Can you elaborate on how you achieved the 4D effects?

[Laughs.] Tediously! The color robin's-egg blue can be blotted out by an image if you combine two negatives and print the positive from them. We shot some of the scenes of Lansing against a blue backing, and then laid that over the live scenes. To have him reach *through* somebody, we photographed him and then photographed the victim, and put the two negatives together. And as his hands were going *into* the victim, we would scrape away emulsion, losing more and more of his hands as his arms moved forward. Then, as his arms pulled *out,* we scraped less and less. It's called rotoscope. Again, as with *The Blob,* the special effects took about nine months.

You sponsored a contest offering a million dollars to anyone who could duplicate the 4D Man's feats on a theater stage. What would have happened if someone pulled it off?

I'd have given 'em a million—because I'd have owned the method! We had a hell of a time getting a backer for the policy—we had to go to Lloyds of London, who brought in fifteen co-insurers to lay off their bet. Everybody was afraid somebody could do it, and I kept saying, "Let 'em do it! I'll cut you in!" I was hoping somebody would do it, but nobody ever tried. Never a phone call or a postcard—nothing.

Why did you switch distributors for 4D Man?

Universal gave me the kind of arrangement I was happy with; Paramount wouldn't, on *4D Man*. While we were at Universal with *4D Man*, I told them I intended to make *Dinosaurus!*, and they said, "Let's put them together." It was that simple.

What was your original concept for that film?

The original idea was a dinosaur picture, but I didn't want to do a prehistoric film. The basic concept was that dinosaurs find their way into contact and conflict with contemporary man. I brought in a consultant, Alfie Bester, who had written a number of science fiction things, and we spent a day in a New York hotel suite bruiting over how to get the dinosaurs from where they were to where we are. He brought up the touch of having them long-buried under the sea and blasted out by men building an island harbor. Then I worked with Algis Budrys, who was a famous science fiction writer; he stayed at my home for two weeks and we came up with all the characters and how they interplayed. In fact *[laughs]*, he came up with a six hundred page synopsis—unbelievable! Dan Weisburd was brought in to write the screenplay, 'cause Budrys was all wrote out.

Where did you shoot?

The location work was done at St. Croix in the Virgin Islands; the balance of it was done at a studio in Hollywood. The budget on that was almost double what the others were; *Dinosaurus!* came to about $450,000. Shooting took about five weeks. The effects, once again, took one hell of a long time. This time we had to build puppets as well as life-size parts for contact. The puppets were motivated through stop-motion animation, which takes a long time.

How did you hook up with the special effects team of Tim Barr, Wah Chang and Gene Warren?

By process of elimination. I had gone all over town—I even hired Willis O'Brien to be my consultant. He kept trying to sell me on stop-motion and I kept saying I didn't want to do it that way. I found some nut that was going to build me two life-size dinosaurs, with three men operating them with pulleys and wires from the inside. He showed me a leg with armatures, real Rube Goldberg stuff—I crossed him off. The next thing we went to was animation, but I just couldn't believe that anybody could animate something that would look like more than a cartoon. One guy wanted to take lizards and stick them in there, but I wouldn't hear of that.

Now I was down to stop-motion, and I went through the list of people that knew how to do that. I met George Pal and he said I ought to talk to these guys, because they had done things for him—some of the Puppetoons, and all the special effects for *The Time Machine*. I went to talk to them, they were excited and I was excited, so we got together.

Were you happy with their effects?

I thought they were excellent for that point in time. The state of the art has improved a lot since then, of course.

The Blob *and* 4D Man *are such sincere, straightforward films, it's disappointing that* Dinosaurus! *spoofs itself.*

Dinosaurus! did have a humorous central portion; Irvin Yeaworth and his wife, Jean, came up with that. I was sort of on the fence about it, but it tickled me so much that I gave in. I was experimental because until that time nobody ever really tried anything like that—mixing this sort of monster movie with humor. I just figured it was new enough to give it a shot, so I did. I take responsibility for it; I could've put my foot down and said, "Nothin' doin'." But I laughed when I read it—I thought it was cute. Looking back on it, it would have been better if we didn't do it.

Why is Mother Goose a Gogo *your only directorial credit?*

A lot of times a movie's credits will say, "Produced and directed by...." I found out on that picture that that was bull. You really can't do both jobs. On *Mother Goose a Gogo* I did both jobs, and I worked myself into a state that it took me about three months to climb out of. I was in on all the arguments with the agents and the managers and the unions, and I was also trying to get performances out of the actors and trying to get the thing to make sense. It ain't easy.

Tell us how you kept busy throughout the '60s.

I was suddenly thrust back into distribution. I was getting my own pictures back and doing very well, and then friends of mine that had made pictures but couldn't find anybody to release them would come to me and I'd help *them* out. And the next thing I knew I was building a distribution organization.

For instance, Wayne Rogers was an acquaintance of mine, and he walked into my office one day tearing his hair out. "I put money in this turkey of a film and now I don't know what to do with it," he told me. "Take it off my hands—just get me out!" I asked him what the title was and he said, *"The*

Producer Harris and director Irvin Yeaworth mixed up an uneven blend of sci-fi thrills and broad comedy in 1960's *Dinosaurus!*

Astro-Zombies." Well, I got turned off by the title. Then when I saw the picture I *really* wanted to vomit! But then I saw an angle: The key art had a zombie — sort of a Frankenstein Monster type — holding this great big machete and grabbing a girl. I felt that had a little marketability about it, and I also could have used a second feature for *Equinox.* So it made good sense for me to pick it up.

How did you latch onto Equinox?

Equinox was a completed 16mm film brought to me by a student named Dennis Muren. You've seen his credits since that time; he got the Academy Award for *Indiana Jones and the Temple of Doom* in 1984. *Equinox* was his demonstration film, and it was *horrendous* — just God-awful. It had a storyline that made no logical sense. I had my son sit down with me one night to look at a print and he walked out after about ten minutes. But I stayed there and went through it, and I saw the seed of something good in it. I bought the picture from him and threw away 70 percent of it. Then I brought in Jack Woods, who is a director, an actor, a writer — really one of the unsung great people of this town. We sat down and tore the picture apart, and came up with the ultimate storyline. We then began reshooting, with Jack Woods directing. Some of it we shot in 16mm, but most of what we did was in 35.

How about Schlock?

Schlock was a film that John Landis had made on spec, and he was taking it all over town. It was rejected by American International, who called me and said I should take a look at it. They thought that maybe I could figure out something and turn it into a movie—I was getting a pretty good name around town for doing that. I took a look at it and I was frightened to death of it, because I had never seen anything like it *[laughs]!* I took the picture into a Hollywood Boulevard sleaze joint and "sneaked" it, and the poor people didn't know what the hell they were looking at. However, enough of it worked to convince me that it was worth pursuing. We dropped some garbage that was in there, went out and shot new sequences, and the picture started to come together. I *still* think it's a strange little "off-center" movie, and it's become a sort of collector's item.

And Dark Star?

Dan O'Bannon knew John Landis, and he asked him to have me look at the film he had done. *Dark Star* was a forty-minute 16mm student film made by O'Bannon and John Carpenter when the boys were going to U.S.C. But what were they going to do with a forty-minute film? They took it around but everybody said it had to be ninety minutes. So they went out and shot fifty more minutes. And it was dreadful, it was *death*—I mean, the opening scene was four guys laying in their bunks, snoring, for five minutes. The bunks looked like Russian army cots, they didn't look like anything on a spaceship. But I felt there was enough *something* there. First of all, it was space; I had never done a space movie, and I figured I wanted to. So at least we had a framework. We threw away a good 60 percent, cutting it way down even below their original forty minutes—some of *that* was padding. We constructed some sets, literally started all over again, shooting in 35mm, and built it back up again. We even shot the meteorite storm and a number of special effects things that weren't in the original picture. And the final result turned out better than I thought it did, because at that time I laid the picture off with Bryanston Pictures, which was emerging, and it turned out to be a cult movie. It's still popular.

Based on his work in Dark Star, *did John Carpenter's later success come as a surprise to you?*

A little bit. I knew he had something, and when he came forth with *Halloween* I was very thrilled for him. And as he proceeded, I was delighted. I think he's a very literate, astute person.

Why did you wait fourteen years to come up with a sequel to a big money-maker like The Blob?

I didn't think it was necessary to make one. My son Tony had graduated from U.S.C. with a degree in music, and he went from there into A&R for a small record label. He was making a lot of money, but he got fed up with it, and he came to my office one day and said, "I'm putting myself under your direction." I said, "Why? I'm not in the music business." He told me that he *wanted* to work with me, that he felt remiss because we had not worked together before. I said, "Well, come in and hang out, see what's going on." After a week, he came to me and said, "Let's make a movie," and I said okay. He reminded me that I had in my drawer a script by Richard Clair called *A Chip Off the Old Blob*. I reread it, it was cute, and *Son of Blob* was the result.

How did Larry Hagman get the job of director?
I had a beach house on the Malibu colony, next door to Larry's. He came over one afternoon, heard us talking about making *Son of Blob* and said, "Boy, I'd love to be in that." He told me that everybody wanted to be "blobbed," every actor wanted to be in a picture like that. He told me that he could put together a cast for the thing, *but* — he would like to direct it. So that's how it came about.

Was the Son of Blob made of silicone as well?
The special effects were done by Tim Barr, of *Dinosaurus!* fame, and they came up with new ways to do them. They were not as effective as the original's. We used a newly developed powdered substance that, mixed with water, gave us a jelly-like consistency. It came in various colors, too, so we didn't have to worry about silicone, vegetable dye and all those other things. We put it on rollers and mounted it right in front of the camera, and it looked like the Blob was rolling right onto the people.

Do you think Son of Blob *was a worthy sequel?*
No. It was too funny and not scary enough.

How did you get involved on Columbia's Eyes of Laura Mars?
That was an idea that John Carpenter came to me with; I was able to take it and get it turned into a picture. That was shot entirely in New York, and the budget was about six and a half million.

Wasn't Barbra Streisand up for the lead in Laura Mars?
She was — for about twenty minutes *[laughs]!* But at the crucial moment she ducked out. She's really frightened of "fright" movies, and when she saw the way the script was going she changed her mind.

Were you happy with the finished film?
I was . . . *fairly* happy with it — not ecstatic. Even though Faye Dunaway had just come away with the Academy Award and it was a coup to have her, I felt she didn't get her face dirty enough, she wore high heels when she should have been wearing sneakers and she didn't look as vulnerable as the gal should have. *Eyes of Laura Mars* was too glossy and too chic, and it lost heart by doing that.

As executive producer, couldn't you have pushed for a grittier look?
I pushed for everything I could, but when you make a picture with a studio it's a combined effort of so many things. And then we went through three changes of administration before the picture got finished; we had a different production supervisor every six months starting from the writing stage forward. About the ninth rewrite, I went in and complained to the production head and he said, "What the hell are you worried about? We still don't have a half million in the script." *Oh, my God!* I thought to myself. And on the other hand, the head of physical production was on my tail about the budget!

You've played small roles in most of your own films, haven't you?
I ran out of the theater in *The Blob;* I was a nightclub extra in *4D Man;* in *Dinosaurus!* I was one of the tourists on the boat; in *Equinox* I was the detective; in *Son of Blob* I ran across the skating rink as the ice was forming; in *Schlock* I was sitting in the movie theater in front of Forry Ackerman, reading a horror cartoon book; and in *Eyes of Laura Mars* I was a dress extra in the gallery.

Can you name a favorite among all your films?
Well, there can't be a contest there, it has to be *The Blob.* When I'm introduced to someone who knows my name but doesn't know what I've done, they hear *The Blob* and a sparkle comes into their eyes. *The Blob* just goes on and on and on; it's a respected movie and I've got to think of it as the best thing I've ever done. I *will* top it, but I haven't done it yet.

*I guarantee you, these cheap pictures will stand up
against any two-hour movie made today. There's
more care and thought in them; even though they
were low-budget, we really cared what we
were making, we really tried. It was
such a ball, and we had so much fun.*

Howard W. Koch

SOME BIG HOLLYWOOD PRODUCERS might act like they don't remember their low-budget roots, but Howard W. Koch is not one of them. A former head of production at Paramount and the producer of such major films as *The Odd Couple*, *Airplane!* and *Dragonslayer*, Koch recalls fondly those days back in the '50s when he was producing and/or directing horror staples like *Frankenstein 1970*, *Pharaoh's Curse* and the all-star terror show *The Black Sleep*.

Getting his start in the movie business in Universal's contract and playdate department in New York City, Koch moved on to Twentieth Century–Fox as a film librarian and then entered production as second assistant director on *The Keys of the Kingdom* (1944). After many films as assistant director, Koch joined forces with his professional benefactor Aubrey Schenck, as well as Edwin Zabel, to strike a three-picture production deal with United Artists that was to start with the Western *War Paint* in 1953. The success of these pictures opened up the deal for more United Artists films by Koch, Schenck and Zabel under the company title of Bel-Air Productions. Koch's first horror films were made at this time.

Following this string of Bel-Air movies, Koch went on to work in TV. With Schenck, he produced *Miami Undercover*, and also worked extensively as a director on such shows as *Maverick*, *Hawaiian Eye*, *Cheyenne* and *The Untouchables*. From 1961 to 1964 Koch was vice-president in charge of production for Sinatra Enterprises, and among his many executive-producer credits during this period was the chilling *The Manchurian Candidate*. He became the production head at Paramount in 1964 and then shifted gears two years later to form his own production unit, which has been supplying major features to Paramount ever since.

Did Aubrey Schenck, Edwin Zabel and you have specific functions within your organization, or was everything done collaboratively?

Aubrey Schenck was the story man—a brilliant story man, and a wild, enthusiastic kind of a guy. He gave me every opportunity I had in my life—whatever break I got was from him. I owe him everything. I was the down-to-earth guy that made the pictures—either I directed them or produced them. I was a "factory picture" maker—I knew what it took to make a film. A lot of producers in those days only knew about finding a script, casting, hiring a director. They didn't know one thing about how the below-the-line was done. Having been an assistant, I knew that pretty well. Edwin Zabel was chief buyer for Fox West Coast Theaters, which was the best chain of theaters in California. He was really our "trigger man," helping us get our pictures distributed right.

What sort of arrangement did you have with United Artists?

Our deal with UA was open-ended. What we would do was, we'd get a title, we'd show it to United Artists, and they'd say, "Here's x number of dollars, go make it." Then we'd write a script for it, check one member of the cast with UA, and then shoot the picture. That was the time of exploitation films—second features were still hot then. All of our pictures, except maybe

Previous page: Director Koch provides some last-minute instructions to horror legend Boris Karloff on the set of *Frankenstein 1970*.

Left to right: John Carradine, Lon Chaney, Jr., Tor Johnson, George Sawaya and Sally Yarnell comprised the ghoulish gallery of mutants in Koch's 1956 production *The Black Sleep.* (Photo courtesy Steve Jochsberger.)

three of them, were second features. We'd come up with a title and then write the story; that's precisely how *The Black Sleep* came about.

When you announced The Black Sleep, *Allen Miner was scheduled to direct.*
     Allen Miner had directed a picture called *Ghost Town* [1956] for us and he did very well — five days, $100,000. We had a nice relationship with him and announced him for *The Black Sleep,* but then when we got deeper into the picture we figured it would take a guy who had done that kind of stuff, knew that genre better. So we switched over to Reginald LeBorg. I'd met Reggie when I was an assistant director at Eagle-Lion, when he was directing a picture with Alan Curtis and Sheila Ryan called *Philo Vance's Secret Mission* [1947].

He'd also done a good job on several of Universal's '40s horror films.
     Reggie LeBorg is a fabulous director — even today he can direct rings around most directors — but he never had the chance to really prove himself. But if you look at *The Black Sleep* and see how slickly that was done — in twelve days! — you've *got* to say he's one hell of a director. And look at the cast we got together for no money — the whole picture cost $225,000.

Horror greats Tor Johnson, John Carradine and Bela Lugosi indulge in some behind-the-scenes buffoonery after shooting *The Black Sleep.*

Can you tell us about the great horror stars you worked with on The Black Sleep: *Basil Rathbone, John Carradine, Lon Chaney and Bela Lugosi?*

Basil Rathbone was the dignified Englishman, just wonderful. I loved to talk to him just to hear him speak. He'd talk to me about his days on Errol Flynn pictures, and how much he loved doing them. He said he did a lot of the swordfights himself. A lovely gentleman, just like Boris Karloff—they were cut from the same kind of cloth. They were hard-working, lovely guys, nothing like the characters you'd see them play.

I had known John Carradine for years, from the days when I was an assistant director at Fox. Carradine had done another picture with us before *The Black Sleep,* an action film called *Desert Sands* [1955]. He was always a shifty kind of guy in life, and by "shifty" I definitely do *not* mean that he was dishonest. But he *lived* the make-believe world of the actor. He really lived in a world of his own, in a dreamworld, and never faced reality.

Lon Chaney I had just directed in *Big House, U.S.A.* [1955], and we really had a great relationship. He said to me, "Look, I'll do anything you want. I know you guys have no money—just tell me how much and I'll show up." Lon was also an amateur chef—he made the best chili in the world. If you loved his chili, he loved you. On the screen you always saw him as a horrible kind of guy, but in life he wasn't at all like that. He was anything *but*—he was a sweet, compassionate, wonderful man. He was great with me, and I was really crazy about him.

Bela Lugosi? Well *[laughs]*, I couldn't figure him out. I don't think he knew he was there! When we opened *The Black Sleep* in San Francisco, we sent Lugosi and a press agent, Chuck Moses, up there for the opening of the picture. Chuck walked into the hotel room one night, and Lugosi was standing on the sill overlooking San Francisco, with the window wide open, saying, "I'm gonna fly!" Chuck cried out, "Wait a second! You *can't* fly!" Lugosi was so drunk, he was going to jump out the window of the hotel! Chuck nearly fainted—he didn't know whether to run and grab him, or to stand there and not disrupt Lugosi's thinking. Anyway, Chuck got him in, called me and said, "What should I do?" I told him, "Put a handcuff on him, take him to the theater, put him on a plane with you and *come home!*"

Both The Black Sleep *and* Pharaoh's Curse *carry an unusual credit line, "Characters Designed by Volpe."*

Volpe is an artist out here in California. He'd read the scripts and then he would draw the characters. Then we'd dress and make up the actors the way he drew them. A very interesting guy; he worked for no bucks, too, very inexpensively. But it helped us—we weren't the great talents of all time. We really needed his direction.

You know, that *Black Sleep* script was really fun to play with; I think more people laughed at it than went with it, although I'm sure there are scary moments in it. I got one of the top brain surgeons in America, who lived in Los Angeles, and used his hands for the brain operation. To this day he's still a neurosurgeon at Cedars of Lebanon out here, and every time I see him he asks, "Where's my second movie?"

The makeup jobs in Black Sleep *are very effective.*

We had more fun doing that makeup; today'd we'd have gotten an award for best makeup, because it was made for spit. We didn't have a lot of money to spend on that.

Bel-Air did pretty well with The Black Sleep, *didn't they?*

When the picture opened, we got some damn good reviews; it did business which was much above what our usual pictures did. In Illinois it played in a double feature with a picture called *The Creeping Unknown,* and a little boy died of fright watching that picture.

Right after The Black Sleep *was finished, you announced that you planned a second horror film,* The Lizard Man *with Lon Chaney.*

I remember the title, but I don't recall what happened with that. I think Lon *wrote* that script, maybe with his wife.

Outwardly, Pharaoh's Curse *seems the most modest of your four Bel-Air horror films, but in many ways it is the most effective.*

The mummy closes in on victim Kurt Katch in a scene from Koch's *Pharaoh's Curse.*

We had planned to make that as a "parasite picture" — to shoot it on location, for around $100,000, after one of our bigger-budgeted features had wrapped up. We had a script developed and we really liked it. But then we had no location picture to put it behind. So we got a little more money — I think that cost $116,000 — and we went back to Death Valley, where we'd made our first success, *War Paint.* The interiors were shot at an old studio on Santa Monica Boulevard. Originally that studio was called Educational, then it became Eagle-Lion, then American National, then Ziv. I think it was during the American National time that we were doing our shooting. *Black Sleep* we shot there, too.

Lee Sholem did a good job of directing Pharaoh's Curse.
    In Hollywood they call him "Roll 'Em" Sholem, because he had cameras rolling all the time *[laughs]!* That picture was made in six days, and it really was a good horror picture. Again, Aubrey had developed a good script, and all the actors worked hard.

While the film's mummy looks good in close-ups, in long shots it resembles an old man in pajamas.
    [Laughs.] That's all we could afford! One hundred sixteen thousand dollars, what the hell could you do? By the way, every once in a while I still see the guy that played the mummy — he's in the State Department or something now! Every time he sees me, he hugs me and says, "See what you did to me? You got me out of acting!"

Unlike your other early horror films, Pharaoh's Curse *has a cast of comparative unknowns.*

We knew what we had to make it for, and that we couldn't afford to pay anybody who was *some*body any real money to be in it. Remember, our deal with UA was, as long as we could make our pictures for price, we'd just give them the title, the lead in the cast, and go on. On *Pharaoh's Curse* I think all we did was give them the title, 'cause at that cost they didn't care who was in it *[laughs]!* It could have been you or me.

How did Boris Karloff enjoy the location trip to Hawaii for Voodoo Island?

He had a ball, he really did. Again, he was the opposite of everything he was on the screen: He was very congenial, worked hard and loved it. We had signed him to a three-picture deal, at $25,000 each, and *Voodoo Island* was our first film with him. We lived very well over there in Hawaii: We stayed at the Cocoa Palms, on the island of Kauai, and Karloff had a nice bungalow. We did all the interiors there, too, because we couldn't afford to do it any other way — coming back and forth was out of the question, we couldn't afford the travel time between.

Two surprising things in Voodoo Island — *first, that actress Jean Engstrom plays a character who is clearly a lesbian. Did you have any trouble getting that past the censors?*

No, I don't think they understood it. And I don't know how much *we* understood it!

The other thing is, you shot a nude bathing scene for the foreign version.

We thought the foreign market would be able to play it, because nudity could be shown in France and several other countries. We planned on putting that scene in the foreign version, but everybody liked the picture the way it was and we weren't going to gain any mileage showing it, so we didn't use it.

Reginald LeBorg told us he was unhappy with the plant monsters used in Voodoo Island.

We had a fellow named Milt Rice who did those plants; he turned out to be one of the best special effects men in the business, and probably is still working. But, again, *money*. He did the best he could with 'em, and I think they made the point.

Effective musical scores helped Voodoo Island *and all the other pictures quite a lot.*

Les Baxter did the musical score for *Voodoo Island;* Les and Paul Dunlap did all our work. I think the music makes the horror work, so thank God for Les and Paul. You know what our deal would be? We'd give Les or Paul $5,000

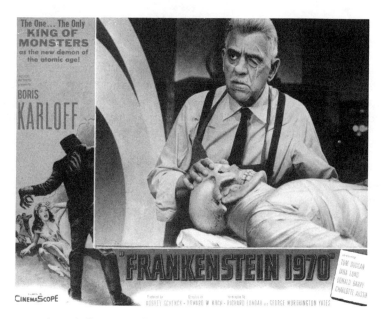

Boris Karloff as the disfigured monster maker in *Frankenstein 1970*.

and say, "Write the score, pay for the musicians, the stage and everything, and deliver the score to us." How the hell they ever did it, I don't know. Les did one of our Westerns, *The Yellow Tomahawk* [1954], in three hours—*three hours* on the music and scoring time! Today's guys get six weeks and $90,000 to do a score.

How did Frankenstein 1970 *come about?*

Remember, we had made the three-picture deal with Karloff—we didn't want to have to pay him, and *not* have a picture. We tried to make a deal to make this second Karloff film for United Artists, but they didn't like the idea. So Ed Zabel got ahold of the president of Allied Artists, a fellow by the name of Steve Broidy, and said, "Steve, would you put up the money for this picture? We'll get a CinemaScope lens, which is a selling point for the theaters, and we'll make it for $105,000." Allied Artists said okay, go.

We were making pictures at Warner Brothers around that time, 1957–'58. I had seen a fabulous set there at Warners from an Errol Flynn picture, *Too Much, Too Soon* [1958], and I knew it was still standing. I went to the production manager and said, "Would you give us this whole stage and the backlot for $20,000?" He said, "What are you, crazy? That set cost $90,000." I said, "Yeah, but it's all rigged and there it is, just sitting there." He said, "Let me talk to J.L." Well, J.L. [Jack L. Warner] happened to like me a lot, I guess because of the few pictures we had done there at Warners—*Untamed Youth* [1957] he *really* liked. He said, "Okay, what the hell, give it to 'em." So we paid them $20,000, Karloff $25,000; that left us $60,000 to make the picture. CinemaScope lenses we got from Twentieth Century–Fox for nothing 'cause Aubrey Schenck is a Schenck and Fox was Joe Schenck. I directed. Nine days' shooting—and I never had nine tougher days in my life, to do that picture in that time. I like directing—in fact, I enjoy directing more than producing—but as a director I don't feel I did such a great job on *Frankenstein 1970*, because I didn't have much time to really think.

By this point in his career, Karloff had begun indulging in a rather overdone, almost self-spoofing style of acting out his "heavy" roles. Did you encourage this broad playing?
    No, but it was very hard for me to direct him because he was really not directable. I was in awe of him, and we just let him go. At that time Boris Karloff had a standing in life, and whatever he did you thought was right, you were afraid to say it was wrong. I was *afraid* to say to him it was too much! That's not right, but again I tell you we weren't great talents, we were just try-ing to make movies. All I was really concerned about was schedule—which is not a good thing to admit, but I had the pressure of the fact that we couldn't go over the $105,000. I just was glad to get the scenes done.

Did Karloff present that problem for LeBorg on Voodoo Island?
    I think Reggie's a little tougher than I am; I think he stood up to Karloff a little bit. Reggie probably got it more the way he wanted it. He's a brilliant director, so overlooked in his life. And at this stage in his life he *still* wants to direct a picture! And I wouldn't be afraid to give him one.

Frankenstein 1970 *is an oppressively "indoorsy" picture, but there* are *several gruesome highlights.*
    In one scene, when Karloff transferred the heart from the living man to the monster, you could see that cow's heart and the blood going through the tubes. That heart looked just like chicken liver. I'd never had chicken liver for dinner. But that night when I came home my wife had chicken liver, and I damn near *died*. I couldn't eat after seeing that heart all day long! And remember when Karloff carried the body parts over to the garbage disposal, dropped them in and turned it on? When we showed that to the Code, they said, "You can't have that sound effect in there, you've got to take it out! Christ, it's the most gruesome thing we ever heard in our lives!" The sound effect now is way down from what it was when we showed it to them.

Now it sounds like a toilet flushing!
    Right! We had to get rid of our original, *crunching* sounds.

Shortly after Frankenstein 1970 *was completed, your third Karloff film,* King of the Monsters, *was announced, but it was never made.*

Zabel and Aubrey didn't live up to the agreement with Karloff. By that time I had left them and gone to work for Frank Sinatra's company. They never made a third picture *or* paid Karloff, and I think it was an unhappy relationship at the end. Maybe Karloff felt badly toward me, too, but as I said I had already gone on with Sinatra and was not responsible. I do think, unfortunately, that before he died Karloff was unhappy with us, that we hadn't lived up to our agreement.

You know, Aubrey Schenck and I made a horror picture that you might not see on our list of credits. I had a friend named William Castle — Bill and I grew up together in New York, where we lived right across the street from each other. One day he called me and said, "Howard, I've got the greatest idea in the world, but I'm afraid to tell it to anybody." I told him to come over to the office. He came over and said, "I want to make a picture like you guys do. I want to call it *Macabre,* and I want to make it with a hook. I got ahold of Lloyds of London, and I made a deal with them: Everybody that buys a ticket automatically gets a life insurance policy for $5,000 against death from fright by watching the picture. That'll be the campaign." I said, "That's the greatest idea I ever heard in my life." Aubrey and I produced it with him, but we didn't take any credit or pay because he had no money. We made the picture for $102,000, then we broke the story about how we would sell it. That's when Allied Artists bought it. All over the United States, the thing did business. *Macabre* grossed over a million dollars, and we all made a few bucks. Bill and I went on from there — I brought him to Paramount when I got in, and of course *Rosemary's Baby* and all those things developed.

Which one of these early horror films is your personal favorite?
Oh, I liked *Voodoo Island* the best. I enjoyed the experience, and the dealings with Karloff. And I like that picture's ambience — the background of the Hawaiian Islands. I just liked the look of it, and thought Reggie LeBorg did one hell of a job. I *love* that picture, I think it's a classic.

Whose idea was it to bring the novel The Manchurian Candidate *to the screen?*
[Sighs.] I wish I could say it was mine. I made a deal to run Frank Sinatra's company: Max Youngstein, an executive at United Artists, had recommended me because of all the pictures I had made for them. Frank, who was not a picturemaker, was supposed to make four pictures for UA, two with him and two without him, over a couple-year period. The day I met Frank he said, "Howard, there's this book I read, I love it, I want to do it. See if we can buy it. It's called *The Manchurian Candidate.*" So I tracked it down and found out that John Frankenheimer and George Axelrod had bought it. It took us a while to negotiate a deal with them as a package, George to produce and write it, John to direct it, and myself to be the executive producer — which *was* the producer, 'cause George was busy enough writing. Frankenheimer's career was

really just starting; this was his third or fourth picture, I think. He was a flamboyant, wonderful kind of kid.

What was your budget on that one?
The picture cost $2,200,000 in 1962—a *lot* of money. Of course, Frank got a million dollars himself, and Larry Harvey got $200,000. So we didn't have much left to make the picture.

One Communist newspaper speculated that Sinatra took the leading role to dispel rumors of his being a Red sympathizer.
Hogwash. Frank thought as an actor he had a chance to play a very confused kind of guy, a character who was brainwashed, had bad dreams, and finally managed to figure it all out. He thought that was a great acting challenge. And Frank worked harder in that picture than in any we had done before or since. He gave it everything he had. And Larry Harvey was a delight. Larry jumped in the lake in New York February 12, and it was twenty degrees above zero the day we shot that scene. I thought he'd die when he hit that water! He had all kinds of rubber clothes on underneath, but he was so shaken I think he drank a bottle of brandy in a minute.

Manchurian Candidate *is easily the most frightening film you've done.*
Oh, I would say so—God, yes. The whole idea of the power of Khigh Dhiegh, that the mind can be controlled—and it *can*, it's been proven. It's such a frightening thing.
I thought that picture was wonderful, and it's a cult favorite to this day. But UA didn't know what the hell to do with it. The word-of-mouth was good but unfortunately not strong enough. You know, that picture took fifteen years to get into profit!

How did you enjoy collaborating with the Disney organization on the recent fantasy film Dragonslayer?
You know, it's funny—we didn't have any real collaboration. The only time I ever saw anybody from Disney was at the preview *[laughs]!* Paramount was in control of the picture, and Disney put up 50 percent of whatever it cost. So the "collaboration" was really nil.

How much creative input did you have on the picture?
I got in so late that I didn't get into the picture until two days before shooting. Most of what I provided was advice and directions, so they wouldn't get themselves into positions they couldn't get out of. Our budget was $12,000,000; we went to $18,000,000. Most of it was because of the cost of the miniatures that were done by Industrial Light and Magic. Not that it was I.L.M.'s fault; it's just unfortunate that we got into heavy expense. I thought they did a fabulous job on the visuals.

Looking back, did you enjoy making the older pictures more than you enjoy working on your newer, "bigger" projects?

I did, absolutely. It was a different time of my life, it was fun, it was challenging as hell. And I guarantee you, those cheap pictures will stand up against any two-hour movie made today. There's more care and thought in them; even though they were low-budget, we really *cared* what we were making, we really *tried*. It was such a ball, and we had so much fun.

These kinds of shows are made as a collaborative effort.
Everyone did everything, which is a wonderful way to work;
I mean, everyone's totally involved, everyone cares.
Though they were seven-day shows and the titles were exploitative,
we wanted them to be the very best we could possibly make them.

—— *Bernard L. Kowalski* ——

YET ANOTHER SUCCESSFUL DIRECTOR who got his career going with the help of Roger Corman, Bernard Kowalski made two of Corman's most luridly titled and enjoyably cheap productions from the '50s: *Night of the Blood Beast* and *Attack of the Giant Leeches*. Although not as visibly successful as other Corman proteges like Francis Ford Coppola and Peter Bogdanovich, Kowalski went on to direct such films as *Krakatoa, East of Java* [1969] and *Macho Callahan* [1970], and, more significantly, to establish himself as an important figure in television with a long and impressive list of credits. To mention a select few, he directed the pilots for *Richard Diamond, N.Y.P.D.* and *The Monroes;* executive-produced *Baretta;* and was co-owner of *Mission: Impossible*. In 1973, he took a break from all his TV work to return to the horror genre with the entertaining thriller *SSSSSS.*

Kowalski got his first job in the movie business at the age of five as a Warner Bros. extra in Dead End Kids pictures, as well as such Errol Flynn vehicles as *Dodge City* and *Virginia City*. His experience behind the camera began at age sixteen when he worked as a clerk for his father, who was an assistant director and production manager. Early TV provided Kowalski's first opportunity to direct on such Western series as *Frontier* and *Boots and Saddles;* he then made the transition to feature-film directing in 1958 when he was hired by Gene Corman (Roger's brother) to make the teen exploitation feature *Hot Car Girl*.

How did working for Roger and Gene Corman compare to working at the larger studios, and in television?

It was a tremendous learning ground. I found that the Corman brothers were the type of producers who would make very tough deals with people in the sense of protecting *their* dollar investment. But I found them to be full of integrity and honesty. I know that no one worked harder than either Roger or Gene on whatever the project they were involved with. Their input was tremendous, and they were very tasteful gentlemen. I'm a big fan of both of them.

Volume upon volume has been written about Roger Corman and his films, but little mention is ever made of Gene. Can you tell us a little more about this lesser-known Corman?

Gene has a tremendous sense of humor, and he is a very highly competitive individual. He's an art connoisseur and a man of extremely fine taste. We were making these movies for sixty-five and seventy thousand dollars, and Gene would practically go to the hospital after each show, such was his total dedication and involvement. He's someone who does know film, does know costs, and is truly a class act.

Any guesses as to why he's been overshadowed by his older brother?

I think it's just that Roger started off and brought Gene into the company. Roger's was just a huge success. Later, Gene made a few attempts at producing

Previous page: Kowalski allied himself with the Corman brothers for his first science fiction effort, *Night of the Blood Beast*. Ross Sturlin flexes his talons in this posed shot.

other kinds of movies, and by that I mean a more expensive, major-feature type of film such as *Tobruk* and *F.I.S.T.*, which were near misses.

Did Roger have any creative input on Night of the Blood Beast *and* Attack of the Giant Leeches, *or was his involvement strictly financial?*
He was involved creatively *and* financially. Roger would supervise the shows, Gene was running the shows. It was an embryonic period for Gene in that area, and Roger, with more experience, was standing back and just guiding Gene as well as myself.

Did you have any choice of material during your time with the Cormans?
It was a matter of reading the material and then agreeing to do it or not. That was the only choice involved.

What were your budget and shooting schedule on Blood Beast?
Shooting schedule was seven days, budget was around $68,000. We shot *Blood Beast* in and around the Bronson Canyon area, and operated out of what was then the Chaplin Studios, which were on Sunset and LaBrea.

Did you have to do any rewriting of the Blood Beast *or* Giant Leeches *scripts, to make them fit in with the way you wanted to do them?*
We did some rewriting as we got into it. These kinds of shows are made as a collaborative effort. Everyone did everything, which is a wonderful way to work; I mean, everyone's totally involved, everyone cares. Though they were seven-day shows and the titles were exploitative, we wanted them to be the very best we could possibly make them. For instance, Danny Haller, who's been directing for some time now, was the art director, and he would pull a trailer onto the sound stage and sleep there, and do a lot of the sawing and hammering himself. It was tremendous fun, because everyone was just doing their best.

The Blood Beast *screenplay was reminiscent at times of Howard Hawks'* The Thing from Another World, *and also used elements from the earlier Corman films* It Conquered the World *and* Attack of the Crab Monsters. *Were these films drawn upon for inspiration?*
I'm sure that the writers were aware of them — we all were. I did not sit down and write with them, but to my knowledge those were probably springboard ideas. I don't think that the writers were intentionally imitative.

Conversely, the 1979 film Alien *seems derivative of your* Blood Beast *and another '50s film,* It! The Terror from Beyond Space.
I'm sure that the same kind of thing happened with that. There were pieces here and there that were springboarding ideas.

What's your reaction when a film like Alien *borrows elements from your early pictures and becomes a huge success?*
You're pleased that you were right in what you were attempting to do. I personally harbor no angers within me. I know it's a creative field and that there are many ways of doing the same thing. Sometimes they're better and sometimes they're not. I thought *Alien* was quite good.

Did you have any say in the casting of these films?
I cast them with the Cormans, who were using a lot of the people that they normally used — an ensemble group. I was happy to use them. If there was anyone I didn't want, I would not be forced to work with them.

What can you tell us about Michael Emmet, who starred in both Blood Beast *and* Giant Leeches?
Michael Emmet and I had worked together on the series *Boots and Saddles;* he was a regular on it, and I had experienced maybe eight of the thirteen shows with Michael having a major role. He was a good, hard-working actor. Coming over to the Corman shows after having worked with Michael, I thought that he was a leading man type that we could afford. I have not kept up the relationship with Michael through the years, so I am not in a position to say where he is now, but he was always just terrific to work with and a thorough gentleman. I still see Ed *[Night of the Blood Beast]* Nelson every now and then; Ed was somebody that was always working very hard, a very decent person and a family-man type of guy. Ed did so many of the Corman pictures, he was a valuable part of the ensemble group.

The alien monster costume seen in Blood Beast *was left over from a previous Corman,* Teenage Caveman.
To save money, the Cormans would often utilize anything that was existing, and incorporate it into one of their new films. One of the philosophies that they approached their filmmaking with was, whenever they could minimize their risk, they had a better chance to have a financial success. So if they had expensive costumes already made, they would try and doctor 'em up; if there were standing sets at the Chaplin Studios from another film, they would paint 'em a different color. A very heads-up approach to being practical in the dollar area.

Did you have a better budget and shooting schedule on Attack of the Giant Leeches?
Giant Leeches went eight days, and that was about $70,000. It was the same general crew as *Blood Beast,* with everybody pitching in together. Now, looking back, there was a funny example of that on *Giant Leeches.* When you're shooting with your camera platform from the water to the shore, you get a water raft that you put your equipment and your people on. It's a rather

Divers (Ken Clark, left; unidentified, right) defend themselves against mutated swamp creatures (Guy Buccola and Ross Sturlin in suits made of raincoat material) in Kowalski's *Attack of the Giant Leeches.*

cumbersome and awkward thing, and it requires somebody *in* the water to propel it.

We were out on a water raft at the Pasadena Arboretum, and I turned to the grips on the show and said, "Push me across to that area over there." They said that Gene Corman wouldn't pay the water rate and that, though they were friends of mine, they just weren't going to get in the water. I understood that and I didn't blame them. So I turned to my brother, who was the script clerk on the show—we both had our bathing suits on—and I said, "Let's go." So while I was directing the show, the two of us were pushing the water raft that day. Later, I went to Gene and said, "Pay these guys the water rate tomorrow. I'm through pushing that raft all over." The next morning Gene was there, took off his clothes, got his bathing suit on, jumped in and pushed the raft all day. He didn't think it was right that he should have to pay the grips more money to get in the water, so the principle of the thing was involved. And I say, Gene would go out and spend $250 for dinner, but instead of giving in to their position, he just did triple-duty all day. And *again,* at the end of the show, Gene, who was so involved and worked twenty-two hours a day, went into the hospital for three or four days, just to get himself healthy, before he'd come back and finish the movie up in postproduction.

We shot all the swamp scenes at this Pasadena Arboretum, a beautiful refuge for ducks and geese. The interiors were done at the Chaplin Studios. The underwater scenes were done in a private home in Studio City. It had a private pool with a viewing glass; we would dress it up with plants and things, then bring the actors in and shoot the underwater scenes there.

Didn't you have some sort of mishap with one of the studio tanks?
We were shooting some scenes on a sound stage, with the leech actors coming out a three-foot tank and into a cavelike area, when the tank *collapsed.* The danger was not of anybody being in the tank or of us possibly getting a little wet, but it happened while all the lights were hot and everything was on. Had anyone been holding onto something and gotten water on them, we could've had an accident. We were all really very fortunate that no one got electrocuted.

Were you happy with the leech costumes used in the film?
No. The two actors playing the leeches were Guy Buccola, a basketball player from U.C.L.A., and Ross Sturlin, a young man that had done stunts on *Boots and Saddles* and played the alien in *Blood Beast.* These two fellows were forced to build the leech costumes in order to get the job. They *were* paid money for the building of them, but the job did come "with costumes." They were made out of cheap, rubberized raincoat material, sewed in a capelike form. Very little money was spent on them, they were always tearing, so as a result they did have a number of problems in trying to maintain the look. Of course, when we'd go underwater, that was difficult because they'd get air pockets in the suit.

You can also see their legs and flippers protruding from the suits.
It was the best that we could do with the time that we had. Unfortunately, on a seven-day feature like that, you don't have an awful lot of time once you've started to make these kinds of corrections. To go back to your original question, "Were you happy with them," in no way were they totally satisfactory at all.

Part of Giant Leeches' *appeal springs from Yvette Vickers' presence in the cast.*
All of us doing the show were really impressed with her, because she had been a *Playboy* centerfold, and we understood why—she had a gorgeous figure. She was hard-working, willing to do whatever she had to do, including some things she didn't like, like going underwater and being dragged around. She was a first-class trouper and a good actress, and someone that we were very happy to be working with. I could say nothing but positive things about her. I worked with her later on *M Squad,* and I saw her again several years ago when I was executive producer on *Baretta* and she was doing one of the episodes.

The grimmest scenes in Giant Leeches—*or, for that matter, in any horror film from that era—are those in which the leeches attach themselves to their victims*

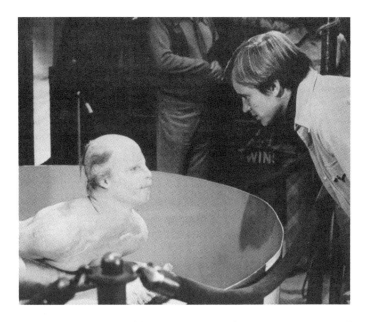

Dirk Benedict marvels at the sideshow snake-man in Kowalski's 1973 sci-fi chiller *SSSSSSS.*

and suck their blood. Did you have any trouble getting those scenes past the censors?
Not really. In those days, Roger and Gene Corman would deal with the censors. They were very effective, total film buffs who knew what the censors had allowed other people to do. They would be about the finest representatives in that area that you could have. They would know what limitations had been imposed on most of the shows that were out, and then they would fight for parity.

How did SSSSSSS come about?
It was an original story idea that Dan Striepeke had; Dan had been a makeup artist, and he and John Chambers were credited with *Planet of the Apes*. Dan went to see Dick Zanuck, and Zanuck had responded to the story. It ended up being the first movie that Zanuck and David Brown made at Universal.

And that's where the film was shot?
We did it entirely at Universal — the backlot and a few of the street areas around it; back near the *Psycho* house; we used the *Virginian* ranch as Strother Martin's place. We shot it, I think, in about twenty-two days.

And your budget?
Since we made it at Universal, with their overhead factors and everything

else, it came to $1,030,000. We had high hopes for *SSSSSS;* we owned a good piece of it, so there was a chance to be in a profit participation basis that might have proved quite lucrative. We've never really received any money on it in the way of profits, but that's a tough thing to do at a major studio. It was quite well received in Europe.

Were you happy with the unusual title, SSSSSS (Don't Say It, Hiss It)?

Yes. I found it to be a title that created a lot of word-of-mouth. Part of how the title came up was, Dan Striepeke and I went to the Hermosa Beach Reptile Emporium during our initial investigation on cobras. The store owner pulled a cobra out—a totally poisonous, lethal cobra—and put it down at his feet. He was between us and the cobra, but it was a very small room, and we heard the sound that it made. That's where we picked up the title of the show. It worked for us.

Did you enjoy working on this one as much as you did the Cormans?

We had a good time making it. Dan Striepeke was a very bright, honest man, full of integrity; Zanuck and Brown were wonderful to work with, thorough gentlemen who had a lot of input; and Strother Martin was just a wonderful human being, a lovely actor and a very funny man.

Did the snakes present any threat during production?

We had a hundred and fifty-five reptiles, and of that, we had like sixty or seventy that were lethal. The King Cobra that we used was absolutely *regal* in the sense that it didn't make mistakes twice. All the other snakes would hit the glass any time you'd go near them, but the King Cobra did it *once,* and then he'd just *look* at you. There were a lot of silly, fun things that we shouldn't have done but we did. The very first day, for instance, I said to my assistant Gordon Webb, "I want you to tell everybody here there'll be no games, no playing around. We're in a position where it could be dangerous, and we'll deal very heavily with anyone that fools around with this." Well, he makes this speech, and the minute he gets done somebody throws a rubber snake at him and he screams at the top of his lungs! *That* was the end of it; after that, everyone was doing terrible things to everybody else all the way through.

One story I enjoy telling on Dick Zanuck: Dick, who was very athletic, very much his own man, would come up to the set every day to offer his comments on dailies, but he never got too close to the snakes. So one of the young snake trainers, who didn't know or care who anybody was, walked up to him and said, "You're one of the big shots with the company, huh?" And Dick said, "Well, I'm the executive producer." And the kid came back, "You're also scared shitless of the snakes, huh?" Dick just looked at him. The kid went on, "Yeah, I could tell. You haven't come anywhere near 'em, and you get away as fast as you can." Dick is the type of person that would swing on someone who would call him that, but he got in his limousine and left. He came back in two hours, walked up to this kid and said, "Put the boa constrictor around my neck." The kid looked at him and said, "You had a couple of drinks, huh?" Dick said, "Uh-huh. Put the boa around my neck." And so they did it. That was kind of fun.

What precautions did you take to safeguard your cast and crew against the snakes?

We had a doctor there at all times, in case anyone had gotten bit by accident. I'd had all of the people that were going to be dealing with the snakes exposed to the hazards, dangers and limitations of the snakes prior to our filming. Everyone was informed as to what we *could* fool around with and what we *couldn't* fool around with. We had no problems, I'm very pleased to say.

One of the highlights of SSSSSSS *is the effective makeup on Dirk Benedict.*

It was done by the best people in the makeup business, Dan Striepeke and John Chambers. At that time they were the very finest — they were Academy Award winners. Dirk Benedict was very patient — some of that makeup that they put on him took six to eight hours to apply. He was a wonderful person, by the way, a super guy. Heather Menzies and he were a wonderful team. It was a little family; all the way through working the picture, we did everything together, Strother and them, all of us. We shared all the good and bad moments.

The most disappointing thing about SSSSSSS *is its too-abrupt, let's-get-this-thing-done ending. Was that a last-minute, money-saving measure?*

No, that *was* the original writing. We didn't know where to go with it from the time that Dirk Benedict was killed. Being of the genre that it was, the intent was to go out on the girl, Heather Menzies, screaming, and the terror of it. I can appreciate where you feel that it was abrupt. Obviously, in some senses, it didn't work for us, but that was *not* done through an economy-cut process.

Which is your personal favorite of the three horror/sci-fi films you directed?

The most recent one, *SSSSSSS,* because the memories are more alive and fresher for me. I'm a giant fan of Strother Martin, and it was one of the latter experiences he had in films. He was such a joy to work with.

*There was a rivalry going on between
Lon Chaney and Bela Lugosi from the Universal days
when they both played Dracula. You see, Lugosi
was the great Dracula, but then something happened
at Universal and they gave the part* [Son of Dracula] *to Chaney.
It came out on* The Black Sleep:
*Chaney was sore at something Lugosi brought up
and it nearly came to a fight. Chaney
picked him up a little bit, but put him down —
we stopped him. We kept them apart quite a bit.*

—————— *Reginald LeBorg* ——————

LOOKING BACK over a career which has spanned a full half-century and encompassed hundreds of credits, Reginald LeBorg is understandably discontent with his too-close identification with "monster movies." He is quick to point out the many different genres his career has embraced, from comedies to musicals and Westerns, as well as the many different positions he has held within the industry itself; to be remembered primarily for films such as *Calling Dr. Death, Jungle Woman, The Black Sleep* and *Diary of a Madman* seems somewhat of an injustice that perplexes and amuses the octogenarian director. Nonetheless, only a handful of directors can equal his output and longevity within the genre (from 1934's *Life Returns* to 1973's *So Evil, My Sister),* and no other director could claim to have worked with as many of the famous horror personages that LeBorg has known. His contribution to the genre is unique and unmatched.

The oldest of three sons, Reginald LeBorg was born in Vienna in 1902. He majored in political economy at the University of Austria and studied musical composition for a year at Arnold Schoenberg's Composition Seminar. His education completed, LeBorg entered his father's banking business and, acting as the senior LeBorg's representative, he traveled to Prague, Hamburg and Paris to transact family business negotiations. During his extended two-year stay in Paris, he studied at the Sorbonne. In the mid–'20s LeBorg traveled to New York to dispose of a collection of paintings in his father's behalf. Remaining in New York, he was employed in several banks and brokerage houses and at an advertising agency. The stock market crash of 1929 wiped out the LeBorg family fortune, and Reginald's interest in the financial world waned. He returned to Europe and his first love, the stage. He worked at the Max Reinhardt School in Vienna, and later devoted much of his time to directing operas and musical comedies for provincial houses throughout Central Europe.

Arriving on the Hollywood scene in the early '30s, LeBorg appeared as an extra in pictures at Paramount and Metro and later staged opera sequences in the Grace Moore hits *One Night of Love* and *Love Me Forever,* as well as other films with operatic themes at Fox, Paramount and United Artists. After a number of second unit assignments at Metro, Goldwyn and Selznick, LeBorg joined Universal, where he turned out band shorts. An eighteen-month hitch with the United States Army interrupted his Hollywood career, which resumed in 1943 with his return to Universal and his promotion to feature film director.

How did you become involved on 1934's Life Returns?

I met the producer, Dr. Eugene Frenke, socially, we started to talk and he told me about the story. I began to point out to him things that I thought were wrong with the story and to offer suggestions, and he asked me if I wanted to write a little bit. He gave me the story and I started to do the screenplay. I didn't do very much on it; I worked only a couple of weeks, a couple of things that I did *he* didn't like. So we had disagreements and so forth.

In 1943 your Hollywood background was largely confined to musical comedies and shorts. How did Universal happen to assign you to The Mummy's Ghost?

Previous page: LeBorg strolls with horror great Lon Chaney, Jr., on the Universal backlot as they discuss their upcoming joint project *The Mummy's Ghost.*

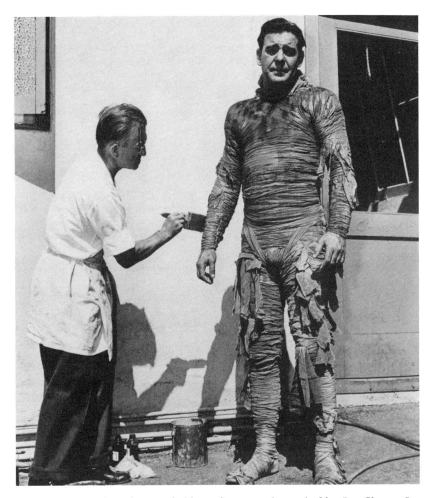

Makeup wizard Jack P. Pierce works his magic on an unhappy-looking Lon Chaney, Jr., in this behind-the-scenes shot from LeBorg's *The Mummy's Ghost.*

The first feature I made at Universal was an overgrown short musical, *She's for Me* [1943]; it had no stars in it, just their stock players. I was supposed to get a comedy afterwards, because I had some comedy in *She's for Me* and Universal liked it very much. Ben Pivar, an associate producer at Universal, had a director assigned to *The Mummy's Ghost*—I don't know who the man was— but I think he had an accident or something, and they had nobody there right then to take his place. Pivar seemed to like me and he said, "How 'bout reading the script?"

What was it like working with Lon Chaney, Jr., in the heyday of his career?

Chaney, Jr., in complete makeup for *The Mummy's Ghost*. (Photo courtesy Steve Jochsberger.)

Well, I *liked* him, he was a nice guy. The only thing is, of course—he drank.

What sort of problems did his drinking create?
No problems, I just had to change my way of shooting. I shot with him mostly in the morning—I tried to get everything in up to 2:00. Then he had his lunch and started on the bottle. He couldn't shake it.

There was a scene in *The Mummy's Ghost* where Frank Reicher brewed tana leaves and inadvertently attracted the Mummy. Chaney limped into the room and Reicher backed against the wall. Chaney's hand went up to Reicher's throat and squeezed so forcefully that Reicher nearly *fainted*. Reicher was an old man, and frail, and Chaney got carried away. Reicher cried out, "He nearly *killed* me! He took my breath away!" After the shooting, I took Chaney to one side and said, "Look, Lon — don't *do* that. . .!" He said okay, but I could tell that he was very happy about it. Chaney always was very — I don't want to say rough, but — he *was* an action man. It was doing it like his father would have done — he was trying to emulate Chaney, Sr., or better him.

In another scene, Chaney broke into a museum at night to steal the body of the Princess Ananka. After a scuffle with a guard, he was supposed to crash through some plate glass doors. I didn't want to endanger an actor by having him go through glass, so I told the prop department to install breakaway glass. The prop man forgot to give the order, and the next day we arrived on the set and the job wasn't done — it was still plate glass. I told Chaney, "Look, the plate glass is still here and I don't want to hold up production. Just push the door open with your foot or elbow." He didn't say anything, he just nodded his head. And when it came time to do the shot, he went *right through* the plate glass. He even injured his hand — of course the Mummy is fully bandaged, but even through the bandages glass penetrated and there *was* a little blood. I said, "See what you did?!" and he said, "I wanted to show you that I had the courage." He was trying to show off his bravura.

In a mid-'60s interview, Chaney said that the Mummy was his least favorite monster role of that era.

Well, sure, because Chaney wanted to act, and the only thing that he invented for the Mummy was the walk — which was very good, incidentally.

What about rumors that Chaney allowed a stand-in to take his place throughout much of the production?

Chaney never had a stand-in during *The Mummy's Ghost*. He was doing it himself, all the time. He may have done this in some of the other *Mummy* pictures but he didn't do it with me. In fact, I baited him a little bit — he wanted to do a picture as a gentleman, and in our next picture, *Calling Dr. Death*, he played in an excellent wardrobe, had a mustache and he was a dandy.

John Carradine really hammed it up as the new High Priest.

Yes, but considering the character he played it wasn't too much of a fault. There were no heavies in that picture other than him — Chaney was no heavy, playing that poor mummy — so we had to have somebody fill that slot. Carradine's voice was sonorous and excellent, much better than the average actor's, so I let him go on. In a picture like that you *can* be a little hammy — it was usually kids and teenagers that went to see that kind of picture.

The role of Amina/Ananka was originally assigned to Acquanetta. Why was she replaced by Ramsay Ames?

In the morning of the first day of shooting [August 23, 1943], Acquanetta was on the set at 9:00 but she was walking very awkwardly—she was scared, I think because this was her second or third film. In the second shot, she was supposed to walk from a lawn, up a couple of stairs and into a house. She slipped and fell, and hit her head, and for half an hour she was unconscious. They took her to the dispensary and gave her smelling salts—she was all right, but she had a slight concussion. Pivar didn't want to take any chances, so the role was recast with Ramsay Ames.

Were you satisfied with the performance Ramsay Ames gave on such short notice?
No, no, no—it was very bad. She was not a very good actress. She later developed, but again, as with Acquanetta, this was her first or second picture.

Did you have any say in the casting of these early pictures?
No, unfortunately, none at all. I got all the stock company. I could only complain. And I wasn't very well liked by some of the people there for that reason—the executives said I was a complainer and a tough guy to work with. There's an old Latin proverb that says, *"De mortuis nil nisi bonum"* ("About the dead, speak only the good"), and Ben Pivar is dead—but I had a lot of run-ins with him.

One of the weak points of The Mummy's Ghost *screenplay is that Kharis is introduced simply wandering out of the woods, with no explanation of how he survived the* Mummy's Tomb *fire or where he spent the years between.*
To me, that seemed ridiculous at first; in fact, I had a fight with Pivar about it. I said to him, "There's no reason! We have to have a motivation!" He said, "Motivation? We've made two *Mummy* pictures already and the Mummy *always* comes out of the woods! Just *shoot* it!" I said, "Well, let me try and find a motivation." So I ran the old *Mummy* films, including the original one that Karl Freund made, and in one of them I found a long shot where a frocked man with a fez goes into an Egyptian temple in Memphis. So I said, "Let's have a scene where John Carradine, the caretaker of the Mummy, goes in there and gets an order to hunt for the Mummy." Pivar liked that idea, and so we took that one long shot, made a negative dub, put it in my picture, and then I shot close-ups in the temple with Carradine and George Zucco as the High Priest. Pivar liked it.

Did you have a hand in the writing of your other pictures?
Every one I did, because I pride myself on being a writer, too. I find a lot of scripts pretty much the same as the others—too much *déjà vu*.

We've always liked the surprising finale of Mummy's Ghost, *with the heroine sinking into the quicksand in Kharis' arms.*

We discussed the finale with Pivar and I said, "Why not let Ananka sink with the Mummy? Why should there always be a happy ending?" Somebody else said, "No, we might make a sequel." I told him, "The Mummy is *always* coming up—Ananka doesn't have to!"

So that downbeat ending was your idea?
It was a steal from the Frank Capra picture *Lost Horizon* [1937], so I can't take all the credit for it. I did take time to shoot it—it took me two or three hours to shoot that climactic chase when I should have only had one shot. I took shots from the back and from the front, shots of the feet and the hands and all that sort of thing. Ramsay Ames was Ananka at the beginning, but after that it was her stand-in, who we dressed the same way and put the makeup on. Incidentally, I shot that chase differently than what Pivar was used to. Chases always ran left-to-right, left-to-right, all the time. I mixed it around. When Pivar saw the rushes, he started to fight with me! He said, "How could you shoot it this way? This has to be a progression!" I went into a cutting room with a cutter and after I pieced it together it was a beautiful chase. Pivar was very satisfied and he asked me to direct his next picture.

That next picture was Calling Dr. Death?
Right. Pivar had confidence in me because I was a fighter who tried to get better and better material. Pivar was sometimes afraid that I would go over budget, but whenever he saw that I *was* on budget, he didn't worry anymore—he stayed in his office and played gin rummy.
Calling Dr. Death was supposed to start a series of *Inner Sanctum* films, *if* it hit. Universal had an option on further stories. We did *Calling Dr. Death* and it got very good reviews.

When Universal initially mapped out the Inner Sanctum *series, they announced that Lon Chaney and Gale Sondergaard would co-star in* Calling Dr. Death *and in all further installments. As it turned out, Sondergaard never appeared in a single one!*
I don't know whether this was the real cause of it or not, but she was a leftist and she and her husband were shooting off their mouths quite often. The war was still going on, of course. Executives there at Universal may have decided to recast it—but I can't be sure, I was not in on any such conference. I just heard one day that she was out, and that they were going to cast somebody else—that's all. They didn't say why, you could only speculate. It happened later on that she *did* find it difficult to get work, and then it *was* due to that situation.

Screenwriter Edward Dein, who wrote Calling Dr. Death, *told us that Chaney could not cope with some of the complicated scientific dialogue that he was asked to deliver in the picture, and that the "stream-of-consciousness" voice-over narration was the result of his inability.*

We had to do a little bit of simplification, that's true, but I think it was not only Chaney but Pivar also. Pivar was very, very crude, not very intelligent, and he couldn't read very well.

Was there a more conscious effort on your part to stylize Calling Dr. Death *as opposed to the other films you directed in this series?*
I put a few different visual effects in there which were absolutely fresh at that time. In one sequence, I had the camera *become* Lon Chaney, with everybody else looking *into* the camera. That's the sequence where Chaney is brought to the house where the wife was murdered—the reporters look into the camera as it moves forward into the house; then J. Carrol Naish, playing the detective, also addresses the camera. Then, the camera pans down to the floor where the coroner is examining the body. The whole sequence was shot this way until Lon Chaney is accused, and *then* you see his face. That was one sequence in the whole film which I thought was a novelty at that time. It was so fresh and new that when Robert Montgomery, who was also directing at that time, saw *Calling Dr. Death* he made a whole picture this way—

Lady in the Lake! *[1946.]*
And that was a *flop!* For one sequence that was all right, but it couldn't sustain an entire film. One critic wrote about *Lady in the Lake* that it was a copy of *Calling Dr. Death* but Montgomery made the mistake of doing the whole picture that way.

In your second Inner Sanctum, Weird Woman, *Evelyn Ankers is cast against type in the role of the sinister Ilona. Was she pleased with the opportunity to play a villainess for a change?*
Evelyn Ankers was a very sweet girl and a very good actress, but no, she wasn't very happy about her part in *Weird Woman*. She was a good friend of Anne Gwynne's, and she had to play Gwynne's enemy in *Weird Woman*—to torment her—and they even had to have a fight at one point because they were competing for Lon Chaney in the film. When Ankers had a scene with Gwynne that was rather macabre, she couldn't do it very well because she loved Gwynne so much that she *couldn't* be mean to her. I gave her a few pointers, and after three or four takes she did it very well.

In preparing Weird Woman, *did you read the original Fritz Leiber story* Conjure Wife?
No, I only read the script. I got the script on a Friday and was told to start shooting a week from Monday. So I had to read it over the weekend and then come in and prepare. That was the norm at Universal: sometimes you'd get two or three weeks in between, if they had no script, but sometimes they had to rush these things out. Of course, me being a hard worker and a fast worker, they gave me the dirt—when they had something they wanted done fast, they rushed me in.

Lon Chaney learns the hard way that acid is no substitute for eyewash in *Dead Man's Eyes,* a Universal *Inner Sanctum* mystery.

Your third and last Inner Sanctum, Dead Man's Eyes, *boasted no supernatural elements, but it* is *an effective B mystery.*

I think so, too, because I like stories that have a basis in medical fact. I think *Dead Man's Eyes* did have pace, and Paul Kelly was very good in it.

What did Lon Chaney think of your leaving the Inner Sanctum series?

At the beginning Chaney thought I would be his *pal,* and when after three *Inner Sanctums* I wanted to do a musical — a Deanna Durbin picture or something — he said to me, "You traitor! We were supposed to do big things together!" I told him, "We'll get together again, don't worry."

Part ape and part woman, Acquanetta contemplates some unsightly leg hairs in this posed shot from *Jungle Woman*.

How did you like working with your Mummy's Ghost *casualty, Acquanetta, on* Jungle Woman?
    She was a nice-looking girl, but she had a squeaky, high-pitched voice. A lower-class Maria Montez. Again, as with Ramsay Ames, she developed a little later, after a few pictures, but unfortunately...

You had to have her at the beginning!
    [Laughs.] Right! At that time, the casting couch was important for the women players, especially for the young starlets. They were put on short money contracts—if they made out, fine; if they didn't, they were let go after six months or a year. In the meantime, the producers had a nice interlude.

What hurt Jungle Woman, *more than Acquanetta's performance, is its surprisingly weak script.*
It was an atrocious script, and a silly idea anyway. But, again, I was under contract. If I had refused it, I would have been suspended without pay, and I wouldn't have gotten *anything* good any more. You had to play ball with the front office.

Jungle Woman *is such a short film, and it uses so much stock footage from* Captive Wild Woman, *you must have been able to get it "in the can" in a very short time.*
I think we made it in one week. Most of these pictures were done in ten days, and this was practically done in seven.

One interesting aspect of the screenplay is its tendency to suggest the presence of the Ape Woman through shadows, moving bushes and branches, etc., and not show the monster until the film's closing seconds.
I tried that especially, because I think you have more suspense that way. If you'd seen the Ape Woman immediately, you wouldn't care about it any more. The story was so bad, I felt I had to do *something* — if I gave it away in the first reel, I would have no more picture.

Were you inspired to do that by the Val Lewton films that were being made at RKO at the time?
Well, I knew Val Lewton very well, and I wanted to work with him, but we never got together. Naturally I saw his pictures and they were good, and there *was* an inspiration, there's no doubt about that. I think that was the only way to make the script palatable.

Was The Black Sleep *conceived as an all-star horror show?*
No. When the script came to me, we had no idea what the cast would be like. Howard W. Koch and Aubrey Schenck, the executive producers, told me they were negotiating for Basil Rathbone and Lon Chaney.

With its all-star cast, The Black Sleep *seems a poorly structured film: Rathbone gets the only sizable role, the others are left to fight for the crumbs.*
Well, Basil Rathbone had a big name. John Carradine was getting old; Chaney was already a sick man — drinking, you know; and Bela Lugosi was practically a wreck, under the influence of drugs. He had a man with him continuously who had to hold him up.

Lugosi's biographers claim that he had been cured of drug addiction by that time and appeared a healthy man.
He was in very, very bad shape. He died a year later.

Were Chaney and Lugosi given mute parts because of their health problems?

Lon's character wasn't mute, he was brain-damaged. And Lugosi's tongue was supposedly cut out so that he couldn't speak, either. The funny thing was that Lugosi came to me all the time asking, "Herr Director, give me more to do—I do not speak!" I laughed, "Well, your tongue is cut out, I *can't* give you more, you can't speak!" He said, "Give me more lines! I've got to do more!" I told him, "You *can't* do more—you're Basil Rathbone's valet, and all you can do is stand next to him and nod." Finally, I compromised: I told him I'd put him into some shots where Rathbone was speaking. So when Rathbone had a discussion with Akim Tamiroff, I put Lugosi in there with them. And he started to *grimace,* while Rathbone spoke—that spoiled the shot! But to placate Lugosi, I took a couple of close-ups of him, knowing they would end up on the cutting room floor. But that satisfied him, and he thanked me.

Lugosi was quoted on the set as saying, "There is Basil Rathbone playing my part. I used to be the big cheese. Now I'm playing just a dumb part."

That's possible. But even Basil Rathbone played better parts than *The Black Sleep*—he was a leading man. Even the greatest stars get old and play character parts when they had played lovers before. That was typical silliness for Lugosi, to be petulant like that.

There was no antagonism between the members of the cast, but each one wanted to steal the scene from the others. When they were together in a scene, each one tried to overact, and I had to hold them down because that would have spoiled the picture. At the end, when the monsters escape into the tower with Carradine shouting, "Kill! Kill! Kill!" they were all overacting in some way, but I let it go because it was an exciting scene and the end of the picture, and there had to be retribution against the mad doctor [Rathbone].

Is is true that, one day on the set, Chaney grabbed Lugosi and hoisted him up in the air over his head?

There was—I won't say *hate*—but a rivalry going on between Chaney and Lugosi from the Universal days when they both played Dracula. You see, Lugosi was the great Dracula, but then something happened at Universal and they gave the part to Chaney *[Son of Dracula]*. There was a terrible rivalry between them before I even arrived at Universal. It came out on *The Black Sleep:* Chaney was sore at something Lugosi brought up and it nearly came to a fight. Chaney picked him up a little bit, but put him down—we stopped him. We kept them apart quite a bit.

Chaney was physically effective as the afflicted Mongo, but his performance was awfully derivative.

Chaney used the walk he had developed on his own for the *Mummy* films, and his whining was from the one good part he had—Lennie in *Of Mice and*

Men [1939]. Lennie became part of him—he was Lennie in a lot of pictures where he shouldn't have been. Whenever there was a petulant scene, he became Lennie again.

Many horror fans are put off by the way The Black Sleep *tries to pass off Akim Tamiroff as a top horror star, even though this was his first genre credit.*
He played Odo, the gypsy, and was supposed to act as comic relief from the horror. He played it very well. We tried to get Peter Lorre for that part, but he wanted too much money. If Lorre had been in it, we would have built the part up.

Herbert Rudley played the part of the young doctor. After the shooting, he showed me one of his own stories, which was well written, and I showed him one of mine. I asked him if he would like to collaborate with me, he said he would love to, and together we wrote a script, as yet unfilmed. It's called *The Flesh and the Spirit,* and it's a new slant on the Mary Magdalene story. It tells how Mary of Magdala and Levi of Jerusalem met when they were teenagers and fell in love.

Where was The Black Sleep *shot?*
It was shot right in the Ziv Studio, the whole thing. The budget was around $200,000, give or take ten. I wanted to do that picture in color; in color it would have made five times as much money. I asked, but they couldn't afford it. It would have cost about 20 percent more.

Did you also have a hand in the Black Sleep *screenplay?*
I always try to bring out the motivation for someone who is "bad"—*why* does he do it? Rathbone played a doctor who mutilated people by experimenting with their brains. The average horror picture does the horror and doesn't explain why. So I wrote the scene where Rathbone vows to his comatose wife that he is going to do everything he can to bring her back to life, even if he has to kill people to do it. You *have* to get empathy for a person like that. I think the scene helped the picture because it gave him stature—he wasn't just a madman. Later on *[laughs],* Aubrey Schenck told me that the writer, John C. Higgins, was furious that I didn't call and consult with him. In fact, I did call him, but he wasn't available so I left a message. He never called back.

One of the best-remembered scenes in Black Sleep *has Rathbone and Herbert Rudley operating on the sailor, peeling back his scalp to expose the brain.*
I called a neurosurgeon and asked him to be technical advisor. He told me exactly how to do it and that, when the brain is exposed, it seeps fluid. So we had a special effects man put a sponge and a hose beneath the operating table and, on cue, he had to squeeze the fluid out of the sponge through the hose and out the brain. That was a different type of horror—it wasn't bloody, as they do it now.

Did anyone ever consider engaging Boris Karloff to play a role in The Black Sleep?

No, I don't think so. I think Karloff was out of the country at the time. I did enjoy working with him on *Voodoo Island* very much. He was not only a wonderful actor, but also a gentleman, very well educated.

Did working on an essentially all-outdoor film like Voodoo Island *present any problem for Karloff?*

No, because the weather was very nice in Hawaii—very mild. It was all shot on Kauai. There was a strip of land in a certain garden there where the flora in each direction was different. All we had to do was turn the camera, and there was a different location. So it was done very economically and efficiently. The budget was, I think, about $150,000.

What about the nude scene that you shot for the foreign version?

Jean Engstrom was playing a character who was supposedly a bit of a lesbian. In the dialogue it wasn't obvious, because we weren't allowed to do it at the time, but there *was* an intimation that she wanted to make it with Beverly Tyler, who played Karloff's secretary. So we had Engstrom swimming in the nude. At that time, we had censorship, but in Europe they allowed nudity.

How did the scene come out?

It didn't come out as well as we had wanted. She said she'd do it, but when the time came she was afraid she wasn't sufficiently well built. I guess we should have looked at her first *[laughs]!* She put on false bosoms and a type of bathing suit that, when it got wet, looked like skin. So it *looked* like she was nude, but she wasn't. Naturally it never looked as good as it could have.

The man-eating plants in Voodoo Island *were also unconvincing.*

The special effects man showed us in a pool in Hollywood how these plants could wind themselves around the feet and legs of swimmers. It wasn't too good an effect, and I told him it had to be better. He said he knew then how they worked and that when we got to Hawaii it would be all fixed. They *never* worked very well at all.

Your next fantasy film was The Flight That Disappeared, *a preachy science fiction meller.*

I'd agree with that. It was a good idea that could have been developed—it was a "message picture." It could have been much bigger, with more money, but it was done in eight days, on a budget that was nothing. It was just an idea that somebody brought in and said, "We can make a cheap picture that has something to say." I like to make pictures with something to say, so I accepted it.

A brutal and graphic knife attack was a high point of LeBorg's *Diary of a Madman* starring Vincent Price and Nancy Kovack.

How would you have improved it with extra money?

We built a set that was just a platform, with smoke and mist around it. With more money, I could have built a bigger set, had more characters in the plane, and had a real political debate. But they didn't want to go into that.

The Flight That Disappeared was an Eddie Small production. I did three pictures for him: *Flight That Disappeared, Deadly Duo* [1962] and the Vincent Price picture *Diary of a Madman*. First I did the two cheapies, *Flight* and *Deadly,* and Small liked them very much, so he gave me the Vincent Price assignment.

Diary of a Madman *seems to have been inspired by the success of the Roger Corman–Edgar Allan Poe films then popular for AIP.*

Possibly. The producer Robert Kent liked this story, *The Horla*, by Guy de Maupassant, and he sold Eddie Small on the idea of making the film. Kent wrote the script and I got the assignment. I felt that the story was a good one and it came out very well—except for the voice of the Horla, which I wanted to distort quite a bit. We made a test of the voice, the way I wanted it, and Eddie Small said, "I can't understand a word!" He wanted the Horla to speak normally, which was wrong.

Did Vincent Price have any enthusiasm about the film or his role, or did he treat it as just another job?

Top: LeBorg displays the poster from 1944's *Dead Man's Eyes* in the living room of his Hollywood home. *Bottom:* LeBorg and Acquanetta display the poster from *Jungle Woman* at a 1987 Universal Pictures reunion.

It was just another job for him. But he did become conscious that I was holding him down. I had looked at some of his other pictures, and I thought he overacted in some. On *Diary of a Madman* I held him down — he started to gesticulate and raise his voice in some scenes, and so I took him aside and whispered, "Tone it down, it'll be much more effective that way." He did, and he thanked me very much afterward. Even the producer, Eddie Small, said afterward that this was the best performance he'd seen Price give.

What kind of budget were you working with here?
Three hundred or three hundred fifty thousand, all shot at Goldwyn

Studios. *Diary of a Madman* was very well received, had good reviews, and did very well. I was very sorry when Eddie Small died right after *Diary,* because he promised me that he might want to use me on other things. You miss out a lot of the time, but that's life, I suppose.

In 1973 you made your last horror film to date, So Evil, My Sister *with Faith Domergue and Susan Strasberg.*
    I thought that picture turned out well, but I got cheated on that. I was called in by the producers to direct; the money was not great, but they promised me a percentage. We shot everything out of the studio, on location—on the beach in Malibu, in actual offices and so on. It came out good and I was paid the minimum—the amount they *had* to pay—but I had high hopes for the percentage. Four weeks later one of the two producers died; the other one, who was just a money man, thought he knew everything, and he came in and started to recut, despite all my protests. Then, eight or ten weeks later, I talked to the cutter, Herbert Strock, and he told me that for the most part they had gone back to the old cutting, what *I* did. Then the producer took the negative and *left;* suddenly nobody knew where he was, nobody could find him. And I'm still today waiting for my percentage, which should have been a fair-sized amount of money—Strock told me that the producer went around with the film, distributing it himself, and then went to Europe, and made a lot of money with it.

You've known and worked with all the great horror stars. Who was your favorite?
    Karloff. He was a gentleman; it was nice to talk with him and to work with him professionally.
    Basil Rathbone was a friend of mine; I knew his wife, Ouida, and used to get invited to her parties. It was very nice to work with him, and he was very receptive to me. We got along very well. In fact, after *The Black Sleep,* he wrote me a long letter from New York. He was being considered for another horror picture by a New York company, and said he would do it only if I directed.
    I liked Lon Chaney personally because he thought I had talent. After our first picture, he was very enthusiastic about my direction and my handling of him. He wanted to become *chummy*—he always called me "Pappy" or "Pops," although I was not much older than him. I didn't want to become too chummy, because I'm not a drinker—whenever he wanted to discuss things, it was, "Come on, have a drink." Well, I can have one beer and that's about all. I had to say no. He even invited me to his home, and I backed out. He thought I was arrogant or something, gradually his idea of the "great friendship" that he would get from me left him, and we drifted apart. Again, I liked him personally, but I couldn't help him emotionally; he wanted to be bigger than his father. Whether this was the only thing that drove him to drink or

not, I couldn't find out—I wasn't a psychiatrist. But I wasn't about to baby him or sit down and drink with him.

Vincent Price I found to be entirely professional and very, very nice, and I enjoyed working with him very much. I was surprised how brave he was in the fire scene in *Diary of a Madman*—I was scared for him, because there was fire all around him in that scene. I had asked him if he wanted a double, and he said no. I said, "Well, it might get really hot, so be careful," and he said, "Don't worry, I've done things like this before." He was a brave guy.

John Carradine I enjoyed working with, because he'd also drink and then start spouting Shakespeare. When we finished shooting *The Black Sleep*, we had a party on the set and he imbibed quite a bit and started to do Shakespeare. I knew a little bit of *Hamlet* and joined in myself. He took me around and we spouted together. It was funny; he does become boisterous.

Bela Lugosi was a typical Hungarian. When he came to me and said, "Herr Director, give me something to do"—when he *begged* me—I placated him; that was all I could do. There are always things that are difficult to do, but you have to overcome them. That's part of the business.

No, [Ed Wood] wasn't flaming around, like I've heard stories of,
wearing this and that and using a megaphone and
acting like an idiot. . . . He never pranced around
on the street in high heels and a wig, he
did it in his own home, and he
was never embarrassed about it.

Paul Marco

CLOSE FRIEND and associate of the late Edward D. Wood, Jr., actor Paul Marco is content in his niche as monsterdom's favorite cop in Wood's low-budget '50s productions of *Bride of the Monster, Plan 9 from Outer Space* and *Night of the Ghouls*. Best known for his role as the clumsy, cringing Kelton in Wood's notorious horror trilogy, the veteran actor has fond memories of his experiences with Eddie D., Bela, Tor (and more!).

Born and raised in Los Angeles, Marco planned on being an actor all his life, taking dancing, singing and drama lessons in high school and later appearing in little theater productions. His work was brought to the attention of television prognosticator Criswell, who predicted on his TV show that Marco would go far in the picture business. A showbiz friend introduced Marco to Criswell and later to Ed Wood, who made Marco part of his entourage. Capitalizing on the resurgence of interest in Ed Wood and his films, Marco keeps busy today appearing at science fiction conventions, hawking Kelton the Cop merchandise and pitching himself and his Kelton character to movie and TV producers.

Were Ed Wood and Bela Lugosi friends, or was it just a professional relationship?

Ed was basically interested in old cowboy actors; he'd be up all night watching Tom Mix and Tex Ritter and all those old Westerns on TV. Ed met Bela, who was down on his luck, and he got the idea to help him—that's when they did *Glen or Glenda*. I didn't know either of them at that time, I came in right after that.

But they did get along well together?

Ed and Bela liked each other instantly—they were like brothers. Eddie was such a likable person, you couldn't say no to him if you wanted to! He was just a real wonderful promoter that would offer you everything—and although he wouldn't always live up to everything, he sure tried like hell.

Who came up with the idea for your recurring character, Patrolman Kelton?

Ed was about to do *Bride of the Monster* and he was wondering what kind of part was in it for me. Actually, there *was* no part that really fit me except for a desk sergeant called O'Reilly. Ed said, "Well, you're not Irish, and you're too young for a sergeant. Let's make you just an office boy, an assistant to the captain." All of us put our heads together to think up a name for this new character; my agent, Marge Usher, said, "How 'bout Kelton?" We all looked at each other—it sounded *so* right that we asked, "Gee, where'd you get that?" She said, "Well, I *live* on Kelton Avenue!" So I was christened Kelton the Cop right then and there. Ed rewrote the part for my personality, which was younger and, shall I say, a bit on the clumsy side—not knowing my work as a policeman. That's how Kelton was born.

Previous page, left to right: **Ed Wood, Vampira, Paul Marco and actress Meg Randall attend a 1955 testimonial benefit for the ailing Bela Lugosi.**

Left to right: Allan Nixon, Vampira, Tor Johnson, Stepin Fetchit, Bela Lugosi, Jr., Paul Marco and Dolores Fuller line up at Bela Lugosi's testimonial benefit.

Makeup man Harry Thomas told us that Lugosi seemed pretty lost on the sets of these films.

I never got that. Bela was always a real sweetheart. He wasn't what you'd call a *loner,* but after all he was quite old when he made *Bride of the Monster.* I remember that he had this tremendous speech to deliver to George Becwar — lots of dialogue. Ed didn't use too many closeups or different kinds of set-ups, and he was afraid that this was a bit too much dialogue for Lugosi. Bela was not sickly, but he *was* tired, and not 100 percent well. So we put all his dialogue on cue cards. Lugosi sat there, me sitting next to him, solemnly studying the lines while I held the cards.

Then came time to shoot. Eddie was very sweet — he treated Bela with all the respect that he deserved. Ed was escorting him to the sofa where he was going to play the scene when suddenly Bela came out with, "Oh, take those cards away. *I'm* going to *do* it!" By this time, the picture was running short on time and money, and allowing Bela to try it without benefit of cue cards seemed somewhat risky. Bela continued to insist that he could do it.

Well, he did it, without even looking at the cards, and the whole crew burst into applause and told him how great it was. Some critics have written that Bela was hammy in that scene, but he was really *feeling* it. This was the last big movie speech that Bela did before he died — his few remaining pictures saddled him with nonspeaking parts. I was there, and helped him. Sometimes when he was acting and doing a very dramatic scene, you could see the tears well up in his eyes. And when in his pictures he would say, "Come to me, I want to suck your blood!" — you'd just go *[laughs]!* Of all the stars that became my friends, he was one of the few that had that magnetism.

So you and Lugosi did become friends?

We became very close friends — I knew the man's warmth and his feelings, and he had so much heart. One night we were shooting in Griffith Park, and he really didn't feel well and he *needed* his shot [dope]. It was very damp and a real black night up there in the hills. Bela walked over to Ed and said, "Eddie, take me home. I've *got* to take my 'medicine.'" Bela didn't call it dope, he called it his medicine. Well, Eddie couldn't go. And Bela didn't trust drivers — you either had to be a perfect driver or a friend he *really* trusted before he'd get in a car with you. We did have a driver on hand, but Bela said, "No, I don't want that stranger! If you won't take me, you have to let me have Paul!" Eddie cried out, "No, he's in the next scene, I can't!" And Bela said, "Okay, then you don't have me either."

Eddie gave in and so I drove Bela home, which wasn't too far away — he lived in a small two-story apartment building somewhere in the vicinity of Griffith Park. It was dark and nobody was there. We entered his apartment and turned on the lights, which were very dim, and Bela said, "Paul, make yourself at home." He motioned for me to sit down in a very old-fashioned type of loveseat. Above it was a huge oil painting of him, from the sofa all the way up to the ceiling. "You're not going to like to see this, Paul," he said. "It's not very nice to watch, but I *have* to have my medicine." I told him, "Please, Bela — do what you have to do, nothing will upset me."

Directly in front of me there was a walk-in closet, and Bela pulled back the drapes and I saw that it was like a small room — I could see a little sink, a table and a hatrack. Off the hatrack Bela took an apron, and he wrapped it around himself very daintily and slowly tied a bow. And then he rolled his sleeves and washed his hands, took a clean towel from a drawer and wiped them dry. Then he opened the sterilizer and took out his hypodermic and his "medicine." This was all so dramatic, it was like I was in a daze, in a fog. This whole heartbreaking ceremony that I was witnessing was so beautifully done, I was spellbound. He put the needle in his arm and took it out — I sat motionless, I just couldn't move. When he was finished, he reversed the process — sterilizing the needle, taking off the apron and so on — just as cleanly and precisely as it was done to begin with. He turned off the light, drew the drapes closed, then turned and smiled at me like nobody but he could ever do. "Now," he said with a laugh, "I think we are ready to go!" And so we went back; it was a long, damp evening up there at the park, but Bela's medicine got him through the night. It was an experience I'll never forget.

Shortly after Bride of the Monster *wrapped up, Lugosi committed himself for treatment of his drug addiction.*

Eddie was very, very concerned about him, and so was Alex Gordon — we all were, because we'd all worked so hard on *Bride of the Monster*. When Lugosi did give himself up for dope addiction, I think it ran in the papers for about five days, and every day the headlines were bigger. Apparently there was *nothing* happening in the world at the time and they had nothing else to write about! It was while Bela was in the hospital that we approached him with the script for *The Ghoul Goes West*, a Western horror film that Eddie was planning. Then Ed changed his mind, and thought it would be better to do a picture called *The Vampire's Tomb*. It was for that picture that Ed shot all that miscellaneous footage of Bela [later used in *Plan 9 from Outer Space*], which had no purpose whatsoever outside of maybe *The Vampire's Tomb* would take advantage of *some* of this material.

What sort of budgets was Wood working with?
I don't think we ever *had* budgets, funny as that sounds. We made these movies for the money we could get or the money that we had. We raised the money as we went along. We'd shoot till we were broke, then Eddie would say, "Gee, I'm going to need $5,000 more" — or $2,000 or $1,000, or whatever — and then he'd go about the business of scrounging up that extra cash. He did everything on a very, very small budget, but it was in his blood — he had to go, go, go.
Bride of the Monster was not made as cheaply as people assume that it was; when [leading man] Tony McCoy's father took it over there was quite a bit of money owed. It isn't the $20,000 picture people think it is, I would say it was more in the $60,000–$70,000 range. Now, *Glen or Glenda* might have been $20,000, but I think *Bride* was considered Ed's first "biggie."

How would Wood go about raising the additional money?
Oh, sometimes Marge Usher would bring in another investor, or a couple of actors would come along who wanted some film on themselves, and so Eddie would write 'em a part. Eddie once told me that he made over a million dollars, and he had nothing to show for it.

What can you remember about the Bride of the Monster *premiere that was staged to raise money for Lugosi?*
Bela wasn't there, he was still in the hospital, but his son Bela, Jr., and Ed Wood were both there, and they each gave a little speech. I took Vampira to that premiere — I was dressed in a tuxedo and she was done up in her costume; Nicky Hilton, from the Hilton chain, drove us there in his Cadillac. When they opened the car door and we stepped out, we stopped the show.

How much money was raised for Lugosi?
Sales were very, very bad and we were all disappointed that more money

wasn't raised, because Bela really did need it. Ed tried very hard selling blocks of seats, and Universal didn't even buy any. You'd think, after all the money Lugosi's pictures had made for them, they'd buy a block. We raised very little money, and that was very, very disheartening.

What can you tell us about Lugosi's marriage?

He married a very lovely lady; Hope and I became good friends, and remained so even after Bela died. She was a wonderful girl. When Bela got out of the hospital, they went around for a while and I think they got married within a week! It was done very hurriedly — so hurriedly, in fact, that one day Ed Wood just slapped me on the back and said, "We're gonna go to Bela's, he's getting married." Eddie was running around with a little singer named Jo at the time; the three of us piled into Eddie's beat-up convertible and we were rushing down Los Feliz Boulevard when Eddie suddenly said *[babbling],* "We've gotta bring something, we've gotta take 'em something! Paul, have you got any money?" I had *some* money, and I said, "Let's take 'em some flowers!" We went into this big Japanese orchard and I gave the guy all the spare money that I had, and we ended up with this huge bunch of long-stemmed gladiolas. As it turned out, this wedding was arranged in such a rush that neither Hope nor her sister Pat had remembered to order flowers. I walked in with the gladiolas, took this big vase into the kitchen and arranged the flowers in it, and set it in front of the fireplace, which is where the ceremony took place.

There must have been at least fifty photographers there, all over the room. When you walked in, all you saw was cameras — *very* few guests. Later on I counted — there were 13 guests, appropriately enough, and *I* was the thirteenth person! Bela was late; he'd had a few drinks, I imagine, because he was — not *drunk,* but — *happy.* Eddie and I met him at the door and escorted him in while Hope put the finishing touches on her makeup and Pat, her sister, set the champagne out. Then we had the ceremony; the photographers were flashing pictures like crazy. It was really very, very touching, a beautiful ceremony. Bela acted wonderfully and Hope just looked so lovely — she was so blonde, and there was such love in her eyes it was just fantastic.

After it was over, all of the photographers left, and eventually the only ones there were Bela, Hope, Eddie, Jo and me. So here we were, driving Bela and Hope to their wedding apartment. We were coming down Western Avenue when Bela spotted this big Italian deli and cried out, "We *gotta* stop here!" Eddie stayed in the car with Jo and Hope while Bela and I went into the store. There were half a dozen people in there, everyone started congratulating Bela on his marriage and he was feeling *good.* We walked out carrying jugs of wine, long loaves of French bread, long salamis, jugs of olives, provolone cheese — my arms were full! They were giving us this, giving us that — I don't think we paid for much of anything, everybody was *giving* us things to congratulate Bela on his getting married.

We arrived at Bela's apartment and walked in — pitch black! Either they

Duke Moore, Mona McKinnon (hidden behind Moore), Gregory Walcott, Tom Keene and Paul Marco greet the Ghoul Man (Tom Mason) with a hail of bullets in Ed Wood's *Plan 9 from Outer Space.*

hadn't had the electricity turned on yet or they didn't have enough bulbs, but there was very little light in this huge, old-fashioned Spanish living room. There was practically nothing in the room except a huge trunk right in the middle of the floor — it looked like a coffin, it was that big! We moved some boxes and chairs around the trunk while Hope got some kind of a tablecloth to spread over the top. Then we brought out all the wine and bread and cold cuts, and we all sat around this trunk like picnickers, laughing and telling stories. That was Bela's wedding dinner.

After Lugosi died, whose idea was it to use this Vampire's Tomb *footage in* Grave Robbers from Outer Space *[shooting title for* Plan 9 from Outer Space*]?*
    We were all sitting around, having a few drinks and talking about what to do with this Lugosi footage that Ed had shot. Ed said, "Let's make a monster picture!" We all laughed, "How much footage have we got? Not very much!" But Ed was very, very clever in his writing, and that's how *Plan 9* started.

Can you tell us a little about assembling the cast of Plan 9?
    It was me who suggested Vampira for *Plan 9,* and Ed went along with that

right away. He said he was only going to use her for a day, for about two hours, and I do think that's about all it was. She did it as a favor to me, because I was her friend, and because it was a Lugosi film—she was a great admirer of his. And now she's more known for *Plan 9* than for anything else she's ever done. I also suggested using Criswell; I had become his close friend and right-hand man, been on his television shows and done personal appearances with him. Criswell wrote his own narration for *Plan 9* and *Night of the Ghouls*—partly because he had a speech impediment, and there were so many words he couldn't quite get out. Ed would tell him basically what he wanted conveyed, and then Criswell would write it to fit his speech.

Now that I had lined up two stars for Ed, I told him, "Now there's something you can do for *me*—I've got two houseguests that are driving me crazy. You've got to do me a favor and write them each a part." It was John Breckinridge and his secretary, David De Mering. Breckinridge was a big socialite from San Francisco—his family owned the Palace Hotel and the Comstock Lode, and his great-great grandfather, John Cabell Breckinridge, was at one time [1857–1861] vice-president of the United States, under James Buchanan. "He's a very flamboyant, articulate and highly educated man," I told Ed. "Why don't we make him the man from space?" And that's how he played his part of the Ruler—he's actually like that in person. His secretary, David De Mering, played the co-pilot of Gregory Walcott's airplane. When Ed Wood died, in 1978, David, who was an ordained minister, presided over the services. And Ed's wife, Norma McCarty, played the stewardess in that same airplane scene.

And the rest of the players came from Wood?

Dudley Manlove, who was a radio man, was Ed's own "find"; "Duke" Moore was a drinking buddy of Ed's. And people like Tom Keene and Lyle Talbot were friends of Ed's, and their little "guest star" scenes were shot in a couple of hours. Tom Mason took over for Lugosi in *Plan 9;* he was also in *Night of the Ghouls*. If you want to see *that* particular "man behind the cape," he was the atrocious actor that shoots it out with the police in the drape room at the end of *Ghouls*.

I think Ed did a masterful job of putting all these little bits and pieces of film together and making a movie out of it. Although he preferred working on *Bride of the Monster* because that was more of a movie, he called *Plan 9* his "little gem."

How did it happen that Plan 9 *was taken over by the Baptists?*

Ed's neighbor J. Edward Reynolds happened to be with the Baptist Church, and in talking with him, Ed mentioned the picture and that he needed x amount of dollars to finish it. Reynolds got involved and brought in other Baptists, and eventually they took it over. Naturally some of them wanted to be actors—everybody does!—and so the two grave diggers in *Plan*

9 are Reynolds and Hugh Thomas, Jr., another fellow from the Baptist Church. Reynolds is the stout one.

One condition had to be met before the Baptists would become involved: Everyone had to be baptized. Eddie had to be baptized, and Tor Johnson, too. Tor was too big to be baptized in the tank, so they had to baptize him in a swimming pool! Then the Baptists took complete control; Ed was in hock up to his eyeballs, and they took over *everything*. Also, they didn't like the title under which we had made the film, *Grave Robbers from Outer Space*, so they changed it to *Plan 9*—which Eddie *hated*. No one really liked that title.

On Plan 9, *you were promised a producer's credit that never came about.*

I was promised the title of executive producer, which is a title usually left in reserve for whoever invests the most money; well, I lost that to Reynolds. And through an oversight my name did not appear in the credits as prominently as Ed had promised. That really teed me off, and I told Ed that *Plan 9* wouldn't have been done if it wasn't for me and that I felt very, very bad about how I had been treated. I was very hurt that he would do this to me, because I was really the closest friend he had. I was very perturbed and I just didn't see him for a while, but then I simmered down and realized, with Reynolds taking over and all, that Ed was caught in the middle. Once we'd patched things up, we stayed close friends until he died.

Your last Wood film, Night of the Ghouls, *teamed you for the third time with Tor Johnson. What do you remember about him?*

He was just a big teddy bear. He didn't speak too well, as you can see in *Plan 9*, but personally he was a pussycat—sweet, generous, charming and a lot of fun to be with. His son Carl, who was a police officer in the San Fernando Valley, was also very nice; he had a small part in *Plan 9*, and he was one of the dead men in *Night of the Ghouls*.

Did Wood ever appear in any of these films?

In *Night of the Ghouls*, Eddie dressed up as the Black Ghost in one sequence! When we couldn't get the girl who had played it in a couple of scenes, *he* put on the same outfit. In fact, he had even doubled for Mona McKinnon in *Plan 9*—he dressed up as her for the scene where she—*he*—is running and falling down, being chased by the Ghoul Man, just before the convertible comes along.

What about the stories that Wood directed in women's clothes?

[Emphatically.] No, he wasn't flaming around, like I've heard stories of, wearing this and that and using a megaphone and acting like an idiot. *I've* never seen that stuff. I'm not saying that I was on the set of every picture he ever made, all the time, but I *never* knew of him getting out of line. He always wore a shirt and tie, always was in a suit when he was directing, to my

Marco (seen here in a 1986 pose) hopes that the renewed interest in the films of Ed Wood will revitalize his own acting career.

knowledge. I never saw him in anything that made me ashamed. Certain people like to knock Ed down because these pictures have notorious reputations nowadays; nobody wants to hear all the good things, they only want to hear the bad. Now, some of the "bad" things you hear about *are* true, but there were also certain little aspects of these films where credit is due. I think Ed deserves a lot more credit than he's gotten from these people who've made a lot of money by deriding him.

Would Wood have been embarrassed to learn that his being a transvestite is now a well-known fact?

No, he was *never* embarrassed about that. If he was sitting at home with his negligee on, and a wig — *and* a mustache, smoking a cigar, with a bottle of vodka nearby, pounding on his typewriter in a most *un*ladylike fashion — and somebody walked in, he'd say, "Hi, sit down, I'll be right with you." But when he went out, he'd always be dressed in a shirt and tie; he never pranced around on the street in high heels and a wig, he did it in his own home, and he was never embarrassed about it.

Why was the release of Night of the Ghouls *held up for so many years?*
According to what Ed told me, the backers decided to use it as a tax write-off. Ed talked about *Night of the Ghouls* quite a bit and tried to get all the rights to it, hoping to get it out, but he never could. And then it began piling up an awful lot of storage fees.

For all its inadequacies, Bride of the Monster *was probably the best picture of the three.*
For Eddie, the favorite was *Plan 9;* as I mentioned before, he called it his "little gem," believe it or not.

Which was your favorite?
I enjoyed doing them all, but *Bride of the Monster* was perhaps my favorite experience. Naturally, since we were working with Bela there was a certain magic on the set, and production-wise and so on that was a bigger picture. And Eddie really *felt* like a director on that one: it wasn't a hodgepodge, he had a script, a *good* script — I think Alex Gordon did a fine job. We all worked hard, and it was more a movie than, say, *Plan 9,* which was made up of pieces. And it really did get a lot of play — it showed in hundreds and hundreds of theaters and drive-ins, all over the world.

What are your feelings about the Worst Films *people who've taken their pot-shots at Ed Wood, Bela, Tor and all the rest?*
Well, naturally, it hurts me very much — in fact, it makes me sick to my stomach. Bela was such a fantastic person, yet people say such awful things about him. And the same for Ed — all these weird things you hear about him directing, they didn't ever happen on the movies I made with him. But through these *Worst Films* people, Ed has finally become a name; he'll live a long, long time in the books, and I hope there'll eventually be a lot of good things said about him, not just the bad.

I think good *science fiction is really one of the untapped frontiers.
Look how much sci-fi has later turned up as fact. One of the
very early science fiction things that I did was
an episode of* Men in Space, *and I designed a spacecraft
that was* exactly *like what turned out later on!
Science fiction is really looking into the future in a way,
and I have no quarrel whatsoever about being identified with that.*

Ib J. Melchior

THE SON of the late Wagnerian tenor and film star Lauritz Melchior, Ib Jørgen Melchior was born and educated in Denmark. After graduating from the University of Copenhagen he joined the English Players, a British theatrical company, and toured Europe with the troupe, first as an actor and later as stage manager and co-director. Just prior to the outbreak of World War II Melchior came to the United States with the troupe to do a Broadway show. After 1941's "Day of Infamy," he volunteered his services to the United States Armed Forces, operating with the "cloak-and-dagger" O.S.S. and the United States Military Intelligence Service. He also served in the European Theater of Operations as a military intelligence investigator attached to the Counter Intelligence Corps. For his work in the E.T.O., Melchior was decorated by the United States Army as well as by the King of Denmark.

After the war Melchior became active in television, directing some five hundred New York–based TV shows ranging from the musical *Perry Como Show* to the dramatic documentary series *The March of Medicine*. In 1959 he collaborated with producer Sidney Pink on the independent sci-fi adventure *The Angry Red Planet*, and he followed up on this early genre credit with screenplays for Pink's *Reptilicus* and *Journey to the Seventh Planet*, Byron Haskin's *Robinson Crusoe on Mars*, Mario Bava's *Planet of the Vampires* and his own *The Time Travelers*. In 1975 his short story *The Racer* furnished the basis for director Paul Bartel's cult favorite *Death Race 2000*, and the following year he was awarded a Golden Scroll for Best Writing by the Academy of Science-Fiction (for body of work). Taking time out from his new career as a novelist, Melchior reminisces about the days when he helped to usher in a whole new Eastern-colored era of AIP terror.

How did you first become associated with Sidney Pink, producer of The Angry Red Planet?

I met Mr. Pink at a party, and he was telling me that he had a story called *Invasion from Mars*. He had had several screenwriters try to write a script on it, and he hadn't liked any of them. I was interested in science fiction at that time, and I'd had a lot of trouble getting directorial assignments because I came from New York and they wouldn't let me work in the Guild out here. The only way you can get in is if a producer says, "This man *must* do my film." So I made a deal with Pink: I said, "I will write a screenplay for you, at scale, provided that if you like it, you also have me direct it, also at scale." So I wrote the screenplay, he liked it and I directed the film, which was released as *The Angry Red Planet*. That's how I started.

Tell us a little about Cinemagic, and what Pink's hopes were for that process.

He really hoped to kind of *invent* a process which would, as he said at that time, revolutionize animation—a process where you just simply photograph people, and they come out as animated figures. Norman Maurer, who later married the daughter of Moe from the Three Stooges, was the inventor of it.

Previous page: Ib J. Melchior earns a living today as the writer of novels with foreign intrigue backgrounds.

The story that I heard is that they were working out of Maurer's garage, and they couldn't get it to work. It did work when they did it slowly, frame by frame, but it never worked the way they really wanted it to. At one point, according to the story that Sid told me, Maurer got so disgusted that he took the lens and threw it against the wall, and it cracked. So they tried it with the crack and it worked *[laughs]!* And *that's* Cinemagic!

What was the advantage of Cinemagic, though?
The advantage, I really don't know. Frankly *[laughs],* I never knew exactly *what* they had intended! In my opinion, what finally came out as Cinemagic wasn't at all what they had in mind when they started. It *was* an interesting effect, but I don't think it was something that could be used other than for very limited things, like *The Angry Red Planet.* The proof's in the pudding — Cinemagic never caught on or amounted to anything.

What were your budget and shooting schedule on Red Planet?
The budget I'm not really sure of; in those days it would have been very small, probably around $250,000. The shooting schedule was very short, only seventeen days. We shot it out at the Hal Roach Studios in Culver City.

Since your list of film credits leans heavily toward science-fiction subjects, can we assume that you're a fan of sci-fi?
Well, I never read science-fiction, outside of Jules Verne and H.G. Wells, until I came to this country. Then I started reading it, and I got fascinated by it. I was really more of a reader than a writer of it; *The Angry Red Planet* was simply the key to becoming a director. But then, once you have done a science-fiction film, that is what you are — you are now a science-fiction filmmaker and that's *it.* Other films that I wrote were more along the lines that I am working in now; they were adventure stories like *When Hell Broke Loose* [1958] and *Ambush Bay* [1966].

There were several interesting special effects in Red Planet.
Like people on short budgets usually do, we ran out of money before the special effects were done. We were planning to shoot the scene where the giant monster's claw crushes the rocks with [actor] Les Tremayne between them; that claw was supposed to have been on a big rig with motors and everything else. The special effects technicians said, "That's going to cost $13,000, we can't do it," and *I* said, "The hell with that, we're going to do it anyway!" So I took two two-by-fours and put them into those claws that we had made — like a scissors. Then we put them on a little cart and just wheeled the cart in! The shot is tight and it looks terrific, but instead of $13,000 it cost $13!
In another scene, we wanted to achieve the effect of the giant amoeba enveloping the spaceship; we wanted a sort of mass to slowly crawl up the sides of the ship and engulf it. What we did was, we took a lot of multicolored Jell-O

Melchior's first science fiction film, *The Angry Red Planet,* featured high-concept advertising and low-budget special effects.

and poster colors and mixed them together. Then we stuck a small model spaceship into that Jell-O and melted it on a hotplate. That, shown in reverse, gave us our effect.

Norman Maurer used to describe you as "a highly excitable young man." Is that a fair assessment?
Excitable? I don't know about that—maybe so. That's hard for me to judge. Of course, *The Angry Red Planet* was a transition, from having done musicals into something which at that time interested me enormously. I *was* enthusiastic—perhaps more so than normally *[laughs]!* I tried to do the best I could with what I had at the moment, which was limited, as you know.

Did you go along to Denmark when Sid Pink shot your scripts for Reptilicus *and* Journey to the Seventh Planet?
No, I just wrote the scripts, which were rewritten to some extent—quite a bit, in fact, in some areas. I have always felt that I would just as soon *not* be that closely associated with those two films. Few people knew that my only connection with them was writing scripts which were considerably altered. I had absolutely nothing to do with the directing of them, or anything else.

Of the two, Reptilicus *seemed to have the greater potential.*
Sid had a lot of good production values in *Reptilicus* because he got everybody to cooperate. Do you remember the scene where Reptilicus chases the people off the bridge? Sid rounded up about twelve hundred people that belonged to an athletic club—those are all the people that ran and fell down into the water. He got them by simply promising some equipment for their club *[laughs]*—he was a *tremendous* promoter. He had five or six cameras set up to cover this whole thing—and he forgot to run them! "Action" was called and the people began running; somebody was supposed to tell all the cameras to start rolling, but nobody did! Luckily, one of the cameramen said, "Hey, I'm going to shoot anyway," and that's what they got.
I have now been to Denmark several times; *Reptilicus* is a cult film there, and the audience has actually memorized the lines! When Sid shot the film, he had Danish actors and he had German actors, and everybody spoke English with a different kind of an accent—some of them very, very badly. Sid knew it was going to be dubbed when it came over here, so he told his actors, "When you speak, be sure to speak distinctly and move your mouths distinctly so that we can dub this." This, of course, is not necessary at all, but that's what he told them. As a result, you have people like Carl Ottosen, the general, saying, "Come ... on ... let ... us ... hur-ry"—it became ridiculous! So now in Denmark they screen it and the entire audience says, "Come ... on ... let ... us ... hur-ry." It's hilarious!

Is is true that AIP initially felt that Reptilicus *failed to meet their standards?*

The Melchior-scripted *Robinson Crusoe on Mars* pitted a human and an alien (Paul Mantee and the kneeling Vic Lundin) against the perils of the Red Planet.

That's right; they weren't happy with it and we had to do some doctoring here. I dubbed it; in fact, six of the voices in *Reptilicus* are mine. I'm a reporter, a police officer, a mayor . . . six small parts. And we did shoot some additional scenes here—some of the early stuff, some of the close-up stuff, close shots of the monster's tail and so on. One scene in there, where Reptilicus destroys a farmhouse, didn't come off at all, so *we* shot the scene of the farmer being eaten by Reptilicus—in fact, the farmer was played by my own son Dirk *[laughs]!* He was about twelve years old at the time, we needed a small person, so we used him. He's always been very happy about having been swallowed by Reptilicus.

Were any of the original Reptilicus *cast brought over for these extra scenes?*
No, none at all — it was all close shots and things that could be done without bringing anybody over. We had next to no money to do it with; Sam Arkoff asked me to try and fix it up, and that's what I did.

And then the same thing happened with the monster scenes in Journey to the Seventh Planet.
That's correct. I saw the original 35mm print that came over here — in fact, I still have it out in my garage! — and *[laughs]* believe it or not, you see the chicken wire on the monsters! Those scenes were all redone; in fact, they even replaced one monster with stock footage of a giant spider from an earlier, black-and-white film *[Earth vs. the Spider]*.

The most ambitious and well known of your early films is Robinson Crusoe on Mars.
Robinson Crusoe on Mars was a big project of mine. I submitted it to [producer] Howard W. Koch and he said, "I am busy at the moment, but I know this is something that Aubrey Schenck would like." Aubrey Schenck and Edwin Zabel were longtime associates of Koch's; they got excited about it and they wanted, believe it or not, a three-and-a-half-hour movie out of it. And I *wrote* a three-and-a-half-hour script! At the same time, I was brought this other property, *The Time Travelers;* I developed that into a script, and started directing it just as *Robinson Crusoe on Mars* was ready to go into production. So I had nothing whatsoever to do with the production of *Robinson Crusoe on Mars*.

Was it Schenck and Zabel who changed their minds about the length?
Right. They got a writer named John Higgins — whom I've never met — to cut it down. He changed a couple of things that I was very unhappy about; for instance, I wanted to show the meeting of two totally alien people that could *respect* each other — *not*, "Me master, you slave." Unfortunately, a line was put in that said precisely that — *exactly* the thing I wanted to get away from! I was very unhappy when I discovered that, but there was nothing I could do about it.

Do you feel that Robinson Crusoe *could have used a better grade of star?*
No, I had nothing against using unknowns; I thought they did a good job. There is some advantage, when watching a film of this sort, in *not* seeing a major star in it. For example, I remember about three or four pictures that were made at the time of the Entebbe incident, and the one that was *real* to me was the one made with Israeli actors — because I didn't know any of 'em! When I see Kirk Douglas or Elizabeth Taylor, it is a *film;* the other way seems so real. I think this is what they tried to do in *Robinson Crusoe on Mars;* they were actors you were not familiar with, and the film was more believable that way. I liked that.

In a book-length interview, Byron Haskin had some very disparaging things to say about your contribution to Robinson Crusoe on Mars. *What might have prompted him to do this?*

I don't know. I knew Byron very, very slightly; before the picture was begun he came to my home a couple of times and I gave him all my ideas on what I had meant to convey in my screenplay and how I saw the whole picture. We got along just fine. What made him say those things later on, I do not know.

Haskin claimed that he *picked out all the Death Valley shooting locations.*

Every location was picked by me—I went there, and I gave Byron a map with every location, and told him which scenes should be shot where. For him later on to say that he did all that is kind of sad, but it happens—there are people who do that.

According to Haskin, your original script was crammed with Martian monsters.

Absolute nonsense! Total, complete and utter nonsense! If he said that, it is an obvious lie. This is no longer something I can accept as having been a mistake. This is a deliberate belittlement. Obviously, in his later years he became terribly insecure. Insecure people have to do that sort of thing. I feel very sorry for him.

He also said the title Robinson Crusoe on Mars *was the only single thing of yours that remained in the picture.*

That is totally and completely and ridiculously wrong. I can only say that I am shocked, that a man with that kind of reputation would belittle himself by saying something like that. Every single solitary person who was involved with *Robinson Crusoe on Mars* will know how wrong that is.

Your Robinson Crusoe *premise seems to have been pirated for a recent film called* Enemy Mine.

And the interesting thing to me is that some of the things in *Robinson Crusoe on Mars* that were not shot, but were only in my original script, turned up in *Enemy Mine*. Almost word for word! It was incredible!

Getting back to The Time Travelers, *how exactly did that come about?*

A young man named David Hewitt had the idea for that film; he and [producer] Bill Redlin came to me and asked me to write it, which I did. Then I became very involved in the project, and David and I evolved the special effects for the film. We used actual magician's illusions—David had been involved in that sort of thing—and we were able to do some absolutely marvelous things, right on the stage, without any optical work. If you had stood where the camera stood on our stage, you'd have seen the same effect that you saw

Step through "The Time Portal" beyond the crack in Space and Time where the fantastic world of the Future will freeze your blood with its weird horrors!

THE TIME TRAVELERS

AN AMERICAN INTERNATIONAL PICTURE IN **COLOR**

STARRING
PRESTON FOSTER · PHILIP CAREY · MERRY ANDERS · JOHN HOYT · FEATURING DENNIS PATRICK

Melchior and special effects man David L. Hewitt used an actual magician's illusions in lieu of conventional effects on *The Time Travelers*.

on film. They were just simply an illusionist's tricks that we modified for our purposes.

We had some fun moments on *The Time Travelers*. Our mutant-actors were actually a basketball team—some of them were Lakers—and I think the biggest guy was about 7'2". These were *huge* guys! We had them running across this field of dead trees, right next to a road that ran through the desert; we were set up in some bushes on the opposite side of the road, shooting these guys running toward us. As we were doing this, a car came along—just as our mutants started running across the road! It came to a *screeching* halt, and there was this little lady inside. And this 7'2" guy went over to her and said, "Lady,

Melchior (left) coaches actor Steve Franken (center) and an unidentified "mutant" on the set of *The Time Travelers*. (Photo courtesy Robert Skotak.)

take me to your leader!" She took off like a shot! And I've always wondered, *what* stories did she tell, and *what* psychiatrist is still saying, "Lady, you are crazy!"

The battle between the androids and the mutants was one of the highpoints of that picture.

We had one guy whose hand was missing in real life; we put a false hand on him, he grabbed somebody's throat and then, *whap!*, someone else hacked at his arm so that his hand stayed around the throat while he pulled his stump away.

Any other memories of the battle scenes?

Well, we had a troublemaker amongst the extras. Remember the scene where the workmen are carrying big boxes to load the spaceship? Those were empty cardboard boxes, you could lift them with one little finger. Just as we were about to shoot, this extra came to me and said, "Mr. Melchior, we have to carry these heavy boxes, and that is time-and-a-half." I didn't have the money for that! And I visualized the battle scenes that were coming up later — were they going to want *triple* time for those? I said, "We've changed our schedule, and we don't need any more extras today. Good-*bye!*" And they left. So then *we* went out and rounded up all the relatives and friends that we could find — we literally got people off the street! We put them in the costumes and shot the whole damn thing. These were the people who did most of the fighting in the battle scenes! By the time the union found out about it the picture was already done; the producer settled with them and that was that. But we would not have been able to finish the picture if it hadn't been for that.

What can you tell us about the actor who played The Deviant?

That's a fascinating story. That man, Pete Strudwick, is a brilliant fellow, a Mensa, in fact. He was born without feet; one hand is like a knob, and the other hand looks like a lobster pincer. I got a telephone call from him one day; he said, "I understand you're doing a science fiction picture and you need, maybe, a monster?" I told him, "Possibly," and he said, "Well, I happen to *be* a monster. Could I come and see you, and possibly get a part?" He showed up at my house, took his shoes off and all, and so we wrote in a part for him — and he did a very, very good job in it. I think he is an inspiration — he has run the marathon several times without feet, he has run up and down Pike's Peak, and he even competed in a marathon against the Marines where half of the Marines did not finish but he did!

How did you get involved on Planet of the Vampires?

That was a story idea that someone, or several people, had worked on in Italy. AIP brought it to me and said, "Do something with this property — it's unusable." I wrote the screenplay, and it was directed by Mario Bava — Mario was very complimentary about that script, by the way. I went to Italy and spent a few days on the set with Mario and Fulvio Lucisano, who was the producer, and ironed out a few problems and what-have-you. I think Mario made a good, moody piece out of *Planet of the Vampires,* and I rather liked it.

Was AIP an agreeable outfit to work for?

I have had excellent relationships with Jim Nicholson, before he died, and with Sam Arkoff, who is still around. They treated me about as good as anybody. The same thing, as a matter of fact, went for Roger Corman, who also had a reputation for sometimes not being the easiest person to work with. He, too, treated me very, very fairly on *Death Race 2000.*

That was based on your short story The Racer?

That's right. I wrote that around 1958, and it's been in at least six anthologies and reprinted in all kinds of magazines both here and in Europe. I had been to the Indianapolis 500 somewhere around 1939, and I sat in the box with the wives of the drivers. There was an accident, and one of the drivers was killed. And the juxtaposition of watching the horror on his wife's face and the excitement of the fans — this, after all, was what they really came to see — struck me enormously. That became *The Racer* — I wrote it as a short story, a serious kind of piece.

Did you approve of New World's black comedy approach?

At first I was *appalled*—after the first ten minutes, I said, "My God, what have they done to my story?" Then I started laughing, and by the time the film was over I thought it was one of the funniest things I had ever seen.

So when you talk about being well treated by Corman, you mean financially.

Right. But also we had some kind of a sequel contract, and although he did not make a sequel, he did do another film which was called *Deathsport* [1978]. It had nothing to do with *Death Race 2000*, but he said, "Look, if it hadn't been for *Death Race*, we would never have done this other one, so I think you're entitled to some money," which he paid me. I thought that was very good of him.

Robinson Crusoe on Mars *is probably your best-known film. Is it one of your favorites, or did the tampering you spoke of spoil it for you?*

Robinson Crusoe, and *The Time Travelers*, are my two favorites among the science fiction things. I would have liked very much to have been more involved with *Robinson Crusoe*, although I do think that Byron Haskin did a good job in directing it and taking advantage of the Death Valley locations that I had picked out. There were a few things that I would have done differently — *differently*, not necessarily better — but I was pleased with what they did with it. *Robinson Crusoe* had a fairly small budget, I think it was about a million and a half, and the same was certainly true of *The Time Travelers* — *that* was done for under $200,000!

What keeps you busy these days?

In 1973 my wife nagged me to write a novel that was based on one of my own experiences as a counter intelligence agent in World War II. I wrote it, it came out and became a best-seller! Since then I have been writing novels with a foreign intrigue background. They have been very well received; they are published, incidentally, in twenty-five countries, which is rather interesting.

Do you mind remaining best known for what you've done in science-fiction?

I don't mind. I think *good* science fiction is really one of the untapped frontiers. Look how much sci-fi has later turned up as fact. One of the very early science fiction things that I did was an episode of *Men in Space*, and I designed a spacecraft that was *exactly* like what turned out later on! Science fiction is really looking into the future in a way, and I have no quarrel whatsoever about being identified with that.

*If [Edgar] Ulmer had a little more
money in his budgets, more time in his schedules,
he would use it. When he had to turn out
the best possible film he could with his back to the wall,
he was marvelous. Turn Ulmer loose,
and God only knows what would have happened!*

Jack Pollexfen

JACK POLLEXFEN may not be a household word, even amongst horror fans, but as producer and writer he was responsible for a number of sci-fi and monster movies from the '50s that are remembered well even if the creator's name doesn't spring immediately to mind. At the beginning of the horror/sci-fi cycle of the '50s, Pollexfen produced the moody cult favorite *The Man from Planet X*, directed by B-movie master Edgar G. Ulmer. Other Pollexfen films include *Captive Women*, a postholocaust adventure; *The Neanderthal Man*, a variation on the Jekyll-and-Hyde theme; and *Indestructible Man*, starring Lon Chaney.

Pollexfen began his professional life in the newspaper business, working his way up from copyboy at the *Los Angeles Express* to reporter on several other dailies. During this period, he also found time to write and produce three plays that he says could be classified today as "off–Broadway—a *long* way off!" He found himself in the movie business when MGM offered him a contract to turn one of his magazine articles into a screenplay. Four years in the Air Force writing training films and manuals during World War II interrupted his movie career, which then got back on track with a series of screenplays for such adventure pictures as *Treasure of Monte Cristo* (1948), *The Desert Hawk* (1950) and other B movies— "sheer assembly-line junk," Pollexfen recalls. Around this time, Pollexfen's producing career got started, in cooperation with his co-writer Aubrey Wisberg.

Our favorite of your science fiction/horror films has always been your first, The Man from Planet X.

The Man from Planet X was always a favorite of mine. One reason, possibly it was the only space film then where Earth people are more or less the heavies. My partner Aubrey Wisberg and I wrote the script with the idea of selling it, but realized it could be made on a very low budget, so we decided to take the production plunge.

A recent book on sci-fi films insists that the most intriguing part of the story — depicting X as a harmless visitor and certain Earthmen as heavies — was not *written into the screenplay and therefore must have been introduced into the story by director Edgar Ulmer.*

Wrong. Making the Earthlings—or some of them—the heavies was a key part of the script from the first. Oddly enough, the idea has been seldom copied. Edgar Ulmer had begun as an art director, working with such personages as Max Reinhardt. His flair was mood. I think if silent films had lasted, he would have become one of the greats.

What was Ulmer like to work with?

No problems for me with Edgar. I thought that, considering the handicap of a six-day shooting schedule and a budget of $38,000, he did a remarkable job. But Edgar and Aubrey developed a feud. Both had that habit.

Previous page, left to right: **Jack Pollexfen, Edgar G. Ulmer and Aubrey Wisberg relax during a break in the shooting of** *The Man from Planet X.* **(Photo courtesy Robert Skotak.)**

I think Edgar could get more on the screen, with less time and money, than any director I worked with. He had a reputation in Hollywood, not wholly unjustified, of being difficult. Incidentally, so did E.A. Dupont [director of *The Neanderthal Man*], who had shot *Variety* [1925], one of the silent screen's all-time classics. Both Ulmer and Dupont, under pressure of time and budget, could get more values than any of the B-budget specialists. But when studios had any say, they generally wanted to settle for the handy hack.

Did Ulmer bring it in for $38,000?
It actually came in at $41,000.

How much creative leeway did you allow the directors who made your films?
On our schedules there was no story leeway on the set. In preproduction I always worked with the director on any problems he thought might arise.

Were you a frequent visitor to the sets of your own films?
As I was generally the production manager as well as co-producer, I was on the set from well before the day's shooting started, to sometime that night when we looked at the previous day's rushes.

Can you tell us about your Planet X *stars, Robert Clarke, Margaret Field and William Schallert?*
We probably looked at a hundred players before selecting Bob and Maggie. Both did excellent jobs. To be truthful, sci-fi does not give the male player too many opportunities, and less to the girl — unless each is lucky enough to have two heads! Bob and Maggie came along at the wrong time in Hollywood's history. Studios were no longer building up contract players, and independents were confined to low budgets for the bottom half of the bill. Incidentally, it was Margaret Field's daughter Sally who won Academy Awards for *Norma Rae* [1979] and *Places in the Heart* [1984].
Both Bob Clarke and Bill Schallert were first-rate, both on and off the set. I suppose you know that some years later Schallert became president of the Screen Actors Guild.

Can you recall anything at all about the actor who played the alien?
He was out of vaudeville, where he did a slow-motion act that combined dance and acrobatics. And he was quite small, about five feet tall. I *don't* remember his name.

The conception of the diving bell–shaped spaceship was quite original and effective.
Ulmer did both the spaceship and the model of the moors. The actual moors we shot were in southwest Los Angeles, and are long covered by tract

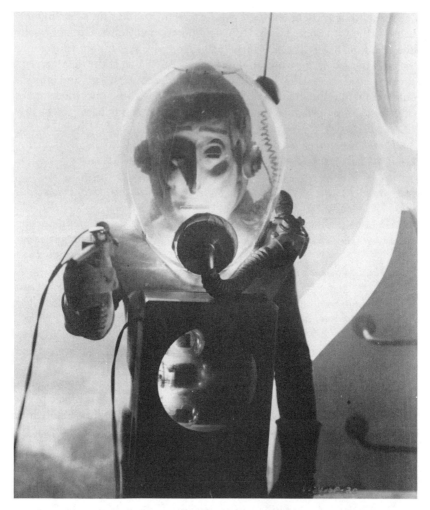

The Man from Planet X. Pollexfen does not remember the name of the actor who played this part — only that he was a vaudeville performer and that his height was "about five feet."

housing. The L.A. Griffith Park Observatory was the telescope location. We also used, somewhat redressed, some of the standing sets at Hal Roach Studios from *Joan of Arc* [1948].

Did you encounter any problems or delays during production?
    The most particular problem we had was that we shot nine-tenths of the picture on the studio stage, and we were using tetrachloride for our fog. Tetrachloride sticks fairly low, which is quite an advantage when you're shooting, because other fogs will circulate around and get up to the tops of the

sets and things like that. But its disadvantage is that, after you've been shooting in it for a few days, you are coughing for the next couple of *weeks!*

Who was Sherrill Corwin, and how was he instrumental in getting The Man from Planet X *released?*
Sherrill Corwin owned a chain of California theaters and drive-ins, and was also one-time president of the Motion Picture Theater Exhibitors. He saw the picture after it was finished and paid us $100,000 for 75 percent. We retained 25 percent. He arranged for the United Artists release. The picture went on to gross well over a million in rentals. Corwin, a most ethical man in the jungles of Hollywood, is now dead. He was not involved in any of our later projects.

Were you completely pleased with the results on Planet X?
If we had had more money to spend on it, there would have been a lot of things that we would have liked to have done. But we were making it on a very, very low budget and had some of our own money in it. So we shot in six days, and I think it was a pretty good picture for six days. Ulmer was an extremely good director for a *fast* picture. He did *not* work out too well if he had any time. His English was pretty shaky, and if he had time enough he'd sit down and try to direct the cast in their dialogue. And his English was, as I say, quite shaky. Ulmer was a difficult person, but a very talented person.

In what way was he difficult?
If Ulmer had a little more money in his budgets, more time in his schedules, he would use it. When he had to turn out the best possible film he could with his back to the wall, he was marvelous. Turn Ulmer loose, and God only knows what would have happened!

What sparked the Ulmer–Aubrey Wisberg feud you mentioned earlier?
I don't remember. Wisberg got into feuds with an awful lot of people — that was probably the main reason I finally broke up with him. He would be irritated if, say, a cameraman who'd worked for us once was not available on the next picture, and things of that nature. Very touchy.

What can you tell us about The Son of Dr. Jekyll, *which was based on an original story co-authored by Mortimer Braus and yourself?*
Not much. Mort Braus and I were kidding one day about outlandish film titles, and we came up with *The Son of Dr. Jekyll.* We thought about it for a moment, thought it might sell, and knocked out a quick story. Columbia bought it at once. We had nothing to do with the production.

Did you or Braus contribute to the screenplay of She-Wolf of London, *which has a plot similar to* Son — *and* Daughter — *of Dr. Jekyll?*

No—neither Mort nor I passed by the *She-Wolf of London*. I never saw it and I doubt if Mort had.

Tell us how you became involved with Albert Zugsmith's American Pictures Corporation, and how the films Captive Women *and* Port Sinister *came about.*

Aubrey and I had a deal to make three pictures at RKO *[Captive Women, Port Sinister* and a Robert Clarke swashbuckler, *Sword of Venus]* when Al, who had been a newspaper and radio station broker, came on the scene. Howard Hughes had been muttering about selling RKO, and Zugsmith conned a couple of RKO executives into thinking he could put together a syndicate to buy the studio. Al didn't have the syndicate, *or* the money, and Hughes at that time had no real intention of selling. However, we found ourselves with a new partner—Al convinced the executives that he should take 25 percent of our deal, leaving Aubrey and myself the other 75 percent, and in return he guaranteed RKO against any losses. We had no losses, which was fortunate, as Al had no money, according to one RKO attorney. Al tried to talk us into an American Pictures partnership, but fortunately we wanted no part of it.

Captive Women *is slow-paced and overly talky, but we've always been fans of this film, with its odd conception of a postatomic world where man has been reduced to near-savagery.*

Our main problem in *Captive Women* was that we were battling Zugsmith too much to pay attention to the production. More serious, Howard Hughes, who normally left us to ourselves, insisted we take Stuart Gilmore as director. Stuart was one of Hollywood's top film editors—had done some of Hughes' most important films—and Hughes had promised him a chance at directing. While there have been exceptions, film editors generally don't work out well as directors. It's one thing to sit before a Moviola and see all the director's mistakes and consider them at your leisure. It is quite different to knock out a low-budget picture where you don't have time to go to the bathroom, let alone do any thoughtful pondering.

Did Captive Women *really have the $100,000 budget—two and a half times that of* Man from Planet X—*announced by Wisberg at the time of the film's inception?*

Never believe *anything* published about budgets. From *The Birth of a Nation* to the latest George Lucas epic, the practice has always been to add a zero or two so the exhibitor won't feel so cheated—as *he* cheats the producer. If I remember, *Captive Women* came in at about $85,000, including a $15,000 writer-producer fee to myself and Wisberg. Zugsmith got $2,500 as associate producer.

The other pictures—*The Neanderthal Man, Indestructible Man, Daughter of Dr. Jekyll* and *Monstrosity*—were independently produced and usually sold outright to a studio.

Why was the release of Captive Women *delayed for almost fifteen months after the film was completed?*
I think some of the delays were hopeless attempts to patch its flaws in the cutting room. It seldom works. However, I was gone from RKO, making some swashbucklers for United Artists.

Captive Women *is really a meaningless title. The picture might have done better if released under its shooting title,* 3000 A.D.
Captive Women was a *god-awful* title. It killed any chance the picture might have had.

Was Port Sinister *initially conceived as a straight adventure film, with the sci-fi angle of the giant crab added as an afterthought?*
The main trouble with *that* epic was that we never licked the story. Actually, it had been initially conceived as sci-fi, with the giant crab in from the start.

What can you tell us about those giant crab scenes?
The crab was a spider crab — tiny body, but legs and claws about three feet long. Not much meat on them, so they are not fished commercially, but they are fairly plentiful on the Southern California coast. In some special effects shots we blew it up to the gigantic monster. It worked fairly well, provided we did not hold on the shot for too many frames. The crab's legs were operated by nylon thread against a dark background. And how it began to *stink!*

In what fashion was Marineland of Florida used during the production?
The pressbook item reporting the participation of Marineland of Florida was strictly a press agent's daydream. The picture was shot at RKO-Pathe Studios in Culver City. The location shots were in Palos Verdes, near Long Beach, California, at a cove called Portuguese Bend.

In a 1973 interview, Albert Zugsmith complained that the casts of these films were forced on him, and that the pictures suffered as a result.
Zugsmith actually had no part in any of our RKO films. The first picture I know of his making was *Invasion, U.S.A.,* released through Columbia. RKO had to approve the two leads and the director. I wasn't enchanted with their choice of players, but the real problem was the directors they dug up.

E.A. Dupont seems a rather offbeat choice for director of The Neanderthal Man.
Ulmer would have been the better director for *The Neanderthal Man,* but he was in Europe at the time. Dupont, considering budget and time, did a decent job. A horror picture is really more of a suspense film than a science film. What you suggest is more than what you show.

I got along very well with Dupont. I much preferred working with directors who had a lot of talent, and also could be rather difficult. I either had to use someone like that, someone the major studios wouldn't touch because they *were* difficult, or I had to use a hack.

Can you comment on the effective man-into-monster sequences in Neanderthal Man?

The transformation scenes were shot in a small special effects room, using a cameraman and a makeup man. It took about half a day. We used red and blue filters, cutting from face to hands, adding a bit more hair, fangs, etc., as we cut back and forth. When the transformation was complete, we switched to a stuntman wearing matching makeup.

Why doesn't that film's saber-tooth tiger have saber teeth?

We were dealing with an amiable but rather large Siberian tiger, and our makeup man became somewhat bashful about adding fangs — especially after the tiger shook them out the third or fourth time! If I remember correctly, we then got a tiger skin rug, added saber teeth to the jaws and put a few quick — *very* quick! — shots into the fight scenes. In shooting monster films, one must be flexible — very flexible.

What hurts many of your early films is the overwritten and unnatural dialogue.

Normally I would write the first draft of the script; Aubrey would *enhance* the dialogue. Another of the reasons we split!

Actually, both horror and science fiction generally need a minimum of dialogue. It is rare that the stories are not, fundamentally, ridiculous. The visual is all-important — which is one reason for the quality of the best of Ulmer's direction. Music, sound effects and so on, all combine.

Indestructible Man *bears a certain resemblance to an earlier Lon Chaney movie,* Man Made Monster. *Were your writers inspired by that older film?*

Man Made Monster played no part in this picture. I wrote the first draft. Sue Bradford and Vy Russell, who get the screenplay credit, were wives of Bill Bradford and Jack Russell, cameramen on many of my pictures. They helped on the second draft.

What prompted you to take on the responsibilities of directing on Indestructible Man?

No director I wanted was available. I had been doing some directing and had my Directors Guild card, so I made the picture. However, I did not want credits as producer, director *and* writer — I thought I would leave such credits to Chaplin and Welles.

John Agar (left) and Arthur Shields comfort a blood-spattered Gloria Talbott in Pollexfen's *Daughter of Dr. Jekyll*.

Many of Lon Chaney's later film roles were of the mute strongman variety.
Chaney could handle dialogue reasonably well. Of course, a talkative monster would tend to be ridiculous. I found him intelligent, probably more so than many actors. He warned me before we started shooting, "Don't make any changes in dialogue, or add new dialogue, after lunch!" — which he drank down rather liberally.

Were you happy with the results on Indestructible Man?
I was reasonably satisfied with it. I thought I did about as good a job of directing as a number of directors we'd used — but I was *not* as good as an Ulmer or a Dupont!

Was it Edgar Ulmer's fine work on Man from Planet X *which prompted you to rehire him for* Daughter of Dr. Jekyll?
Yes, Ulmer, as I have said, was an excellent director, at his best when he had his back up against the wall budget-wise. We shot *Daughter of Dr. Jekyll* in an old L.A. mansion, and the establishing shot of the mansion and the car driving up were done in miniature.

Did you have to secure permission from Columbia to remake, in a distaff version, the story [The Son of Dr. Jekyll] *you had written for them?*
The Son — and the *Daughter* — *of Dr. Jekyll* carefully ducked anything in

common that could not be traced back to Robert Louis Stevenson's original story, which was in public domain.

Did you use doubles for the monsters in Daughter?
Stuntman Ken Terrell doubled for Arthur Shields in the fight scene. His guttural, animal-like roars came out of a sound effects library. The fanged girl-monster was also played by a double. We shot the scene in a recently burned-over woods, using ultraviolet film to get a weird effect.

What in Daughter of Dr. Jekyll *could possibly have inspired its surprising Legion of Decency "B" rating?*
I don't know why that picture got the "B" rating. The mental processes of the Legion at times verged on fantasy.

What became of two sci-fi/horror thrillers you announced in 1958, The Astonishing 12-Inch People *and* The Brain Snatchers? *Did* The Brain Snatchers *evolve into the much-later* Monstrosity, *which has a brain-transplanting premise?*
The Brain Snatchers did turn into *Monstrosity*—certainly the worst picture I was ever involved with, and incidentally the only one that did not eventually climb into the profit column. Alas, I have to confess I did the first draft of the script. B films were collapsing; the studio financing the film turned out to be heading into bankruptcy. We had shot about half. Tried to patch it together in the cutting room—but that was a task beyond human hands.

When was that film made? It wasn't released until around 1964.
I guess that was shot around '58, with fundamentally an amateur crew. *Everything* went wrong with it. The major reason for this was that it was the only picture I ever tried to make without a first-rate, professional crew. That was a lesson to me.

Did you at least save money by using amateurs?
Not really. The budget was about $25,000, but it ran up to around $40,000 by the time we finished it. Joe Mascelli was a pretty good cameraman, but he was no director. I ended up doing most of the directing.

Isn't that Bradford Dillman doing the narration?
Dean Dillman, Jr. [co-writer and co-producer] is his brother. Brad did help out on the narration.

And The Astonishing 12-Inch People?
I simply dropped that. The handwriting on the wall was clear. B movies were dead.

Of your many sci-fi and horror films, do you have a favorite?

    The Man from Planet X, because it was my first production, and one of the first sci-fi films made with sound.

A least favorite?

    Monstrosity. The name describes it.

My pictures were great, they were fun. . . .
It was a great life — but, I sure wouldn't want
to be doing it now. The pressures are too great. . . .
I've had it — forty years is plenty. It's fun to reminisce,
but I don't want to get back into that routine.

Lee Sholem

IF THERE'S ONLY one Hollywood name that's synonymous with speed and efficiency, then it has to be Lee "Roll 'Em" Sholem. In a forty-year career Sholem has directed upwards of 1300 shows, both features and television episodes, without once going over schedule—a feat practically unparalleled in Hollywood history. In the 1950s he turned his talents toward the area of science fiction when he took the directorial reins on the feature *Superman and the Mole-Men,* the film which introduced George Reeves in his best-remembered role as the Mighty Man of Steel. After helming nine episodes of the *Adventures of Superman* teleseries during the '51 season, he returned to the genre for 1954's *Tobor the Great* and then branched off into horror with 1957's *Pharaoh's Curse.*

Sholem learned the motion picture business by starting out in the cutting room some time in the 1930s. "The first week I worked a hundred and eighteen hours, the second week a hundred and twenty-six, and the third week a hundred and thirty-eight, and then passed out!" he recalls. A lengthy association with *Tarzan* producer Sol Lesser brought Sholem in contact with the celebrated William Cameron Menzies, from whom he learned the key to expedient production, and later led up to his first directorial assignment on Lesser's *Tarzan's Magic Fountain* (1949).

Do you remember how you became involved on Superman and the Mole-Men?

I got involved when the guys who were writing and producing the show asked me to do it, and so I went to work on it. That was Bob Maxwell and company. National Comics owned *Superman,* and they're really the ones that got the whole thing going. It was an interesting movie, a cute little show.

Was George Reeves cast as Superman before your involvement in the production?

Yes, he was. It was a lot of work building him up to play the Superman character—he had a good physique, but his shoulders needed padding and so on. But what a sweetheart—everybody loved him, you couldn't help it. He had no ego, none of this crap that you get from most of these guys. And he could tell stories—I mean, he really could rattle 'em off, one after another. He was very much like another actor that I used to work with, Alan Mowbray. Alan would start telling a story, he'd get about three-quarters of the way through, and the cameraman would interrupt and tell him that everything was ready. He'd stop right there, I'd yell, "Roll 'em!" and he'd go right into his lines. And when I'd say, "Cut!" he'd go right on with the story just as though nothing had happened *[laughs]!* It was remarkable, *incredible,* and George was very much like that.

Where was Superman and the Mole-Men *shot?*

At a studio out in Culver City, RKO-Pathé. The oil fields seen in the film were within a stone's throw of the place—they were within two hundred yards

Previous page: Lee Sholem in a 1987 pose. (Photo courtesy Ed Watz.)

The low-budget feature *Superman and the Mole-Men* introduced George Reeves as the Man of Steel and spawned the popular *Adventures of Superman* teleseries. And, yes, that *is* an Electrolux vacuum cleaner the little guys are aiming.

of the studio lot. We'd shoot *Tarzans* there, too, and we had a hell of a time keeping those derricks out of the picture! The budget on *Mole-Men* was, I guess, about $275,000, and I think it was shot in approximately four weeks.

How much input did National Comics have in the production?
They had nothing to do with it. A V.I.P. from National Comics came out to visit one day, and I was introduced to him. He was a very nice man. But that was the only visit that I saw from National Comics! From then on, *never* during the shooting was anybody representing the company out here.

How did you earn your nickname "Roll 'Em"?
[Laughs.] When I'd be waiting on the set and my assistant would say that we were ready, I'd get the cast out and I'd yell *[loudly]*, "All right—r-r-r-roll!" And everybody in the place knew it! Then when the scene was over, I'd yell *[loudly and very sharply]*, "*Cub*-hut!" And they could tell by the way I would yell *cut* whether it was a print, or if we were going to do it again.

On the average, how many takes would you go before you'd print?
Normally I would get any scene within three or four takes. You *have* to. You can't go ten, twelve, fifteen takes, waiting to get something absolutely

perfect—none of the shows I made required that. They were all action shows, and so if some guy missed a beat or something like that, it really wasn't all that important.

Do you prefer to work that fast?
[Emphatically.] I sure do. Also, by knowing exactly what I was going to do, I could walk on the set in the morning and say to the crew, "Eleven shots from now I'm going to make a dolly shot, from *here* to *there.*" By knowing and telling them that, it gives them a chance, whenever they have a few minutes' break, to go ahead and lay the track, put the dolly on there, and set a camera and tripod on it. So by the time we got to that eleventh shot, everything was ready! *This* is where you save the time. If you wait until you're just about to do that particular shot, your company could sit on its ass for anywhere between forty-five minutes to an hour and a half while they're preparing the damn thing.

How did you like working with Phyllis Coates in the Superman *movie and TV show?*
She was just a very, very nice gal, willing to do anything. I'll tell you an anecdote that concerns her: We had stuntmen doing fights on that show somewhat often. We had both George Reeves and Phyllis Coates in fight scenes in one day—and this one day was *not* a lucky day for us. *Both* of them got knocked cold. These stuntmen would throw a right or a left hook, and if their timing was off, even just a little bit, look out! That day it was; one of the stuntmen actually punched Phyllis Coates and knocked her out! Later we were shooting a scene where George was supposed to run and crash through a door. The prop man or the construction man who made the door made it out of balsa wood, but he put two-by-fours in the son of a bitch *[laughs]*! And George was knocked cold! He was supposed to go right through, but he hit those damn two-by-fours dead on!

Any mishaps during Superman's *flying scenes?*
We never had an accident with any of that—we did a hell of a lot of testing. The takeoffs we achieved by yanking George up into the air on piano wires. We had the same guy who worked with Betty Bronson on *Peter Pan* [1924] involved on *Superman,* and the effect was marvelous. In most cases, the tricky part is the lighting—those piano wires had to be painted to cover up their shine, and also so that they would blend into the background. When George would leap out a window, he was simply diving onto cardboard cartons which would break his fall. We got the actual flying scenes by having him lie on a body cast—it looked like a spatula, almost. He'd lie on this thing with his arms out and we'd have the wind machines going. Later, of course, that body cast had to be masked out, and it would look as though he was actually flying.

What do you think of the new Superman *movies?*
Good. But, I mean, when they spend money like that, they can do a *lot* of things that we couldn't do. These new pictures cost twenty million, thirty million, forty million. . . .! I mean, what the hell, if you've got *that* much money —

You'd better *end up with a good movie!*
And how!

How many days did it take you to shoot an average Superman *episode?*
Two and a half.

And how many set-ups a day?
I've *done* ninety *[laughs].* . . .! I can give you an example of how we used to work: We were doing a *Superman* episode, and we did ten pages without a break. We started with an insert and pulled back to a shot of a man picking this object up off the floor. As he started to look at it, another person came in, and it kept building until there were ten people in the room! The scene just flowed right on till, toward the last couple of pages, everyone had left but two guys, and *they* walked from that one room, which was a sort of a living room, into a laboratory which was next door. And the scene went on in *there* until the ten pages were completed; we did it in one take!

Where did you learn to work like this?
I learned by working with a man by the name of William Cameron Menzies. He was an art director, and he was the best. He was *miraculous.* He couldn't direct, but he could sure lay out the show. Bill Menzies was working on a picture called *Our Town* [1940], produced by Sol Lesser. Menzies was brought in as the art director, and he sketched the entire show. But he had a problem, and that was drinking. I was the assistant director on the show, but my biggest job was to keep him off the booze, *or,* to keep him off it at least long enough for him to get the job done, and then let him go out and have his drinks. I learned to block my shows, so that I knew where I was going. Blocking means to lay out the show with *hieroglyphics,* more or less *[laughs]* — laying it out with pencil and paper, and knowing where your camera is going. As long as you know your sets, you can plan your action. That way, when your actors show up in the morning, you can walk through the entire scene with them, and they'll know exactly what lines they're going to move on, what props they're going to use, where they'll hesitate, where they'll pick up the tempo and so on. All these things are figured out prior to any actor appearing on the set, and it's so much easier that way to explain to them what you want done. I literally could do a show backwards — I could go from the back page of the script to the front, and know exactly what I was doing.

Did Menzies actually sit down and teach you this, or did you learn by observing him?

Menzies taught me the idea of blocking. He was a great artist; I'm not *[laughs]!* I would sketch things the easiest way possible, but *he* could draw; he did everything in charcoal, and it was magnificent. His artwork was so great that I would guess that a museum could be filled with it.

How did you get started in the business?

I got started as a director of plays when I was with the *New York Times.* We started a little group back there called the *New York Times* Theater Guild, and we put on thirty-two different plays. I directed about half of them, and acted in a few. I'd been brought up in California, and we had a lot of friends in the picture business, one of whom was a director named Hobart Henley. Henley said to me, "Lee, if you want to go into directing, it's all well and good, go for it. But quit when you're ahead — when you have done as much as you feel that you ought to — and *relax*. The pressures are great." And they are — it's a tough racket, a tough business. I was in the business for forty years, I directed 1300 shows and I never was late. I always brought 'em in on time.

Many of your early credits were on the Johnny Weissmuller Tarzan series. How well did you get to know Weissmuller?

Very well. Weissmuller was just a doll to work with, just a hell of a guy. He wasn't the most intelligent guy in the world, and so those *Tarzan* and *Jungle Jim* parts were perfect for him. They didn't require a lot of brains, they just required a good physique. And Weissmuller was a master at swimming, and at keeping his trunk out of the water when he'd swim. Even in his older age — he was still playing Jungle Jim when he was in his fifties, and that's pretty damn good. His body wasn't *great* anymore — he did do a little drinking, and when you do that, something's got to give!

The first Tarzan film you directed was Tarzan's Magic Fountain *with Lex Barker. What's the story on him?*

He was an egomaniac — I mean, *really* an egomaniac. He had a birthday while we were shooting one of these *Tarzan* pictures, and the crew got together and purchased a great big mirror for him *[laughs]!* He was *built* — God, he had a nice physique — and he did very well in the business; he made a lot of pictures in Europe after he finished playing Tarzan. He was a real egotist, and that's about as much as I can say for Lex.

You know, my *wife* discovered one of the Tarzans. We were up at the Sierra in Las Vegas: I was looking for a Tarzan and she knew it, and she looked over and saw this handsome hunk of beef who was a lifeguard there. His name was Werschkul. I asked him if he was thinking that possibly he'd like to be an actor; he hadn't thought about it. I said, "Well, you'd make a good Tarzan, and they're looking for one in Los Angeles. I'm going to try and set up a meeting with you and a man by the name of Sol Lesser, who is producing."

That was Gordon Scott, right?
Right. My wife also gave him that name. He came up to our house one day and we agreed that the name Werschkul didn't sound too good for a Tarzan — or for *any* actor, for that matter! So she suggested the name Gordon Scott, and he grabbed it.

Did you ever help discover any of the Janes?
At one point, Lesser was looking for a new Jane and I found a young gal that I thought was just *marvelous* for Tarzan's mate. She didn't have to be a great actress, but she had to be attractive. A girl by the name of Marilyn Monroe. I just thought Marilyn would have been perfect. Well, Lesser didn't think so. I had her out *eight times* to see him, and eight times Lesser remained undecided. And, needless to say, he never did cast her.

Who ended up with the part?
He finally ended up with a gal by the name of Vanessa Brown for that picture *[Tarzan and the Slave Girl, 1950]*. She was a quiz kid, and Lesser had fancied himself as a man who had a great knowledge of words. He'd put long words into his scripts so that you'd literally have to look 'em up in the dictionary to understand what the hell he was writing about. He'd get the thesaurus out and find words that he thought would work, and he'd throw 'em into the script to make everybody think he was a genius! And he was more of a horse's ass *[laughs]!* Anyway, he chose Vanessa Brown because of her knowledge of words and her diction. And she was no bargain herself. There was a situation one day where she had about three words to say, and she asked, "What is the underlying *meaning* of this?" In a *Tarzan* picture *[laughs]!* "What is my feeling here? What is my attitude?" Oh, you never heard such shit!

After Superman and the Mole-Men, *your next science fiction film was 1954's* Tobor the Great.
Tobor was not an easy picture to make. There was a lot of action, a lot of hard work, a lot of nights and lots of days. I think we shot it in about two weeks.

What do you remember about your robot suit?
The suit that Tobor wore was expensive — I think the guy who put that together had been working on it for probably five months. It was utilitarian. The guy that worked in it had a tough time — it wasn't easy for him at all. It was no big problem, though, because we really didn't have him doing very much. But the guy worked out in the suit for about four weeks — what for, I'll never know! One *day* would have been enough.

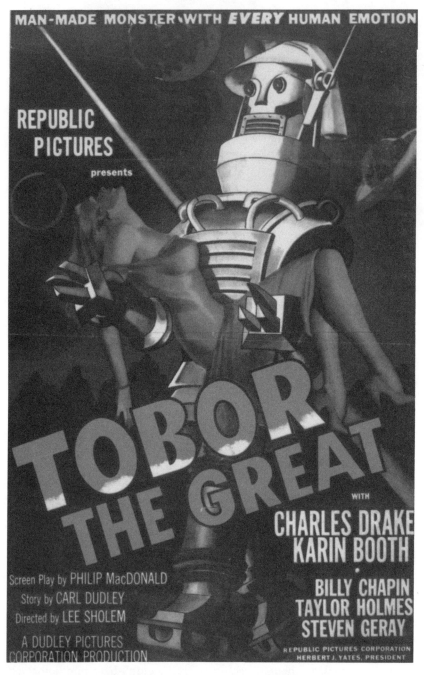

Made on a low budget at Republic Studios, Sholem's *Tobor the Great* was a kiddie-oriented sci-fi adventure remembered mainly for its mechanical star.

Unidentified man, director Lee Sholem, makeup man George Bau and assistant director Paul Wurtzel gang up on the shrivelled (and unidentified) star of *Pharaoh's Curse*.

And where was Tobor *shot?*
At Republic, in the Valley. But that wasn't made by Republic; the producers of *Tobor the Great* simply rented the studio space and the crews and everything else.

Then, in 1957, you made your only horror movie, Pharaoh's Curse.
I made *Pharaoh's Curse* for a producer by the name of Howard W. Koch. Howard is a doll of dolls; I've known a lot of guys in this business, and there *isn't* a nicer guy than Howard Koch. He used to work with a guy by the name of Aubrey Schenck, and I directed three pictures for them.

How did you get hooked up with Koch and Schenck?
I was shooting a show with Jon Hall, and the operating cameraman said to me, "Lee, when you get finished today, what are you doing?" and I said I was going home. He said, "Well, I've got somebody you ought to meet, a producer named Howard Koch. I'm going to go down and talk to him, and you'll probably be hearing from him." I got home and the phone rang, it was Howard Koch, and he said he'd like to have me come down and pick up a script for a picture *[Crime Against Joe,* 1956] he wanted made in Arizona. So I picked up the script, came home and read it, and called him up. He asked me, "Can you shoot it in seven days?" and I told him, "Yeah, I think so." And he said, "Well, then you'll be leaving for Arizona day after tomorrow."

So we go to Tucson, where [director] Les Selander was already shooting a Western for Howard. He was shooting first, and then after he was finished I'd move in and do my show. I had a week to prepare, and in that time I blocked my show. Now came time to shoot, and Howard came on the set. He'd never seen me shoot; up until a few days before he'd never even *heard* of me! He came on the set as I was shooting my first scene. He watched, and then he came up to me and shook my hand and said goodbye. I said, "Where are you going?" and he said, "Back to Los Angeles." I said, "Well, that's a hell of a thing — I'm just starting your show, and you're taking off." And Howard said, "Lee — you're going to do *fine.* "

P.S.: we finished that picture in *five days [laughs]!* And then he gave me another one *[Emergency Hospital, 1956]* and *another* one *[Pharaoh's Curse].* The total for these three shows: seventeen and a half days, for three features.

Where was Pharaoh's Curse *shot?*

The exteriors were done in Death Valley. We flew out of Burbank, early in the morning, and landed in the desert just as the sun was coming up. The company and cameras and all the equipment were all on trucks, and they were there already. We started at one end of the canyon in Death Valley and worked all the way down to the other end. We moved with the sun. We shot all the desert exteriors, finished the day's work and came home. One day! That was really one for the books.

You created lots of atmosphere in the tomb scenes.

Those were shot at American National. And you'd be amazed how little area we used in shooting those scenes. We did that by constantly redressing the sets: We'd put a piece or a prop in front of the camera, in the foreground, and we'd have a couple of run-bys. Then we'd move the pieces around, and you'd think it was a whole different area — but we'd only lit *one!*

What can you tell us about Doomsday Machine?

Oh, Christ — I didn't even know that was *released!* I kid you not! I'll tell you what happened on that damn thing: They had two directors in on that show, and they called me in to see if I could make anything out of it. Everything was just a hodgepodge — I don't know why they let the director carry on as long as they did. They had nowhere to go, they didn't know what to do. They knew they had nothing, the cutter was proving that — they couldn't even cut what they had! It was a monstrous job — it was a patch-job more than anything.

You get a director's credit, though.

Well, I guess because I saved it — as much as it could be saved *[laughs]!* I really don't remember how I got hired for that; I know the guy behind that picture was using his own money. And a lot of money had been spent. I had my own ideas about how to fix and finish the thing, and when I told him he asked *[sheepishly]*, "Can't we get away with just doing it *this* way. . . ? I haven't got that much dough." And then they had to go out and borrow more money—he had a very tough time.

Doomsday Machine was a tough job. When you go in to patch a show, you find that you've got certain sequences that *haven't* been shot and others that *have*. And you've got to shoot added scenes, and retakes, and God knows what else. That was a *mess* when I got ahold of it.

Do you have any particular favorites among your 1300 credits?

No, no—I enjoyed 'em all. They were great, they were fun. It was enjoyable, it was a great life—*but*, I sure wouldn't want to be doing it now. The pressures are too great. Everybody wants a picture done in so many hours, and you're under the gun from the time you get there in the morning till you leave at night. I've had it—forty years is plenty. It's fun to reminisce, but I don't want to get back into that routine.

I'm a writer, and to write the right things
is more important than getting a lot of dough for it. . . .
Today, nobody lives better than I do.
I have an estate, fifty acres overlooking the mountains,
and every night I say "Heil Hitler!"
because without the son of a bitch,
I wouldn't be in Three Rivers, California,
I'd still be in Berlin!

Curt Siodmak

AN INTERVIEW with Curt Siodmak offers the rare opportunity to speak with a man who was an important contributor to both the classic Universal horror pictures of the '40s and the sci-fi/horror cycle of the '50s. As writer or director, Siodmak has been associated with the superb *The Wolf Man*, the Karloff-Lugosi vehicle *Black Friday*, *Son of Dracula*, the all-star horror show *House of Frankenstein*, the Val Lewton masterpiece *I Walked with a Zombie* and, in the 1950s, such sci-fi standards as *Earth vs. the Flying Saucers* and *Donovan's Brain*. A prolific novelist and short-story writer as well, he is currently working on a novel called *Siblings*, inspired by his relationship with his brother Robert Siodmak, the great director who made such *film noir* and thriller classics as *The Killers*, *Phantom Lady* and *The Spiral Staircase*.

Born in Dresden, Germany, in 1902, Curt Siodmak worked as an engineer and a newspaper reporter before entering the literary and movie fields. It was as a reporter that he got his first break of sorts in films: In 1926 he and his reporter wife hired on as extras in Fritz Lang's *Metropolis* in order to get a story on the director and his film. Siodmak's first film-writing assignment was the screenplay for the German science fiction picture *F.P.1 Antwortet Nicht [Floating Platform 1 Does Not Answer]*, based on his own novel. Compelled to leave Germany after Hitler took power, he went to work in England, where he adapted the novel *Der Tunnel* for the film *Trans-Atlantic Tunnel* and co-wrote the script for *Non-Stop New York*. He then moved to Hollywood in 1937 and got a job at Universal on the picture *The Invisible Man Returns* through his director friend Joe May. "It was one of the first pictures that Vincent Price starred in," Siodmak recalls. "It went over well, and I fell into a groove."

While writing your three Invisible Man films — The Invisible Man Returns, The Invisible Woman *and* Invisible Agent *— were you limited in what you could write by what the special effects department was able to do?*

No, *I* told the special effects department what they *should* do. We had a kind of competition: I thought of the most impossible things, and John P. Fulton really came through with it, every time.

Were you comfortable with sci-fi/comedy on The Invisible Woman?

That was charming. Yes, I like comedies, and I also wrote a lot of musicals for Universal, for people like Ginny Simms and Susie Foster. John Barrymore was in *The Invisible Woman*, and he was at the point where he couldn't remember one line anymore. He had to hold the pages of dialogue at his side so he could read them.

On Black Friday, *Boris Karloff was originally slated to play the college professor who is turned into a Jekyll-Hyde character, and Bela Lugosi was supposed to portray the brain surgeon who is responsible for the transformation. When the film was made Karloff became the surgeon, Stanley Ridges played the*

Previous page: Curt Siodmak is flanked by twin female fans in a '50s photo. (Photo from the archives of Forrest J Ackerman.)

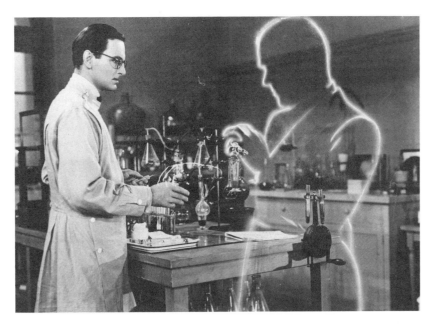

The Siodmak-scripted Universal film *The Invisible Man Returns* went over so well that Siodmak was instantly typed as a sci-fi/horror writer. John Sutton and a not-quite-invisible Vincent Price share this posed shot.

professor, and Lugosi took on another villainous role. What prompted this role-switching?

Karloff didn't want to play the dual role in *Black Friday*. He was afraid of it; there was too much acting in it, it was too intricate. So they took Stanley Ridges, who was a stage actor, and he filled the part. Karloff was smart enough to know that he might not come off too well in the role. Karloff had a very dark complexion, and I've often wondered where it came from. I think he had a little shot of Indian blood or something. A very friendly, very kind Englishman.

Bela Lugosi ended up playing a gangster in *Black Friday*, and that didn't turn out well at all. Bela never could act his way out of a paper bag. He could only be *Mee-ster Drac-u-la*, with that accent and those Hungarian movements of his. And he was a *pest!* He would call me up and say, "Curt! Please! Put me in your picture!" He was very unrealistic.

When you wrote The Ape *for Monogram, you made a lot of changes from the play and the first film version.*

Oh, sure. Whether it was *The Ape* or *The Climax* or even *I Walked with a Zombie*, I never used the original material. I used my own stories. In *The Ape*, Karloff played a scientist who discovers that fluid taken from the human spine can be used to cure a crippled girl, played by Maris Wrixon. That was an idea which *I* had.

While writing movies for Universal, did you know in advance who would be playing the various roles?

Yes, they told me who would be in the pictures before I would even start to write them. On *The Wolf Man*, for instance, I was told, "We have $180,000, we have Lon Chaney, Jr., Claude Rains, Ralph Bellamy, Warren William, Maria Ouspenskaya, Bela Lugosi, a title called *The Wolf Man* and we shoot in ten weeks. Get going!"   .

Was The Wolf Man *written as a vehicle for Lon Chaney, Jr.?*

Yeah. Well, actually Boris Karloff had originally been assigned to that title [in 1932], and he wanted to play it, but then another job came along and *The Wolf Man* with Karloff never came about. But I created the *character* of the Wolf Man. Of course there were some werewolf films before—not many, but some—but none with that sharp definition of character.

Was any research required in writing The Wolf Man?

A tremendous amount. Books and books on lycanthropy. Every time I write a story, you wouldn't *believe* how many books I read. Then, if it's a science fiction story, before I write I pick up the telephone and I call the most important men I can think of in their fields. And all the things are checked and rechecked.

You know, I have the bad luck in life of always being ten or twenty years ahead of my time. I wrote a book called *F.P.1 Does Not Answer,* the story of a floating platform in the ocean where the airplanes land between Europe and America, to refuel. I wrote that in 1931, and there's *radar* in it. And the weather stations of today are exactly the same construction. I wrote another book about twenty years ago called *I, Gabriel,* and in it I had *microchips.* Ten years before they *invented* microchips!

The Wolf Man *is such a definitive treatment of the werewolf theme that today it's difficult not to confuse the actual legends with your film's innovations.*

That's right. I wrote that little four-line ditty for *The Wolf Man*—"Even a man who is pure in heart. . ."—and nowadays, film historians think it's from German folklore. It isn't. I made it up!

A few years ago, I got a letter from a Professor Evans, from the University of Alabama, citing the parallels and similarities of construction between *The Wolf Man* and the Greek plays. At first I thought to myself, "This guy is nuts," but it was true. In the Greek plays, the gods tell a man his fate, and he cannot escape; in *The Wolf Man*, when the moon comes up Lon Chaney knows there's going to be a killing. In the Greek plays, the gods are domineering; in *The Wolf Man*, the father of the family is domineering.

The movie certainly made a lot of money for Universal.

After *The Wolf Man* made its first million, [producer-director] George

Lycanthrope Lon Chaney, Jr., hovers over an unsuspecting Evelyn Ankers in a posed shot from Curt Siodmak's *The Wolf Man.*

Waggner got a diamond ring for his wife, and [executive producer] Jack Gross got a $10,000 bonus. I wanted $25 more a week, and they didn't give it to me.

I never got a raise from Universal — *never.* "You get your raises outside, and *then* we'll pay you more," they told me. Basically I never pushed it because — this may sound silly — money doesn't mean as much to me as an objective in life. I'm a writer, and to write the right things is more important than getting a lot of dough for it. The other people make the money, and try to cheat you out of yours. I cannot be bothered. I mean, my time and my mind are much more important to me than fighting to get money out of some lawsuit. Today, nobody lives better than I do. I have an estate, fifty acres overlooking the mountains, and every night I say "Heil Hitler!" because without the son of a bitch I wouldn't be in Three Rivers, California, I'd still be in Berlin!

How much creative input did George Waggner have on The Wolf Man?
    I never talked to George except on Thursdays. I'd go into his office and give him all the honey I could think of—told him how big a man he was—and I figured, "The guy *must* know that I'm kidding." He never found out. I couldn't really sit down and talk to him about these pictures, because he'd say, "I don't want *my* ideas, I want *your* ideas!" So he never talked to me. But he was a nice man, and we had a good relationship. His idea of fun was to drink beer, sing songs—he was very German in his tastes. My brother Robert did a picture for him called *Cobra Woman* [1944], and they couldn't get along at all. Robert was much more individualistic than I am. For me it was a *job*. I went from one picture to the next.

What kind of relationship did you and your brother have?
    We had a sibling rivalry, Robert and I. When I was born, my father took little Robert to my crib and said, "Here's your new brother." And Robert said, "I don't want your new brother!" You know, like a dog who doesn't want a second dog around *[laughs]!* When we were in Germany, Robert had a magazine, and when I wrote for it I had to change my name. He wanted only one Siodmak around. This lasted seventy-one years, until he died!

And you only worked with him on one picture in America?
    I *never* worked with him in America.

What about Son of Dracula? *You get a story credit.*
    That's another story. Robert got his start in Germany, became very famous, made the big pictures, and then Hitler threw us out. He started in France and became very famous there. Then he came to America, where nobody knew of him. Finally he got a job at Paramount making B pictures— *West Point Widow* [1941], *Fly by Night* [1942], things like that. They forced him to do *this* shot and *that* shot, and Robert didn't want to do it. One day an assistant said to him, "I thought you were such a big director! Why don't you fight to do it your own way?" Robert said, "Because this is Paramount shit, this is not a Siodmak picture!" So they fired him. That's when Robert got a job at Universal directing this picture I had written, *Son of Dracula*. Next thing I knew, I was out. He had me fired and took on Eric Taylor as a writer!

We've been told that Robert Siodmak concentrated on getting one "perfect" sequence into every movie. The rest was just framework for it.
    Yes. Robert once said, "Only five minutes of my pictures are okay. The

Spooky posed shot of Lon Chaney, Jr., and Louise Allbritton from *Son of Dracula*. Siodmak had a writing job on this Universal film until his brother Robert came in as director and had him kicked off the picture.

rest is routine." I think Robert was one of the best directors you have ever seen. His pictures, they are classics.

We've heard that your brother and Lon Chaney had a dispute on the set of Son of Dracula, *and*—

—and Chaney took a vase and hit him over the head! Chaney was drunk—or at least I imagine he was drunk. Secretly he must have sneaked a few, then went up behind Robert, took a vase and hit him over the head with it!

All these people, if you knew them, had sad stories behind them. The father of Lon Chaney—the old man, Chaney, Sr.—was a very cold man, and he used to beat the boy all the time. Lon told me he had to go into a shed and be beaten with a leather strap, sometimes for things he hadn't done. This *killed* him, mentally—he became an alcoholic, and always needed a father figure to tell him what to do. He'd drink on the set. I stopped that when *I* directed him.

Tell us how the Wolf Man *sequel,* Frankenstein Meets the Wolf Man, *came about.*
Never make a joke in the studio. I was sitting down at the commissary having lunch with George Waggner and I said, "George, why don't we make a picture, *Frankenstein Wolfs the Meat Man*—er, *Meets the Wolf Man?*" He didn't laugh. This was during wartime; I wanted to buy an automobile and I needed a new writing job so I would be able to afford it. George would see me every day and ask me if I had bought the car yet. I said, "George, can I get a *job?*" He said, "Sure, you'll get a job, buy the car." Well, the day finally came when I had to pay for the car. George asked me that day, "Did you buy the car?" and I said, "Yes, I bought it." George said, "Good! Your new assignment is *Frankenstein Wolfs the Meat Man*—er, *Meets the Wolf Man!* I'll give you two hours to accept!"
And then you had to sit there and think, "What can I do?" Now is when you need a basic idea. My idea was, the Wolf Man, as was the tradition now, wants to die—he doesn't want to be a murderer. And Dr. Frankenstein knows the secrets of life and death. So he wants to meet Dr. Frankenstein. The Monster, on the other hand, wants to live forever. In an early script I wrote a scene which I knew definitely would be thrown out. The Monster is walking along with Chaney and Chaney says, "I change into a wolf every night." And the Monster says, "Are you kidding?"

One weak aspect of the Universal horror films is that the monster characters would turn up in sequels, often with no explanation of how they escaped destruction at the end of the previous picture.
That became a kind of gag. We finished the pictures in such a way that the next writer *couldn't* revive the characters. We'd freeze them in ice, cremate them, whatever. It was a game. Then *you'd* get the assignment, and you had to do it yourself!

It's never clear what happens to Maria Ouspenskaya at the end of Frankenstein Meets the Wolf Man. *Are we supposed to assume that she dies, or not?*
She died in the meantime *[laughs]!*

What can you tell us about House of Frankenstein?
The idea was to put all the horror characters into one picture. I only wrote the story. I didn't write the script. I never saw the picture.

Most of your early films lack a conventional hero type. They either have tragic heroes, like Chaney in the Wolf Man *pictures and Robert Paige in* Son of Dracula, *or unsavory or unscrupulous protagonists [Karloff in* The Ape *and* Black Friday, *Robert Alda in* The Beast with Five Fingers *and several more].*

This comes again from Greek mythology: a man who is guilty without being guilty, through some inequity, a defect in character, or something like that. My heroes are never *bad* people. I wrote a play called *Song of Frankenstein* — a musical — and in the story, everybody is a monster, *except* the Monster! The Monster is only twenty-four hours old, so why should it be mean? Nobody has hurt it. But *people* go through life and *they* become mean, see? That was the theme of it.

How did you get involved on The Beast with Five Fingers?

They had a few different scripts for that film, but they couldn't lick it. So they called me in. I had the idea that the hand was only in the man's mind. *This* made it, so they gave me the assignment, and a year's contract afterwards. I had Paul Henreid in mind for the [Hilary Cummins] part. "I won't play opposite some goddamned hand!" he said, so they took on Peter Lorre — which was, to me, too obvious. With Paul Henreid, it would have been a better picture. The special effects department did an excellent job.

Were you pleased with director Robert Florey's handling of the film?

I wanted to direct it; that was my whole objective. They wouldn't let me. Florey supposedly was very unhappy about the thing, and didn't want to do it. Luis Buñuel supposedly worked on it; I don't believe it. I never met the man.

You used some of the better situations of the short story, and built a very interesting and largely original film around that framework.

The widow of William Fryer Harvey, who did the original story, hated the film. She had sold the short story to Warner Bros., and it didn't turn out exactly as her husband had written it. But it was a very short story, so how can you make a big picture out of it? You have to add to it.

How did you enjoy working with Peter Lorre?

He was really a sadistic son of a bitch — liked to look at operations. He really was the type, a very weird character.

Jack Warner reportedly was unhappy over the way The Beast with Five Fingers *turned out. Did this ever get back to you?*

I only met the man once. One day he called me into his office and asked me not to become a Communist. That was all he ever said to me.

Val Lewton was known for his contempt for the kind of horror films being made at Universal during the 1940s. Did that cause any initial tensions when you worked with him on I Walked with a Zombie?

Oh, no. Why would he engage me if he had so little respect? He certainly liked my stuff, or obviously I wouldn't have gotten the job.

What was Lewton like?
He seemed like a lovely guy, very erudite, very interesting. But later I gave him *Donovan's Brain* to read, and when I came back to him he said, "It's not a good book." There was already a kind of friction between us, because he liked people he could dominate. He couldn't do it with me, because I was independent.

How did working with him compare to working at Universal?
Oh, he was brilliant, constructive and intelligent — much more interesting than any of those Universal guys. Producers at Universal were businessmen who would see that pictures came in on time and for the money. They never contributed anything of any literary value.

Did Lewton have a hand in the writing of I Walked with a Zombie?
Nobody helped me with *I Walked with a Zombie*. Of course, Lewton and I discussed scenes, and if he objected to something, I came up with an alternative suggestion. Ardel Wray came on the picture after I left; I never met her. Maybe Lewton had had enough of me, and that was why he hired somebody else.

Which of the three major movie versions of your novel Donovan's Brain *do you like best?*
I have not seen them. I saw half of one, and walked out. Republic made the first version. Herbert Yates [president of Republic Pictures] called me one day and said, "Siodmak, you are crazy!" I said, "Why am I crazy?" He said, "A scientist like Dr. Cory, he doesn't live in a little hut in the desert. He lives in a *castle!*" He put a damn castle in the story, and von Stroheim running around it like a rat! "And," Yates went on, "I have a new title for you — *The Lady and the Monster*. And *The Lady* will be *Vera!*" — Vera Hruba Ralston, the ice-skater, Yates' girlfriend. So I quit. And I never saw the picture.

Then they did it again — Allan Dowling made it, and it was called *Donovan's Brain*. Nancy Davis Reagan was in it. And in this one *God* destroys the brain with a lightning bolt! So I didn't see it. Then they did it again in England. The title was *The Brain*, with Peter Van Eyck. In that one, he invented a cancer cure. Why a cancer cure?!

If I had to be reborn, I would like to be John Huston. John Huston was about to do *The Maltese Falcon* [1941], so he took the Dashiell Hammett book to his friend Allen Rivkin, who was a writer, and asked, "How do I write a screenplay?" Allen Rivkin took the book, marked the scenes in continuity and said, "Take the book and shoot it." And so he did. I never wrote *any* of those *Donovan's Brain* scripts — they wouldn't let me. I had a contract to *direct* the

Allan Dowling version, but they paid me off. There was a guy over there, Tom Gries, that didn't like me. He had these advertisements made for the film saying, "Based on the famous book." Period. He didn't want to mention my name! Gries was the producer and he wouldn't let me direct it because of a personal dislike. He was the meanest son of a bitch I had ever seen.

Why did you decide to become a director in the 1950s?
I wanted to show my brother Robert I could direct. My first film, *Bride of the Gorilla,* is one of the pictures I like most for some reason. It was a marvelous idea: Raymond Burr has an affair with Barbara Payton, who has an older man for a husband. The husband gets bit by a snake and Ray Burr doesn't help him, lets him die — so he's a murderer. But his conscience doesn't permit that, so every time he looks in a mirror he sees an animal. Because an animal can kill without being punished, he's free of guilt. *They* made a gorilla out of it — I didn't even want to show that. *They* called the film *Bride of the Gorilla;* my title was *The Face in the Water.* It had real characters, and a story. Today's horror film directors, they have a mattress with two hundred and fifty gallons of blood coming up out of it, and *that* they call a picture *[laughs]! This* was development of a character.

There is one shot, toward the end of the movie, where you do see the gorilla, and not through its own eyes.
They forced me to do that — sometimes you can't fight 'em. But I like that picture anyway. And, can you believe, only seven days' shooting? Wow! And I got good performances out of them. Directing is 80 percent public relations and 20 percent directing. You have to put your people at ease. I made my people as comfortable and happy with their scenes as I could, and I got better performances out of them.

There are some interesting parallels between Bride of the Gorilla *and* The Wolf Man.
Possibly there are. I wrote the script on speculation, because I wanted to direct something.

How did The Magnetic Monster *come about?*
Ivan Tors came to me with ten minutes of a German picture called *Gold,* which had tremendous special effects shots, but he had no story. So we formed a company and I wrote a script around the footage and directed the picture. It cost $105,000.

Richard Carlson was a partner in that company also, wasn't he?
Yes, he was. He died of alcoholism, too. They're all unhappy people, actors. Most of them start to fade, and they cannot take it. I later wrote a picture for Carlson to direct, *Riders to the Stars.*

What can you tell us about Curucu, Beast of the Amazon?
I had no money at that time, so I wrote *Curucu*. The idea behind it was
very interesting, actually: The people in the Amazon jungle can shrink heads,
and a girl who studied medicine realizes that if she can find out the process,
she can use it to shrink cancer tissues, tumors and what-not, by injection. My
agent got a couple of other guys, Richard Kay and Harry Rybnick, aboard to
produce. It was done in Brazil for $155,000. I shot it down there, in the
jungles. I never recovered, physically.

Beverly Garland's presence in the cast really enhances that picture.
I'll tell you a story about her. I remember I wanted to shoot a scene by
the big waterfalls in Argentina. I figured I could make rubber face masks of
my stars and put them on extras, then shoot some long shots by the falls in
Argentina without having to bring the stars along. We went to this company,
Beverly Garland and I, to have a mask made. It was a horrible process. I
couldn't have done it, to have your face covered up with all this stuff and to
have straws up your nose so you could breathe. Beverly didn't want to do it
either, but there was already a naked rubber body of an actress, Carolyn Jones,
made for *Invasion of the Body Snatchers*. Beverly saw it and said, "Well, if *she*
can do it, *I* can do it!" and she went through with the thing. She's a brave,
tough lady.

You had an entirely Brazilian crew on that one, didn't you?
Portuguese. And I learned Portuguese very quick, to see what those sons
of bitches were saying behind my back!

What about your follow-up film, Love Slaves of the Amazon?
That was very tough, because I never knew what I had. I had forty thousand feet of film. You couldn't import film. By law, you could only develop
in the country, and they had no color labs. So what do you do? At one point
I asked my production manager, "How much film do I have left?" and he said
ten thousand feet. I said, "Wait a minute! I'm not half through yet!" So I
rehearsed every scene and got it in one take, and came back with the picture.
I could never see dailies, and so by *memory* I knew where to put the shots.

*About this time you also got involved with some television horror pro-
grams.*
I directed the pilot for *Tales of Frankenstein*, but no one ever picked it
up. I *told* them, "You cannot carry a whole show with nothing but Frankenstein stories!"

How about the made-for-television No. 13 Demon Street?
I had a title, *No. 13 Demon Street,* and I knew a guy named Leo Guild,
who was connected with an outfit called Herts-Lion. I met Kenneth Herts, who

Director Siodmak (with hat) checks the pulse of Frankenstein Monster Don Megowan in this candid shot from TV's *Tales of Frankenstein.*

made a deal for the pictures to be made in Sweden, and so I went over there to direct them. Twelve or thirteen episodes I shot. Herts-Lion showed them to CBS, but CBS didn't take them. Half a year later, NBC came out with *Thriller* with Boris Karloff — same idea, everything. Then Herts-Lion double-crossed me — they took three of the shows, put them together, put a frame around 'em and put Herbert Strock's name on it as the director. They made a feature out of it, and called it *The Devil's Messenger.* I wasn't even mentioned in the credits, but I'm glad of that. I never saw it.

Actually, some of those episodes did come out okay. I think they were better than the *Thriller's,* in story values.

Lon Chaney worked on that series, too.

Chaney went over to Sweden also, but he only played in the framing device. The frame was very interesting: The camera was on a house, and a storm was brewing. The camera went into the house, and a strange guy in a hirsute suit came forward — you never saw who it was — and he talked to the camera about the worst crimes he committed in his life, and how he is condemned to stay there in that room for eternity. He was a Wandering Jew. Then the camera went to the window and we'd show the show. At the end the camera would pull back through the window, out the door, and the wind would blow it shut. It was a good frame.

Compare the Lon Chaney of 1941's The Wolf Man *to the Chaney of* No. 13 Demon Street.

Well, he was already deteriorating, believe you me. He was a drunk, an alcoholic.

What is your opinion of the horror films of today?

Today, the approach is different. The special effects have taken over. There's no humanity in it any longer, no personality. We have drifted now into a soulless picturemaking business which is based on effects and cruelty. The pictures we did had no violence, only implied dangers.

You know, there's a parallel between time, history and horror pictures. When we made those pictures throughout the Second World War, we couldn't show an American with a machine gun mowing down five thousand Japanese. Nobody would believe it; it wouldn't work. So we had the Gothic stories. People would get rid of their fears and walk out of the theaters *knowing* it was a fake, a fairy story. When the war ended, the bottom fell out of the horror film business. Then, when they began testing the atom bomb, it all started again. And today, with the threat of a war, a *holocaust,* these films are as popular as ever. In times of peace of mind, there's no place for horror films; times of fear — like now — bring out the need for violence in people. This reflects, in my opinion, a fear of the people of *tomorrow.*

Everything seems so glamorous when you look back. It wasn't. It was a struggle for life, all the time. As soon as you finished a job, you were *out* of a job and trying to find another one. I took every job that came along in my life. I have thirty-four pictures running on television now and I don't get a penny out of them — not one cent. But look at the credits. Those guys are all dead and I'm alive. *Who's winning?*

I remember when I was doing these pictures,
my kids were ashamed of me, they felt I was pandering.
I said, "Look, we've got to eat — they're fun to do
and I don't mind." Now they're clamoring for me
to collect the posters from these films. . . .

———*Herbert L. Strock*———

HERBERT L. STROCK was involved in the early years of '50s science fiction and horror, first as an editor, then as a director, and worked steadily in the genre through the early '60s. The movies he has directed have ranged from the serious-minded science fiction of Ivan Tors to the no-holds-barred exploitation-horror of Herman Cohen. For Tors, Strock worked on *The Magnetic Monster,* a sci-fi thriller that made ingenious use of stock footage from the 1934 German film *Gold,* as well as *Gog,* a story about robots and sabotage in a space-station-in-the-making. From these relatively sober thrillers, Strock then went on to collaborate with AIP's Herman Cohen on three sensationalist horror pictures: *I Was a Teenage Frankenstein, Blood of Dracula* and *How to Make a Monster.* These movies, along with *The Devil's Messenger* and *The Crawling Hand,* have established Strock as a prolific and memorable horror craftsman.

Boston-born Strock's introduction in the movie business was as director of the Fox Newsreel crew, visiting Hollywood stars in their homes. After serving with the Ordnance Motion Picture Division, he found employment as an editor at MGM and later moved into the infant medium of TV, where he produced and directed *The Cases of Eddie Drake,* the first-ever motion picture film to become a network series. His first fantasy film credit was as assistant to the producer on *Donovan's Brain,* a film initially slated to be directed by Curt Siodmak but ultimately helmed by Felix Feist. Today the head of his own postproduction facilities, Strock looks back with disarming candor on a science fiction film career that has spanned four decades.

Curt Siodmak told us that producer Tom Gries dropped him as director of Donovan's Brain *because of a personal dislike, and described him as "the meanest son of a bitch" he had ever seen. Do you know anything about this?*

Despite what Mr. Siodmak told you, Tommy Gries was a lovely, lovely man. I knew him when he used to work on the *Daily Variety;* he was a very intelligent young fellow and became a damn good director. I was very excited about the fact that Curt was going to direct *Donovan's Brain,* and I wanted him to stay on the picture. But it seems that in discussions of how things were going to be done, Curt became the stiff, Germanic, immobile person, and would not listen. Gries and the producer, Allan Dowling, became very upset; I pleaded with them to keep Curt on, that I would guide him through, but behind my back they bumped him. And it was too bad, because Curt did feel very badly hurt. I tried to explain to him what had happened, and I also very much wanted to be his friend, but he kept sloughing me off and did not want to discuss it. He was extremely sensitive and extremely hurt. I can't understand his attitude toward Tom, because it wasn't a personal dislike at all.

I replaced Curt Siodmak a few times in my life: once on *The Magnetic Monster;* once on a TV series *[No. 13 Demon Street]* that was being done in Stockholm, Sweden; and then of course there was the situation with *Donovan's Brain.* As I said, I tried to get him to stay on the picture and tried to get the producers to keep him on, but it didn't work and he blamed me for this for the rest of the years. I haven't seen him in many years.

Siodmak places all the blame for his removal on Gries. He didn't mention you at all.

No, he told me that he blamed me for his losing *Donovan's Brain.* He also was very hurt when he was later thrown off of *The Magnetic Monster,* and that had nothing to do with me. I started out as editor on *Magnetic Monster,* and I just mentioned a few things to the producer, Ivan Tors: I told him that I thought Siodmak should get in closer with the camera, that he should do this and that, and so on. Apparently Siodmak resented these intrusions from the cutting room; he and Ivan had a fight and he was off the picture.

Curt has many negative feelings; he always had a chip on his shoulder because of the fact that he could never follow in the footsteps of Robert, his brother, who *was* a fairly good director. Curt just couldn't get his own projects going the way he wanted to do them.

What was it like working with Ivan Tors?

Ivan was charming to work with. He was a very open-minded, even-handed producer who knew his business.

Tell us about your experiences on The Magnetic Monster.

The Magnetic Monster was a picture written by Curt Siodmak. Ivan and Curt and Andrew "Bundy" Marton and Laslo Benedek were the Hungarian clan in Hollywood—there was a sign over their writing department at MGM, *Being Hungarian Is Not Enough.* They all took care of each other, and that's how Curt was working with Ivan. After two or three days into *Magnetic Monster,* Ivan was very unhappy with the dailies, and one day he called me and said, "Come on down to the sound stage." I said, "I can't—if I come down, you won't have your dailies on time." He said, "To hell with the dailies—come down to the stage." So I jumped on a bicycle and went down to the stage. Here was Richard Carlson, Ivan Tors, the cameraman and Harry Redmond, the special effects man—standing around, doing nothing! The script supervisor, a charming lady by the name of Mary Whitlock Gibsone, said, "They want you to take over the picture." I said, *"What?!* I'm not a director, I'm a film editor!" And she said, "This picture uses *so* much stock footage from the German film *[Gold,* 1934] we have, and you know *exactly* how everything must go together"—and Curt couldn't understand it. Ivan came over and said, "Don't worry, I've called the Directors Guild, you're in the Guild, take over." So *[laughs],* I was called upon to instantly become a director! I went over to the cameraman, asked him what was being shot, he told me and I said, "Well, that's not the way to do that, let's do that *this* way, and *this* matches *this"*—I didn't even have to *look* at the stock film, I knew it so well. And I directed the picture.

Speaking of Andrew Marton: When I took over this picture, "Bundy" said to United Artists, "Don't worry about the new director, because if he doesn't do it well, I will break my contract at MGM and *I* will take over the picture. That's how much faith I have in Herbie." And that's how I became a director.

Now, what exactly was the problem with Siodmak?
The problem with Siodmak occurred on the third day of shooting. He had shot some interior elevator sequences with Richard Carlson and King Donovan, and these intimate shots felt like they were shot in a barn—he used the wrong lens, he was too far away and so on. Scenes weren't playing, the man was falling behind schedule—he was *lost* somehow, I don't know what happened. That's when Ivan yanked me out of the cutting room, fired Siodmak and gave me the picture to direct.

As you can readily imagine, it was difficult to plot out the scenes at night that you were going to shoot the next day—I am a firm believer in production preplanning, which I had taught at U.S.C. for years. I would plan and come in and shoot, and then I also had to edit the film at night—so it was a real chore. However, the day after we finished, we showed what is known as a rough cut, and in fear and trepidation I ran the film with Ivan Tors and Richard Carlson, who was a partner in the project. I kept slinking down in the seat saying to myself, "Well, I gotta fix *that*," and "I gotta speed *that* up," and "That's not a good match." But when the lights came on, Carlson and Tors got up and *applauded,* and thought I had done an excellent job. They were both very happy.

Now, the upshot of this story is, I tried to get a poster from this movie recently, it was sent to me by a friend in New York, and it has Curt Siodmak's name on it as director. That was my first picture, and my name is on the film as director and film editor. And apparently no one bothered to tell United Artists—or if they did, it didn't drift down. The poster went out with Curt's name on it—which is to this day galling me. *I* directed that picture...!

I hate to be the one to tell you after so many years, but you don't *receive screen credit as director. The only time your name appears is as editorial supervisor.*
I just don't understand! I remember ordering—I *think* I remember ordering!—my name on it as director. However, it could be there was a legal shenanigan pulled by Siodmak against Tors, I don't know. I know I was a member of the Directors Guild, and if anything we should have had co-credit. But if I recall correctly, he only shot three days on that film, and I had to redo a lot of the stuff that he did. There was very little left that he had done; in fact, if I am right, there can't be more than six scenes that he shot.

Mr. Siodmak took the credit for directing Magnetic Monster *when we spoke with him.*

I did just about all of that movie; I don't know why he claims he directed the picture because he didn't shoot one-tenth of it.

Was the documentary flavor and the extensive location photography on Magnetic Monster *Ivan Tors' idea?*
    I did all the exteriors—this was my idea, *not* a Tor-ism. We were short on the movie, and we decided to go out and get some reality. I went out with a camera crew and shot all this stuff. When Richard Carlson went to work at the Office of Scientific Investigation, that was shot at the McCullough Plant at the Los Angeles Airport. I just walked up to the door and asked them if we could shoot in there, they said certainly, and we shot it right inside that place.

How did you like working with Richard Carlson?
    Carlson was a good friend of Ivan's. He was an actor with a photographic mind—he would merely look at a script, ask you what it was about, and then learn the lines that you wanted put on film immediately. He was a very pleasant man to work with.

What was he like as a director on Riders to the Stars?
    He was very capable. Carlson was originally brought out to Hollywood by David Selznick as a writer, became an actor, was very astute as a writer, very astute as a director, and knew quite a bit about editing. We got along like two peas in a pod; in fact, when he later did the TV series *I Led Three Lives* at Ziv, it was he that insisted that I come over there and take over the series because he felt that he and I were most compatible. Carlson directed *Riders to the Stars*—with my assistance—and I edited and was associate producer on that picture. We went to the U.S.C. Centrifugal Force Department, and we actually photographed Bill Lundigan in a centrifuge and spun him around and got the effects that we wanted from him. I did that directing, by the way.

Your next film for Tors was Gog *with Richard Egan.*
    Right. That was made in 3-D, shot with a magnificent cameraman by the name of Lothrop Worth, who I still see today. We had two cameras running simultaneously, through optics, to give it the 3-D effect which you saw when you put on the special glasses. Well, the funny part about it is, *I* can't see 3-D because I have monocular vision. So I had to rely on a Dr. Gunzburg, who was technical assistant. He guided me through this thing, and we had at that time one of the best 3-D versions that could be shot because we used it for effect and did it so it wouldn't hurt the eyes of the audience. And I'll never forget going to the preview of that picture, when Gog fired his arm of fire out into the audience and everybody screamed—and it didn't affect *me* at all!

All three of your sci-fi features for Tors were intriguing and sometimes exciting, but were belabored by talky scripts and a heavy emphasis on "science fact."

Scientist John Wengraf struggles in the neck-breaking grip of *Gog*.

That was another Tor-ism. Tors had a great intrigue for *The Scientific American* magazine, he became very over-talky in what he wanted, and you were stuck with that. The key was to try to find a way around the original talkativeness—that was *deadly*—that was written into the scripts, and you would have to fight Ivan a bit on how you wanted to rewrite those scenes. He rarely allowed us to rewrite, but when we did he went along pretty much. I completely rewrote *Battle Taxi* [1955] with a friend of mine, Richard Taylor. It looked so much like a documentary and a hurrah-hurrah for the Air Force Rescue Service that we didn't think it would make an entertaining film, and so we inserted where we could things that made it a dramatic film. We tried to do the same with *The Magnetic Monster, Riders to the Stars* and *Gog*—in fact, Taylor and I did a tremendous rewrite on *Gog,* and Ivan finally agreed that if we did certain things certain ways, he would go along. But he wanted that "science fact" *slammed* into the pictures, and that's the way we had to do it. He was in love with scientific facts.

The second half of Gog *is terrifically fast-paced, in contrast to the first half and to the other Tors pictures.*

We felt that *Gog* was bogging down, and I just took the bull by the horns and edited that picture a different way than was originally intended and made it work.

How were the twin robots, Gog and Magog, operated?

The robots were operated by a midget named Billy Curtis—he got inside, and was able to turn them, walk around, move the arms about and fire the acetylene torch which was in one arm. Billy was inside of those damn robots until I thought the guy would die! We had a terrible accident in these two films, *Riders* and *Gog,* with a brilliant man—an optical engineer, I think he was—by the name of Maxwell Smith, who in making some of the special effects for *Riders to the Stars* had an implosion at his home, due to a leaky oxygen or hydrogen tank in his living room, that blew off his right arm and cut a hole in his left leg. He did recover—we all ran out and gave blood. Ivan leaned very heavily on Max and Harry Redmond. Harry was into explosive effects, whereas Maxwell was into making gadgetry work so that we could photograph it.

Do you remember your budget and shooting schedule on Gog?

I think the budget was two hundred and fifty or three hundred thousand dollars, which was *nothing*—especially shooting 3-D with two cameras running all the time—and it was up to me to save money and come in *under* budget because Carlson had gone over budget on *Riders* and we wanted to get even. The shooting schedule I really don't recall, it was probably no more than fifteen days because in those days we had to shoot extremely fast. By knowing exactly what was needed in the cutting room, I would not waste a lot of film. However, I do remember one incident when an operative cameraman left the switch on in the camera and we went to lunch, and he ran out eight or nine hundred feet of film in each magazine, which was sixteen or eighteen hundred feet of color down the drain.

Why did Carlson go over budget on Riders to the Stars?

Carlson went over because he was trying to *act* in that picture and *direct* it and *rewrite* it and so on. Also, he was not sticking to planning. He was into color and into perhaps a larger production than he expected, he needed help and he asked me—he said, "Would you come down and direct the scenes that I'm in?" I did; I co-directed with him and enjoyed it very much. I liked Dick quite a lot.

Since space mirrors are being considered for use as part of President Reagan's "Star Wars" antimissile system, it's interesting to find them an integral part of the story of Gog.

The idea of using space mirrors was Ivan's. As I said, Ivan was into the *Scientific American* magazines, and he got a lot of these ideas out of there. Ivan was a darn intelligent writer—I didn't like the *words* he used, but his ideas were always very, very good.

Did you prefer Gog's *working title,* Space Station, U.S.A.?

You know, that's something I don't even remember! I think today it would have been a better title than *Gog,* but at the time I think *Gog* was good because it was fascinating and intriguing, and referred to Gog and Magog in the Bible.

What was it like working with a cast that included Richard Egan, Constance Dowling [Mrs. Ivan Tors] and Herbert Marshall?

I must say that Richard Egan was a pleasure to work with. He was, I would say, at the height of his career at the time — he was about to get a contract at Fox, if I remember right — and he was a really good guy. Gig Young was up for this part, and I felt that Egan was right and Gig Young was wrong. Right or wrong, I met with Gig, had a long talk with him and convinced him that this picture was not for him. Constance Dowling I loved dearly, she was a sweet, lovely woman — probably not the finest actress in the world, but very competent, easy to get along with. Because she was Mrs. Tors made no difference; she was just a member of the cast, and never pulled any rank or anything. Herbert Marshall was at that time probably one of the nicest — and *biggest* — actors I had met to date. Marshall had a bad leg; I believe he had it amputated in the war, around the knee. And it pained him terribly. If you study the film, you can see his slight limp. He came to me one afternoon, on the side, and said, "Herb, is my limping too obvious? Is it bad for the scene?" And I blurted out, like a jerk, "Oh, no, no, it's a good gimmick." And he looked at me and said, "Gimmick? With this pain, I'd hardly call it a gimmick." I will never forget that as long as I live. I felt terrible, I apologized, and he, being the charming Englishman that he was, understood. I was terribly hurt when he passed away.

There was one thing I particularly liked about this cast: They did *what* I asked them to do, *when* I asked them to do it and *how* I asked them to do it. We did a lot of moves: I was on a boom, I moved around on a crab dolly so that I would get motion into this film. I remember that I had a magnificent art director whom I had stolen from MGM, William Ferrari. Despite the fact that I was busy editing *Riders and* tackling *this* one, Bill and I worked out an idea of mine about color being used to emphasize the mood of a scene. I did a lot of research at U.C.L.A. about the impact of certain colors on the emotions. Bill and I worked out the earthy colors in certain scenes, the blue in the cold scenes, and reds and oranges in the warm scenes. And we were very clever in devising ways of cutting costs on sets, and making the same eighteen- or twenty-foot passageway work for different places in the movie. He was very clever at this, a fine art director.

Why did you edit The Magnetic Monster, Gog *and, later,* The Crawling Hand, *in addition to directing?*

At that time I felt that I could edit what *I* wanted the way *I* wanted it faster, and would therefore save money and time. Having come from the cutting room, I guess I couldn't shake loose the fun of being at a Moviola and making things work.

After making these Tors films, you spent several years working at Ziv-TV directing Science Fiction Theatre *and many other shows.*

Ivan Tors also came to Ziv through Richard Carlson; he ended up on *Science Fiction Theatre,* and I worked with Ivan on many of those. I enjoyed working on that show with actors like Victor Jory, Gene Barry, Gene Lockhart and others that the studio would hire because it was a prestige series. But eventually Ivan came to resent the fact that I would want to rewrite certain things in order to make them work better. There was really no argument between us, but he resented a little bit and I was moved off *Science Fiction Theatre* onto other series—as well as doing one of those every once in a while.

Ziv, for your information, was the name of a man—it was a Midwest firm and a man by the name of [Frederic W.] Ziv was the head of it. They were big in radio, and got into TV. He had people running the outfit that didn't know anything about the picture business—one was a mattress salesman! It was very, very tough teaching these people how to make films, because they had their own ideas. I did an unbelievable number of shows over there—*I Led Three Lives, Favorite Story, Meet Corliss Archer, Men of Annapolis, Highway Patrol, Harbor Command, Dr. Christian,* one after another. I enjoyed working over there except for the fact that the people we were working for really did not have any motion picture knowledge. It was very difficult fighting them when you knew they were wrong but they insisted things be done their way. It was like banging your head against the wall.

How did you end up working for Herman Cohen?

The way I got to work with Cohen is very interesting. Herman was on the Ziv lot at the time we were doing all these television shows. He would come down, unbeknownst to me—I didn't know who he was!—and he would watch me shoot. And he would see how fast we were going—we were always on budget, always or most of the time ahead of schedule. He came to me one day and asked me if I would be interested in doing a feature with him. I said I had a vacation coming from Ziv, I was sure I could get time off and I would be thrilled to do his picture. And that was *I Was a Teenage Frankenstein.*

What did you make of Cohen at the time?

I thought Herman was a strange bug—he had an ego that knew no end. He wanted things *his* way and *that's* the way he wanted them, and he wanted a director that would do things his way. He was a very wishy-washy guy who tried to be very pontific, which he couldn't be. He had no guts. I had very little respect for him and I guess he knew this. I remember that on *Teenage Frankenstein* we were shooting at two or three o'clock in the morning in a place called Hancock Park, which is a high-class neighborhood of homes; this Frankenstein Monster was running around in the backyards, and we were hauling cable and so on. I remember Herman and I had a terrible fight over something, I don't remember what it was, and I told him where he could go

Adolescent monster Gary Conway contributes a cultural interlude to Strock's *I Was a Teenage Frankenstein.*

and what he could do with his picture, and I would quit. And everybody on the crew was behind me, they *wanted* me to quit. But when it got down to the nitty-gritty, I just felt it was the wrong thing to do and it would be spread all over town that I walked off a film, and I stuck with it. But from that day on Herman and I did not get along too well. It was strange, however, that when he wanted to do *Blood of Dracula* and *How to Make a Monster* he took me to lunch and we walked around the block and he told me of *my* shortcomings and he told me about *my* attitude, and would I want to do the pictures? It was so strange that he would even come to me! I said, yeah, I'd do the pictures, because I wanted to do some more features and get away from the sausage-grinding-out of those hundreds of Ziv television shows I was doing. We made a deal, at a little better money, and he was easier to get along with on these two.

Did you contribute anything to Cohen's scripts for these pictures?
I would receive the scripts, practically finished, and I would say, "These stink," "These are bad," "This should be done *this* way" or "This should be done *that* way"—and we would work it out together. I tried awfully hard to correct a lot of things. You find that a writer, especially of this caliber on these pictures, really doesn't read the dialogue out loud, and you have to do that because actors have to speak the lines and they have to mean something. Sometimes alliteration or sentences that are backwards are very difficult for an actor to remember, and I would rewrite those. There was never any argument with Herman about rewriting dialogue, but restructuring was a real problem. The script supervisor was the same one I had on *The Magnetic Monster,* Mary Whitlock Gibsone, and she had broken the script down and tried to explain to Herman some of the mistakes. I remember having violent arguments with Herman over story points, over illogical things in the script, over time warps that were absolutely ridiculous—you didn't know where you were or when this was supposed to happen or how it happened. And he just didn't want to listen, till finally Mary and I got together and rewrote and did things that we thought *had* to be done. After much arguing, Herman finally accepted.

Your three Cohen films, as well as quite a few Cohen films you did not direct, are all very similar in plot structure. Was Cohen helping to write these scripts, or was this pattern something he insisted his screenwriters perpetuate?
Most of these plots and basic storylines came from Herman, as I remember. I believe that he did contribute to the screenplays, corny as they were—and now that you look back at them, they were really thin. And you're right, they *were* alike—I think he insisted that the screenwriter do this, otherwise he wouldn't work with him!

The major flaw in Teenage Frankenstein *is its heavy-handed emphasis on the repulsive aspects of the story.*
All this was done for Cohen's shock value, and I tried to get things done a little differently. I tried to do things in a tasteful way. I remember when we had Whit Bissell use the electric saw to cut off the leg, what I did was use the *sound* of the saw hitting the bone and you *felt* that it went through the bone—you never saw it. And then we lifted this phony leg through the scene. I remember when the censors ran this picture, they were furious. I had to run it again and explain to them that my effect was great—they loved the effect— but I did *not* show the leg being cut off, which they insisted I did.

What about your stars Whit Bissell and Gary Conway?
I probably used Whit in more different films than anyone else in town.

He was a very capable actor, always knew his lines, always on time—he was "Old Mr. Reliable," and he could play almost anything you wanted him to. Gary Conway was not that great an actor but he was a nice kid—a little sticky at times, but I had no real basic problem.

What prompted you to end Teenage Frankenstein *and* How to Make a Monster *with color sequences?*

Herman couldn't afford to do these pictures in color, so we did them in black-and-white and then for shock value made the last reel in color. This was a Cohen-ism, if you would want to coin a term.

What was it like working with a largely teenage cast in Blood of Dracula?

The casts in all these Cohen pictures were pretty untrained, untried—some of them had never done things before, others had made a few pictures, but they were easy enough to get along with. The only problem was, you never had enough time to really rehearse and get things the way you would like to have them. I remember when I was doing these pictures, my kids were ashamed of me, they felt I was pandering. I said, "Look, we've got to eat—they're fun to do and I don't mind." *Now* they're clamoring for me to collect the posters of these films, which I have been able to do.

Do you recall anything about Sandra Harrison, who played the teenage vampiress?

I found Sandra in readings, and I tried to get her involved in doing this show because she and I had a rapport—there was sympatico between us. But Herman didn't want her. At *all*. We read many, many other people until I finally convinced him that I wanted Sandra to do it. I think she is in New York now, doing some television commercials or something. In fact, she called me a few years ago and we had a few minutes together. Louise Lewis, who played the villainess, did a lot of work in AIP pictures, and she was married, if I remember right, to Robert H. Harris, who was also in many of these pictures. She was a very good actress. I do believe she is still alive, but I don't think she's active in the industry.

Where did the idea for How to Make a Monster *come from?*

It was either Cohen's idea, or AIP's, to combine Teenage Frankenstein and Teenage Werewolf in *How to Make a Monster*. I don't know where this story came from, but at that time we were told by many people, including a man, very famous in the business, Robert Lippert, that pictures about pictures don't make money. And I had fear and trepidation in doing this thing. I think the crew and the cast enjoyed it more than I did—it was a tough one to do.

Was Michael Landon offered the opportunity to repeat his Teenage Werewolf role?

Teenage Frankenstein (Gary Conway) grapples with Teenage Werewolf (Gary Clarke) in this posed shot from Strock's *How to Make a Monster.*

I don't think Landon was offered the opportunity because I don't know whether Herman and he got along that well. Also, I think Landon had already made too much of a name for himself and Herman couldn't afford him. Gary Clarke replaced him — not a bad kid. I thought Robert H. Harris, who passed away recently, was a little heavy-handed, a little overdone, and we had to constantly sit on him to try to pull him down. He had a tendency to run away with the lines.

Where were the studio exteriors photographed?
I think they were shot right on the Ziv lot. Because I know Cohen wouldn't let us go anywhere—we had no money for location shooting—I'm pretty sure it was shot right there—that's the old Educational Studios on Santa Monica Boulevard, which by the way is now a market.

It's always seemed to us that pictures about pictures must be especially fun to do.
How to Make a Monster was not that enjoyable because I had a lot of interference from Herman; he was always hanging around and watching what we were doing, making sure it was what he wanted. On the other pictures he was busy preparing these, so therefore he didn't interfere as much. This was one of the last ones, and he had more time to hang around. I do remember that he hired a cameraman who was related, I believe, to the assistant director. The cameraman and I just couldn't seem to hit it off. I would say to him, "I want to do the following shot. . ." and I would walk away *knowing* it could be done. Then in a few minutes I'd come back and see I'd have a completely different setup, and he would tell me that what I wanted to do wouldn't work. I resented this, and I pleaded with Herman to replace him. He was about ready to, because he was unhappy with some of the dailies, but he decided it was dangerous and he stuck with him.

I remember we had a fire scene. The wax masks were on a wall with these curtains, and when the special effects man ignited the pilot before the camera was running, the curtains caught on fire. We had the fire department standing by but I wouldn't let them put it out. I grabbed a camera, turned it on, yelled to another cameraman to grab the other camera, and we photographed part of the wax melting. *Then* we had the firemen put it out, and I was able to use these pieces later on. That was quite a mess.

Of your three films for Cohen, do you have a favorite?
No, I don't; I never liked any of them, really. *Teenage Frankenstein* was the most fun to work on because I had Lothrop Worth as a cameraman, and enjoyed that. I think *Blood of Dracula* has been listed in somebody's book as probably the worst Dracula film ever made—which is *[sarcastically]* a great honor.

Have you worked with Herman Cohen since?
After these pictures, I *have* talked to him but I've never been able to work with him—nor would I want to work with him, I don't believe.

About that same time you worked on a TV series called The Veil, *with Boris Karloff.*

The Veil was originated by Hal Roach, Jr., and it was done at Hal Roach Studios. I remember we had a lot of fun; I started out editing these, and then finally I wound up directing them. Karloff played a wide variety of magnificent roles—in one episode he would play a policeman from India, in the next one a British bobby, in the next a maharajah, then a doctor, then a lawyer and so on. This man was absolutely sensational. He was as easy to work with as anyone I've ever known, he was like putty in your hands. He would always know his lines; he knew everybody *else's* lines. I would tell him not to show up until 10:00, to take it easy—he was no spring chicken—but he would be there, ready to be in makeup at 8:30 in the morning no matter what I told him. He would stay after I told him he was finished—I tried to finish with him earlier in the afternoon so he could get some sleep, but he would stay. I'd say, "Don't *worry* about it; when I'm doing the other man's close-ups, I'll play your part off-camera and he can react to me." But Karloff felt it was much more charming if *he* stayed and *he* did the part, and the actor could get the proper reaction from *his* eyes. I mean, they don't come like this anymore. He and Ed Wynn were the two most professional people I have ever worked with. I was very, very sorry to see that series end. After that we went to San Diego and did the pilot for a show called *Mann of Action* with John Ireland, and right after that Hal Roach, Jr., got in trouble—the studio owed money, they got tied up with the Mafia and were sold, and all the pictures went down the drain.

Shortly after that you got involved on the Swedish-made horror TV series No. 13 Demon Street.

That brings back horrible memories. This was done for a company called Herts-Lion International, which has gone bankrupt. They had a Swedish motion picture studio, Nordisktonfilm, making this series in Sweden, with Curt Siodmak's scripts and Curt directing. The first five or six came back, and I was called by a Kenneth Herts, who was the president of Herts-Lion, to come and look at them. I ran these quote-horror-unquote pictures at home and my kids were roaring with laughter all over the floor over this corny, junk film that was supposed to be exciting horror films. When I went back to Kenneth I told him these were probably the worst scripts, the worst acting, the worst assembly of anything I had ever seen in my life. I never could understand Curt Siodmak; I always thought he was a sensible man but everything I've ever seen him do has been rather pedantic and ill-advised. It was like he just didn't know what he was doing. Ken insisted that I go to Sweden and remake them—so once again in my life I am replacing Curt Siodmak. Ken had already sent one editor over there to try to straighten them out, but the Swedes did not react pleasantly to him—he was a miserable, arrogant son of a bitch. The Swedes were putting up all the money so it was dangerous, but I went.

I met with a Mr. Hammerbaek, who ran the company, and the production manager at a club over there. At first Hammerbaek pretended that he didn't speak English—he had had it with Ken Herts and also with Curt, and I think he had it in his craw to get even with the Americans. It seems the American side was constantly blaming *them* for everything that was wrong with the series, but there was nothing wrong other than the screenplay and the direction. I noticed when I was talking, there was a light in Hammerbaek's eyes, so I *knew* that this man understood English. But he was waiting to find out where I was coming from before he would level with me. I assured Hammerbaek through the production manager—the production manager interpreted until Hammerbaek started to speak English—that they were not at fault, it was strictly a matter of stupid interpretation, a drunken Chaney, Jr., and all that crap. So finally Hammerbaek decided that I knew what I was doing, and he gave me carte blanche. He put up a lot more money, we reshot, we put some exteriors and action in, put a live score in and so on. I remade four of the messes that Siodmak left.

Did you work with Chaney, Jr., in Sweden?

No, I did not have Chaney to work with over there. When I got back, Ken called me and said that he wanted to put some of these episodes together into this *Devil's Messenger* film. We took three of the shows and strung them together with the Hell sequence, which I wrote. We had what I would call a half-assed crew—everything was done for spit and chewing gum. It was no fun—we rented a cheap stage and built this Hell set and played this stupid movie, and then I had to reedit and put it all together. Herts merely took the episodes and created a feature film and reaped all the money with no expense, the Swedes having paid 99 percent of the cost. I'm *still* owed about $10,000 on that picture which I have never seen to this day.

Herts changed his name and opened up a new company, and several years ago he conned me into believing he had found God and that he was a changed man. He had a half-baked story about a monster in Colombia and he wanted me to direct this picture *[Monstroid]* if I would do it for the expenses involved plus the trip to Colombia with my wife and daughter. My wife would be in charge of wardrobe, my daughter the script supervisor. I acquiesced, figuring it would never get off the ground. When it *did,* I was conned again into letting him use half of my building for his office. We were going to shoot in 35mm color and we were going to use my cameraman. I completely wrote the script— all he had was a storyline that was just terrible. I wrote the whole movie with a friend of mine and registered it with the Writers Guild. All of a sudden we're *not* going to Colombia, we're going to New Mexico, because I didn't realize Herts had trouble with the Colombian government—he had ordered a monster built down there at a cost of $10,000-plus, and had never paid for it.

Every location that he picked was absolutely unusable. My production manager, the cameraman and I picked all new locations with the help of the New Mexico Film Bureau. Now came casting. For our star we got Jim Mitchum, who sounded and looked like his father but . . . is problems. All of a sudden, everything was downgraded. Herts doesn't want to take my cameraman, he doesn't want to take my production manager—they cost too much money. Also, we're going to shoot in 16mm. I should have *walked.* I didn't. Actors came out of sewers. The word "actor" is actually a misnomer—these were human beings that couldn't spit and walk at the same time. We didn't have the time to teach them to act, we had a cameraman who had his own ideas, we had no one on the crew we could rely on. We shot this miserable mess for almost a month. I came back, put it in a rough cut, and then Herts and I had an argument and he had an argument with some of his backers. I've never seen a dime. To this day I have not been able to collect a penny of the $60,000 for the screenplay, the editing and the direction. *This* was the same guy that did *The Devil's Messenger.*

Why does he get screen credit for direction on Monstroid?
That is also a viable lawsuit, but I don't want to get into that because I don't *want* credit on it! The picture doesn't make any sense at all because he skipped story points—this guy has absolutely no story sense, no artistic integrity.

How did you get involved on The Crawling Hand?
The Crawling Hand also came to me through this Kenneth Herts. A man by the name of Joe Robertson had brought him a script, a science fiction/horror picture, and Herts asked me if I would read it. It was just awful. Some friends of mine and I had written this *Crawling Hand* a couple of years before, and it was very visual in the writing. I said to Robertson, "Let me show you how it should be written." So Robertson looked at our script for *The Crawling Hand,* and said that the guy he had putting up the money would put up money for *this.* The budget would be $100,000, it would be in black-and-white, and he wanted me to direct it. I made a deal with the writers and we went into production. Joe Robertson was the kind of producer that left you alone—he never bothered you, you did what you wanted. In fact, he was trying to *help* and would do things that would cost you money, like taking the pieces of film left over at the end of the shooting and sending them to the lab for processing when there's nothing on them! But he was a very charming guy and I know him today—he's in the soft-porn business at the moment.
As I told you, the budget was $100,000, it came in for ninety-eight some-odd. If I remember right, that picture was shot completely on location—we never once set foot in a studio. Even the computer banks and stuff were shot at the U.S.C. Computer Division Center. It *is* a minor film, it was made for peanuts, as I said, but it was a lot of fun to do.

Were you satisfied with the performance of your star, Rod Lauren?
I was not. I felt that Rod was a one-dimensional actor with a one-octave range, and I like larger ranges between people, to get highs and lows. Also,

Strock poses with actress Sirry Steffen during a break in the filming of *The Crawling Hand.*

we had this Miss Ireland, Sirry Steffen, in the lead—she wasn't much of an actress, but she was a doll to look at. We had nude scenes to do which Sirry Steffen didn't want to do. She would only do it if *I* put the body makeup on her; she trusted me implicitly—because I'm a prude, I guess. We shot the scene, it was never used. I found it rather difficult to maneuver these people. Mechanically, it wasn't too bad, I was able to stage things the way I had envisioned them in writing the script, but I found that interpretation and subtleties were missing because the actors really didn't have the experience.

Conversely, your supporting cast included a large number of screen veterans.

We just felt we could get these people, who had some sort of a pseudo-name which would help the picture, for less money because they weren't working, and that's exactly what happened. I had worked with Richard Arlen in some of the science pictures that Ivan was doing at Ziv; a very good actor, very good friend. Alan Hale was another actor I had worked with before; also Ross Elliott, Tristram Coffin, Syd Saylor and Arline Judge, whom I liked very much. We got them all together for very little money and made this picture. Another one of my mistakes: I could have had Burt Reynolds, who read for a part, but I didn't think Burt was good enough; at that time, he was a stuntman. So we wound up with Kent Taylor, who was a bit of a problem. He was never on time and he never knew his lines.

It's hard to picture Burt Reynolds in the part played by Kent Taylor. Was the role rewritten?
No, it was the way Taylor played it. We changed a little bit of it because he couldn't remember some of the long dialogue. Apparently he hadn't worked in a long time and was out of practice. He wasn't a bad egg, but he didn't have the professional attitude of getting in there and getting the job done. He was not showing up on time; begging off at lunchtime to go somewhere, promising to be back in an hour and not coming back for three or four hours, things like that. It wasn't a drinking problem — I don't know what he was doing or who he was seeing, but he was never on time.

Who designed the mechanical crawling hand, and how was it activated?
The mechanical hand was designed by myself and Charlie Duncan, an old-time special effects and powder man. He and I worked out the mechanical hand, which had little prongs in its fingers and a battery-driven motor on wheels. We just put a torn sleeve on it. Of course we couldn't make this hand crawl up stairs and up bannisters, and at times it would get stuck. So I merely donned a glove and it was my hand that did the actual crawling in those situations.

Have you been involved on any other horror or science fiction film projects in recent years?
A few years ago I took over a picture with Richard Benjamin, Lana Turner and Teri Garr called *Witches' Brew,* which a director by the name of Richard Shorr had started. He and his partner Donna Ashbrook got the movie with an NBC show-of-the-week commitment and started to make the picture. Apparently they didn't get along too well; Shorr was taken off the movie and I was asked to complete it. I shot about a week, wrote and redirected many scenes, and edited the picture. It was a lot of fun working with Lana Turner and Benjamin and Teri, who are all very, very capable. Lana was of course full

of fear and trepidation *against* Shorr; he berated her terribly. He would scream at me about certain things and I finally just barred him from the cutting room once he was taken off the movie. It *is* a good picture, it cost about six or seven hundred thousand dollars, and it was a lot of fun.

My acting days are behind me now. I saw Audrey Hepburn
on TV the other night, and talking about her career she said,
"I did my thing. Let the kids do it now." And that's
how I feel. Thank God I don't have that burning desire
that some people really have — I think that'd be
horrible to live with.... My Emmys and my Oscars
are my children, and I like it that way.

Gloria Talbott

IF THERE'S A LESSON to be learned from the sci-fi films of actress Gloria Talbott, it's just that you can never be too careful in picking your friends. She was the girlfriend of a rampaging one-eyed giant in *The Cyclops*, legal ward of a werewolf in *Daughter of Dr. Jekyll*, bride of an alien invader in *I Married a Monster from Outer Space* and romantic rival of an ageless murderess in *The Leech Woman*. But what the onscreen Gloria Talbott apparently lacked in discriminating judgment, the real-life one compensates for with exuberant charm and earthy wit.

Gloria Talbott was born in the Los Angeles suburb of Glendale, a city co-founded by her great-great-grandfather. Growing up in the shadows of the Hollywood studios, her interests inevitably turned to acting, with the result that she participated in school plays and landed small parts in such films as *Maytime* (1937), *Sweet and Lowdown* (1943) and *A Tree Grows in Brooklyn* (1945). After leaving school she started her own dramatic group and played "arena"-style shows at various clubs.

After a three-year hiatus (marriage, motherhood and subsequent divorce), Talbott resumed her career, working extensively in both television and films. A showy "sweet young thing" role in Paramount's *We're No Angels* (1955) failed to pave the way to top stardom, and the talented actress soon found herself a fixture in B-grade Westerns and horror thrillers. Although long retired from the acting profession, Gloria Talbott remains a '50s favorite for sci-fi fans.

How did you become involved on The Cyclops?

I think I was just simply sent the script, they met my price, and I was *in* — although I had no idea what I was in *for!* I remember that the first day of shooting was on Alvera Street, in the oldest building in Los Angeles, where we did the scene where I'm talking with the Mexican governor. Just seconds before we were going to start, Bert I. Gordon said to me, "Gloria, I want to ask you something. I saw *We're No Angels*. I just don't understand how you let Peter Ustinov and Aldo Ray so overpower you in that picture. You came off looking like a little weakling compared to their performances." I was stunned. I said, "Are you *serious?* I was playing a little girl! A sweet little girl who fainted a lot! What in the world are you *talking* about?" And he said, "Well, I just don't know why an actress would allow them to take the scenes away from her."

To this day I don't know if he just wanted me angry in that one scene — but if he did, he did a very good job! I was absolutely infuriated, and I stayed mad at him throughout the rest of the picture because I thought that was one of the dumbest things I'd ever heard. You'll remember that in that first scene my character is agitated? Well, it's *not* all acting! I was mad as hell that first day — I came very close to crying, I wanted to quit. I told Tom Drake about it — I liked him enough to confide in him that Bert Gordon had already gotten me to the point where I was ready to puke — and he said, "Oh, the hell with him, Gloria. Forget that crap and just say the lines." Thank goodness he had

Gloria Talbott fans got a double dose of their favorite leading lady when Allied Artists co-billed *The Cyclops* with *Daughter of Dr. Jekyll* in 1957.

that attitude, because that helped me a lot. I just tried to stay away from Bert Gordon as much as I could.

What kind of a director was Gordon?
He was like a man possessed because he did have to get it finished quickly; this was all done in five or six days. But he certainly had it well organized — and I'm sure that his wife had a hell of a lot to do with that. His wife was so sweet — she was doing the script supervising, the wardrobe, making cookies, *everything* — and he was so *mean* to her, like she was "the help." He had a disregard for actresses, I do believe — or maybe females in general. He just wasn't a particularly pleasant person.

Gloria Talbott, James Craig and Tom Drake in *The Cyclops*.

How did you get along with co-stars James Craig and Lon Chaney, Jr.?

James Craig was an enigma to me. He never once said, "How do you do, Gloria?" or "My name's Craig"—he would say his lines and go away. And it wasn't just *me*—he was that way. So we had absolutely no rapport. I don't know whether he was having terrible personal problems or what, but he would do the scene, then just sit down and not talk. He was not cruel or mean, but he didn't want to have very much to do with anybody.

And Lon Chaney?

Lon Chaney was just a dear, sweet man, with such a vulnerability that you wanted to wrap him in cotton and take him home. His mama came up to Bronson Canyon and brought him lunch, which I thought was dear, and brought him an air mattress. They blew it up, and he laid out in the sun and went to sleep on it! I thought that was charming. He was a bear of a man, but kind and sweet. I loved him.

What about Chaney's notorious drinking problem?

Lon Chaney was a darling, darling man—but drunk as a skunk! I don't drink and I've never done drugs, but those things probably hurt a lot of people in the '50s—they were passing out amphetamines in the cafeterias! I remember that all the scenes that took place on the Cessna were shot in a mock-up on a little tiny stage on Melrose that I think Bert Gordon rented for the day. Lon Chaney and Tom Drake were in the two front seats, and James Craig and I were in the back. Well, both Lon and Tom were absolutely *smashed.* James Craig was nipping a little, too, but nothing like what was going on in the front! And in this *h-o-t,* tiny mock-up I was getting blasted from the *fumes!* It was such close quarters and so hot that I was ingesting alcohol through my skin, I was getting absolutely stoned, and by the time we got out of there I was *weaving [laughs]!* If you watch that scene, you'll see that every once in a while I look a little sick—well, I *was!* That was a funny piece of business.

Did you come in contact with the actor who played the Cyclops?
    Only the time that the boa constrictor almost killed him! I did not know the stuntman; we were all so busy that I didn't even get a chance to watch them apply his makeup. But we were all there at Bronson Canyon, and I was watching them shoot the scene where he fights the snake. Well, the snake did manage to get around the actor, and it started to constrict around his throat and his chest. It got hairy—the actor went down, he was in trouble. And the handler was scared to death. What I think he did was take a stick with a little nail in it, and somehow used it to make the snake let go. There *is* a little bit of it in the film, but I'm not sure how much. That was scary.

Where else besides Bronson Canyon was The Cyclops *shot?*
    There was a scene in the jungle that we shot at the Arboretum—James Craig and I are chased by a giant lizard, and we run into a pond. We tried it once, and we kept running on *top* of the pond! And we all realized that there was at least twenty years of *duck shit,* cement-hard, forming a surface that went out a good ten feet. And, I swear to God, they yelled, "Cut out a piece of the duck shit so we can get the actors in!" I actually sat there and watched them bring out a chainsaw and hack out a big area for James Craig and me to wade in, where the duck shit was still floating around in pieces. I'm amazed neither of us got salmonella—I mean, it was horrendous! And I thought to myself *[laughs],* "*This* is glamor? *This* is fame and fortune?" I just wanted to go home...!

Any other recollections on The Cyclops?
    One funny thing, when it was premiered. They opened a new theater in Redondo Beach, and the first picture they played was *The Cyclops.* It was a "sneak preview spook show"—they didn't tell the people what the picture was. This theater was huge, and it was packed. I was there, with my agent, and my folks, and my little boy. The film progressed past the point where the Cyclops was seen for the first time; James Craig and I returned to camp, and I said, "I feel sorry for that giant, I pity him, and I don't know why." Beat. Beat. "There's something about his *face...*"
    Well *[laughs],* when I was saying it, it made sense to me as an actress—I was seeing my old lover's face somewhere in there. But within the context of the film it was one of the funniest lines I had ever heard in my *life!* The people

Doing what a scream queen does best, Gloria Talbott lets out a yelp in director Edgar G. Ulmer's *Daughter of Dr. Jekyll.*

caught on — it started low, people tittering, and that started a roll. Pretty soon everyone was hysterical, *screaming,* stomping their feet and rolling in the aisles. And for the first time in my life I saw my agent get scared; he whispered to me, "Darling, I think it's time for us to go." He thought they might turn *angry!* And we left the theater while this was still going on! Since then, they have cut it — thank God! — but it was a classic line.

Were you happy with the results on The Cyclops?

I was amazed. There are parts that are corny, but considering the time involved; the amount of locations we went on; how quickly we did it; some of the not-too-reliable actors; and Bert I. Gordon's personality — considering all that, I think it's not bad. I'm not ashamed of the film; and I'm not ashamed of *Daughter of Dr. Jekyll,* either.

What did you enjoy about Daughter?

I felt that it had a good, interesting script; I loved Arthur Shields, I thought he was by far a better actor than his brother, Barry Fitzgerald. He was certainly a wonderful gentleman. And I worked with a *nice* director, Edgar Ulmer — I liked him a lot. He was . . . *[laughs]* kind of insane, and I love people who are quirky and funny. He just was easy to work with — he was not a Douglas Sirk, who thinks he can get a performance out of somebody by scaring them to death. He was affable and fun — a pixie, sort of.

Also, I had some good lines in the film, like, "If you love me, you'll kill me"—I really *felt* it, and I can still make myself cry when I watch that scene. And I thought that the cameraman did wonders with my face. If you don't light my face just right, I look *funny*. Well, this man was indeed a photographer, and I was vain enough to be very happy with the way I looked in the film. And, again, we did it in something like five to seven days—not on a stage, but in a house. It was on Sixth Street, near Hancock Park, where there are great, *wonderful* old mansions; it must have been the Beverly Hills of seventy years ago. That house was fascinating—I'd never seen a kitchen like that, never seen a dumbwaiter, never seen such a library or such a glorious staircase. It was a real experience.

The first time we met, you told us about a "dumb mistake" you spotted in Daughter.

In the scene where I come down for breakfast, in the background is a lace curtain. If you look closely, you're going to see 1956 Chevys, Fords, etc., going by on Sixth Street—and since John Agar and I drove up to the house in an old Stutz Bearcat to establish the period, these new cars flying by spoiled the whole mood. I didn't pick up on it, either, as we were shooting, and it just drives me insane whenever I watch it. It *was* a dumb mistake.

What do you remember about working with Agar?

John was another enigma to me; I can honestly say that John didn't seem to have much personality. He certainly was not gruff or mean, or standoffish, like James Craig was on *The Cyclops,* but he would do his scene and then just go sit.

Why did a stand-in take your place in the nightmare scene?

Quite frankly, I never gave it any thought. I *think* that they didn't believe that I could turn into that rather sexy, demonic-looking creature; that would have taken a lot of makeup and a lot more time. They did that scene after I was gone, and whoever that was that they brought in was wonderful.

And overall you're pleased with the way the picture came out?

As a matter of fact, I was amazingly surprised at it. I didn't think it was going to be anything—it was another one of those "wham-bam-thank-you-ma'am" shoots—and yet it turned out to have a lot more content that I might have hoped.

I Married a Monster from Outer Space *gave you your most dramatic sci-fi role. How did you enjoy the experience?*

I loved working at Paramount, I was very much at home there; the money was terrific; and I did like the role, although in a sense it really was written one-dimensional. I tried my best to put some dimensions into her. I think there could have been more of a character development, and I was anxious to play with it. One scene I liked was when I was trying to seduce Tom Tryon into bed; I was trying to be flippant and cute, and I was getting *nada*. So there was a change in character there. And there were lots of scenes where I was scared — and I can really play scared. I've been frightened in my life — horribly frightened! When I was a kid I had an older sister who was gorgeous, and the boys would follow her home and peek in our windows. We had six years of peeping toms scratching at our windows, but we were so poor we didn't have a phone to call the police. It was like living in a horror movie — scary as hell!

Did you like working with Tom Tryon?

Tom and I had worked together in two or three *Matinee Theaters* and we liked each other a great deal. I remember a day when we were at Lake Sherwood, which is where we filmed the scene where one of the aliens drowns; we were laying on the grass, between takes, and he was watching this great big plane being refueled in midflight by a smaller one. He must have watched for about fifteen minutes, I looked up finally and started watching, too, and he said *[softly]*, "They just had *sex* — right up in the air. . . ." Well *[laughs]*, he didn't say it to be funny, he was looking at it as a writer. He *is* a writer, of course — he wrote *The Other*, which is still one of the scariest movies I've ever seen. That movie haunts me, I thought it was wonderful. So he was very introspective, very *into* himself, but always professional, always gave 100 percent. One thing I do remember is that Tom didn't like the monster outfits. Originally they had tiny spangly jockstraps for the aliens to wear, and Tom just freaked out when he saw that. He said, "This is ridiculous — it'll look like monster Rockettes!" He was absolutely right, and they did change them.

Gene Fowler, Jr., directed seven pictures, some of them very good [I Married a Monster, I Was a Teenage Werewolf, The Rebel Set], *and then went back into editing.*

Gene Fowler put a *lot* of himself into these pictures; I know that he was worn out at the end of *I Married a Monster*, I could just see it physically. I know he took the picture home with him every night, he slept with the script — it never came out in agitation, but I could see it coming out in tiredness. But I liked doing pictures with Gene, he was a sweetheart, and it was a delight, an actor's dream, to work with him.

So everything went smoothly on I Married a Monster?

I enjoyed the whole experience, except for the first three days. One side of my face was swollen because I had an abscessed tooth, and for a few days, while we were shooting the scenes that took place in the living room, they had to shoot around that. One other thing I remember is that the man who wrote the movie, Louis Vittes, was so *intense,* and so insecure that we weren't going

Talbott's wedding party assembles in 1958's *I Married a Monster from Outer Space.*

to do it right. When we'd be rehearsing a scene he'd sit way back in a corner somewhere, but then just before we were ready to shoot he'd get on the floor directly under the camera. He knew his script inside out, and he would sit there and silently *mouth* every word! And he went absolutely insane if we left out an "a" or a "the"! He was not being unkind, I think he was just scared. But it was driving both Tom and me crazy to have the guy down on the floor saying the lines! Finally I had to go to the producer and ask him if this could be avoided — I didn't want to hurt this fellow's feelings, but it was distracting as hell.

Do you think that the notoriously silly title helped or hurt I Married a Monster?

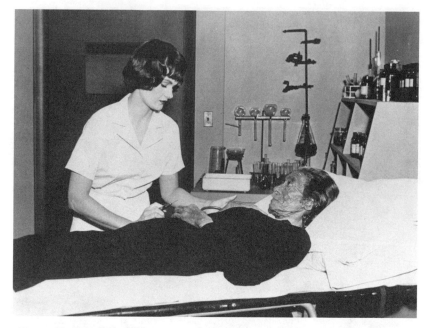

Nurse Gloria Talbott ministers to wizened Estelle Hemsley in *The Leech Woman*.

I think the title *killed* it; I think people went in expecting to see a funny movie. But now that it's so well known, I can't think of a better title — in fact, I believe now that the title has helped make the picture! But, again, at the time I thought it was sad that *I Married a Monster from Outer Space* was our title because I felt it was a better movie than that.

Was your shooting schedule quite a bit longer than on the other sci-fi jobs?

I think we had almost three weeks; compared to *The Cyclops* and *Daughter of Dr. Jekyll* this was a *big* movie *[laughs]!* And it was an enjoyable experience because we were not rushed. We did do a lot in a short period, except this time we ended up with a picture that some people now call a classic. All in all it was an excellent experience.

Can you tell us about working with the cast of The Leech Woman?

Grant Williams was a very interesting fellow — another one of those "inside-himself" people. I would come on the set and he would say, "Oh, God — pure woman!" — and then leave it at that! He was always easy to work with. Phillip Terry was another James Craig — do a scene, go sit in a corner. But the star, Coleen Gray, was wonderful. I remember that as we were getting ready to shoot the fight scene, she said to me, "I'm little, but I *am* strong." Well, about two weeks before I'd had a fight with Steve McQueen in one of his *Wanted: Dead or Alive* episodes—he grabbed me, I tried to get away from him and I really gave him a fight. It was fun because I wanted to see if he could hang onto me—it was a twirling, twisting fight where I actually picked him up on my back at one point and went around in a circle, which he couldn't *believe*. So when Coleen Gray said that, I thought to myself, "Well, if I can almost outdo McQueen, I can sure handle *you*, lady!" But, by God, this little bitty person wasn't kidding! She picked me up, *threw* me in the closet—incredible! But she was very much a lady; I liked her and she was very good to work with.

Did you enjoy the opportunity to turn "heavy" in your last scene?
Yeah, it was fun—although it was kind of weird, because I didn't get much of a chance to work up to it. I mean, it was the least of my challenges. I've got to admit *[laughs]*, I made that picture because I wanted to buy a horse for my son, and *The Leech Woman* got him a really nice horse and saddle!

The way you pull the gun on Coleen Gray, and expect to take her to the airport at gunpoint, really was ludicrous.
I know, the entire time I was holding the gun I was thinking that this whole thing was ridiculous! But I thought, "Oh, well, the horse is pretty, he's brown, I like him, so let's keep going, Gloria!" Anybody who tells you they're acting just for the love of it is in the hierarchy of 5 percent. For most working actors there's usually a monetary consideration involved in it. But how nice to be paid for something that isn't that hard, and that you like to do!

Why did you retire from acting after An Eye for an Eye *[1966]?*
I'd been working a long time, and I decided that I wanted to be with my new baby, Mia, who was born in '66. I wanted to be a mom, and I haven't regretted it—Mia's been such a joy to me. And then meeting and marrying my new husband, Patrick, has filled my life. Mia's about to get married, my son has a son, I'm a grandma—I mean, I'm *heavy* into family! The only time I miss acting is when I see a part that somebody's fluffing, or doing absolutely wrong. I get to the point where I want to scream—and so I turn the channel.

Do you ever think about getting back into the business, or are your acting days behind you now?
They're behind me. I saw Audrey Hepburn on TV the other night, and talking about her career she said, "I did my thing. Let the kids do it now." And that's how I feel. Thank God I don't have that burning desire that some people really have—I think that'd be horrible to live with. It's been fun, it's been interesting, I've enjoyed rehashing it with you—but I don't believe you've heard any mournful sounds coming from me, have you? No "my-my's" or "why didn't I get *this* part or *that* part?" My Emmys and my Oscars are my children, and I like it that way.

[The Curse of the Living Corpse *and* The Horror of Party Beach]
opened in Fort Worth and Dallas in a multi-drive-in situation. . . .
I remember we went to one of those back-to-back drive-ins:
on the other side of the screen from our films
were Move Over, Darling . . . *and* PT-109 . . . , *which was*
about $18,000,000 worth of pictures. And I'm thinking,
"Oh, God, what are my little black-and-white,
no-name pictures doing competing with these?"
The results came in the next day
and we outgrossed them. Double.

Del Tenney

FEW HORROR/EXPLOITATION PICTURES have established as unique an appeal as *The Horror of Party Beach*. A movie with something for everyone, it combines such '60s elements as the surf craze, sports cars, teenage sex, radioactive waste, bikers, rock'n'roll, a rumble and monsters. The man behind this heady package was a resourceful Connecticut-based independent named Del Tenney, who also made *Psychomania*, *The Curse of the Living Corpse* and *I Eat Your Skin*, an exploitation legacy not easily forgotten.

What was your background before you began making pictures?
    I was born in Mason City, Iowa, in 1930. When I was twelve, my parents moved to California, to join the war effort, so I lived in Los Angeles all my school years. I went to Los Angeles City and State colleges, got interested in the theater at the age of sixteen or seventeen, became an actor and actually made a living at it for most of my younger adult life. I worked my way through college as an actor in things like *The Drunkard*, and did extra work in films like *Stalag 17* and *The Wild One* [both 1953]. I had such classmates as Bob Vaughn, Zev Bufman, James Coburn, Alan Arkin, Bobs Watson—on and on and on. I graduated in '53 from Los Angeles State College, which at that time was considered one of the best drama schools in the United States. In '54 I came to New York with very little money, and I was going to be an actor. I worked at various jobs—working in restaurants, being a detective—but mainly I supported myself working in summer stock. You could make a decent living at it—it was nothing to write home about, but *[grandiosely]* I was a de-*vo*-ted *ac*-tor. I think by the time I finished acting in '62 I had had fourteen years of summer stock and thirteen years of winter stock.

What made you decide to quit acting and get into filmmaking?
    At that point I decided that I really didn't want to be an actor anymore; the struggle was not worth it to me, and I really wanted something a little more secure. You know, when you're an actor, even though you *have* a job, you're *looking* for a job—always. I guess I wanted to be my own master—it was just a matter of growing up. I decided that I really liked the production end of the motion picture business; I'd always been on the outskirts as an actor, and I was fascinated by the technical aspects of filmmaking, editing, special effects and all that stuff.

What were your first behind-the-scenes jobs?
    I started as assistant director on several very low-budget pictures—down-and-dirty stuff. Back then there was no such thing as hard porn; it was all soft porn. In those days it was pretty risque stuff; today you'd look back at it and

Previous page: **Aside from handling the chores of writing, producing and directing, Tenney also played the mystery killer in *The Curse of the Living Corpse*. The bathtub victim is Tenney's wife, actress Margot Hartman.**

A strong cast bolstered Tenney's first film, the mini-budgeted *Psychomania*.

you wouldn't blink twice — it's done on television now! We did things like *Orgy at Lil's House, Satan in High Heels,* and a couple of shorts for what would have been considered porno producers.

How did your first horror film, Psychomania, *come about?*
My wife [actress Margot Hartman] and I started to work on a screenplay

that was based on a true story. She had gone to Bennington College, and at one point a girl disappeared—later they found her body, she had been murdered, but they never found the killer. And we thought that would be a good basis for a relatively scary murder mystery—which is basically what *Psychomania* turned out to be. My wife and I did the screenplay, which is not on the credits.

Someone named Robin Miller gets screenplay credit.

I don't even know at this point who Robin Miller is *[laughs]!* My wife and I did a treatment, and then I did the screenplay. I really didn't like it; in those days I didn't have enough confidence in myself as a writer, because that was really the first thing I'd ever done.

What were your budget and shooting schedule?

I think we did that picture on $42,000—my father-in-law put up most of the money for it. Nineteen or twenty days of shooting with actors, then maybe a week of pickup stuff.

Did you have a hand in the directing of Psychomania?

I directed a lot of it—but, again, I didn't have confidence that I could do it. A friend of mine, Dick Hilliard, was a very talented, all-around sort of filmmaker, just a few years out of Princeton. I had worked on a couple of his pictures that never saw the light of day. We really worked together on *Psychomania,* but I gave him the credit for directing it. Most of the action stuff, I did. Having my theater background, I found out as we went along that I could work with the actors better than he could, because he was really not a theater person. So a lot of the more intimate scenes I also certainly had a great hand in.

Psychomania was a nice picture to work on because our cast were all stage actors and very accomplished people. Shepperd Strudwick was, of course, a wonderful actor, and Lee Philips was quite hot at the time. I remember Roddy McDowall was also under consideration for that Lee Philips role—we knew we couldn't afford a *major* star, but we wanted somebody that people would recognize.

Many of the Psychomania *supporting players—Jean Hale, James Farentino, Dick Van Patten, Sylvia Miles—went on to Hollywood stardom.*

When we were preparing to cast after the screenplay was finished, what I did was ask myself what actors I knew that fit the roles. In those days, and today still, we use a lot of our friends—nepotism, you know. I knew Jimmy Farentino quite well, and Sylvia Miles and I had been on the road, along with Hugh O'Brian, in *The Rainmaker.* You must understand that by now I'd been in the theater and had been in summer stock, and I knew practically every actor in those days. My wife was also in that picture.

The only prints of Psychomania *that turn up today are loaded with negative splices and abrupt scene changes, suggesting some major cuts.*
Well, it was cut and then it was added to. We went back and shot a lot of the so-called "sexier" scenes with Lorraine Rogers and Jimmy Farentino, because the distributor wanted more sex in it. *Psychomania* was kind of an exploitative film—really a soft porn, I guess, although it's so mild compared to what's going on today. Our original title was *Violent Midnight*—I don't know where *Psychomania* came from.

The distributor probably came up with that, to invite confusion with Hitchcock's Psycho.
Well, that's what they were going after in their selling of it. We had a lot of fun making *Psychomania,* and it really turned me on to moviemaking. We looked at all these pictures as kind of off–Broadway filmmaking.

Did you make money with Psychomania?
Psychomania was a relative success. I didn't make a *lot* of money on it, but we ended up with a few bucks in our pockets, which I thought certainly made it worthwhile.

Tell us about Alan Iselin, your co-producer on The Curse of the Living Corpse *and* The Horror of Party Beach.
Alan Iselin's family had about thirteen drive-in theaters in and around Albany. He approached me and said, "Gee, I'd really like to get into the movie business. I have an idea: You put up half the money, I'll put up the other half, and we'll make two pictures—strictly drive-in fare. I'll come up with two titles that I know I can sell—I can even build a pressbook right out of the titles before we even start on the screenplays. Can you do it for $100,000?" I said, "Aw, why not?"—because what did I have to lose? So he came up with *The Curse of the Living Corpse* and *Invasion of the Zombies.*
I decided that I was going to try an experiment: to shoot these things back-to-back. We built a sound stage in a studio here in Stamford, the old Gutzon Borglum Studio. In those days, my father-in-law owned it—it was his summer house. He gave us the place and we turned it into a mini–sound stage. My wife and I wrote both original scripts.

Again, as with Psychomania, *this isn't reflected in the credits.*
Credits? I didn't care about credits, *nobody* cared with these things. They were always done kind of tongue-in-cheek and you never knew how they were going to turn out. And, obviously, they are not the greatest films in the world.
I gave myself seventeen days apiece to shoot with actors, and got together a bunch of people who were friends and film nuts for my cast and crew. We did *The Curse of the Living Corpse* first. As you know, that was the first film

Robert Milli reacts to a sword across the face in Tenney's *The Curse of the Living Corpse*.

that Roy Scheider was ever in; Scheider is a wonderful man. Candace Hilligoss was quite a nice actress; we had worked together on a couple of plays, and I thought she was a good choice for the ingenue role. I'd seen her in a very strange film called *Carnival of Souls,* and I think that I hired her on the basis of that.

Have you ever appeared in any of your own films?
    I'm in almost every one of them! It was always a case of the-actor-never-showed-up or we-need-somebody-on-the-spot. Let's see—most of the shots of the masked character in *Curse of the Living Corpse* is me. In *Psychomania* I was in the bar and I break up the fight between Lee Philips and Jimmy Farentino. In *Horror of Party Beach* I play the gas station attendant who lets the gas spill over. And in *Zombie [I Eat Your Skin]* I did a lot of the stuntwork—the diving, and other stuff.

Curse of the Living Corpse *has some elements in common with a Roger Corman picture that was new at the time,* The Premature Burial.
    Never saw it. It might be possible that I was subconsciously inspired by the original Edgar Allan Poe story, because I read all of Poe's works. Alan Iselin had come up with the title *Curse of the Living Corpse* and, realistically, there are only so many plots you can make out of that!

Where did you shoot your exteriors for Living Corpse?

Most of *Living Corpse* was shot on the grounds of the Gutzon Borglum estate—we had about ten acres there, and a river; the bog was right down the road. It was a lot of fun. The big trick was to get six or seven minutes into the can every day. Two takes was exceptional, three takes was almost unheard of. And this shows in the films—they're not good films, and were never meant to be.

Living Corpse *seems almost a prototype for today's splatter films with its slasher-killer, mutilation murders and nearly nude scenes.*

I did have some problems later with *Living Corpse*. In those days, they had the Legion of Decency, and on that board were priests and nuns and so on. They came up to me and said that they were going to give *Living Corpse* the equivalent of today's X rating—not because of the excess sex and bloodletting, but because of something that never entered my head. There's *matricide* in *Curse of the Living Corpse,* when it turns out that it's Roy Scheider who's killed the mother. I told them, "Well, I never even *thought* about that—I mean, the man's *insane!"* You get so wrapped up in these pictures that you don't think about who's killing who, you just do a murder a reel. That's the formula.

Twentieth Century-Fox saw *Curse of the Living Corpse,* which as you know has some good things about it. We told them about *Horror of Party Beach,* which I was just starting at that point, and they said, "If *Party Beach* is at all decent, we will distribute both of them, but we have to see it first."

How did Iselin's proposed title Invasion of the Zombies *wind up as* The Horror of Party Beach?

Invasion of the Zombies / Horror of Party Beach started as an evolutionary story about atomic waste speeding up evolution, changing a fish into a man who becomes a monster, "the man of the future"—big, tall, no hair, features changed. *That* was the original idea which I had for that, which I still think is a very interesting idea and someday, maybe, I will do that film. Then Alan and I tried to work the music into it, the Del-Aires and all that stuff, and tie in some kind of a beach-blanket beat. We wanted to bill it as "The First Monster Musical." I don't remember which of us changed the title to *The Horror of Party Beach.*

Are there any anecdotes you can recall concerning the production?

The third or fourth day of filming, we were going to shoot a sequence where there's kind of a drag race, using a local group of motorcyclists called the Charter Oaks—the Hell's Angels of Stamford, Connecticut. Well, as you know, people go crazy when a camera starts. This guy from the back of the pack, a crazy, decides he's going to do something different than what was planned. He puts the pedal to the ground, passes the lead guy, clips his handlebars and knocks him over! You've got to understand, there are forty of these motorcycles cóming up behind them! Anyway, they start crashing off the road and into the woods and somersaulting, and one of them smashes into the camera car—! Well, to make a long story short, four or five of the bikers end up in the hospital, and one of my lead actors is among them with what we thought might have been a broken back. Obviously he was out of it for about three months, so there was no way that we could go on with him. We even had to shut down shooting for a few days.

The point I'm trying to make here is that these guys were *really* rough characters. I had made them all sign releases that if anything happened, I was not responsible for their *bikes* or their *lives,* or *anything.* We had an editing room set up in the studio so that we could look at the rushes, and late one night I was working with the editor and rewriting the script because one of my lead players was out of commission. All of a sudden I hear the motorcycles roaring in the distance, getting closer and closer. Sure enough, they pull up in the driveway and walk in with their leather jackets and their long hair and their beards, smelling like a fish market. So I grin: "Hiya, fellas! How ya doin'?" But I'm thinking, "God, these guys are *mad!"* because, after all, there'd been thousands of dollars worth of damage done to their bikes. And, since two police cars had crashed on the way to the accident, the mayor and the police department were not too inclined to help me at this point. There was this sort of pause, and they're all standing around, shuffling their feet, and I'm thinking, "You've had it, brother—you're gonna get wiped out." So one of them finally says, "We wondered whether you would show us the film. . . ." All they wanted to do was see the film! I had shot it from three different angles, so they sat there *all night* running this footage over and over and *over,* until I wanted to throw up.

Who designed and constructed your Party Beach *monster costumes?*
Those were built by Bob Verberkmoes, who was a set designer out of the theater. I didn't like the monster suits he came up with, but he thought it was funny—campy—that people were gummed to death with hot dogs instead of sharp teeth. I didn't think it was particularly funny, but I let him have his way. The monsters' heads were well above the heads of the actors inside; the actors had to look out through a hole in the neck, if I remember correctly. And those suits were very hot—we shot that in the summertime.

What's become of them?
I have no idea. I did have one of them hanging around here, and my kids used to put it on every once in a while, and at Halloween. They're gone now. I mean, you're talking twenty years ago. I wish I still had it!

After Party Beach *was finished, you had to show the print to Twentieth Century-Fox.*

Radioactive waste spawns a band of scaly sea monsters in "The First Horror Monster Musical," Tenney's *The Horror of Party Beach.*

And I was afraid that Twentieth Century–Fox was going to see it for the piece of crap that it was! The day we were to screen it for the Fox head of distribution, I had a guy who had played one of the monsters secretly putting on a monster suit in the bathroom while we were getting ready to project. All of a sudden the distribution man says, "Excuse me, I have to go to the bathroom." So I'm thinking, "Oh, Christ, I've really blown it now!" A minute later I hear, "God *damn* you, Tenney!" And he comes tearing down the hallway into the screening room, runs up to me, shaking, red in the face, yelling, "You almost gave me a heart attack! How could you *do* that to me?!" Well, of course, everybody in the place thought that this was one of the funniest things they'd ever seen in their lives.

And Fox decided to take the pictures.
Right. We had spent at that point, clear through to the answer prints, $120,000. Remember, our original budget was $100,000, so I was feeling a little bad about the fact that I went over budget 20 percent. We opened in Fort Worth and Dallas in a multi-drive-in situation. Alan and I flew down there with the executives from Twentieth Century–Fox because it was the first opening and a big deal. I remember we went to one of those back-to-back drive-ins: on the other side of the screen from our films were *Move Over, Darling* with

James Garner and Doris Day and *PT-109* with Cliff Robertson, which was about $18,000,000 worth of pictures. And I'm thinking, "Oh, God, what are my little $120,000, black-and-white, no-name pictures doing competing with *these?"* The results came in the next day and we outgrossed them. *Double.* Of course Twentieth Century–Fox was impressed and they really shot the works, did a big job of promotion—it was one of those flukey things. The pictures made a lot of money. Unfortunately most of the money Alan and I made went to taxes. That's the way it worked in those days.

You broke up with Iselin shortly after that, didn't you?
     Alan wanted to hire me to do his next picture, *Frankenstein Meets the Spacemonster;* he didn't want a partner, and I didn't want to work for somebody else. So then I made *Zombie [I Eat Your Skin].*

We've always felt that Zombie *lacks most of the qualities that make* Living Corpse *and* Party Beach *such favorites today.*
     After the success of *Living Corpse* and *Party Beach,* Twentieth Century–Fox came to me and said, "Listen, my friend, you've got to go union on your next picture. That's the only way we're going to distribute it." So that's why I had so much trouble with *Zombie;* it was no longer off–Broadway filmmaking. I was stuck with four makeup men, eighteen electricians, so on and so forth. That was my so-called "big" picture—it was a fiasco.

That was shot in Florida, right?
     The whole thing was shot in Key Biscayne, when Key Biscayne was nothing but a jungle. And *hot?* Oh, my *God!* We got all sorts of jungle rot and fever and malaria—you wouldn't believe it. The local doctor finally came to me and said, "What is going *on* here? Twenty people come to me every day from your cast!"
     I remember, there was one sequence where Heather Hewitt is swimming across this little inlet, way out in the jungles of Key Biscayne, and Bill Joyce dives in after her. That took about half a day to shoot. Well, we later found out that four of the largest sharks ever found in that area were seen in that bay the next day! That scared me a bit—I never did tell Bill or Heather.

Zombie *went through a lot of different titles before it ended up as* I Eat Your Skin.
     It was originally called *Caribbean Adventure.* The reason I called it that is, I didn't want the people of Biscayne Bay to know I was making a horror picture. We knew that we were going to call it *Zombie,* or *Zombies,* or maybe even *Invasion of the Zombies,* but *Caribbean Adventure* was our shooting title so that everybody would think it was a James Bond–ish kind of thing. I remember calling that film *Voodoo Blood Bath* for a time, too.

What were you planning to do about a second feature to go with that film?

I was going to make another picture to go along with *Zombie;* I had a cute screenplay called *Frankenstein Meets Dracula.* Unfortunately I had trouble getting a distributor for *Zombie.* The whole market fell apart at that point: Hammer was making big pictures with Christopher Lee and Peter Cushing, and then the big, color, star-studded horror/disaster film cycle started. And I knew it was time for me to get out of this business—I could see investing $100,000 but I couldn't see sinking two, three million into a picture. Then it stops being fun and it becomes big business. So I got away from low-budget filmmaking—but I will say that it was quite a wonderful, rewarding experience, because I learned a lot about all aspects of the business.

Of your four horror films, which would you say is your favorite?

I think *The Curse of the Living Corpse.* It makes a lot more sense than the others, and I think it has a little more artistry in the photography, and in the direction. I took some extra time, had good actors working for me, and the story sort of fit together. Plus, I knew more about filmmaking at that point, having had the *Psychomania* experience.

Were you discouraged by the unfavorable reviews your films got at the time, or by their presence on Worst Films *lists today?*

Those kinds of things don't bother me. I didn't make these films for art, I made them because I thought it would be fun and we could make some money on 'em, which is exactly what happened. Goodness knows, I found it amusing when my friends used to come up to me and gasp, "How could you *do* all these terrible films?" I told them, "Listen, I cry all the way to the bank."

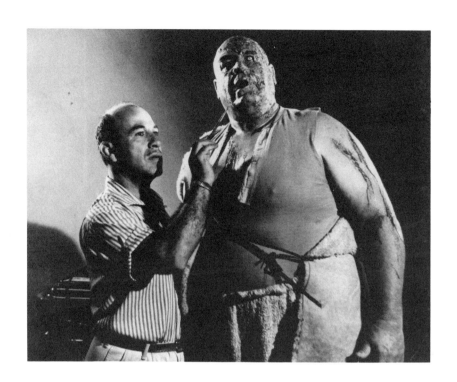

Everything is pressured on these low-budget pictures.
Sometimes they'd say, "We've got to get this thing done today,"
and they'd start cutting pages out of the scripts.
And this hurt me, because I figured that someday
the makeup was going to sell these pictures.
It wasn't the hackneyed stories or
the poor acting; it was the makeup.

Harry Thomas

DURING THE exploitation/horror boom of the 1950s, makeup man Harry Thomas was associated with some of the most memorable personalities and pictures of the period. He worked with Roger Corman, Edward D. Wood, Jr., Tor Johnson and Richard E. Cunha, and contributed to such films as *Frankenstein's Daughter*, *Cat Women of the Moon*, *Killers from Space*, *The Neanderthal Man*, *Port Sinister*, *The Little Shop of Horrors* and many more.

Thomas began his career in the 1930s when one of his first jobs was at MGM working under the renowned makeup artist Jack Dawn and his associate, William Tuttle. He is best known for his work on horror movies of the 1950s in which he almost invariably had to make something out of nothing, but he has also worked more recently on such features as *Logan's Run* (1976) and *The Hand* (1981).

Did you have a fondness for horror or science fiction movies before you began your makeup career?

Yes. I especially enjoyed the Frankenstein films, and I was very thrilled when I later worked under Jack Pierce. He was a little, feisty man that I enjoyed knowing; I respected his genius. I used to visit him over at Universal in the 1940s.

Universal treated Pierce pretty shabbily during his last days at the studio. Was he ever bitter about that?

Yes, he was kind of bitter. Jack had a miraculous way of doing these horror makeups with Egyptian cotton, spirit gum, collodion, lens paper—very similar to the way I work. I believe his pride was hurt, and I don't know whether or not he resented the fact that Bud Westmore went in there and took his place. I believe that Universal mentioned that he was getting older, and they wanted somebody who would work faster, and do prosthetics; that was their excuse. I don't think anybody's ever compared with what he did. Universal was very, very ungrateful in doing this to a man whose pictures all made a lot of money. The makeup artist didn't get the recognition or the appreciation in those days—not like today.

I never like to work in a major studio. I did work in a lot of them; you did *all* the work and you got no credit. The man whose name does get up there on the screen never even came down on the set. It was very interesting, but the pay was low and the department heads never came to view your work. People who do nice work, or think they do, like to get some kind of appreciation. That's all we need, we human animals. Being independently working most of the time, I would get a little bit more for myself than I would if I worked under a department head. There was a couple of hundred dollars difference per day.

Previous page: Thomas applies final touches to the makeup of man-mountain Tor Johnson on the set of *Night of the Ghouls*. Thomas says he had to stand on a box to reach Johnson's face for these touch-ups.

One of Thomas' first Hollywood jobs was as an extra in films like Laurel and Hardy's *Pardon Us* (1931). Thomas is standing to the right of Oliver Hardy.

How did you become interested in working in the movies?

I was interested in *art*—I did some artwork during the Depression. That's when I had an opportunity to get into the motion picture business and do makeup and various other things. Early on I worked at Hal Roach; I did some atmosphere [extra] work, a little costuming, a little of this and a little of that. They had no unions to speak of in those days—you could do whatever you wanted to do, if you were willing, and nobody jumped on you. Today it takes five union people to move a makeup table, and they get after you if you try and do anything yourself.

Do you enjoy the many extra creative opportunities that come from working on a horror or sci-fi film?

Oh, I just love them. You know, I used to work here in my house, even when I didn't have a picture, and create things on my own. I used *my* face, because my friends wouldn't cooperate; they said, "I *eat* hamburgers, I don't want to *look* like one!" So I made myself up. For *The Neanderthal Man*, for instance, I didn't have anybody that would sit, and I worked on that by myself, on my own face.

Did you make up the Mole-Men for Superman and the Mole-Men?

Oh, I did the whole thing. The producers wanted to use children as the

Mole-Men at first, but I fought against that. Midgets are easier to work with, and their faces are older and more porous. I brought those midgets into my house and I took the size of their heads. I put bald caps on them and stuffed them with cotton to make them look a little larger than their faces. I crossed the eyebrows, and then, to make it a little different, I laid a little tuft of hair down near the mandible—the bone below the ear. Every one was different— they all had this to identify themselves. I wanted to make them look sympathetic—not horrible or scary, but lovable little creatures from another part of the planet.

And you later did the Adventures of Superman *TV series?*
Right. It was very nice work—I enjoyed it. I even did the first episode *[Superman on Earth],* and I made the parents progressively older while the kid grew up to be the Mighty Man of Steel.

What was George Reeves like to work with?
George was very pleasant; he sort of kept to himself, and wasn't a glib person. He had a sensitive personality. We got along very well; he told me that he was a nightclub singer at one time, so I'd go into his dressing room, say "Now, George, I like to sing, too," and we'd sing a little ditty together. So he *was* human, even if he did come from another planet.

How did the hectic pace of TV compare to that of the low-budget movies you worked on?
Television was a lot more hectic. They had budgets and schedules, and they don't want to go over—or *under*—because of the union demands for overtime, meal penalties, etc.

How did your makeup for The Neanderthal Man *evolve?*
To give it a little authentic touch, I went to the library and looked at several primitive people—the Cro-Magnon, the Neanderthal and a lot of others. I made up Robert Shayne. The Neanderthal Man was laid with cotton, spirit gum and stuff like that, the way Jack Pierce would do it. After I'd make Shayne up, I'd make a double up, because Bob didn't do all the running and chasing, or the tiger attack. When he died in bed, I think they reversed the process: Shayne had all the makeup on, and I took off the pieces so he'd look like he was changing back to normal.

The transformation scenes in that film are interestingly done and rather effective.
They could have spent more time, and photographed it a little better than they did, but everything is pressured on these low-budget pictures. Sometimes they'd say, "We've got to get this thing done today," and they'd start cutting pages out of the scripts. And this hurt me, because I figured that someday the

makeup was going to sell these pictures. It wasn't the hackneyed stories or the poor acting; it was the *makeup*.

You also made up the servant girl as a Neanderthal Woman for a series of still photographs seen in the film.
The girl was very lovely; her eyebrows were fascinating, very heavy, as I recall. I left 'em that way; sunk her eyes; did the teeth, and all that sort of thing. She changed, but not as much as Shayne did. The minute we started that picture, it was makeup, makeup, makeup, all the way to the end. The Neanderthal Man worked a lot—it didn't just pop up once in a while to scare you. This thing they played to the hilt.

What can you tell us about the saber-tooth tiger sequences seen in the film?
The tiger was very playful, just a big cat, like you'd have for a house pet. It weighed four or five hundred pounds—a beautiful animal—but it *wouldn't* get ferocious. I made the tiger's trainer up as the Neanderthal Man for the scene where the tiger jumps the monster. The cat wanted to lick his face and purr. In those days, I don't think they had the Humane Society or the restrictions they have today. They took a stick and poked the tiger from the back so he could look furious, but they never accomplished that.

What about the design of the alien eyes in Killers from Space?
The producer-director W. Lee Wilder wanted to get ping-pong balls and cut them for the eyes of the aliens, because he didn't want to pay the price I asked, which wasn't very much. I made the eyes out of plastic and colored them, gave them a light film for the sclera and put a hole in the middle so the actor could see. Again, it was a hurry-up thing—what I wanted to do was punch the plastic eyes through cotton or lens paper, then seal all that to the face so it would look like they came out of the eye sockets themselves. They wouldn't give me that time, nor time to shade the sides of the eyes to give it some dimension and feeling.
The main alien—did you notice his eyes *move?* What I did was put another pair of eyes over the first pair and pull them back and forth with strings. That was my own idea; I just couldn't see the picture without animation. I wanted to see those eyes move, and when it worked, that made my heart feel real good because *then* the audience believed it.

Throughout the '50s, you contributed to a number of Edward Wood's films. What was it like working on a Wood set?
It was like a big, happy family. Eddie Wood was a happy-go-lucky type of person, really jovial, easy to get along with, rather good-looking. At that time, to me he looked pretty young for a producer-director. Eddie always used players who hadn't worked very much, or stars that were slipping. He would

Thomas manufactured a devil on the spot and then also appeared as an extra in the hallucination scene from Ed Wood's transvestite tract *Glen or Glenda*. Thomas can be seen in the center, between a blonde and a brunette; Wood is on the floor.

get these people and shoot hundreds of feet of film on them, like he did with Bela Lugosi. I'd say to Woody, *"What* are you going to do with all this film?" and he'd tell me, "I may make another Lugosi picture and not even use him." But it was kind of a sad thing: Lugosi, in two of the pictures I worked with him on, did not know what he was doing. One day Bela came to me and said, "Harry, vot am I doing?" I said, "Well—you're *acting!*" "But vot kind of acting? He tells me to look this vay, that vay, stare out this vay. I have no script, I don't know vot I'm doing!" Eddie would direct, at random, whatever came to his mind.

Did you make up the Devil for the hallucination scene in Glen or Glenda?

Yes. There was a fellow with a very strong accent who lived in an apartment next to Quality Studios. He'd come over to the set, and one day I said to Eddie, "Jeez, why don't I make him up to look like the Devil himself?" So I took his hair, lifted it up, took some of Max Factor's hair gel, wrapped it around and dried it so it looked like horns. I brought his eyes up, built his nose up in the middle, and I think I put a little chinpiece on him. And he looked like a devil!

So that bit wasn't even in the script until you suggested it to Wood?

Oh, I helped him a *lot*. Woody'd come to me and whisper, "What do you think I ought to do?" I didn't tell him, honestly, what I thought he ought to do with these pictures *[laughs]*, but I'd make suggestions, like the one with the Devil. You know, I'm in that scene, too, when the Devil and all the people are pointing down at Eddie on the floor. I also made Eddie up as the girl—I put lashes on him, and *[lisping]* he was very *thweet*. I think Woody played that part real good—it was supposed to be a transvestite that led this closet life. *Glen or Glenda* was a little bit ahead of its time. Had there been more money in it, a little more quality and time, I think it would have been a successful picture.

How well did you get to know Tor Johnson?

Tor and I were pretty good friends, and I got him a lot of work—whenever I'd get a job, I'd recommend Tor. I got him work in *The Unearthly*, and I got him other jobs with Wood. Tor was a big Swede—he was actually "The Super Swedish Angel" at one time in wrestling—and a wonderful character. A big, big, *big* baby! Tor was so big, I had to get a little box and stand up on it to touch him up. Otherwise I think I only came up to his navel *[laughs]*—really, he was a huge man! One day Tor said to me *[Thomas now doing an on-the-money Tor Johnson imitation]*, "Harry, I want you to come over to the house. The missus and I are going to have a little snack." I told him I'd be very glad to. I dared not let him sit in my car, because the seat would break—he weighed about four hundred and fifty pounds. We went over to his house and he brought out whole barbecued chickens. I said, "Gee, I just want a little piece." Tor looked at me and said, "You eat it all! You gotta! It's just a little snack, before we eat the big meal!" I said, *"What* big meal?" Next he brought out all these various cheeses—Tor's father had a farm in Sweden. And he *kept* bringing on food. So finally the main course was coming, and this I still can't believe: huge roasts of lamb and big roasts of pork. By the way, the forks and knives were extra big, and the spoon looked like a small shovel. *Everything* was made special! And when he'd walk across the apartment floor, the boards would sink, and you'd think there was a slight tremor!

Tor said, "The little woman's coming home soon." I pictured her in my mind as some little dainty, transistorized woman. Then, down the hall, I heard *thump, thump, thump,* and then a knock at the door. And here's a big woman—not as big as him, but good-sized. Very pleasant, very sweet, nice-looking woman—but big! *Thump, thump, thump* down the aisle again, the knock at the door, and there was his "baby boy" Carl. These people were huge. The son was as big as Tor was!

Outside, I heard dogs barking—Tor had three German shepherds. I said, "Oh, let 'em in, I wanna pet 'em!" They came bursting through the door, three big, beautiful dogs, and they got under the table. Every chance I got, I'd take a little food off my plate and slip it to these dogs. Otherwise, I wouldn't be here today speaking with you!

Tor was like a great big kewpie doll. After dinner, he took one of the bed-sheets and made a diaper out of it for himself, with a huge pin. He said to me—he called me "Little Tor"—"You don't mind me being comfortable? You enjoying yourself, Little Tor?" These were *such* dear people—you've never seen such a happy family in your life.

One of your more elaborate makeups for Tor were the burns on his face for Night of the Ghouls.

All I used was some collodion and some Naturo Plasto—undertaker's wax, used by all the morticians to reconstruct cadavers. I used it quite fre-quently.

Tell us about making up Sally Todd for The Unearthly.

That was very simple; it took me about half an hour to do that. I put hair gel all over her face, then I took Egyptian cotton, wrinkled it up and put it over the gel. Next, I took some liquid makeup, dipped a brush in it and made highlight and shadow.

Certainly the best-remembered part of The Unearthly *is the closing scene where the two policemen find the cell full of monsters in the basement.*

I had all these things at home—rubber pieces, hair, eyes, pieces of leftover makeups from other pictures. I grabbed whatever I could, and stuck it on these people. Tor Johnson's son, Carl, was in there—he was the biggest, tallest fellow, and he had rubber on one side of his face, pulling it down. I just threw it together. If they had given me more time, I'd have done a lot better, really.

What's disappointing is that all these monsters are seen for only a few seconds in the film.

They should have stayed on a few of them. I worked on them, one by one, putting at least fifteen or twenty minutes into each, which is a lot of time when you're working on a budget and under strain. But I did all right. They looked good.

Did you contribute to the walking tree in From Hell It Came?

No, the tree was made, all I did was spray it. I don't know who made that tree; it could have been Paul Blaisdell. Whoever made it did a beautiful job. What I contributed to that film was the radiation burns on the natives. I used some egg seal that stretched the skin, Bosco chocolate for dried blood and so on.

It was also around this time that you did two makeup jobs which have received a good deal of criticism: the title characters in Voodoo Woman *and* Franken-stein's Daughter. *How did you become involved with* Voodoo Woman?

There was a man by the name of Les Cook, that I first answered to; he was supposed to produce the picture for American International. He had a different title for the picture, and I suggested *Voodoo Woman;* it was far better than the title he originally had, which I've forgotten. I told Les that *Voodoo Woman* would look a little better on the marquee, and it might attract people to the box office. Les and I sat around and talked about the movie—they didn't have a script yet. Les used to tell me what the story would be like, and Les said, "I want you on this picture." Well, *he* never did it; whatever happened to the poor guy, I don't know, I never heard from him again.

I made the skull-head, and laid the hair on it. When I took it over to Sam Arkoff, he liked it, and we made a deal right there. I asked Arkoff, "Now, what have you got for the body?" I suggested at that time that they should put a scary, Inner Sanctum shroud on it, and make the hands up, sort of skeletal. Then, they could put a bit under the mouth so that whoever was in the mask could bear down on the bit and the mouth would open. And leave the eyes free to animate. Arkoff said, "Oh, we've got something already made up." I had never seen it; I was never on the set. All I did was make the head and bring it to Arkoff. I was very surprised when I later saw pictures of it, with this hideous costume they had used in another movie *[The She-Creature].* They had every opportunity *not* to put my name on the credits if they didn't like my mask; every opportunity not to *use* the mask—they could have gotten something that would have been more befitting to the horrible suit, which looked like a butcher who had meat cleavings all over his gown!

Some of the people who eventually worked on Voodoo Woman *charged that your mask did not become their monster suit.*

I believe that petty jealousy is the only vice that gives no pleasure. I think that's what it was. *They* didn't do the head.

What about Frankenstein's Daughter?

You know, a lot of times you get blamed for something that you tried hard to change, and nothing happened. I made up Harry Wilson as the Monster; I stretched cotton, used liquid plastic to make it stiff, painted over with liquid makeup and put it on him, partially with spirit gum. I didn't think *he* was Frankenstein's Daughter, I was only taking orders from the producer and the director. For some odd reason, these producers never gave me scripts; they cost two dollars, I think, and that could have bought a reel of film! When the scene started and the little man who played Donald Murphy's assistant said, "Look at that—*she's* alive!" I blew a gasket! I thought that Frankenstein's Daughter was Sandra Knight, 'cause I worked on her first. I wanted to change it right then and there.

So you wanted to do a new makeup on Wilson and then refilm those first monster scenes?

Oh, God, yes. Absolutely. I spoke to Richard Cunha, the director, and I said, "They won't buy this out there! I feel this is the wrong thing to do." Really, I'm not to blame for that. Being the producer and director, they could have done something about it then. They could have made the monster an *it* or a *he [laughs] — Frankenstein's Nephew!* I wanted to make Sally Todd up as the monster, but the producers didn't think she was big enough to fight and look menacing. If they had given me the time, I would have made up Sally Todd to play the monster. Or, I could have made this big fellow, Harry Wilson, look like Sally Todd. I could've put a wig on him, and put organdy over his eyes like Jack Pierce did on *Frankenstein.*

Richard Cunha told us that he wanted to hire Jack Pierce for Frankenstein's Daughter, *but he was unavailable.*

They would have *never* given Jack Pierce time to do that. Jack used to take an awfully long time to do something, but he'd do it really well. He wouldn't slop things together like that, and he wouldn't have worked as cheaply as I did. You know, I worked fast on those things, to get 'em out. I didn't get four or five hours, I'd get four or five *minutes!* I did all the makeup — there wasn't anybody else.

Mr. Cunha credited a Paul Stanhope for Harry Wilson's makeup, and for Donald Murphy's acid face.

Stanhope was never on the set, and there was no other makeup man but me. They couldn't afford it! They said they were going to throw the acid in Murphy's face, so just sprinkle a little blood on him and have him raise his hand to cover his face. I said, "Oh, no, no, let's make him look burned." You know, when you get on a low-budget picture, you *plead* with these people — you can see the future of it. So what I did — in less than five minutes — was, I put hair gel all over Murphy's face, then took large pieces of lens paper, wrinkled them up and pinched some little holes out, stuck them on him and painted chocolate into the holes. All this time they're yelling, "Hurry up! Hurry up! What are you doing now?!" I said, "It won't take a minute, let me do it. It'll be effective." Later on, they didn't even say thank you — they didn't say a damn thing. And now they've got the nerve to give the credit to somebody else! If they didn't like my work on *Frankenstein's Daughter,* why did they carry me over to *Missile to the Moon?* They should have shouldered some of the responsibility and accepted the blame for having a man do that female part. Now, don't let them blame *me* for that — I was not responsible!

Another filmmaker with whom you worked on several occasions was Roger Corman. How did you enjoy working for him?

Roger's a nice fellow; I did his first picture, *Monster from the Ocean Floor,* in 1954. He was very, very cooperative, and probably never realized that

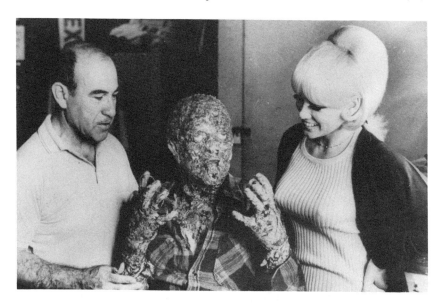

Top: Thomas and actress Mamie Van Doren flank radiation-burn victim Charles Kramer on the set of 1966's *The Navy vs. the Night Monsters.* (Photo courtesy Robert Skotak.) *Bottom:* Harry Thomas (second from right) is still active on the Hollywood scene, teaching makeup and cosmetology as well as tackling the occasional film assignment.

someday he'd be a tycoon or a great movie mogul. He's a hard-working fellow and he's got a lot of foresight. Anybody who works as hard as that has my greatest admiration. On *The Little Shop of Horrors* Roger was very nice to me.

I like Corman a whole lot, and the more I could do to help him, the better.

What do you remember about The Bride and the Beast *and* Terror in the Haunted House?

For *The Bride and the Beast,* I laid some hair on the gorilla suit; a fellow by the name of Ray Corrigan was inside it. All I did was fix the eyes a little bit and spray the suit, which was already made. Ed Wood wrote that picture, but I never saw Ed on that set at all.

And Terror in the Haunted House?

I remember putting ax prints on people, and making some heads. You know, I've never seen that picture, and I would like to. There was some subliminal stuff in that, that I worked on, also. I just can't remember that picture!

What did you do for The Navy vs. the Night Monsters?

I made up the radiation-burn victim. He was not in the script, and it was a last-minute thing. An assistant director came to me and said, "I want this man burned to a crisp—and you've got a half hour or less. You think you can do it?" I told him, "I *know* I can do it"—there's always a way to improvise, if you just use your little head. Some men were packing fragile glasses and props in a barrel, and when I walked by it I saw all this excelsior. I took some out, went to a mirror and put it on myself—hair gel, the excelsior, liquid makeup, black pancake for highlight and shadow—and it looked like radiation burns! "I think I've got it!" I said to myself, as I smiled in the mirror. You know *[laughs],* this gives me aesthetic pleasure! When I was finished with the actor, by God, you've never seen anything so effective. They *loved* it! And, can you imagine, they didn't hold the camera on him long enough, but they used that one frame to blow up and put on the posters!

One of your more memorable makeups from the 1960s was seen in She Freak.

The actress playing the She Freak was a very pleasant girl, but she didn't want to be hurt. You get a lot of people who are very sensitive or allergic to makeup. I knew she was worried; when they start asking questions, you sort of back down on the hard chemicals and go with the simpler things. I guaranteed her that everything on her would be *edible.* I made her up as the She Freak out of kitchen stuff. The eyes were broken eggshells, pierced with a hot icepick. The hair was done with flour, water and food coloring. I took an orange peel, cut it into teeth and let it dehydrate for three or four days until it became solidified like rawhide. I put syrup on her arm. You've got to think of these things to use as substitutes. When we were finished, she asked me, "What shall I do with all this stuff?" I told her, "Peel it off and eat it!"

Do you have a favorite among your many horror makeups?
The acid-burn makeup in *Frankenstein's Daughter,* because I did that so fast, just minutes. I like that, and I also like the changes in *The Neanderthal Man.* That was a challenge to me.

What keeps you busy these days?
I'm teaching all kinds of makeup techniques at Joe Blasco's school, which is probably the best makeup school in the country. I also teach skin care and cosmetology at another school. Every day of my career has been a pleasure. It's the only job I've ever had where you get paid—*good* pay—for having fun.

*I've seen many producer friends go down the drain
because of what directors do to them. Because directors
are interested in getting something* worthwhile. *I don't
blame them for wishing to do that, but it doesn't fit into
the shoestring-type picture. It's the wrong chemistry.
My directing is what is adequate for
the type of films I wanted to put together.*

——————— *Jerry Warren* ———————

WITH ALL DUE RESPECT toward the man himself, it is hard to think of any horror filmmaker who made movies that were as cheap or as ridiculed as Jerry Warren's. Whether making shoestring quickies like *The Incredible Petrified World* or *Teenage Zombies,* or rehashing Mexican imports like *Face of the Screaming Werewolf,* Warren could be counted on through the late '50s and early '60s to deliver the lowest common, campy denominator in horror. Despite their low quality, or more likely because of it, these pictures have managed to consistently draw an audience through the years on late-night and early morning TV.

Like many quickie producer-directors, Warren proves to be more interesting than the movies he made. When speaking about his pictures, he doesn't entertain any delusions of adequacy, and he offers an intriguing look at the scruffy underbelly of Hollywood production.

Warren says that he grew up with the same natural inclination that every other kid growing up in Los Angeles had: He wanted to get into the movie business. He first pursued this ambition by playing small parts in such '40s films as *Ghost Catchers, Anchors Aweigh* and *Unconquered.* A producer once made a big impression on Warren when he said, "In this town, producers are the ones that have it all." Warren subsequently took the producer's plunge in 1956 with the horror film *Man Beast.* "At the time," says Warren, "the Abominable Snowman had gotten a lot of publicity, and there hadn't been many films on it. I had been a fan of it, I studied the phenomenon and it seemed like a natural for my first picture."

How did you go about getting Man Beast *into production?*

Some of my friends helped me somewhat; they told me things to watch out for on a first effort. Being very inexperienced and naive, it wasn't easy. *Man Beast* was made at a little tiny studio on Santa Monica Boulevard called Keywest Studio. I had to use actors who really had no film experience at all; as a matter of fact, I cast practically the whole thing out of the Pasadena Playhouse because I couldn't afford professional actors. I used 90 percent from there and 10 percent from other little theater groups.

Did you use clips from another picture in Man Beast?

Yes, there was a lot of mountain-climbing footage that we bought from Allied Artists Studios. I assume it was originally from a Monogram picture.

Where did you get your Yeti suit?

We got it from a Western Costume–type outfit on Highland Avenue. I can't say for sure, but I think it was the same suit that was used in *White Pongo,* which was a much earlier "white gorilla" picture. We changed the face, and had different people in it at different times.

Can you tell us your budget?

Let's just say it was about one-half of what the normal low-budget picture

Previous page: A behind-the-scenes glimpse of producer/director Warren from *The Wild World of Batwoman.* (Actresses unidentified.)

The mid-'50s fascination with the possibility of Abominable Snowmen sparked Warren's first production, *Man Beast,* in 1956.

cost in those days. This was very, *very* low-budget. I remember I needed a Mongolian village, because I had to establish where the characters were. We filmed around Bishop, California, which is a snowy ski area; we had ice and glaciers, that was no problem, but nothing to establish that it was Tibet. We couldn't possibly build a village, and naturally we couldn't go to Tibet. So I took my actors and we climbed over the fence into a major studio and shot our scene on *their* Mongolian set! We got our scene, and then climbed over the fence and out again. I was a good fence-climber in my younger days, and it really didn't seem weird to me, at that age, to do such things.

Who did Rock Madison play in Man Beast? *His name heads the cast list, but he doesn't seem to be in the movie.*
He was in the Yeti suit!

Did he appear in any other role?
Yeah, but we had to make some changes that cut what he did way down. Other than playing the Yeti, he may not even be in the picture anymore.

Like Roger Corman, you put together a small stock company of players who appeared in picture after picture.
Certain people I felt good about working with, and through the years some of them became my friends. In Hollywood, if you're known for making

movies you get hounded by actors all the time, and a lot of them are very unreliable and present all kinds of troubles. I like to use the people that give me the least amount of problems; that's why I stuck with John Carradine for a lot of pictures.

A gal by the name Bri Murphy worked in different behind-the-scenes capacities on your various films, and even did some acting.
    Bri and I were *married* at the time! She worked with me on *Man Beast, The Incredible Petrified World* and *Teenage Zombies*. The only time she did any acting was in *Teenage Zombies*.

Was she any relation to G.B. Murphy, who was your production supervisor?
    That's *her*—Geraldine Brianne Murphy. G.B.M. Productions was one of our companies back then. I lost track of her, but she later directed a couple of pictures somewhere along the line.

How did you enjoy working with John Carradine in your various pictures?
    John Carradine is a grand old man. The first picture that I used Carradine in was *The Incredible Petrified World*. When I found I could get John, I spent the whole night expanding his part, because at that point his role was not a lead, it was just one of the scientists. The possibility of getting Carradine came about very suddenly, so I spent all night building up what I was going to shoot with him in the next few days. I wrote all kinds of crazy jargon to explain why a cable snapped and a diving bell was lost. I concocted dialogue where he explains what happened—it was immensely long and complicated, and made *no* sense at all—just because I was going to have Carradine!
    The funny thing is, when I was done I said to myself, "I hope he can learn this!" because the whole thing was full of ridiculous phraseology that made no sense whatsoever, and it was *l-o-n-g* and drawn out. I was thinking, "Nobody can remember all this stuff, but I gotta try." The first take, he does it *word-for-word*, absolutely perfect. Then, when he gets behind the camera and I get the reverse on the guy that he's talking to, he does it *again*, off-camera, and doesn't even look at the script! The guy has a photographic memory, and he is absolutely amazing. That was my first experience with him; he is such a marvelous actor that you can count on him for anything.

Have you appeared in any of these pictures?
    On *Petrified World*, I sat on the plane next to John Carradine. I thought I'd do a Hitchcock.

Petrified World is probably the most accomplished of your early pictures, but what cripples that film is its tame survival-and-rescue story.
    We had a monster who was supposed to play a very important role in that

picture—a real terrific-looking monster. We made the monster outfit in Hollywood, before we went to Arizona to shoot the picture. The base of the outfit was a black rubber scuba-diving suit; we painted it with bright colors, made a great big head, goggle eyes, big claws and all that. It was an earth monster, something that was supposed to be living down in the center of the earth.

The funny thing is, by the time we got to Arizona, the suit had shrunk, particularly the legs. Jack Haffner, the actor who was supposed to wear it, had big thick calves. The suit had been designed and fitted to him. When we got to Arizona and went down into Colossal Cave, he said, "I can't zip up the legs! This thing's *shrunk!* You're going to have to get somebody with small calves." So we started looking around amongst ourselves for someone that might have skinny legs. We had picked up a young black fellow named Willie from the unemployment office in Tucson to work as a laborer. Everybody was lifting up Willie's pantlegs and looking at his calves. And he was so *scared!* I told him, "Willie, I'll put your name on the screen! You can tell your friends, 'That's *me* in that monster suit!'" But he was terrified, and would not put it on! Finally we put it on Bri, she being so small. Her legs would go in because they were small enough, but she didn't fill out the top and it was too heavy for her. We shot the footage with Bri wearing the monster suit, but it looked so terrible that we had to cut that completely out of the movie.

Where was the rest of Petrified World *shot?*
We shot in Catalina, which is a little island twenty miles from L.A. We took our cameras underwater, and I directed underwater. We built a diving bell and sunk it off Catalina, so our people could swim up out of it. Then, when we were finished, we figured, "Let's just leave it there." I'm sure that in the years that have passed, that shiny half-dome way down on the bottom there has been spotted by many scuba divers who thought they were seeing a flying saucer! It looked exactly like a U.F.O., and we just left it there.

Robert Clarke was a good choice for leading man.
Bob Clarke is one of the nicer people in Hollywood. Actors are sort of a flakey bunch; Bob has a lot more intelligence than most and he's a very, very nice guy. And he's also a very adequate, dependable actor who can always come up with a good performance.

It certainly appears that you took more time and effort with Petrified World *than with most of your other early films.*
I probably did. I got a lot of flack on *Man Beast,* and some of the reviews were unmerciful—they really pounced on it. By the time I made the second picture, I thought that I ought to try and make it better. But in those days quickies were acceptable. You didn't have to go all-out and make a really good picture; you'd just make the kind of thing that was *weird.* But with *Petrified*

No, it's not a projectionist leaving the scene of a Jerry Warren triple bill; he's the victim of evil experiments in Warren's *Teenage Zombies.*

World I did try to make something that was a little better. I didn't with the third, though—not on *Teenage Zombies,* not at all. I just put together a picture that was long enough to play the lower half of my double bill.

How long does it take to put a film like Teenage Zombies *together?*
    I wrote the script in a week, sitting around a pool in Las Vegas, and I shot the movie in five days. Five days! And the budget was so low that it was preposterous. I remember sitting in a big screening room at RKO with the King Brothers. They were running *Teenage Zombies,* and Frank King said, "Tell me, how much did this picture cost you?" When I told him, he just fell over laughing! This huge bald man—all he could do was roll around roaring with laughter! He couldn't *conceive* of such a thing, because the price was so low that it was utterly, utterly preposterous. It was one-tenth of the lowest possible budget you could think of! I made it so cheap that it was really ridiculous; as a matter of fact, in one sequence, I ran out the whole magazine of film shooting the scene. There were no cuts—it was all the master shot, the whole thing going on for ten minutes. I just did it like a stageplay. I mean, you can't do it any cheaper than that—that's one-to-one shooting!

Katherine Victor is the only horror film "personality" that emerged from your pictures. Can you tell us about working with her?
    Katherine is a very sweet lady who's done a lot of these kinds of pictures,

Warren hoped to capitalize on the mid-'60s *Batman* craze with *The Wild World of Batwoman* with Katherine Victor.

for other people as well as for myself. She specialized in being "the spooky woman," and still does, as a matter of fact. She always was very, very dependable, and did a good job in everything that she and I were associated with. She's a good friend.

Would you agree that Teenage Zombies *is the film you're best remembered for?*
    I think it is. Wherever I go around the world, particularly Europe and places like that, they all know *Teenage Zombies*. If they're the right age, that's the picture that really clicked with them. They somehow liked it, but why they did I can't tell you *[laughs]!*

Was Invasion of the Animal People *your first sci-fi import?*

Animal People was really not an import; that was an American production that was shot in Northern Sweden and the Arctic Circle. Virgil Vogel directed the stuff over there, I directed extra scenes here. I did my scenes for *Animal People* in color, and I don't remember why. It was released in black-and-white. That was all done in English language.

The American dialogue and narration in your horror imports often tackle curious and abstract topics like man's conception of time, our image of the universe, things like that, which don't advance the plot at all. Were you trying to get points of your philosophy across, or was that all—

Gobbledegook. Definitely. I separate my private life entirely from the movies. I'm very, very serious about my researches and endeavors on the reality of the whole universe, and I would not try to inject my philosophy into a movie because I just don't think it can be done successfully. So anything I wrote was gobbledegook. Strictly ridiculous.

Why are so many of your imports from South America? Did you have a fondness for the films being made down there?

In Los Angeles there's a big Mexican movie market, because a lot of Mexicans live in L.A. There's a very, very big distributor called Azteca Films, and the president of that was a friend of mine. It was just a natural thing to get leads into possible Americanizing of those kinds of pictures. In other words, I, not being a great traveler, didn't want to go to various countries and try to put co-production deals together. Mexico is close, Azteca is right in L.A., the president was a friend, so it was just a natural, easy way to make movies without an exceptional amount of work.

Why didn't you simply dub these foreign films from beginning to end, and save yourself the bother of shooting additional scenes?

Those pictures that I imported were very low-budget to begin with. They did every cheat possible in their original versions—they wanted to build them up time-wise and they did it with dialogue scenes. Some of these Mexican films did that like mad; they're very, very budget-conscious down there. Therefore, I would have to delete an awful lot, for this reason or that. Sometimes their dialogue scenes were so lengthy, so bad and so impossible to dub that we had to cut big pieces out. And suddenly the character who was talking is somewhere else, and I was left with a big hole in the story! I'd bridge it—try to make it make sense—by sticking in something, like a shot of somebody who'd say, "He's gone down to the saloon," or wherever. When you see something that I shot stuck in there, it was probably done to try to take the curse off of something else. Mine was usually the lesser of two evils.

The people who poke fun at your movies—and there are lots of them!—sometimes judge your talents as a director by the static American scenes in these imports.

Those *l-o-n-g,* talky scenes you're speaking of now were never in the original theatrical versions. I had a television distributor who insisted on more length—that was the reason for those scenes. I didn't shoot that stuff until those pictures were ready to be released to television. The TV distributor said these things must run eighty-odd minutes, and most of them were down around sixty-five, seventy minutes, which was fine for theatrical showings in those days. But he insisted on fifteen, eighteen minutes *more.* So the only thing that I could do was to shoot lengthy dialogue scenes and stick 'em in. When these things were originally released, they were much faster moving, and they didn't have those long dialogue scenes at all.

It's apparent that more care went into pictures like Man Beast *and* Petrified World *than into the added scenes in the imports.*

Oh, yes. Absolutely. *No* care went into those! In those days, they were buying this kind of stuff for television a lot. Rather than get involved in a picture from start to finish, which takes a lot of work, I'd find something to use as a frame and hang my hat on it. I'd shoot one day on this stuff and throw it together. At that point I was in the business to make money. I never, ever tried in any way to compete, or to make something worthwhile. I did only enough to get by, so they would buy it, so it would play, and so I'd get the few dollars. It's not very fair to the public, I guess, but that was my attitude toward this.

People think that the Richard Webb who stars in your Attack of the Mayan Mummy *is the Richard "Captain Midnight" Webb.*

No, certainly not. Whoever this Richard Webb was, he couldn't have done very much in the picture, and I don't even remember the guy.

Probably the best-known actor to regularly appear in your Americanized imports was Bruno Ve Sota.

Aw-w, Bruno was a *great* guy. I just can't say enough good about Bruno; I wish he was still around today. He was very talented and a good actor. And I always liked to use Bruno because he could take over directing if necessary. He knew what shoestring budgets I was on, and he never gave me any fuss about money or anything. He knew the problems of directing, the pressure, what you're up against. He was not like actors who only think about their egos and their own selves, and have no concept of what it is to try to make movies, which is very, very hard work. He knew he had to wing it fast, do this and get that before the sun went down, and that there was no time to be a prima donna. That set Bruno apart.

Tell us about a picture you worked on without taking credit, House of the Black Death.

House of the Black Death was a movie produced by a friend of mine, Bill White. Bill had always wanted to make movies; he had worked for me as an actor, and had been around the business a long time. He finally got his opportunity and put *House of the Black Death* together. Then, apparently, they got into real trouble. They shot half a movie, with a pretty good cast—Lon Chaney, Jr., Carradine, Tom Drake, Andrea King—but they also had some production people who gave them a lot of problems. And it was one of those things where Bill wasn't experienced enough to put his finger on it and hold it together. Anyway, they had a terrible mishmash of a movie—it *wasn't* a movie, it was a bunch of film. Somebody took over the project, contacted me and asked if I could make a movie out of it. I looked at as much film as there was, told them I thought I could do it and made a deal with them to finish the picture. The whole thing was laid in my lap and I functioned as *everything*—as producer, as director, as editor, putting music in it, the whole works. It came out *bad* but it came out playable, too, and it did pull out some money for the people who backed it. That's what they were after.

Did you work with Lon Chaney on House of the Black Death?

I didn't have anything to do with him on *House of the Black Death* because all of his scenes were in the can by the time I got there. I did work with him on *Face of the Screaming Werewolf,* and he was a trouper. He didn't like doing this kind of film; he didn't like being classified as a werewolf at all. After he did such a fine job in *Of Mice and Men* [1939], he wanted to be Lon Chaney in pictures, not the sort of character whose face changed. But that's precisely what he had to do. Although he didn't have to do that in *House of the Black Death,* he did play the werewolf in *Face of the Screaming Werewolf,* and it was the same old thing with the slow dissolves and hair growing on his face. He did *not* like that, but in Hollywood people do the things that they have to.

Weren't you courting legal disaster doing a film like The Wild World of Batwoman *at the height of the* Batman *craze?*

No, I don't think so, not at all. It had nothing to do with Batman, it was Bat*woman*. But, yes, there was a big lawsuit, which I won. But it went on and on and on, so by the time I won it, the whole craze was over.

Was it you who changed the title to She Was a Hippy Vampire?

Well, yeah, but I didn't *have* to because when they finally made a settlement on the lawsuit, there was no demand that I change the title at all. But as I said, the craze was over, so to come out with a *Wild World of Batwoman* four years later would have been ridiculous.

Jerry Warren (right) and sculptor Jerry Syphers with the star of 1965's *Curse of the Stone Hand.*

What kept you busy between Batwoman *[1966] and* Frankenstein Island *[1981]?*
    I was no longer interested in the movie business at all. I lived on my ranch ... a different kind of life.

So what brought you back for Frankenstein Island?
    Frankenstein Island came about in a funny sort of way. I hadn't seen Katherine Victor in years, and she came down to see how we lived. She started talking about newer pictures, and how there were so many pictures out like the ones we used to do. I don't think I'd seen a movie, *any* movie, in almost fifteen years. I noticed that low-budget horror films were playing, and cleaning up. I figured that, since inflation was very tough, maybe I'd try and make a movie again.

The passage of time did not seem to affect your approach to picturemaking.

As I said, I don't think I'd seen a movie since maybe the mid–'60s. I didn't see what was happening, and I assumed that I could still make 'em like I used to. But they had changed an awful lot. I didn't update *Frankenstein Island* enough to really compete with what was out.

I changed *Frankenstein Island* a lot for the television version. I brought it up to date, shot new stuff, put in explosions and special effects and cut out an awful lot of bad stuff. It's not like the version that you see on prerecorded cassette; I really sharpened it up to make it more acceptable. It's never going to be anything like *Star Wars* or those big pictures, but it's much, much improved over the original theatrical version, which is the version that's on cassette now.

How would you describe your talents as a director — good, bad or indifferent?

I can only say that I have never gotten serious over such a thing. I only direct because it costs too much to *hire* a director. I do all my own editing as well, because directors have their own concepts and they fight with their editors. I don't want fights. To me, life is too short to be involved in hassles with egos. I feel that the easiest way is to control the whole thing, do as much as I can myself and hire as few people as possible. Even though I would *love* to sit back and let somebody else do all that work.

Most directors have aspirations — they figure, "People are gonna see this, and I wanna get another job through this." Before you know it, he's screwin' around, foolin' around, and the picture goes on and on. You can't survive on a shoestring budget with directors like that. If you want to eliminate all that and just make a vehicle designed to be merchandized and make a little bit of money, the easiest way is to control it yourself and not get involved in such things. I've seen many producer friends go down the drain because of what directors do to them. Because directors are interested in getting something *worthwhile.* I don't blame them for wishing to do that, but it doesn't fit into the shoestring-type picture. It's the wrong chemistry. My directing is what is adequate for the type of films I wanted to put together. I have never seriously wanted to be a director, or to do great things.

I was talking with Leon Blender and Sam Arkoff, friends of mine at American International Pictures, several years ago, and I was telling them how much flack I used to get on my pictures. And they told me how much they used to get on *theirs!* And their pictures, to my estimation, were really good stuff. Compared to mine, at any rate. I knew these guys for years, but they didn't reveal until recently that they were getting tremendous flack at the time they were making films, and people in the industry looked down upon them like they were the worst creeps that ever lived. *Now* their films are nostalgia, and acceptable. Theirs and, hopefully, mine.

*I love toys, and in the movie business they give you
a half a million dollars' worth of toys to play with
on every picture. And they give you real live dolls
to work with and splash blood on and shoot up—
it's like playing cops and robbers all your life!*

Mel Welles

AS PART OF the classic Roger Corman stock company, actor Mel Welles joined Dick Miller, Jonathan Haze, Ed Nelson, Bruno Ve Sota and others in lending his unique talents to such ten-day wonders as *The Undead, Attack of the Crab Monsters* and the famous Film That Was Shot in Two Days, the cult favorite *The Little Shop of Horrors.* His later experiences included overseas productions like *Island of the Doomed* and *Lady Frankenstein.*

Prior to his Hollywood acting career, the New York–born Welles held a variety of jobs, including clinical psychologist, writer and radio deejay. After some stage work he wound up in Hollywood, where he made his first film, *Appointment in Honduras,* in 1953. Other early credits included *Gun Fury, The Racers, The Silver Chalice, Abbott & Costello Meet the Mummy* and *The 27th Day.* In 1956 he teamed professionally with longtime acquaintance Roger Corman and played offbeat supporting roles in the maverick producer's *The Undead, Attack of the Crab Monsters* and *Rock All Night.* His best and favorite role, as Gravis Mushnick in *The Little Shop of Horrors,* was one of his last before leaving the U.S. in the early '60s and forging an acting-producing-directing career in Europe. Welles has racked up a total of fifty-eight features, three hundred and fifty TV appearances, twelve producer-director credits and an incredible *eight hundred* voice-over assignments during a career in which he has traveled two and a half million miles and worked in twenty-eight different countries.

Early on, was there any particular niche you were eager to fill in forging an acting career?

I kind of wanted to be a character *star*—my design was to do what Peter Ustinov wound up doing. The problem I had was lack of focus, in that after a while acting appeared very childish to me, and was not as provocative or as challenging as other parts of the business such as producing, getting the whole package together and directing. The other facets of the motion picture industry appeared much more enticing, so therefore I never really focused on my acting career.

Throughout my career, I have traditionally done many, many different things at the same time—in fact, that's kind of how I stay young, by learning a new skill every year. A few years ago I learned how to read, write, arrange and orchestrate music, and the last two years I spent becoming totally computer-literate. I'm in my sixties now, and in the last dozen or so years I've probably learned to master more things than I did in my formative years!

Do you remember how you first came in contact with Roger Corman?

I had known Roger Corman since his first picture because Jonathan Haze was a very good friend of mine, Dick Miller is still one of my best friends and Chuck Griffith, who wrote many of his early films, *is* my best and closest friend to this day. So I knew Roger and we were kind of friends, but I was just generally too busy to do his films or to join his "repertory company."

Previous page: **A giant claw makes short work of Prof. Deveroux (Welles) in Roger Corman's** *Attack of the Crab Monsters.*

How would you describe the professional relationship you had with him?
My professional relationship with him was always good, but . . . at that
time, he showed up as an entirely different person than he shows up as today.
He was eager to try new things in those days and he was very, very decisive.
That's what made him a great low-budget picturemaker: He could make a
decision instantly if time was being wasted or money was flying out the window. Of course, with the kind of pictures he made, it wasn't a question of being very discerning or perceptive, or making an extraordinary comment on the
human condition. The wonderful thing about horror films is that black is black
and white is white, and there are very few grays that show up. Until *A Bucket
of Blood* and *The Little Shop of Horrors,* the formula was basically pretty
standard—kind of like making the same picture, with a few variations, over
and over again.

Did you enjoy the offbeat character you played in your first film for Corman,
The Undead?
The character I played, Smolkin, who sang evil nursery rhymes throughout the picture, was one of the best characters that I ever played. I played him
kind of insane, and what was wonderful was that one of my reviews compared
me to Stanley Holloway in one of his Shakespearean gravedigger roles!
Chuck Griffith wrote that script completely in rhyme, in *couplets,* the first
time; it was a wonderful script and it probably would have been *the* cult film,
rather than *Little Shop of Horrors,* had it been shot that way. But either Roger
or someone at American International Pictures didn't think that it was commercially viable to do it that way, and at the last minute a decision was made
to rewrite the script without that.

Where was The Undead *shot?*
We shot that picture in an empty supermarket on Sunset Boulevard, and
we almost died of asphyxiation from all the creosote fog that was created in
that place. We also shot at what we call The Witch House here in Beverly Hills.
Some years ago, on the corner of Carmelita and Walden, someone who I would
presume was a set designer or art director of some kind built a very nice house.
But he built it like an absolutely authentic witch's house! We used that Witch
House for exteriors, and we shot the beheading scene out in the back. The rest
of the exteriors were actually all *in*teriors.

Did Corman give you creative freedom in shaping your characters?
Generally, yes—he was really busy with the actual filmmaking process,
and he didn't have time to tell you much about them! That's why he kept a
repertory company and always used the same group, because he could rely on
them to do a competent or adequate job under any conditions. Since he made
like ten, twelve pictures a year, an actor could always depend on Roger: If you
called him up and you needed a job, you could count on a week's work. But

Welles (left) played the demented gravedigger opposite Dorothy Neumann (center) and Pamela Duncan in the Corman quickie *The Undead*.

that's *all* you could count on, because with the exception of only a few films, they took a week to write a script, a week to prepare the film, a week to shoot it and a week to finish it!

How did you enjoy working with the other members of the cast of The Undead?

Richard Garland was a nice chap, but he and I never got very close because I'm an intense investigator into the nature of one's being, and I live in questions a lot more than answers. Richard at the time was kind of a complacent guy that looked to escape the activity of living—to have it happen to him rather than to *make* it happen. I found Pamela Duncan very stiff and very affected, like she was very full of being a movie star—which probably is the reason she never really became one. Allison Hayes was a great person to work with because she was very loose—earthy and relaxed. She was a very pretty, attractive lady; I liked working with her because she had no pretenses or ostentation. She was just very real. What I really enjoyed on that picture was working with my colleagues like Dick Miller, Billy Barty, Val Dufour, Richard Devon, Bruno Ve Sota—Bruno and I were very close. I don't remember the name of the actor who played the knight on the horse, but he was like a Western actor and he had kind of a Western accent. And in medieval times it seemed kind of absurd and incongruous to hear that accent coming out of his mouth! I got kind of put off—I couldn't help but giggle whenever he talked to me—so instead I did the whole scene talking to the horse! Since I was supposed to be a nut anyway, I guess it was all right.

Would you agree that, even within the realm of monster pictures, Attack of the Crab Monsters *had a story that was just too farout?*

That, in my opinion, is one of the worst pictures ever made. I think the only thing that saved that picture was the title—comedians all over the country began to crack jokes about it, and it really became a pop-art kind of cartoon. But aside from what the picture was, the making of *Attack of the Crab Monsters* was nothing but fun. Fun and absurdity. That picture was made about the time that pictures like *Them!* were being made. When they made *Them!,* I think they spent about twelve or fourteen thousand dollars for each of those giant ants. Roger spent a few *hundred* dollars building that crab. Chuck Griffith did the second unit underwater stuff on that picture, and when they went to Catalina to do that, they discovered that the crab was made out of Styrofoam, and so it wouldn't sink. They tried winching it under the water, and it exploded *[laughs]*—there were all kinds of fun things that happened. There were problems, but they were problems you could giggle about. Of course it was a farout story, but no more farout than some of the ones we're seeing today. Again, it took a week for most of those scripts to be written *[laughs],* and nobody had time to fill the holes.

You also had a strong role in a non-horror Corman, Rock All Night *[1957] with Dick Miller and Abby Dalton.*

Rock All Night was one of the more interesting pictures to me. There was an Emmy Award–winning television show called *The Little Guy* that starred Dane Clark; Roger bought the film rights, which I thought was very courageous of him, and had Chuck write it into a rock script to emulate the success that *Rock Around the Clock* [1956] and all those pictures were having. An interesting thing about the character I play in the picture, Sir Bop: Chuck, with my advice, wrote the part for a character *I* used to write for, Lord Buckley. He was a comedian who has a large cult following, even today. He was the first one to do "hip" talk—he did some very famous pieces like "The Nazz" and stuff like that, and I wrote some of that material for him. If you've seen a picture called *High School Confidential!* [1958], you'll remember that John Drew Barrymore does a routine about Columbus in front of the history class. I wrote that piece of material, and also the poetry and jazz piece that Phillipa Fallon does. Actually, I was the technical director on *High School Confidential!* for the "pot" language on that picture; *[sotto voce]* I was an expert on grass, in my day. Anyway, that's the kind of stuff that Dick Buckley did, and Sir Bop was written for him. Then he disappeared somewhere, so I played it myself — dyed my hair silver and tried to do him the best that I could.

Because of the language in *Rock All Night,* Roger got really worried that nobody would understand the picture. So I wrote a dictionary called *Sir Bop's Unabridged Hiptionary: A Lexicography for Hipsters of All Ages.* A couple of million of them were distributed with *Rock All Night* so that people would not get confused when the characters talked about their short or their iron [their cars] or their kip [bed]. At that time, nobody knew anything except *groovy* and *dig,* and they only knew *those* because Steve Allen and Frank Sinatra had used them on television. The rest of hip talk nobody knew except musicians, carnies and subculture people.

I think people get the impression that you're a little like some of the characters you play — amiable; a little bit of a con man; aggressive but pleasantly so.
I'm not like them at all. I'm a very super-educated, professorial type, and a family man — I have five children, ranging in age from thirty-six to seventeen. I *am* amiable, and I have a terrific sense of humor, but I don't have any accent — in most of my pictures, I have an accent. Although I'm certainly not "a little bit of a con man," in a way I *am* a wheeler dealer. I can't sit idle waiting for the phone to ring, so I'm always creating some kind of action. And if there were no problems in my life, I would create a few so that I'd have some to solve!

Was it Roger Corman's success with low-budget pictures that inspired you to get into production in the '50s?
No, not at all. As I said before, I always found acting rather childish. In putting a creative jigsaw puzzle together, the producer has the provocation and the challenge in seeing that everybody gets what they need in order to be able to successfully translate the story to the screen. And the director gets a chance to play with *toys.* I love toys, and in the movie business they give you a half million dollars' worth of toys to play with on every picture. And they give you real live dolls to work with and splash blood on and shoot up — it's like playing cops and robbers all your life!

How many pictures did you produce in the '50s?
I made *Killers' Cage* [1958], and then Chuck Griffith and I started to work on a picture called *The Trouble Giants,* which we had to close down because we got involved in a jurisdictional dispute between the IATSE and NABET. *The Trouble Giants* was a film about Israel which we were making in the Imperial Desert near Indio. We tried to make it on a shoestring budget and so we didn't use the IATSE, we used NABET. But in the middle of it the IATSE spotted us and dropped a picket line in by helicopter! I also did a couple of pilots and things like that before leaving for Europe.

Welles (right) gets serious with Jonathan Haze and Jackie Joseph in the classic *The Little Shop of Horrors.*

Weren't you originally slated to play the coffeehouse beatnik in A Bucket of Blood?

That role was written for me, but I just wasn't available for it—I was off in Mexico making my own picture, *Killers' Cage,* at the time. Chuck Griffith always wrote a role in every script for me; in fact, he's just recently written a picture called *Ghost of a Chance,* which is kind of a horror comedy, and there's a part in it for me. So I'm hoping that it'll be funded and done sometime in '88.

Is it true that Corman made The Little Shop of Horrors *in two days on a bet?*

No, not to my knowledge. A lot of stories have come out about *Little Shop of Horrors* that I was certainly not aware of, although I could not swear they were untrue since I was not privy to everything that happened. In actuality, the way it happened was this: Chuck wanted to write a comedy/horror script, and he wrote a *Dracula*-type comedy very much like *Love at First Bite.* It was called *Cardula,* and it was about a Dracula character who was really a music critic, and it kept him up at night going from club to club. It was a real funny script, but Roger didn't like that. Then Chuck wrote a script called *Gluttony,* about cannibalism, but Roger didn't like *that.* And then he wrote *Little Shop of Horrors.*

You know, one of Roger's ploys was to do pictures that he could shoot on sets that were already erected, and rent the sets before they were struck. By doing that, he saved oodles of money and got a lot of production value. Well, that shop was already constructed on the set at Kling Studios. Actually, what made Roger do the picture was that Chuck and everybody convinced him that we would be able to shoot it *tout de suite* because we would rehearse it, and do the exteriors ourselves. We made him a package that he couldn't really resist. But there was no bet about it that I know of; that's a nice story, but I don't think it's true.

Dick Miller told us that practically everything you and he did in Little Shop *was ad-libbed.*
    Absolutely none of it was ad-libbed. Dick Miller and I used to talk to each other in accents all the time, and use Jewish expressions in conversation. But every word in *Little Shop* was written by Chuck Griffith, and I did ninety-eight pages of dialogue in two days.

Is it difficult to maintain a sense of humor when you're under pressure to make a movie in two days?
    No, we weren't under pressure. We got together and rehearsed the lines for about three weeks before we got on the set, so we were all very well prepared and we did it like a play. Roger had two camera crews on the set—that's why the picture, from a filmic standpoint, really is not very well done. The two camera crews were pointed in opposite directions so that we got both angles, and then other shots were "picked up" to use in between, to make it flow. It was a pretty fixed set and it was done sort of like a sitcom is done today, so it wasn't very difficult. And sense of humor? Hell, that was a real love project—everybody on the film knew each other and was having a good time. Jackie Joseph, Jonathan Haze, Dick Miller, Chuck Griffith and myself were all very good friends; the first patient in the dentist's chair was Chuck Griffith's father, and Myrtle Vail, the woman that played the mother to Seymour Krelboined [Haze], was Chuck's grandmother. Chuck's mother was Marge and his grandmother Myrt of the first soap opera in the United States, radio's *Myrt and Marge.* Even the extras on *Little Shop* were friends! It was an exercise in love.

How involved was Roger Corman in all of this?
    Roger, who gets a lot of accolades for having produced and directed this film, really didn't have a lot to do on *Little Shop* because we were so well rehearsed. As I said, it was a love project, and we "stole" a lot of time—we did fifteen minutes of exteriors for a total of $1,100. And Roger wasn't around at all for the whole chase sequence and things like that—that part of the picture was produced by me and directed by Chuck Griffith.

How were you able to produce all the exteriors so cheaply?
    We paid the children who ran out of the tunnel five cents apiece, and all

those winos on Skid Row we paid ten cents a shot. The winos would get together, two or three of them, and buy pints of wine for themselves! We also had a couple of the winos act as ramrods—sort of like production assistants—and put them in charge of the other wino extras. We got a funeral home to donate the hearse that was in the picture—in fact, there was a real stiff *in* the hearse when we had it!

We shot all night in the Southern Pacific railway yard for two bottles of Scotch, presented to the guy who managed the yard that night. That was kind of a coup, because Twentieth Century–Fox had shot all day long in that same yard and it cost them something like ten or fifteen thousand dollars. We got a train with a crew, and had them back away from an actor; in the film we showed that footage in reverse, to make it look as though he was struck by the train. We cut it a little shorter than we could have, because they felt that seeing someone actually getting hit by a train was a little brutal for a comedy.

Didn't Little Shop *run into problems on its first release?*

We couldn't sell the picture for a year. The reason was that the exhibitors in the United States, who were largely Jewish at the time, thought the picture was anti–Semitic. They thought that, not only because I did it in a Jewish accent and because I was a little more worried about the cash register than about what was going on, but because we had a woman character in the picture whose relatives were always dying. We called her "Mrs. S. Shiva." And in the Jewish religion, when somebody dies in your family you *sit shiva*—sitting shiva is the mourning process. At the time the exhibitors thought that was kind of irreverent, so on the first swing around, with Filmgroup, the film got cold responses. The way *Little Shop of Horrors* finally got out was that Mario Bava, Italy's horror film director, had made his first picture with Barbara Steele, *Black Sunday*. American International bought it, mounted a sensational ad campaign for it and needed a companion feature—all those pictures went out in double bills in those days. So they agreed to put *Little Shop* out with *Black Sunday;* the ads didn't even mention the title of our film, just, "Plus Added Attraction." That's how *Little Shop* got out, and then of course word-of-mouth carried it.

Would you say that Roger Corman gave you your best acting opportunities?

No. I had a wonderful part in *Hemingway's Adventures of a Young Man* [1962], and *Soldier of Fortune* [1955] was a great character, although we don't see much of it these days in the television version. Of course, the best part I ever had was in *Little Shop of Horrors,* but it wasn't really because of Roger, it was because Chuck Griffith created the character based on things that I would say when I talked with an accent. The character was written for me, and there was no question about the fact that I was going to play it. And in playing the role I rose to the cause—it's always nice when you have a part written for you. I'm kind of sorry I didn't get a shot at doing it in the new movie [the 1986 musical version of *Little Shop*].

You know, recently I did another role like it, in *Dr. Heckyl and Mr. Hype*. We tried to do the *Little Shop of Horrors* thing again, only this time with Chuck Griffith directing and Oliver Reed starring. It's kind of an arty, fun picture, but it isn't outrageous like *Little Shop*. And the reason it isn't is because of the way Oliver Reed played his character—we all had to tone down or we would have sounded crazy, because *[imitating Oliver Reed]* he plays everything very *intense* and *low* and *serious,* and everything is *whispered.* His sense of comedy wasn't real farcical, like in *Little Shop,* and so we didn't accomplish what we set out to do. And of course Cannon Films didn't really know how to distribute it, so it didn't go anywhere. But it remains one of Oliver's favorite pictures, and there's a very interesting look to the film because we shot it in all the French and Swiss Normandy–type locations in Los Angeles. There was a spate of that kind of architecture in L.A., and we picked all those locations so the picture has a weird look to it.

We enjoy talking to people who've worked with Roger Corman, but many of them have come away with less-than-fond memories.

Well, *I* have a lot of fond memories, but Roger himself is not an easy man to deal with. He's pretty self-indulgent, he's insensitive to other people's needs and wants—and he really doesn't care about it anyway. Somewhere along the line he sees his function as giving you an opportunity, so therefore I guess he considers that he has implicit permission to exploit you in any way that he wants to. I could go into a lot of stuff—he and I are not terribly friendly, although I just did a picture for Julie Corman called *Chopping Mall.* Roger and I are kind of friendly when we see each other, but we don't talk that much, and my experiences with him in recent years have been nil. You know, he *did* distribute my *Lady Frankenstein* picture [in 1972], and I've got to say this: In that particular instance he saved my ass. I had made a deal with a guy in New York to do that picture, and then some shenanigans with a letter of credit made the deal impossible. I had the sets built, the stage rented and about a hundred people employed in Italy, and I was suddenly without the necessary financing. So I got on a plane, came to California, went to see Roger and he rose to the cause. Now, I'm not saying that he didn't take everything that he could—in fact, I had to give him the picture in perpetuity and all of that—but nevertheless he did rise to the cause and work with me on it.

People windbag and gossip a lot about things, but in reality it's only their interpretation or their perception that we're getting. Everybody knew everything about Roger when they went to work for him—everybody went in with their eyes open, so they have nothing to complain about. And there are some things about Roger that are incomparable; he's a hard man to deal with, but he keeps his word down to the last letter. He provided, throughout those years, more work for actors than any other single producer around. He also gave people opportunities to play parts they would never otherwise have played, and to direct, and to write, and what-have-you. Like what a minor league is for professional baseball players, that category of picture was a place where you could sharpen your skills, and then go on. So that could still be considered a major contribution. Also, you could redefine all that to *opportunity* if you want to—you don't have to consider it burden and responsibility to work for Corman, you can redefine it to be opportunity and possibility. Look how many people have used it as a springboard.

What prompted your decision to relocate to Europe in the 1960s?
    Well, actually, television here; I created such polemics in the film industry that I found myself doing a lot of television and I didn't like it. A lot of *Rin Tin Tin, Circus Boy, Captain Midnight, Peter Gunn,* that sort of stuff. It was good work, but it wasn't my idea of anything. So I went to Europe to direct two pictures for a German producer: I had bought a short story from *Playboy* called *The Skin Diver and the Lady,* and they were going to finance that if I directed a picture for them called *Maid from Nymphenburg.* I went to Europe with my family, but those pictures never happened. On my way back I stopped in Italy, and got involved in the directing of a picture called *Le Teste Calde.* There we had a robbery in which everything we owned in life was stolen—we were left just with the clothes on our backs. I got very angry, and I said I was going to stay there until I got even. I stayed, and by the time I got even I loved it, so Europe was my headquarters for a long time.

What recollections do you have of acting in The She Beast?
    That was a wonderful experience, for several reasons. Michael Reeves, the young man that directed the picture, was only twenty-one years old. It was his first picture, he was very young and a couple of us were veterans, so he let us help him direct the picture. Michael was a wonderful boy, and Ian Ogilvy, who played the lead in *The She Beast* and also plays the son of *The Saint* in that English series, was a real nice boy, too. Chuck Griffith was in the picture—he's one of the "Keystone Cops"—and so was Amos Powell, another writer we know, and a longtime friend of mine, "Flash" Riley, who stars in the musical *Bubblin' Brown Sugar* all over the world now. He played the witch. It was a fun picture—we were all living and working in Rome and having a good time living the *dolce vita.* The producer of that picture was Paul Maslansky, who produced *Police Academy* [1984] and is now a very wealthy producer; that was his second film. I had done the looping on his first film, *Castle of the Living Dead.*

Some unwelcome comedy hurts The She Beast *a lot.*
    Paul couldn't make up his mind whether he wanted to do it as a comedy or not. It was a real farcical script, and by watering it down they kind of spoiled things. We made that entire picture in Italy and looped it there—in Italy you

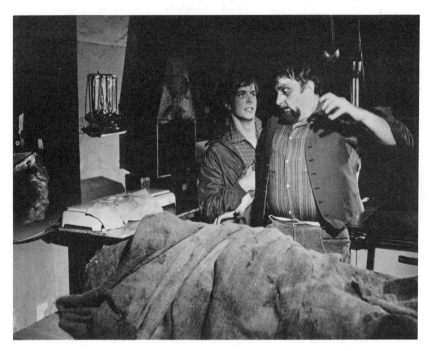

What's under that blanket? Ian Ogilvy can't get Mel Welles to tell him it's *The She Beast.*

don't make direct-sound pictures because you can't keep an Italian crew quiet long enough *[laughs]!* Like all Italian pictures, it was shot and then dubbed. In Italy they make pictures with three scripts—they make the deal on one script, they shoot another and loop another in the dubbing room!

How did Island of the Doomed *come about?*
      A chap named Nick Alexander and I had a company called Compass Films in Rome, and we developed some properties. When nothing happened with that company and we divided up, I inherited the properties. One of them was called *Island of Death.* So I made a deal with a Spanish friend of mine and made it as a Spanish-German co-production in Spain, with Cameron Mitchell and with George Martin and Elisa Montes, who are Spanish actors. In all European countries, the industry is subsidized by the government, and each government has a ministry that controls that. If you make a Spanish-Italian or a Spanish-German co-production, your principal people are supposed to be from one or the other of the co-producing countries. I put co-productions like this together and directed the pictures, but could not go on record as being an American. I had to direct *Island of the Doomed* under the name of Ernst Von Theumer. Actually, he was the German co-producer, and I just used his name.

Does Island of the Doomed, *which is a movie about a monster plant, owe its inspiration to* The Little Shop of Horrors?
No, not at all. It's not about a carnivorous plant, it's about a *vampirical* plant. And it's a *tree*, not a plant. I didn't create the script anyway; it was done by a writer, independently of me.

Can you tell us a little about the film's special effects?
[Laughs.] We built a tree that was supposed to run electronically; it cost $30,000 in Spain to build it. And then it didn't work. So we wound up using the old-fashioned trick of pulling the branches with wires. The close-ups of the flowers opening and the pistil with the saliva on it attaching itself to the neck and sucking the blood were achieved on a special effects stage in Germany.
At the very end of the picture I wanted lightning to strike the tree and set it on fire, burning both the tree itself and the evil baron [Mitchell] who was trapped in its clutches. For a week I kept asking the special effects men—who had not accomplished *anything* correctly up till then—whether that effect was in place. And they kept telling me that, yes, it was, and explaining about the magnesium powder that would be used. On the night we were supposed to shoot it, they brought out the chemicals, and they had bought magnesium *salt* instead of magnesium *powder*. It was enough laxative for three movie companies *[laughs]!* We ended the picture without the fire because I didn't want to go an extra day, and there was no way to get magnesium powder late on a Sunday night.

After a promising start on stage and in legitimate pictures, Cameron Mitchell has wound up a top star of low-grade horror films. Can you describe working with him?
He wasn't terrific to work with in those days; he was an okay guy but at the time he was expatriated and he had some tax problems in the United States, and he was really unhappy about working in Europe. And when he did *Island of the Doomed* he was on an unusual health kick in which he ate twenty-six cloves of garlic every day—which kept everybody, especially the actors that he worked with, in misery! But I think he's a consummate actor and a real serious, wonderful worker. He's very interesting in the choices he makes as an actor, and he always brings something special to his roles.

Were you happy with the way Island of the Doomed *turned out?*
Oh, *very* happy—I can't tell you how happy! The film was made on a budget of like $4.23 *[laughs]*, and it sold very well all over the world.

What's the story on Lady Frankenstein?
I read a script called *Lady Dracula,* which was given to me by a guy who said, "If you want to make this picture, I'll give you the money." It was one of those dream things that can happen to a filmmaker—it's never happened

Welles (center) clowns with unidentified monster actor and screen veteran Joseph Cotten during a break in the shooting of the Italian-made *Lady Frankenstein*.

to me before or since. So I said, "Fine" — and then I questioned him a little bit and discovered that he didn't have the rights to the script but he was sure he could buy it. But in fact the fellow who owned the script didn't want to give it up, he wanted to make it himself. Because I was in the mood to make a Gothic horror picture, I went to England and got Eddie Di Lorenzo to write a script called *Lady Frankenstein*. The interesting thing about *Lady Frankenstein,* historically, is that it was the first Gothic horror film with an explicit sex scene in it. Another thing about it that I liked was Roger Corman's poster of it in this country. It said, *"Only the monster she made could satisfy her strange desires."* That was a very interesting campaign. *Lady Frankenstein* was shot at the oldest studio in Rome, Depaulus Studio. It was mouthed in English except for about four or five parts, but it was very well dubbed.

That was done about the time that Joseph Cotten seemed to be trying to make a name for himself in horror films.

Joseph Cotten's a great man, a dyed-in-the-wool professional. At the time he was traveling around, doing all those pictures in Europe, and enjoying his new entrance into the horror field. One of his best friends is Vincent Price, and Vincent always gave him hints on how to play those parts. In a horror film, regardless of whether it's a comedy, the guys in the film have to play it seriously. Cotten's wife Patricia Medina was there with him, too; she and I had worked together, years before, on a film called *Duel on the Mississippi* [1955] at Katzman Studios. Actually, the truth is that Joseph Cotten only worked a short time in *Lady Frankenstein*—his character was killed early in the piece. He was in it to get the name value.

You seemed to be out of the business for several years in the '70s.
Around 1972 I went from Europe to Southeast Asia, where I did get out of the film business and into the concert business—I became the Sol Hurok of Southeast Asia. I produced huge concerts all over Southeast Asia, with big orchestras and symphonies. I was very successful with that.

And back to the U.S. after that?
What happened was, my family and I came back to America for a visit—two of my kids had never *seen* America, and my wife, who is Australian, had never been here either. We came here and I fell in love with this place again. All the things that I kind of ran away from seemed to have been dealt with, and I was very impressed by everybody's energy—everybody was going to seminars and workshops, doing things and having classes. So I went back overseas, took half a year to close out all my obligations, and moved back here in 1976.

In what capacities are you working today?
I'm working mostly behind the camera—not directing, but doing post-production supervision. My passion and love right now is, I give effectiveness workshops to studio executives and key personnel in the entertainment industry. These are workshops on how you are when you're being effective and how you are when you're *not*. I've been giving these all over the U.S. and all over the world.

You've worn a lot of different hats in your career. Which facet of filmmaking have you found the most rewarding?
[Emphatically.] Producing. The ability to be able to give key people what they need to do their jobs properly is very provocative. Most people don't know how much goes into making a film. There are about four thousand steps, and if you blow any *one* of them, you could blow the film. It's so complex, and a fortune is spent in a very short period of time. Even on a low-budget picture today, you spend a couple of million dollars in four weeks or so. With that money you could open up several luxury restaurants, buy real estate or do a lot of other things. Instead you wind up with two small cans, which may or may not be worthless. They may also be worth $300,000,000—that's the thrill of it. But the interesting part about producing a film is to be able to creatively secure for your director, art director and so on, the things that they need in order to do their work. *That* I find very exciting and challenging, and I hope I can continue to do that and to help other people do that. That's really important to me.

Index

Every movie title is followed by year of release. Television series, stage plays, radio shows, etc., are identified as such in parentheses. The titles of novels, short stories, and magazines appear in quotation marks. Page numbers in **bold** indicate photographs.

397